# RIDING THE BULL

# RIDING THE BULL

## MY YEAR IN THE
## MADNESS AT MERRILL LYNCH

# PAUL STILES

TIMES BUSINESS

RANDOM HOUSE

LIBRARY OF CONGRESS CATALOGING-IN-PUBLICATION DATA

Stiles, Paul.
Riding the bull : my year in the madness at Merrill Lynch /
Paul Stiles.
p.    cm.
ISBN 0-8129-2789-3
1. Stiles, Paul.   2. Stockbrokers—United States—Biography.   3. Securities industry—United States.
4. Merrill Lynch & Co. (1973–   )   5. Bond market—Developing countries.   I. Title.
HG4928.5.S75    1997
332.6'2'092—dc21
[B]                                                                              96-52232

Random House website address: www.randomhouse.com
Printed in the United States of America on acid-free paper
98765432
First Edition

Design by BTD / Robin Bentz

*This book will always be for
Sarah*

# A U T H O R ' S  N O T E

*Riding the Bull* is a true story. It is a personal account of one man's Wall Street journey, in all its diverse elements. But since the term "true story" means different things to different people, I feel the need, here at the beginning, to explicitly describe what I mean by it.

This book is almost completely the product of personal experience. I watched, listened to, or participated in nearly all the events described. A few interviews rounded out the picture, confirming what I had heard through the grapevine. The rest is drawn from the public record.

Writing a memoir does pose its challenges, of course. I have had to decide what to include from the past and what to throw out. Here I enjoyed a kind of luxury: since the first draft of the book was twice the size of the final one, I was able to sort through a lot of chaff to find the wheat. My criterion for selection was the book's central theme. Anything that did not directly pertain to the core story was removed.

I have also been subject, as we all are, to the limitations of human memory. This problem was minimized by the fact that I began this book just two months after the final events within it occurred, but certain natural limitations still applied. When reconstructing dialogue, for instance, it is sometimes impossible to remember past conversations word for word. On the other hand, some of the most memorable lines in this book *are* word for word; by definition they have stuck in my mind. In any case, the substance of each conversation has been related with complete accuracy. With the exception of one passage translated from Spanish, I have quoted no conversation I did not hear myself. In a similar vein, I have based all market prices, in the few places where they occur, on historical data, but specific trades are, by necessity, often fictional trades representative of what was happening at the time, rather than actual trades.

Some further concessions have been forced by the act of writing this memoir as a *story*. In a few instances I combined a number of conversations into one, for the sake of brevity, or sequenced an event to make sense in terms of the larger narrative. The reader is better off for it.

I have also changed many of the names in this book, as well as some identifying details, to avoid any confusion about my purpose in writing it. Make no mistake about it: this book *is* a "tell-all," but not about any particular individual, office, corporation, or city. It is a tell-all about a system, a very powerful system in which we are all involved. Individuals, offices, corporations, and cities do enter into the story, of course, but only insofar as they serve to illuminate the larger picture.

A few names have survived intact. These include people named in news stories (Mexican politicians, for example); Merrill Lynch executives Dave Komansky, Dan Tully, Charles Clough, Edson Mitchell, and Michael Stamenson; former *Wall Street Journal* columnist Foster Winans; my friends Jim and Lou; my former neighbor Rebecca; the omnipresent Dr. Zizmor; and my family members, especially Sarah and the Little Beast. Otherwise, any similarity of names to those of real individuals is purely coincidental.

Rest assured that this litany of exceptions has had only a superficial impact on this work. The deeper integrity of the story has not been affected in the slightest. Throughout this book, and the three thousand hours of writing that went into it, I have sought to get at the nature of things—to crack open each event and expose its guts: what it meant, what it felt like, and how it relates to the rest. The result, I hope, is a cohesive picture of a market society at work, one worthy of being called the truth.

Paul Stiles
Annapolis, Maryland
August 1997

We hold these truths to be self-evident, that all men are created equal, that they are endowed by their Creator with certain unalienable Rights, that among these are Life, Liberty and the pursuit of Happiness.

—The Declaration of Independence, 1776

But Natural Selection, as we shall hereafter see, is a power incessantly ready for action, and is as immeasurably superior to man's feeble efforts, as the works of Nature are to those of Art.

—Charles Darwin, *The Origin of Species*, 1859

First the piston travels downward and the fuel-air mixture is injected into the cylinder. Then the piston rises, compressing the mixture. At the apex of the stroke the spark plug fires, igniting the mixture, driving the piston back down, and turning the crankshaft. Finally the valves open and the rising piston forces the exhaust from the chamber. Thus we have completed one full cycle in the four-stroke internal combustion engine: intake, compression, power, exhaust.

—William Cave, *The Heart of the Machine*, 1994

# CONTENTS

# RIDING THE BULL

# P R O L O G U E

*Merrill Lynch World Headquarters*
*December 20, 1994*

We stand in a fortress of finance, four granite arrows set in a quiver and slung from Manhattan's long arm. It is morning, during that brief lull between the global conference call and the opening of the market. Behind me people are sifting through newspapers, sipping coffee, preparing for the day. Another day at the World Financial Center, North Tower.

Outside lies a bright and tranquil world. The view wraps around us, stretching from the twin towers of the World Trade Center, across the southern tip of the island, and over the Hudson to the Jersey shore: blues of water and sky, blacks and grays of metal and concrete, the glint of sunlight on glass. Down below, the orange Staten Island ferry is plowing toward us; in the distance the Statue of Liberty raises a tired arm; still farther lies a thin line of horizon and open sea. It is a tourist's postcard, a panoramic cliché, a snapshot I tuck away to remind me of this moment of silence, and of something beyond Merrill Lynch. Then I pull myself away and turn toward the circle of traders, the trainee phone in my hand. The picture fades.

It is my second day on the Trading desk. After ten months of scraping my way through the bruising strata of my group, I have finally been given my golden ticket to the world of bond trading. Yesterday, my first as an official trader trainee, I allowed my defenses to slip and thought that this would matter. I arrived wrapped in the warmth of a pleasant vision: I would sit down with the traders and be accepted by them. No longer would I be one of the faceless crowd hovering around the desk. No longer would I be ignored. The scraping was over, the training could begin.

It took less than ten seconds to shatter that illusion.

"You can't sit here," said Justo Lamberti, the Argentina trader.

"I'm starting today," I informed him. "I'm on the desk now."

"I need my space. Sit over there."

Over there was an empty chair, next to an empty trading position. How I was supposed to learn the business of bond trading by myself was not explained; but it was a mystery paralleled by many others in my mysterious world, where the normal rules of business—and society—did not apply.

So I sat down in my designated spot and looked aimlessly about, fighting a familiar wave of frustration. I was tired of scraping to get ahead. For the past ten months I had been doing nothing else. I had arrived at Merrill Lynch International Emerging Markets without any experience at all, thinking that I would be trained; but in my group, new people weren't trained, they were abandoned to their initiative—and then prevented from using it. Questions were met with impatience, contempt, belittlement, or simply ignored. This forced the new man through a succession of stages: first surprise, then consternation, dismay, frustration, possibly even some anger, and finally the realization that he had two alternatives: quit or beat the system. For that was the ultimatum raining down from above: deal with it or depart. There were plenty of others behind you.

Faced with these alternatives, I learned to scrape. In fact, over the past ten months I had turned scraping for information into a science. I could judge from someone's expression whether it was safe to ask a question, how many I could get away with, and what kind—never a simple one. I knew that certain times of the day were best—in the morning, before the market opened, and after it closed—but only if it had been a good day. I had plugged myself into all the information resources I could find—economic research, industry journals, private message systems—and learned how to observe without getting in the way: how to stand with something in your hand as if performing an official function, how to listen to what was going on around me while typing. In general, I had learned how to vacuum my surroundings for knowledge while avoiding the sting of rebuke, and in the process developed a basic understanding of the bonds, countries, economics, and markets that made our business run.

Meanwhile I had begged my pride for clemency, as I did yesterday. Sitting there alone on my first day, mocked by a formidable array of computer screens, I thought I deserved better. I was thirty, which is near the edge of too old to learn bond trading. I was scraping from people my age, or worse—younger. But I knew the rules: deal with it or depart.

It was time to scrape.

The problem was, I doubted whether scraping would suffice anymore. Scraping in my office was hard enough, but scraping from the traders was nearly impossible. In the heat of a hectic trading session, they focused intently on their screens, a phone in each hand, watching the market move while salesmen yelled at them for prices, blotters flew around the desk, and money was lost or won. Tension rose accordingly. In this atmosphere, a misjudged question was like sticking a pin in a swollen balloon—the trader would turn and all the frustrations of the market would burst from his mouth, sending you slinking away like a disciplined school-boy. Even in slower periods, the time to explain was rare, short, and often inter-rupted—and few felt responsible for taking it. I have enough to worry about, their faces said, without having to worry about you.

So after a frustrating morning of trying to teach myself the basics, I finally de-cided that extraordinary measures were called for: I needed a trainee phone. I say extraordinary because no one in my office had yet dared employ one. Normally a trader's phone is a simple handset—or headset, if you preferred—attached to a long cord that plugs into a jack below his position. But a trainee phone comes with a double jack, allowing you to piggyback a trader's line onto your own and listen to his conversations. This, I thought, would give me a tremendous advantage, for I knew from my previous employer, the National Security Agency, that there was no better way to collect intelligence than by eavesdropping.

The idea also presented its challenges, however, for trainee phones are less than universally admired. While the trainee certainly benefits from listening to a trader at work, the trader only puts himself at risk. Yes, he might put this lad on the path to righteous profit, but what was in it for him? What if his wife called, and wanted to talk about that particular problem they were having? What if—er—that other woman called? And what about that headhunter trying to lure him to Salomon? In the jargon of the market, trainee phones offered the trader unlimited downside and no upside. They were a bad trade.

But I was a desperate man. The question was not if, but where to find the phone—and quickly. Merrill Lynch Technical Services seemed like the logical answer, but that was like asking the Department of Motor Vehicles for overnight plates. I tried the few traders I knew, but word seemed to have got out that their sex lives were being monitored; there were no such phones to be found. So in desperation I turned to the only other alternative: I began to scour the floors of the World Financial Center myself.

This was no easy task. One did not just pop around and visit other areas of Merrill Lynch without a good reason. They were like foreign lands, places where strange things like municipal bonds and mortgage-backed securities—unknown in the emerging markets—were traded, and where a new face was often greeted with suspicion. But to my advantage, I was a veteran scraper; and, if nothing else, this was a scraping challenge. Entering these strange rooms, I immediately became one of the local faceless hoverers, a man who could blend in anywhere and look on unseen. And within an hour, I returned from a distant desk with my borrowed prize, swearing—to myself anyway—that I would one day return it.

Now I stand here on my second day, clutching my hard-won prize and ready to employ it. While I admit to some kind of perverse satisfaction at the thought, there is a great urgency underlying my mission, for both myself and my organization. It has been a bad year for our business—no, a *disastrous* year. In fact, 1994 has been the worst bond market since the Great Depression, and leading the plunge have been the bonds of developing countries, the so-called emerging markets. Throughout the early nineties, the emerging markets were one of the hottest investments on Wall Street, in some cases yielding returns of 60 to 70 percent per year. But since the Fed's first interest rate hike in February, they have steadily declined, bringing our market to its knees, and my group with it.

Looking over our small trading floor, I see enough empty seats to remind me of that, and the urgency of my task. But I can't help from thinking that this bear market has created my trading opportunity—which, in Wall Street psychology, makes it a positive trend. When a market suffers, the flow of trades, what traders call liquidity, dries up, making it difficult to determine the market price of a bond—the key to successful trading. Consequently, in order to expose us to more flows and vital market intelligence, my group has decided to establish a new trading position, one dedicated to trading with our competition, the other emerging markets groups of Wall Street—something we generally avoid due to its lack of profitability. The new Street trader is me.

Naturally, this makes me happy. People are lining up in my office, and in business schools across the country, to have the chance to trade bonds. It is the prestige job, the money job. But there are two problems with the idea. The first is that I know nothing about bond trading. My tenure at Merrill has been spent in various marketing jobs, far from the cry of bid and offer, hit and lift, the intricacies of trading strategies, the dynamics of market movements, and even the advanced equipment surrounding the desk. Yet according to our head trader, Diego Barbero, I am supposed to start calling on the most formidable banks in our business— Bear Stearns, Lehman Brothers, Goldman Sachs, ING—and soon. It is a sweat-producing thought. These firms have the sharpest traders on the Street. I am facing Goliaths unarmed.

The other problem, of course, is that no one will give me a slingshot. And yet according to Barbero, I have only a short time in which to prove myself, or he will be forced to go outside the organization and hire a more experienced hand. We have no choice, he said during our one abrupt meeting, the market is simply too bad. What he did not say, of course, is that they are trying the cheaper alternative first; but in any case, I must get up to speed as soon as possible, and the trainee phone will help.

The question is, where to use it? As I survey the desk now, it is abnormally quiet. The Christmas season is upon us, the time of year when the market is traditionally dead. But on this twentieth of December it is especially so, for exhaustion is playing a role as well. The entire market is licking its wounds, trying to forget about the past year and hoping for a better '95. Basically, everyone just wants to go home.

Our traders are no exception. Most of them have already fled on vacation, leaving a skeleton crew behind. Apart from myself, there are only two trading assistants, who don't dare take vacation, and one trader, Juan Fuentes, who has just arrived.

I perform the continual assessment of the scraper: less activity, perhaps, but some breathing room at least. And it's good that Fuentes has been stuck here on Christmas week. Though one of the junior members of the desk, he is also one of the best. Perhaps I can learn from him.

I pull up a chair beside him and sit down. "Hi, Juan."

"Hi."

Fuentes doesn't even lift his head. He continues to focus on his large computer monitor, pulling at his scruffy black beard. It doesn't surprise me. As long as the market is open, he is always intense, unreadable, pensive, a compressed spring of concentration. On the weekends, he releases this pent-up pressure in fits of rugby, often returning Monday with a gladiator's bruises on his face. But that is a Fuentes I don't know. The Fuentes I know is the man who trades Mexico.

"Anything going on?" I ask.

Fuentes shakes his head and continues to focus on the screen. A young Mexican, nearing thirty, he came to Merrill Lynch two years ago from Mexico City, where he worked at Mexico's largest bank and learned the market well. He has since proved himself to be an extremely able trader. Like many of the best, he has a mind like a computer. He can estimate bond prices from yields, and yields from prices, with startling accuracy, and has a tremendous memory for numbers. During our daily conference call he stands in front of the speakerphone reciting the latest auction prices of various Mexican treasury instruments without virtue of notes. When he uses his Hewlett-Packard financial calculator, his fingers blur upon the keys.

These talents have placed Fuentes in charge of our Mexico book, our single largest country position. Under normal circumstances, he is responsible for trading Mexican par and discount bonds, the restructured debt of the Mexican government; *cetes,* the Mexican treasury bill; and *tesobonos,* a dollar-based version of the same. But today, amid the slumber of the market and the absence of the other traders, he has been left to trade Merrill Lynch's entire emerging markets trading book—some $600 million in bonds.

The added pressure shows in his movements. While the rest of the office yawns, his focus bounces around the trading position, checking the broker screens, muttering prices to himself, typing them into his position report, then jerking his head back to the screens. The three other major trading books he has inherited—Argentina, Brazil, and Venezuela—each has its own menu of bonds, which have been trading in London since three this morning, New York time. Now he must quickly learn their new price levels and update his computer models before the market opens in New York.

"Mind if I plug in a phone?" I ask.

Fuentes doesn't appear to hear. He has turned to his Bloomberg monitor, that vast reservoir of financial information, and is checking his messages. I lean over his shoulder—some salesman in Tokyo is asking him for prices—and am about to speak again when my scraping alarm goes off. There's too much tension in the air, it tells me, and Fuentes can be painfully sharp with his tongue. With his heavy accent, he can fire at you like a machine gun, a rat-a-tat-tat that sprays until he runs out of ammunition.

I sit back down and analyze the risks, like a good trader. If I wait to ask again, I continue to lose—and even then he may say no. But to break his concentration now, moments before the market opens, is to invite hot lead from an Uzi. So why ask at all? I look at Fuentes, who is still turned away, and my simmering frustration overwhelms me—fuck it! I'm a thirty-year-old man! I've got a job to do! Reaching forward, I quickly unplug his phone jack, insert it into my trainee jack, and plug the mated pair beneath his desk.

Moments later I am still congratulating myself when Fuentes's phone rings. I know it is ringing because I can hear it in my headset, but Fuentes doesn't move. It rings again. He keeps typing. He can't hear it—and suddenly I realize why. I have inadvertently disconnected his phone.

My spirits freeze. A trader's phone is his lifeline, his source of income. I have done the unmentionable. But how? The phone keeps ringing, sparking a moral brushfire in my mind. Should I tell him? That could be a million-dollar call. . . . Then the repercussions strike home. Are you kidding? Let it ring!

Suddenly Fuentes starts, his eyes focused on the touchscreen that serves as our phone system. His extension is blinking rapidly. He turns toward me with a puzzled, impatient look and fiddles with his phone jack.

"What is *this*?"

"Just a minute!" In a movement so fast neither one of us can see what I'm doing, I yank out the trainee phone and replace Fuentes's single jack. He sits up, all questions preempted by a sudden ring in his headset, and begins to talk in Spanish.

Whew! Sagging back in my seat, I study the trainee phone, wondering what went wrong, and how I can be so tired this early in the morning. There's a switch in back—that must be it. I flip it and wait for another chance. My shirt sticks pleasurably to my back. For some reason I'm actually enjoying this, it's so silly. Grown men—

Fuentes hangs up and returns to his Bloomberg without pause. As soon as his head is turned, I quickly pull out his phone jack again, plug it into mine, reach beneath his desk . . .

"What are you doing?"

My head snaps up; Fuentes's eyes are focused on me.

"Just putting in a line, that's all."

He looks beneath the desk, kicks at the new jack. "What is that?"

"A trainee phone," I admit.

"A trainee phone," he repeats. Suddenly I realize he's never seen one before. Seeing my opening, I rush through it.

"I'm supposed to train with you today. I'm starting on the desk. I'm going to be the new Street trader."

All this comes out rather breathlessly, but it's enough to send Fuentes back to his work. He has better things to think about.

I draw in a slow breath and let it silently escape. That was close.

Leaning forward, I study the broker screens attentively. They stand piled up in front of us like building blocks, a group of small square monitors from different vendors—Eurobrokers, Chapdelaine, Tullett & Tokyo—that form what is known as the inside market, the trading monopoly of the broker-dealer community. It is here that the Street trades with itself. All the major emerging markets are represented, with the best bids (to buy) and offers (to sell) for each bond. With New York now open for business, there is a brief flurry of activity as people adjust their positions to reflect developments in London. Every so often a price blinks a few times and disappears, another two-million-dollar trade complete.

I sit watching the first few trades come and go. Part of the new man's game is trying not to look the part, so I'm serious, attentive. My eyes wander the different screens like an old pro, feeling the pulse of the market.

"Where's the peso?" I ask.

Fuentes takes me literally and points to his large computer monitor, which is divided into different sections of news feeds, graphs, and prices. A large fluctuating figure resides in one corner, still reflecting yesterday's close.

"Three point four six four seven," I observe, brimming with understanding. Yet my acting gets in the way of my learning. Yes, I know that's almost three and a half pesos to the dollar—but is that good or bad?

I look back to the screens. A few years ago they didn't even exist, but now they stand as testimony to the growth of the world's developing countries, and our market. Each price is someone's bet that a particular bond—the debt of a struggling nation in Latin America, Asia, Africa, or Eastern Europe—will go up or down. Almost anything can move the price—news stories, political events, economic statistics, technical factors—but underlying them all is the simple notion that a bond, and a country, is only worth what someone is willing to pay for it.

"Good morning."

I look up to see Miguel Forte entering the trading floor. Our former head trader glides by in a long cashmere coat, *The Wall Street Journal* tucked under one arm, his morning fruit cup in his hand. One of the founding members of our group, he has recently been set adrift in a quiet palace coup and now roves about as Minister Without Portfolio—an unfortunate fact for the rest of us. A quiet Panamanian with unflappable nerves, he was the best manager we had.

He disappears into his office, the only one in the room.

Fuentes picks up his phone and hits one of the direct dial buttons.

"Morgan."

"Can you give me prices on Mexico?" Fuentes asks.

The J. P. Morgan trader recites his latest bids and offers: "Pars at sixty-three to a half, discounts eighty-three and three eighths to seven eighths, Aztecs ninety-nine and a half to a buck."

"Nothing done."

Fuentes hangs up and thinks a moment. Like Merrill Lynch, J. P. Morgan is one of the big "market makers" who trade with each other on demand. But Fuentes had no intention of trading: he was just collecting intelligence.

He grasps a wiry microphone, turned up in front of his face like a sun-starved flower. "I'll buy Mex pars at sixty-three."

"Mex pars at sixty-three," a voice confirms, coming over a little speaker called the squawk.

A price of sixty-three suddenly flashes on the Eurobrokers screen, alerting the inside market to our bid for the Mexican par bond. A little dot beside the price indicates that it is ours.

"You want to buy Mex pars?" I venture safely, hoping to extract some insight.

"Yes."

So much for insight.

Fuentes continues to study the market while keeping his bid in sight. His intense focus appears unnecessary: the entire market is asleep. The broker screens have settled down, the news out of Latin America, carried on the Reuters and Dow Jones feeds, is a slow trickle of background stories, and the ailing thirty-year U.S. Treasury bond, our benchmark, is scratching a dead man's EKG. The peso hasn't moved either, but Mexico City is in a different time zone: trading doesn't begin until ten.

I peer over the stack of computers. Across the divide sits Sales, forming the other loop of our figure-eight trading floor, and the second half of the Sales & Trading equation, that profit engine of Wall Street. Unlike the broker screens, Sales is our link to the outside market—our investor base—the mammoth mutual funds, the pension funds, the insurance companies, and the speculative hedge funds that have turned our backwater bonds into a major industry. They rely on us for product, we rely on them for clients. It is a profitable marriage, though not without its share of acrimony.

While mostly present, Sales is quiet today; they have had a rough year too. Three of our four salesmen sit in a row, chatting casually about last night's basketball game. Meanwhile the Undertaker looms over them, making their banter sound out of place, even forced. A humorless envoy from Risk Management, the Undertaker has been with us off and on since the decline began, watching our every move, reporting to his superiors. He stands in a typical pose, hands clasped behind his back, watching the screens with an impassive face. Now, as if reading my thoughts, his thick glasses tilt upward and he blinks at me with his owlish eyes.

Mickey Gurevich, our hedge fund salesman, stands up between us, his phone in hand. "Juan, can you give me an offer on five million Argy discounts?"

Fuentes looks immediately to the broker screens, checking the current prices of the Argentine discount bond. He considers his current position in that bond, and his view on the direction of the market, and comes up with an answer.

"I'll sell five million at sixty-seven and a quarter."

Gurevich sits down and relays the information to his client, one of the big hedge funds.

"Nothing done," he announces across the divide.

Fuentes returns to his screens.

The morning plows on as slowly as the Staten Island Ferry. I wonder how long it will take to get up to speed at this rate. I have been sitting here for an hour now and learned nothing. The market is dead. And it will continue to be dead for another week at least, maybe until the first of the year. By that time I'll be calling Goldman Sachs, getting laughed at, losing millions—and my job.

A ring sounds in my headset. Fuentes answers in his accented English. "Merrill Lynch—"

A Spanish voice bursts in. I can't understand Spanish but I know urgency when I hear it: breathlessness is the same in any language.

I glance at Fuentes. He sits tense and motionless, leaning forward as if restrained by an unseen harness. For once his eyes are not fixed on a screen but stare dully into space, as if turned off in order to focus on his ears. His fingers have ceased their constant beard pulling and now grip the edge of the desk.

The line goes dead as quickly as it sprang to life. Fuentes has said nothing. He turns, looking through me and down the deserted trading desk, still unseeing. Then he slides back his chair, pushes himself unsteadily to his feet, totters somewhat, as if in shock, and finally looks across the room, awakens, lifts the phone up over his head, and pointlessly shouts:

"SELL MEXICO!"

The salesmen's heads all turn in surprise as Fuentes, spurred on by his own advice, bursts into action. He grabs the black microphone curled in front of his face and punches the direct line to one of the broker screens. "Sell Mex pars, sell discounts!" He moves to another without waiting for a reply. "Sell Mex pars, sell discounts, sell Aztecs!"

Sales looks on in disbelief. Has Fuentes lost his mind? In less than five seconds he has sold ten million dollars of bonds—and is still going strong. Fear takes over and they edge back cautiously to their desks. "What's up?" one of them calls out.

But Fuentes is still in motion. Having blitzkrieged the screens, he grabs a phone and moves on to the Street, his window of opportunity quickly closing.

I press the headset tightly to my ears.

"Chase."

"I need prices on Mexico," Fuentes says flatly, hiding his excitement.

"Let's see . . . ," a lazy voice replies. "We've got pars at sixty-three and an eighth to three eighths . . . and discounts at eighty-three and three eighths to five eighths."

"Are you good for five million?"

"Sure," a voice easily agrees.

"I'll sell you five discounts at a quarter and five pars at sixty-two."

"Okay, you're done."

Fuentes immediately punches another button, the direct line to Chemical Bank. But the trader there isn't so ignorant. By now, barely twenty seconds after hearing the news, Fuentes's actions have lit up the screens and Mexico is moving down. Something is wrong, the trader suspects, something he doesn't understand. He puts Fuentes on hold.

Fuentes hangs up and quickly calls J. P. Morgan. "Are your prices still good?"

Gurevich suddenly leaps to his feet, pressing his headset to his ears. "There's a rumor in the market! Mexico's broken the Band!"

Seconds later the screens explode into life, blinking like sparklers. Fuentes steps back as if blinded. The news has struck the market, sparking a wave of selling—not just in Mexico but in the entire emerging markets. Argentina, Brazil,

Venezuela, Mexico—they're all going down. He stands with the phone in his hand, looking helpless. He's never seen anything like this.

"You just bought Mex pars," a voice announces over the squawk.

"Fuck!" Fuentes erupts. In the excitement he has left his bid on the screen, and paid the price: someone has just sold him two million dollars in bonds—bonds quickly losing their value.

A door flies open behind us and Miguel Forte bursts from his office. He pulls up in front of the screens like a decelerating horse, muttering, "Ay, ay, ay!" through his fingertips. "What's going on?"

"They're devaluing the peso," Fuentes spits back, rat-a-tat-tat.

"*¡Hijole!*" Forte exclaims. He turns back to the screens, his eyes blinking as fast as the prices themselves. He has never seen anything like this either. Then his discipline takes over and he settles into his usual stance, crossing his French cuffs and rocking back and forth on his heels while thinking the problem through. The Mexican peso trades within a narrow range set by the Mexican government, known as the Band. If the price rises to the top of the Band, the central bank normally steps in and buys pesos, driving it back down. This long-standing policy is the cornerstone of the Mexican economic plan, a plan that has sparked a major recovery, brought Mexico to the edge of investment-grade status, made it a partner in NAFTA, a darling of investors, and the flagship of all the emerging markets. But now the Band is gone, swept away in some surprise, unexplained act, and it is anyone's guess where the peso—and the emerging markets—will end up.

Forte quickly senses all of this. The question is, what does it mean for the prices glittering on the screens? There are many schools of thought on how to divine the intentions of the market, but he bases his trading strategy on psychology, rather than the technical analysis that drives some; and this action, he decides, is going to yield some very bad psychology.

"Where is the peso now?" Forte asks.

Fuentes checks his monitor, does a mental calculation. "Up seven percent already."

"What's our position?"

One of the trading assistants immediately produces a stack of trading blotters, which list our total holdings in each bond. I know what Forte's thinking: he wants to know if we're long or short. If we're long, we own bonds—not where you want to be in a falling market. But if we're short, we've sold more bonds than we own and can replace them later at a lower price—and a profit.

"Miguel, are you trading?" one of the salesmen shouts. It is the pug-nosed Brazilian, Bruno Rocha, our mutual fund specialist, standing with the phone in his hand. I look across the divide: the rest of Sales is on the phone too.

Forte nods absently, his eyes on the blotters.

"Scudder wants a bid on twenty-five million Mex pars."

*Twenty-five million!* Forte's head snaps up. *It's been a year since we had an order that size.* He drops the blotters on the desk and looks over the screens. He has to be careful. He can't afford to give bad pricing to a valued client like Scudder, one of the largest mutual fund companies in the country. But he doesn't want to buy their bonds, either, not when the bottom is falling out of the market. Instead he tries to walk that fine line between them both, known as a bid-to-miss.

"I'll pay sixty-two," he says.

"Sixty-two!" Rocha objects, his commission in peril. "It was sixty-three five minutes ago!"

"The market's falling."

"But this is Scudder, Miguel."

"My market is sixty-two, Bruno."

Rocha looks downcast, grits his teeth, and speaks rapidly into the phone. He nods a few times and hangs up. "Okay, you bought twenty-five million Mex pars," he says, quieter this time.

A trading assistant gets working on the blotter.

Forte isn't happy. *He should have lowered his bid further.* But it tells him something about the market. "Keep selling," he tells Fuentes. "Open a strong short position."

Fuentes is grinning, slapping his hands on his desk. He realizes how closely he has escaped disaster. "I'm already short," he announces.

"You're short?" Forte says incredulously. "Even after that last trade?"

"I'm short five million."

Forte smiles; *some good news at least.*

The feeling is temporary. By now the market is in a frenzy. The screens are blinking frantically, all our lines are flashing, and the phones are ringing around the office. We can't hope to answer them all.

Gurevich pops out of his chair across the divide. "It's confirmed on Reuters. A fifteen percent devaluation."

"It's fixed at fifteen percent?" Forte asks.

"That's what they're saying."

Fuentes glances at the peso spot price and whips out his calculator. His fingers dance across the keys. "It can't be—it's gone through fifteen percent already."

"Miguel!" Rocha shouts. "I need another bid—ten million Mex discounts for Templeton."

Dick Sullivan, our insurance company salesman, pops to his feet as well. His best client wanted a bid on twenty million Brazil IDU bonds: "That's their whole position."

"Juan, take Mexico," Forte says. "I'll get the rest. What's going on?" he asks Gurevich. "Are they setting a new Band?"

"I don't know, all I know is what Reuters is saying. Juan, I need a bid on five million pars *and* discounts—quickly. It's Steinhardt."

"Miguel," says Rocha, "I've got Templeton holding."

"Hold on . . . Okay, ten million Mex discounts . . . I buy those at . . . eighty-two and a quarter."

"Eighty-two and a quarter? That's your bid?"

"Who's next?"

"I'm still waiting on those IDU bonds," Sullivan says.

"How many?"

"Twenty."

"Okay . . . I buy twenty at eighty-four and three quarters."

"You're done at eighty-two and a quarter!" Rocha shouts.

"You're done at eighty-four and three quarters!" Sullivan yells.

The two trading assistants are writing frantically on the blotters, trying to keep up with the flow.

"Stiles!" Forte shouts. I move quickly to his side. "We need to put you to work." He hands me a stack of blotters and turns back to the screens.

I sit down at the desk, keeping my head below the volley of trades passing back and forth above. You've got to be kidding me, I'm thinking. I've never used these sheets before.

Guerra, one of the trading assistants, leans over to me. "Just write the trades down as you hear them. Don't wait for them to tell you. We'll add them up later."

I take his advice as best I can. Meanwhile the carnage continues around me. Overwhelmed by the tide of selling, we are buying back millions of bonds from panicked investors—bonds rapidly losing their value—then turning around and dumping them at a loss. The nightmare of the brokerage firm is upon us.

"Okay, guys. Guys!" Forte says, taking command of the desk. "Let's do an exercise!" He stands in the center of our circle, holding the phone to his chest, collecting our eyes. "We sell five million Mex pars, sixty-one or better. I'll take Chase. Juan, you take Salomon. Marcello—Citibank. Stiles—Chemical."

I freeze in my seat. I have heard of an exercise. It is a way of quietly taking out a big position without moving the market against you in the process. But I have never participated in one. I have never even done a trade before. I don't know how! I feel like screaming. But that would be suicide.

I tentatively pick up the phone, as do the others. We're all staring at Forte.

"Okay guys, ready?" He looks around. *"Now!"*

Four fingers punch four buttons, sending four calls out to the Street. In the split second before mine is answered, I run through the basics in my mind. First, I want to sell the Mexican par bond. Second, I want to sell five million dollars of them. Third, I want to sell them at a price of sixty-one or better—that means higher. Fourth, I don't want to screw up my first trade.

"Chemical."

"Bid me five million Mex pars, please."

"I'll take five at sixty and seven eighths."

I think a second—"No thanks"—and hang up the phone, chagrined.

"Okay guys, what did we do?" Forte asks a moment later.

"I sold five."

"I did too."

"Chemical was too low," I say.

"So was Citi."

"So we're short another ten," Forte says. "What's the total?"

"We're still long fifteen million Mexico," Fuentes's trading assistant says.

"What about the rest?"

Guerra flips through his blotters. "We're long twenty-five million Argentina, long fifteen Brazil, and long eight Venezuela."

"Fuck," Forte mutters. He begins gnawing on the end of his phone.

"Morgan calling for prices," Fuentes announces.

*"Fuck!"*

Another voice comes over the squawk, a salesman from another group. "Juan? What's going on in Mexico?"

"I can't talk now!" Fuentes yells, his voice wavering unnaturally.

Forte rattles off bids and offers for J. P. Morgan.

"Scudder again!" Rocha shouts. "Ten million Argy par."

"A bid?" Forte asks.

"Yes, a bid! Of course it's a fucking bid!"

Forte keeps his calm, checks the market. "I'll take ten at forty-two."

"Forty-two, you say?" Rocha checks with his client. "That's no good. Juan, I need a bid on ten million Mex pars as well."

"Hold on!"

Fuentes has seven lines on hold. He's hitting them one by one but can't put a dent in the stack.

"Juan!"

"Just a minute!"

Juan is checking the peso, checking the screens, putting more people on hold, talking to his trading assistant. Another assistant arrives and I back out; there is no room for me anymore. The market is already down three and a half points and still falling. The peso continues to plummet.

"My God, the market's crashing," I hear someone say. I turn around: a crowd has collected behind the desk, full of people I don't recognize—except for the Undertaker, perched on a chair like a curious buzzard.

*"Juan!"* Rocha is insistent. "I need a fucking bid on Mex pars—now!"

"All right!" Fuentes flares. "I bid fifty-nine."

*"Fifty-nine?!"*

"Yes, Bruno, my bid is fifty-nine!"

Rocha lifts his phone to the air. "How can it be fifty-nine? It was just fifty-nine and a half!"

"That's the market!"

"I know it, but my client—"

"Look!" Fuentes explodes, rushing the equipment separating him from Rocha. "The market is fifty-nine because the fucking peso has devalued and the market is falling and I have ten fucking people holding and I have a position to run and that's where I make my fucking market!"

"That's fine, Juan," Rocha pleads, "but I have a client—"

"I don't care about your client!"

"He said his market is fifty-nine," Forte interrupts.

"I know, Miguel, but—"

"It's fifty-nine, Bruno."

"I know, but—"

"I said it's fifty-nine! Now that's it!" Forte makes a cutting motion through the air with his hands and turns back to the screens.

Rocha slinks back to his chair, mumbling, "We're losing our jobs here. . . ."

Forte once again takes command of the floor. "All right guys, let's go again. We sell Argentina par bonds, forty-two or better."

By this time another trader has arrived, rushing back from his Christmas vacation. The exercise commences, then another, then another, and on it goes like this for the rest of the day—the volatile market jerking spasmodically back and forth, the desperate calls of investors coming in waves, the flood of blotters spreading across the desk, and the continued screaming of the salesmen and traders as millions of dollars flow through their hands, leaving them stained with red ink. Meanwhile I stand back and watch with the rest of the crowd, wondering if I am witnessing the end of the emerging markets, and my short Wall Street career. The thought only raises a smile.

# 1

## I N T A K E

### 1

We lived in a cottage by a river in Maryland. It was a modest little box, with a top floor lined with windows and two bedrooms below. The windows looked out on the river in winter; the rest of the year the oaks that surrounded the house leafed out, lifting you high into the canopy of a forest.

The interior had that cozy warmth that springs elusively from smallness of size and the imprint of time. A large brick fireplace stood in one corner, suitably blackened by the years. The floors were hardwood and worn. The kitchen had cloth draperies bright with flowers, white wooden cupboards, and the feeling of summers by the shore. A serpentine staircase led below, as if into the bowels of a ship. We took that feeling as a theme and decorated the upstairs like a sea captain's study, replete with curios from the Far East. In back was a small patio bordered by a steep drop-off to a marsh. Standing by the edge, looking back at the house, you beheld a simple, practical square; yet one offset, in some humorously defiant act, by a small cupola, to which we added the colorful flag of Maryland, like a cherry planted atop your favorite dessert.

The house sat on three and a half acres, most of it salt marsh. This provided my wife, Sarah, and me with a welcome privacy and the company of nature. A green-and-yellow garter snake lived under the kitchen steps. Fuzzy moles tunneled beneath the front yard. Squirrels chattered from the trees. And there was a variety of birds, from the great ospreys that circled above the marsh to the delicate little hummingbirds that paused in midair to inspect you. We had raccoons too, a whole daring family of them that made nightly commando raids on our garbage cans. We finally acquiesced and put our scraps out on a plate.

The finest quality of our cottage was its close proximity to Annapolis, the historic capital of Maryland. Beyond the marsh and across the river, the city's spires and cupolas rose above a ruffle of green. The town center was a good mile's walk, one we often made. During our three years as Annapolitans, we developed a strong appreciation for this uniquely American place, and the principles that make it work.

Once an important Colonial port, Annapolis is spread across a broad peninsula that reaches out toward Chesapeake Bay. The city is interlaced with numerous waterways, inviting the bay into its heart. The brick Main Street slopes from its summit, historic St. Anne's Church, straight down into the water. Standing at the top, one looks down through an attractive channel of shops to the boats lined up at City Dock, the busy harbor, and the bright plain of blue beyond. From the water, one looks up into the outstretched arms of a Colonial *polis*, a city on a hill, crowned by a steeple. It is this handshake with nature that gives the town its character. The bay provides the crabs that grace the tables, the fishing, sailing, and boating that occupy the weekends, and the calming views that fill so many windows. Without nature, Annapolis would be a ghost.

History also plays a central role in Annapolitan life. Walking around the central historic district, you soon find yourself warmly embraced by it. Annapolis was settled in 1649 and has one of the finest collections of eighteenth- and nineteenth-century buildings in the country, now diligently preserved. A handful are museums, but most are still viable parts of the town, shops, inns, taverns, or private homes. Many are brick, with slate roofs, wrought-iron fences, and private gardens, secret enclaves where one can catch a glimpse of blooming flowers, ivy walls, patio, and chairs. Others are wooden, with clapboard sides and a fresh coat of paint. They all share that slight lean, an unevenness of sill and pane that speaks of ages past. The streets also show their age, being of varying widths, and with sidewalks to match. Long ago, some prudent hand gave them a regular geometry, but without the chill of the modern grid: the major thoroughfares radiate from three merry traffic circles.

The heart of historic Annapolis is the waterfront, three sides of shops and taverns facing a small harbor. In 1774, local patriots burned the brig *Peggy Stewart* there, along with its cargo of tea—a Tea Party often ignored in the history books. The city was a bustling commercial port back then, full of fishing boats and schooners laden with goods. Today a few watermen continue that tradition, mooring their scallop draggers and crab boats downtown when the summer crowds subside; but for the most part the marine industry has turned to recreation. Annapolis has become the Sailing Capital of America, a haven for scores of marinas, boatbuilders and sailmakers, and a popular cruising destination for sailboats from around the world. In the summer months parking becomes a problem on the water as well as the land.

This nautical heritage would be enough for any city of thirty-three thousand, but in Annapolis it is matched by a lengthy tradition of government, reaching back to Colonial times. Annapolis is the capital of the Free State, and, though not many people realize it, it was the first capital of the United States as well. The city is crowned by the resplendent white dome of the Maryland State House, where George Washington resigned his commission in the Continental Army in 1783, and where the Treaty of Paris was ratified the following year, ending the Revolutionary War. The spirit of that time still surfaces each January when the Maryland legislature, the oldest such body in the nation, convenes for ninety days with all the clamor of a constitutional convention—and resonates in our national anthem, whose composer, Francis Scott Key, attended St. John's College across the street. Such sentiment does not, however, spare the politicians from the vibrant pen of the Annapolis *Capital,* a daily owned by America's oldest newspaper publisher. Perhaps it was they who nicknamed it "The Crab Wrapper."

Life in Annapolis is still dominated by what may be called Colonial virtues. The town shares the industriousness of its forefathers, a sense of community, and a strong belief in personal freedom. But what makes Annapolis stand out—and the principal secret of the town's success—is the Aristotelian sense of moderation that holds all of this in balance. In business, Annapolitans are neither cutthroat nor complacent but play a serious intramural sport. In temperament they reflect the climate: something midway between the excessive warmth of the South and the chill of the Northeast. Community spirit is suitably strong but always voluntary, never subject to the draft. The principal threat to it—the modern penchant for the self—is likewise restrained: there is no glitz or glitter to the town. People with money, and there are many, typically try not to show it. The one regular exception is the ritual circling of boats in the channel by the City Dock, where the summer crowds gather. No wonder they call it Ego Alley.

Opinions are also muted in Annapolis. Like the settlers who first arrived in Queen Anne's name, Annapolitans practice a selective tolerance, drawing the line at manners but steering clear of questions of philosophy. This is aptly demonstrated by the town's two educational institutions: St. John's, a small, freethinking liberal arts school that teaches solely by the Great Books; and the U.S. Naval Academy, which teaches conformity to military principles. The two coexist across the street from one another yet butt heads only in an annual croquet match, braced by gin and tonics. Yes, it is no accident that one of the city's oldest roads is Compromise Street.

The Annapolitan model is best seen in the practice of sailing, the town's ruling passion. The city is host to a number of yacht clubs, each with its own attitudes toward the sport, and a multitude of marinas. In the warmer months the whole town appears to be sailing after work. Races are held for all different classes of boats, from million-dollar yachts to small craft towed home. The highlight is the dramatic Wednesday night finish by the Spa Creek bridge, which is typically thronged by onlookers. At the same time there are also plenty of people in Annapolis who *don't* sail, and this is fine too. A nonsailor, like myself, could walk the docks for a lifetime watching the boats come home and never feel chastened by their crews or, as many do, he could inquire about the sport and quickly be shown the ropes. It's up to you.

To be fair, there is one thing that Annapolitans are completely *un*balanced about and that is their town—specifically, any proposal to change it. We experienced this firsthand when the old drawbridge in front of our cottage was slated for replacement by the state. The bridge was truly dilapidated; in one instance an enormous counterweight fell off the rising spans, narrowly missing a passing boat. But the citizens, convinced that restoration was paramount, immediately formed a Save the Bridge committee and marched on the Governor's Mansion. In the end the failing structure was still replaced—but with a shining white arch trimmed with brick, lined with elegant lamps, and entered through twin pillars embossed with the bronze seal of the City of Annapolis.

I would be remiss not to add that such measures have failed to take hold outside the historic district. Once you enter the zone of twentieth-century development, the land is scarred by strip malls, fast-food joints, and row after row of cloned town-house developments with nauseating names like Heritage Landing. Major shopping complexes have sprung up all over the periphery of the city, clogging traffic everywhere and making you wonder in what direction progress is going. But things could be worse. Saved by its shallow harbor, Annapolis never grew into a Philadelphia, a Boston, a Baltimore, a New York. Instead of a slew of modern urban ills, what you find throughout that small brick enclave is the true measure of a great city: happiness. I've never met anyone who didn't like it there.

One of the joys in the history of a place is when your own intertwines with it. Sarah and I met in Annapolis, and the city figured prominently in our relationship. I was a naval officer at the time, fresh out of cryptology school; she was teaching elementary school in a neighboring county. A mutual friend introduced us in a downtown tavern one chilly February evening and we hit it off immediately. The following fall we celebrated our engagement in the Maryland Inn, one of the historic inns of Annapolis. The next May we were married in St. Anne's Church, the brick crown atop Main Street. The rehearsal dinner was a crab feast held in a restaurant overlooking City Dock.

Soon thereafter we moved to the cottage and life settled down to a regular rhythm, one that changed with the seasons. During the summer the downtown area is thronged with tourists and becomes a continuous party. The fall is noted for the annual boat show, the largest in the country, when sailboats from all over the world pack the harbor. The holidays bring the annual Parade of Lights, a nighttime procession of boats lit up like Christmas trees; and First Night, an evening of artistic events culminating in a spectacular New Year's fireworks display when the whole town fills the City Dock. Then a generally mild winter sets in, a time of reflection in Annapolis fortified by fires and cocoa. Throughout the year we also enjoyed our close proximity to Baltimore, with its lively inner harbor and funky Fell's Point; and Washington, where we were members of the Smithsonian. When searching for more rustic pleasures, we would drive across the Bay Bridge to Maryland's Eastern Shore, where there are charming coastal villages and miles of open road, or to the horse country north of Baltimore. And, of course, we enjoyed the serenity of life in our cottage, with its simple pleasures. We went for long walks. We set up an aquarium and stocked it with fish from the river. And we made an important addition to the family: Tugger, a Jack Russell terrier with the fighting spirit of a Marine division, who arrived one day in a shoe box and soon turned into the Little Beast. It was a good life and we knew it, a life in true Annapolitan style: in balance.

Then I started thinking about money.


I must admit I had never given much thought to money before. Indeed, when I think back on it now, there seems to have been a great conspiracy to prevent me from thinking about money at all, one in which I was a willing participant.

When I was growing up, money was never an issue in my family. This is not because the Stiles clan is particularly well-off. Both my parents are schoolteachers and our roots have not granted us much largesse. In fact, though the Stiles family as a whole can trace its name back to the England of 1296, the family genealogy, a hefty tome prone to charitable judgment, admits that "On both sides of the Atlantic, the Stiles family has held a respectable, though not exalted position." In the New England branch, of which I am a lifetime member, this heritage is reflected in a sturdy line of frugal stock, the kind common to the region. In our house, economic decisions were based on a single unwavering principle: buy only what you need and save the rest. Consequently, since our needs weren't great, we never worried about money. Beneath this fiscal policy lay a more important philosophy regarding the worth of money itself. It wasn't that money was unimportant, it was that if one pursued what one loved, enough money would result from it. The profession mattered most.

In my high school no one talked about money either. I went to the Roxbury Latin School, a small private all-boys day school in Boston. Founded in 1645, it is the oldest school in continuous existence in North America (as all its graduates are required to say) and a permanent fixture in my heart. Formed in the British public school mold, it carries on the very best of that tradition, providing its students with a classical education, a vigorous athletic program, and the timeless values of Western Civilization. It is a school that knows what it is about and is unafraid to say so. "Above all," says the school catalog, "we want our students to become men of character: knowing right from wrong, having the courage to stand—alone if necessary—for what they believe is right, and willing to use their influence for the good of others." To this end, the school's main objective, in the language of its founder, is "to fit students for public service both in Church and Commonwealth"—a noble goal, tinged with duty, that it has faithfully pursued for over three hundred and fifty years.

I carried that view with me to Harvard College, where I graduated in 1988 with a degree in government, and where I continued ignoring money. Like most universities, Harvard enjoys a thick layer of insulation from American society. It is a place where ideas triumph over life's fiscal questions. I had also won a U.S. Navy scholarship, which freed me from the pressure of tuition bills. Instead I concentrated on more interesting, if less practical, concerns, generally in the realm of foreign affairs. It wasn't until graduation was approaching and my classmates began interviewing for jobs that I developed the faint sense that something in my thinking was amiss. Looking up momentarily from my ruminations on the Cold War, I noticed a lot of people focused on Wall Street. Odd, that, I thought. All those good minds wasted on those tiny figures in the back of the business section. What did they see in it?

Five years later I thought I knew. If there is a perfect recipe for youthful disillusionment, it must be a few years spent in the bowels of a government intelligence agency. In my case, it was the National Security Agency, the center of code making and breaking and the blackest hole of them all. To the uninitiated, this may sound like an interesting, even sexy, place to work. But in reality, it was an eye-opening look at a malevolent bureaucracy, a place so overbudgeted and underscrutinized that there were actually people wandering the halls without a job or a desk. Add to it the fact that I worked in the Congressional Affairs office and the recipe becomes even more deadly. Consequently, as soon as my service commitment expired, I left, having discovered what the American people already know: their government is incompetent, self-serving, and freely abuses their trust. But as a result, I felt like a colossal fool. I had swallowed a pack of lies about public service, I decided, someone else's sweet-sounding dream. I had been a naive, idealistic kid. And I had paid the price for it. While I had been toiling in a mindless bureaucracy, my friends from college had been getting ahead and making money—in some cases, lots of money. Perhaps those guys who went to Wall Street had been right after all.

My short experience in the world of marriage has taught me that the best way to make a difficult decision with your wife is to take a walk. If you stay inside, the question traps you, and squeezes. But if you go for a walk together, it seems that all you have to do is keep moving and eventually you'll reach the answer.

In the summer of 1993 Sarah and I were taking lots of walks. I had been kicking around for a while since leaving the navy, to the detriment of our bank account, and now I needed to get on the ball and get a serious job. For the first time there was more at stake than just paying the rent. Some of our friends were buying houses and having children, and I knew that Sarah was thinking about both. She had even mentioned a 401(k) plan to me once, inspiring a wince. A retirement plan? I thought that life was just beginning!

We generally took our walks in the afternoon, led by Tugger, who lived up to her name. There was a deserted marina near our cottage that served the purpose well. Not only did it offer a scenic view of the Severn River, but no matter how bad things got, the only place to run was into the water.

"The thing is," I said on one of these jaunts, as the Little Beast towed me along, "if I get a job on Wall Street, there's a decent chance I can retire by forty. That's not something we should ignore."

"There's no guarantee that will happen," Sarah pointed out.

"I know—but look at Jim."

I was referring to Jim Ortiz, a college friend of mine who had gone to Wall Street and made himself a millionaire.

"Maybe he got lucky," Sarah said.

"Maybe we can too."

"How do you even know you'll get a job there?"

"I don't. But we have to decide what we *want,* first."

Sarah kept her eyes on the dock. The little slats of wood clicked beneath our feet, taking us farther out over the water.

"And you want to be a banker?"

"No, I just want to make us some money."

"Why not find something around here, then?"

"Like what?"

"I don't know. Anything."

I looked across the river. Annapolis was there all right, but what work was available? I was a former naval officer—hardly a rare commodity in the area. I would need some kind of training program in a new profession, probably in Washington or Baltimore. But compared to Wall Street, the idea didn't hold much attraction for me.

"I can make a lot more money in New York," I said.

"But we love it here," Sarah said simply.

How could I refute that? Not with that view staring me in the face. But there was something else lurking beneath the surface. Now that I was focused on money, Annapolis just didn't feel like . . . success.

"Besides," Sarah added, "New York is dirty and expensive and full of crime and the people are hell. *Everyone* knows that."

"There are millions of people there," I scoffed. "It can't be all *that* bad."

"I used to go there all the time in high school. It's fun to visit, but living there *sucks.*"

"If we make enough money, we'll be fine."

We kept walking. With the tide going out and the quiet broken only by the occasional cry of a gull, the whole idea of moving to New York took on an unreal quality. Could it really happen?

"And what about *my* job?" Sarah asked.

I cringed. I'd hoped to avoid that one. Sarah had just left teaching to work for an educational software company, a job she loved. She would travel to various public schools and instruct teachers how to use computers in their classrooms. The problem was the pay: same as teaching.

"I know, I know . . . I'm not saying this is *easy.* But the fact is we have to make an economic decision here, and if I can pull this off I can make enough money for both of us. Besides, maybe they can transfer you to New York."

"Ha!" she cried. "Work in the New York public schools? Are you *kidding*?"

"Maybe you can work outside the city somewhere."

"What about my master's?"

I cringed again. Sarah had recently enrolled at Johns Hopkins and was taking the first course toward a master's degree. She was enjoying it tremendously.

"Can't you transfer to Columbia or NYU?"

"I'll lose my credits."

"Oh . . ." I fumbled for something to say and came up empty-handed. Luckily Tugger chose that very moment to bound ahead, pulling me and my thoughts with her.

"Hey!" Sarah called out. "Slow down!"

"This is a strong beast!"

"She weighs ten pounds!"

I halted the dog with a nervous laugh and looked down into the water. There was nowhere left to run: we had reached the end of the dock.

Sarah came up behind me. "You did that on purpose."

I turned around. "Look, hon, I'm not saying this is an easy decision. I'm not even sure it's the right one. But we've got to make it and we may have to live with it a long time. Do you want a nice house on the water someday? Do you want to send our kids to good schools? Then we need to pick up and go where the money is. And we need to do it now, before it's too late."

She turned away, her voice firm. "All right—as long as it's not revenge."

I frowned. "What does that mean?"

"You know what I mean."

"At least it's not a *lie*," I said. "No one on Wall Street is saying they're doing it for *you and me*. They're doing it for the *money*—and that's it."

"And you can live with that?"

I looked off at the skyline, so near but so distant. The white dome of the State House was sinking into the trees.

"I'm not sure what else is left."


## 2

From a small cottage in Maryland, Wall Street seems very far away. I knew that a few hundred miles to the north men were donning their suits and doing battle with financial instruments. But I had no idea how I was going to vault myself into their midst. The more I thought about it, the more I realized how little I knew about Wall Street, what job I wanted there, or how to get it. Like most people, I knew that Wall Street was a financial middleman, moving money from lenders to borrowers and skimming off profits in the process. The rest of my knowledge came from the media. I had read *Liar's Poker* and *The Bonfire of the Vanities,* seen the movie *Wall Street,* and heard of various scandals that had rocked the Street in recent years; and from this I had gleaned that Wall Street was a financial Hollywood, a fabled land of money, celebrity, power, and corruption—but one where, if you kept your head down and played your cards right, you might escape with a pile of cash and have the last laugh.

he problem was, I wasn't the only person thinking this way. To my generation, all Street has become the land of opportunity, a magnet for our best and brightest. Competition is fierce. Each year thousands of hard-nosed students line up at the best schools in the country for the chance to interview with one of the Street's fabled firms. In large part, of course, this is because we want to get rich, but it is also because we have swallowed the mythology of the Street. We hear fantastic stories about someone losing $300 million and we think, hey, maybe I can *make* that much money. And while much of this mythology is based on the acts of notorious financial felons, most recently of the Boesky-Milken variety, their activities, in fine American fashion, only seem to lend the Street that much more panache. One Wall Street profession, bond trading, has even become the premier job of my generation, its practitioners knighted with the humble title Masters of the Universe—a spark that leapt from *The Bonfire of the Vanities*. Many would doubtless challenge that assertion, but the social facts are hard to ignore. In today's culture, if you say you're a trader for one of the Street's household names, you are likely to inspire envy in your friends, respect in your elders, and the attentions of the opposite sex. If you say you're in education—that's nice.

Aside from the competition, I also had my work cut out for me in other areas. I had a Harvard degree, it is true, and this was worth some misplaced confidence. But I had no M.B.A., which was the most common ticket to the Street, at least among my contemporaries. Nor did I have any experience in finance. In fact, I didn't even like economics, which I viewed as the *Gray's Anatomy* of society—without illustrations. On the other hand, I did have certain intangibles working in my favor. I have long been a believer that the best path to take is the untrodden one, because it separates you from the crowd. Here I felt my intelligence background could come in handy, regardless of its realities, which I vowed to keep to myself. Furthermore, I have always considered the unknown to be full of opportunity, rather than pitfalls. Most people, I think, take the opposite view, which narrows their options in life considerably. On the whole, however, my greatest advantage was that I was blessedly ignorant of the odds against me. If I had known what they were, I would never have tried to get a job on Wall Street at all.

Since I knew so little about my chosen career, my first step was to try and fill in the holes—or at least narrow the chasms. I spent the next week or so in the library poring over whatever books and articles I could find on Wall Street. There were many. Too many, I discovered. Wall Street was a big operation. So one night I called my one good friend in the market, Jim Ortiz, to try and narrow the scope of my efforts. In college, Jim had been famous for earning his tuition in Las Vegas, and for shuffling a deck of cards in one hand. His gambling prowess stemmed from a natural ability to estimate odds in his head, a fact that had also endeared him to Goldman Sachs, which had hired him directly from school. What made Jim really unique, however, was that mated to this quantitative ability was a most un-

numerical heart. Jim's most treasured possession was a collection of fiction ⟨
followed him everywhere. He had the ability, rare among bankers, to talk abo⟨
books as well as bonds.

I reached him in Tokyo, where he had just left Goldman Sachs for Lehman
Brothers—two names that were already on my list.

"You're *what*?" he laughed when I told him the news.

"You heard me."

"I knew this bull market couldn't last."

"Funny. Listen, I don't have a clue what I'm doing."

"Neither do I. And they're paying me a million a year!"

"I'm serious. What should I go for?"

"Depends on what you want. Do you know anything about banking?"

"I don't even know what a bond is."

Jim chuckled. "That's all right, it's not that hard. First of all, you've got commercial banks and you've got investment banks. Commercial banks take deposits
and make loans. Investment banks underwrite new issues—they buy new bonds
from issuers and sell them to investors, taking their cut. The fact is, the line between them is getting pretty hazy, but that doesn't matter to you. What matters is,
investment banks pay a lot better."

"Why is that?"

"Who knows? They just do. I guess it's supply and demand, like everything else.
Hold on."

Jim came back a moment later. "Sorry, I was doing a trade. Where was I?"

"Investment banks."

"Oh yeah. When people say 'Wall Street,' they're talking about downtown investment banks; commercial banks are mostly midtown. I don't think it matters
which one you work for—not right now—as long as it has a good training program.
You'll be paid the same everywhere. The question is what kind of job you want."

"That's what I'm asking you."

"Well, you don't want to be an investment banker, that's for sure."

"How can I work for an investment bank and not be an investment banker?"

" 'Investment banker' means you're one of the guys who talks to companies,
arranges financing, brings in new deals and all that. You don't want that. You'll
work sixteen hours a day for three years making copies for a bunch of assholes.
The thing to do is Sales and Trading. That's what I do. You can still make a boat-
load of money and you don't have to work weekends—you only work when the
market is open. And you don't need an M.B.A. either. Look at me!"

"Sales and trading of what, stocks and bonds?"

"Sales and Trading just means the institutional brokerage business—selling
stocks and bonds to major financial institutions."

"You do both?"

e laughed. "Man, you *are* new to this. No, they're completely different."

"Then which one is better?"

"It depends on what you like. Bonds are more quant than stocks—quantitative, I mean. You'll hear that term a lot. They're more open to mathematical analysis. Equities are more story driven. You know, you talk about a company and its earnings and all that." Jim paused. "If I were you, I'd stick with the bond market. Right now we're in the biggest bull market in history. You'd be stupid to pass that up. You've got some math, don't you?"

"Yeah, but it was a long time ago."

"You'll pick it up."

"Don't I need to know what a bond is first?"

"Man," Jim laughed, "do I have to teach you everything?"

"I've read the books, but they're not written in English."

"A bond is simple," he explained. "You lend someone a thousand bucks for ten years. They give you a bond that pays you interest at some interval—say eight percent every six months. That's called a coupon payment. Then when ten years are up you get your principal back. All you've done is lend someone money for a certain amount of interest. See?"

"That's it?"

"No, of course not—that's it for *now*."

"Thanks, you're a prince."

"I'm just glad I'm not paying for this phone call."

"So what should I do next?" I asked as tactfully as possible.

"Well . . . all my friends are back at Goldman. Why don't you go up there and take a look around? Have an informational interview or two."

I smiled. "That sounds great."

"Let me give them a shout and I'll get back to you."

I hung up the phone, contemplating Neil Armstrong. It was one small step forward for Stiles, one giant leap backward for Wall Street.


While waiting to hear back from Jim, I continued my research, confident that I had narrowed things down to the essentials. I was looking for a job in Institutional Sales & Trading with a major Wall Street investment bank, one that would give me the training I required. I knew early on that I wouldn't have the luxury of choosing which one. I would simply approach them all and take whatever came my way—hopefully something more than rejection letters. But before I went any further I knew that I would have to narrow the scope of my interest in the market. Thanks to Jim, and the booming bond market, I had decided to settle on the world of fixed-income investments, but there were also specific instruments to choose from—corporate bonds, municipal bonds, Treasury bonds, mortgages—each its own Sales & Trading specialty. Considering how little I knew about any of the, the most logical strategy, it seemed to me, was to settle on one, learn as muc, about it as possible, and take my case to all the major firms. The problem was they all seemed the same to me: equally dull. For a novice, reading about financial instruments is like perusing an auto parts sales manual. It does not produce much encouragement. As I sat there scanning old *Wall Street Journal* articles on a microfiche reader, I began to wonder whether or not I could force myself to do this at all.

I also began to seriously doubt whether I would succeed. Wall Street firms are nothing if not intimidating. They project an image of money, power, and success in life, a bulletproof suit built from the rigors of finance. The longer I looked at annual reports, international operations, hard-nosed advertisements, and monstrous earnings, the smaller I seemed. Who were these sharp-tongued, robotically efficient superpeople manning the trading desks of Wall Street anyway? And what were these firms but nations unto themselves, bestowing upon their citizens unimaginable wealth?

Then I stumbled upon my first articles on the emerging markets.* Now here was a story I could sink my teeth into: the world's developing countries were booming. From Latin America to Asia to Eastern Europe, economies that had been stagnant for years, and in some cases generations, were making great strides forward due to the end of the Cold War, economic reforms, and the interest of foreign investors—especially investors from America, where interest rates were at a thirty-year low. Wall Street was playing a major role in this development. Major firms were expanding into the former Third World and underwriting new stock and bond issues, financing growth. At the same time a new market had sprung up for these securities and was growing at a dizzying pace, fueled by the mammoth U.S. mutual funds and centered on a coterie of banks in New York.

I read the news with relief. Compared to the numerical efficiency of the U.S. Treasury market, which left me gasping for air, the emerging markets seemed bursting with life. They were whole nations, different cultures, and far-off, exotic places. They had an air of adventure about them completely lacking in the developed world of finance, the product not only of their foreign locales, but of their very rawness. Growth was rapid and subject to sudden change; information was

---

* The term "emerging markets" is, in equal parts, a product of changing times and opportunistic marketing. Before there ever were "emerging markets," there was a "Third World," a term suffering from unpalatable connotations of poverty and disease, political instability, and economic hopelessness. To avoid these, "Lesser Developed Countries" was devised, a term that dominated the eighties. Then some Wall Street marketing whiz came up with "emerging markets," a term that focused on economics and growth—both of interest to investors. The term stuck and even has a purely financial definition: countries that are not investment grade.

omplete, and often wrong; unknowns abounded; and events were extraordinary, om political uprisings, natural disasters, and financial crises to armed conflicts. All of these factors lent the financial details a much richer flavor. How did one trade Peruvian bonds anyway? And why had they gone from three cents on the dollar to sixty in just a few months?

Best of all, from a practical standpoint, the emerging markets made my résumé seem almost relevant. I had always had an affinity for undeveloped places, and an interest in their progress, albeit from a political rather than an economic standpoint. I had studied international relations in college, which had later come in handy in the intelligence business, and had also done a fair amount of foreign travel. Granted, the financial aspect of the developing world was still unknown to me, but with a little positive thinking I figured I could bend my résumé into shape and squeeze it through the door.

A glimmer of hope rose in my mind. Yes, the emerging markets . . . that makes sense. Perhaps it would even mean some travel or living abroad. The thought gave my confidence a needed boost, the kind that comes from finding your direction. Maybe this whole Wall Street idea will work out after all, I thought with relief. Maybe I can have my cake and eat it too. I can do something interesting and worthwhile and make money at it. I can be a banker without submitting to the cold embrace of the numbers.

That is, if someone will hire me.

### 3

My first stop on the road to Wall Street was, quite naturally, Harvard. The Harvard name is something with a very practical value, as all its graduates know. And since the university has a strong connection to Wall Street, it popped into my head right away. I was especially interested in Harvard's Office of Career Services, which I knew from my student days. OCS is the manager of the Lottery, a complex system, set forth in a lengthy set of rules, by which interview slots are apportioned among graduating seniors. I had never had need to use the Lottery before, since I had a service commitment to the navy, but now I badly needed a winning ticket.

My timing turned out to be serendipitous. Harvard's annual fall job fair was just a few days away. And the director of OCS, Ms. Dorothy Winthrop, consented to meet me beforehand. I drove up from Annapolis with the highest hopes. Mother Harvard was on my side.

I found the Office of Career Services in a white wooden house on a narrow Cambridge side street—an appropriately benign location for an organization that not only sounded like the euphemism for a CIA operation, but which, according to legend, operated much the same way. It had an aura of covert connections strong enough to inspire genuflection in even the hardiest undergraduate. Sarah was with me, but soon found herself back in the street. A prominent sign just inside the entrance explained why: HARVARD STUDENTS ONLY. It didn't even matter if you were married to one.

I presented myself to the receptionist and waited for Ms. Winthrop in the adjacent library, which was full of career reference material. A few studious researchers eyed me suspiciously: more competition, their faces said. Turning away from them, I noticed an intriguing sign on the wall: MAY NOT LEAVE REFERENCE AREA. DO NOT PHOTOCOPY. Curious, I flipped through the set of well-worn binders beneath and felt a warm prickle of excitement. Enclosed were survey forms listing the names, phone numbers, and professions of Harvard graduates the world over. I removed one binder labeled BANKING and found scores of men and women at all the Wall Street investment banks, with detailed descriptions of their jobs. I gripped the binder in triumph—networking paradise! Deep inside this quiet sanctum, I had accidentally discovered the Harvard family jewels. I looked around—did anyone else know? Of course they did! Grabbing some loose copy paper, I began scribbling wildly.

Eventually I was given the nod to go see Ms. Winthrop and located her in the attic. She was sitting in a tiny office eating an apple and looking over a newspaper, a small window casting some light upon her efforts. Her hair was gray and pulled back in a severe bun, and a pair of wire-rimmed glasses was perched upon her nose. The sight of her caused me to pause in midstep. I had expected more regal quarters for such an arbiter of human futures, and an august presence in them. What I found looked more like a librarian on a lunch break.

She asked me to have a seat and looked over my résumé. It was an uncomfortable moment. Apart from the word *military*, I had *intelligence agency* attached to my name, two labels that fail to inspire much sympathy in the Harvard administration.

"Now . . . what is it you want to do?" Ms. Winthrop asked, as if she couldn't imagine.

"I'm interested in a job on Wall Street."

"I see." She twitched her head in dismay. "I fail to see the application here."

"I'm interested in the emerging markets."

"Ah!" she chirped, as though an emerging markets investor herself. But a closer look at my life yielded only impatience. "Mr. Stiles, first I should say that Wall Street positions are extremely competitive."

"I know it won't be easy."

"Literally thousands of people apply there every year, and only a very few make it."

"That's what I hear."

"Do you follow the market?"

"Yes."

"Regularly?"

"When I can."

"So you have a subscription to *The Wall Street Journal*?"

"Well . . . not yet."

A deep inhalation. "We have students here who study the market *every day*," she said proudly. "It's their whole life."

"I know I'm coming from a different background."

"I can see that." She tapped my résumé edgily. "But I also have to say that I have a pretty good idea what Wall Street firms are looking for. They call here all the time—*once a week*, it seems."

"Do you think they might appreciate military experience?"

"Possibly. Possibly." She drew in her cheeks. "But we have students at the *Harvard Business School* who can't get a job on Wall Street." She clucked in dismay. "Believe me, I know. I hear about it *all the time*."

I felt a flush climbing up my face and fought to ward it off. Was it anger or embarrassment?

"All I want is an interview or two, just to see if it's right for me."

"A lot of people would." Ms. Winthrop peered over the top of her reading glasses. "But Wall Street interviews are very hard to come by, Mr. Stiles."

"I was hoping to use the Lottery."

She quickly drew back with a pained smile. "Oh no no. The Lottery is for undergraduates . . . You've been doing other things."

"Have any graduates ever used it?"

She looked behind me, avoiding my eyes. "Yes . . . but only in rare circumstances."

I waited, but Ms. Winthrop said nothing. Apparently four years in the military did not qualify me for a job interview.

"Are there any other resources I should look into here?"

"We have a reference library downstairs. The librarian should be able to help you."

"I see."

Ms. Winthrop glanced over her untidy desk, as if pressing matters awaited her there. "Is there anything else?"

"No, I guess that covers it."

I stood, and she handed me back my résumé. "Good afternoon, Mr. Stiles."

I found Sarah waiting on the steps outside. "How'd it go?" she asked.

"Just like you," I said. "Couldn't get past the gate."

●  ●  ●

I walked over to the job fair alone; Sarah was meeting some friends. Harvard hosts two undergraduate job fairs each year, fall and spring, and though five years out of school, I was attracted by the opportunity to meet scores of eager employers. The event was held in cavernous Memorial Hall, the university's Civil War memorial, an immense Gothic cathedral near the edge of Harvard Yard, and was in full swing when I arrived. The fair was set up like a dog track: a large oval for walking around, flanked by tables of employers on either side. The greatest single presence, I soon discovered, was the Wall Street banks. All the major firms were there, as they were every year—Salomon Brothers, J. P. Morgan, Merrill Lynch, Morgan Stanley, Goldman Sachs, Lehman Brothers, CS First Boston—along with some I didn't recognize. And behind each of their tables was a recent Harvard graduate, preaching the merits of his or her new firm. This didn't surprise me: the Ivy League–Wall Street connection grows stronger every year, and private job fairs certainly don't hurt. But what a grand contrast it was, to look up into the rafters of that old cathedral, named for all those Harvard graduates who had died holding the Union together, and to look down and find Wall Street.

I plunged on, thinking of the last time I had been on campus: graduation, 1988. I had listened, without much comprehension, as the president of the university, Derek Bok, addressed the packed Yard on the declining role of Harvard graduates in American public life. Of my senior class he noted "only 7 percent say that they are interested in government and far fewer will actually make a career in public service. Less than 2 percent of the students plan to teach in public schools, and virtually none are interested in the ministry for which the College was founded." Bok attributed this dramatic shift in values to market forces. "When I left the Law School in 1954, the starting salary for Wall Street firms was $4,200, while starting teachers could earn $3,600. Today the Wall Street salary is between $70,000 and $75,000, and teachers get $17,000 to $18,000." What he didn't add was the obvious: the former educators, public servants, ministers—and naval officers—were now bankers.

The room crept past in a noisy blur. I stopped at all the major banks, talking to their representatives, collecting business cards and slick brochures, and asking about the emerging markets. No one knew much about it. Meanwhile I was joined by scores of curious undergraduates, clad in T-shirts and jeans and carrying book bags, who were stopping by between classes. They approached the tables tentatively, unsure about this next great step in life, flipped through a few brochures, phrased a few innocent questions, and tottered off. In turn the Wall Street representatives greeted them in one of two ways. There were those who obviously felt uncomfortable in their new suits, and who were prone to talk as if still back in college—"Yeah, well, it's a pretty cool firm." And there were those first-year analysts who liked their wingtips, their silk ties, and the starch in their shirts. They stood resolutely behind their tables, torn between the need to converse with these lowly undergraduates and the imperatives of maintaining their new position—which, given that they had survived the interview process and a few months on the Street, was undoubtedly on a higher plane. They said things like "We're currently seeing a burst in M and A activity," and "We're looking for people with diverse quantitative skills for our expanding derivatives business," making a lot of undergrads run for cover—or even graduate school.

I left the job fair presently, needing some air, and took a slow walk through the Yard. It was a beautiful October afternoon. Cambridge was covered by a pure blue dome, bringing out the deep greens in the grass and the ocher in the brick. Passing through the high walls, I entered a familiar enclave of weathered Colonial buildings, lawns and pathways, flying Frisbees, and students lounging beneath the shade of great elms. And yet the whole place felt different now. Reaching Memorial Church, I looked up at its shining white columns and felt the strongest desire to go inside. I soon found myself standing alone behind rows of silent pews, facing a deserted altar. Shafts of light slanted through the arched windows, full of dancing motes of dust. Then I walked around the outer aisle, staring at the walls. They were literally covered with the names of the university's war dead, inscribed in sheets of marble and organized by class and conflict: World War II, Korea, Vietnam. Beneath the spire was a separate Memorial Room built in honor of the World War I casualties, for whom the church was named. It was a dim and somber place, like a tomb, with light barely filtering in. A bell stood in the center, inscribed IN MEMORY OF VOICES THAT ARE HUSHED. And above, circling the room in a frieze, were the words of former university president Percival Lowell: WHILE A BRIGHT FUTURE BECKONED, THEY FREELY GAVE THEIR LIVES AND FONDEST HOPES FOR US AND OUR ALLIES, THAT WE MIGHT LEARN FROM THEM COURAGE IN PEACE TO SPEND OUR LIVES MAKING A BETTER WORLD FOR OTHERS.

## 4

From the Au Bon Pain coffee shop on Broad Street, Goldman Sachs didn't look very impressive. Just another New York building reaching for the stars. Nor did the rest of Wall Street, for that matter. I had made a quick journey from one end to the other, expecting to see something extraordinary, something that said I had arrived at the world's financial capital, and been disappointed. There was a nice statue of a bull, but otherwise it was just more Manhattan.

The real action was going on in my body. There was a very hollow feeling in my stomach and some excess perspiration to match. My hands were wobbly too. I had made the mistake of nervously downing two cups of coffee without any breakfast, perhaps the last thing you want to do before a job interview. It's like hitting the accelerator when you want to brake. Added to that had been my reintroduction to New York. In the short time it took to go from Penn Station to Wall Street the city had seemed intent on revealing itself to me.

The first incident occurred at Penn Station, when a young man dragging a bass guitar put his hand on the door of a taxi that had pulled up ahead of the cab line.

"Hey! HEY!" a burly, spectacled man in a houndstooth sport jacket blared behind me. "Can't you see the line here?"

The musician made a dive for the backseat.

"Oh no you don't!" The burly New Yorker sprang from the line as if from a slingshot, his face a tempest. "Get out of there! Get out of there! *Get the fuck out of there!*" He nearly ripped the cab door from its hinges. "What the fuck do you think this is, huh? Huh? Jesus Christ, you're not from around here, are you?"

The last thing I saw of the offender was a big bass guitar bumping down the sidewalk.

From this incident I gleaned my first important lesson of New York: New York is a fuck town. In other locales, the musician's action might have generated surprise—"How rude!"—and perhaps a moderate rebuke—"Hey, what the hell are you doing?" But not in New York. In New York, anything less than fuck is for wimps. There is even a T-shirt available on the street announcing 100 USES FOR THE WORD FUCK in which the various noun, verb, and adjective forms are placed in context, front and back. It's compelling reading.

I heard a few more examples before I even reached Broad Street. My driver cut someone off in traffic—and suddenly there he was at the next light, pounding his fist on our windshield. "Hey, you fucking asshole! You think you can just cut me off like that? Watch where you're going! Yeah? Well, *fuck you too!*"

Come to think of it, I probably should have driven. I-95 at rush hour would have been a lot more relaxing. But there was nothing I could do about it now: the time of my interview had arrived. Straightening my suit, I pleaded with myself to relax and walked across the street into the world's most prestigious investment bank.

Goldman Sachs stands apart from the rest of Wall Street. This is because Goldman is a private partnership, the last major one on the Street, and while this implies a different legal status, one in which the partners, rather than the stockholders, own the firm's capital, the real reason for its luster is all the money those partners make. For most bankers Goldman Sachs is the fairy-tale castle at the end of the financial rainbow. Inevitably, when discussing the firm, people will say—it's mandatory, it seems—"Of course if you make partner there, you're set for life." This, anyway, is what I heard time and again before even setting foot in Goldman. And by all accounts it was true. By the time the fourth quarter of 1993 rolled around, rumors of tremendous profits at Goldman were circulating around the Street, spoken in hushed tones. "Did you hear? Goldman is going to top *two billion* this year!" The reason for those low voices, of course, was the thought of all the money those partners were going to make. Just a few knights in that one big castle. The average partner would take home a few million at least, the story went. The chairman, twenty-five.

Such numbers uprooted my points of reference and sent them sailing into another world. What would it be like to work in a place where salaries were spoken of in millions and not thousands? I couldn't fathom it. It all seemed like sheer fantasy. But it did explain a few things. I had always wondered who could afford those Luxury Homes and Estates in the back of *The New York Times Magazine* and now I knew: they were all Goldman Sachs partners! And here I was, sitting in one of their reception rooms, deep inside their granite edifice, somewhere in downtown Manhattan, with an orange security pass stuck to my chest and a handful of résumés in my leather portfolio; here at the gate to the castle. I felt like Dorothy demanding to see the Wizard. Goldman Sachs, the top-earning firm in Wall Street history. The thought certainly did lend a shine to the place. And it seemed to give the employees a boost as well. The hallway looked like Penn Station: crowds of people were passing back and forth in front of me at an abnormal clip. Where were they all going? And who were the rich ones? It was hard to tell. They all looked my age.

Eventually a secretary came out to collect me and led me down the hall. My friend Jim had set up a meeting between myself and Yakov Silver, the head of Goldman's bond options trading desk—a big step for someone still struggling with the definition of a bond. Options are a type of derivative, the complex, high-tech financial instruments that have burst upon the market—and sometimes cratered it—in recent years, so called because their value is derived from some other instrument or index. This adds a second tier to the world of finance, one that owes its success to the computer, and which, after two days in the library, had stymied my best efforts at comprehension. The growth of this cyberfinance has also changed the social landscape of Wall Street, presenting another challenge. To meet the growing demand for derivatives, Wall Street firms have scoured whole new regions of society looking for people with the quantitative and computer skills necessary to create, analyze, and trade these esoteric instruments. In the process they have bred an entirely new species of banker: the quant. You see them everywhere now, staring at their screens, pecking at financial calculators, bringing the technological edge and the competitive edge ever closer together.

Yakov Silver was one of them. Indeed, from what I had heard, he was practically the archetype of the movement. Silver had dropped out of law school weeks from graduation to put his math background to work in the nascent field of bond options at Goldman. In a short time, his mathematical models had made the firm so much money that he had left the other bankers scratching their heads. None of them knew how he did it. And Silver was smart enough not to tell them—unless he made partner, that is. This presented the firm with a cultural problem. Silver was not your typical button-down Goldman banker. His dress, his manner, his speech, his gestures—they were all odd, or at least slightly off. He would arrive at a partner's pool party unshaven, wearing a black T-shirt, and, instead of mixing with the well dressed, stand in a corner by himself sipping ice water. But this was Wall Street—in the end, only the money mattered. By the time he was thirty, Silver had been made a Goldman Sachs partner, planting the flag of the quants on the highest hill in town.

"Helloooo," Silver said as I entered his office. "*Wel*come." He glanced up from his laptop. His face was large, pale, and triangular, with big eyes and patchy stubble. His curly brown hair looked slept in. So did his black T-shirt, which hung loosely on his thin frame. "Good to meet youuuu," he added and resumed typing.

*Mens sana in corpore sano,* I thought, shortened to *mens sane.*

I sat down across from him, portfolio by my side, and looked around. Aside from Silver and his laptop, the room was bare. So this is the legacy of the Information Age, I thought. The quants shall inherit the earth and fill it with empty rooms.

Down at my feet, two spotted socks wiggled beneath Silver's desk.

"So you are a friend of Jim's."

"Yes."

"He told me a little bit. Do you have any questions?"

He lifted his head to stare at me and pressed his fingers together. He had very long, thin, white fingers and they bent backward until I thought they would break.

"Well," I replied, surprised by the rapidity with which he had thrown the ball in my court—or was that the point? "I'm very interested in bond trading . . ."

Then I launched into my preset speech. I had worked on it on the train until it sounded genuine enough. It was an attempt to show why I should be hired as an options trader while concealing the fact that I knew nothing about options, had no interest in them, and was not even a quant. What I really wanted, of course, was an entrée to the emerging markets, but this was my only foot in the door. You don't want to be picky at the world's most profitable investment bank.

"Okayyyyy," Silver said when I was done, seemingly satisfied. "What did you think of the National Security Agency?"

Now there was a difficult question. How do you explain what it is like to work in a government bureaucracy? If you tell the truth, there will be no reason to hire you. But at least I had secrecy to hide behind.

"Interesting," I said coyly.

Silver flipped out a few more innocent questions and we had a conversation, of sorts. As I spoke, he would grunt at times, and moan at others, both in a neutral fashion, letting me know that he was listening but not what he was thinking. Sometimes he would cock his head at an angle and nod; other times he would type a few keys on his laptop. It made me distinctly uneasy—or was it supposed to?

My unease was magnified by the mystery in the air, the mystery of how I would or would not get hired by Goldman Sachs. This was never addressed. Instead it lay below the surface as if we were having a friendly chat, not a job interview. What is the procedure here? I felt like asking, but something held me back, a feeling that this would be a faux pas. This game had certain rules, I suspected, and one of them was never to admit there was a game at all.

Finally there was a long silence in which my future hung suspended. I was either moving on or reboarding the train.

"Why don't you go out to the trading floor and talk to the options desk?" Silver said.

"All right," I happily agreed. Moving forward had already become a matter of pride.

I expected Silver to say something further but he didn't. "How do I get out there?"

"My secretary will show you."

I turned to go, and the door suddenly opened in my face. No one was there. I looked back in surprise: Silver was smiling.

"It's electronic," he explained, his hand on a button.


My first view of a trading floor was, appropriately enough, like walking through a souk, a noisy, crowded bazaar that assaults your senses from all sides. There appeared to be one long, black, continuous pile of computers with wires so jumbled and randomly ordered that I immediately wondered what would happen if any one of them failed. In front of these disorderly rows sat lines of men and women, many of them speaking into phones, the rest of them staring at screens covered with colored lines of information. The computers were obviously grouped according to some rationale, but the general effect was of a sea awash with people and technology: as if the good ship IBM had gone down in stormy weather and this is what had floated to the surface.

"So where is the bond market?" I asked Silver's secretary as we weaved through the wreckage.

She laughed at first, as if I were kidding, then looked oddly at me. "This is it."

I looked around in surprise. Up until this point, my idea of a financial market had been the view of the New York Stock Exchange seen on the nightly news: a group of screaming lunatics running around a floor littered with paper.

"This is the bond market?"

"Part of it, anyway." She halted behind one chair in a long row—"This is Diane"—and left me with a worried look.

Diane had her back to me. "I said forty-five!" she was screaming. *"Forty-five!"* She slammed her phone down on the desk. "Fucking idiot!"

"Diane?" I asked gingerly.

"What?!"

"Yakov Silver sent me out here."

"Yeah, he just called. Hold on—okay, they're two points out of the money . . ."

I looked around the desk while Diane fielded three calls in quick succession. "The only trader ever reprimanded for being too rude," Jim had warned me about her. Oh well, I had more important things to worry about. Like what a trader *was.* Until this point the term had failed to form an image in my mind. But now I saw that a trader was someone who had more computer screens than a NASA ground controller, with more information than anyone could possibly keep track of, and the phone skills of the average collection agent.

"No, I want ninety-two. I said ninety-two! Right. See ya." Diane swung back around. "So what do you want to know?"

I hesitated. Where should I start—economics, bonds, the meaning of life?

"How options work."

She scowled at me. I grinned at her. Miraculously, it worked.

"Read this," she laughed, handing me a monstrous textbook. "Anything else?"

My visit with Diane didn't last much longer; there wasn't much else to say. So I wandered back to see Silver, who offered me a tuna sandwich. While he sat quietly typing on his laptop, I ate, wondering what to do next. I still needed an entrée to the emerging markets group, so I told him I had an additional interest in that area.

"Good," he replied. "I'll talk to them. Anything else?"

"I have a meeting in a few minutes with Jack Hale."

"Don't let me keep you."

I stood and hesitated; should I?

"I'm also wondering how this whole thing works. I'm not sure how to proceed."

"You're seeing Jack Hale."

"Yes, but after—"

"Don't worry," Silver said. "You're among friends here."

I tried to read him but couldn't, and forced a smile. I always feel uncomfortable when people say things like that, especially after you've just met them. Do they really mean it?

Jack Hale stared at me from behind his desk. He looked like he was going to explode. His face was flushed, his teeth slightly bared, his gray hair raked back over his head. Luckily, his expression had nothing to do with me. Hale was a partner in J. Aron and Co., Goldman's commodity trading and foreign exchange division: he always looked that way. In the past twenty years, he had worked his way up from the bottom with the tenacity of a street fighter. It showed in his accent, which was reminiscent of different streets from those the average Goldman partner had traveled; and it showed in his face, which advised you not to forget it.

Ironically, my presence in Hale's office was the result of the Harvard family jewels. Once I had my entrée to Goldman, I used it as leverage in other parts of the firm: "I'm going to be visiting Yakov Silver next week and I was wondering if you would have some time to see me . . ." One of the jewels, a partner at J. Aron, had agreed, then gone out of town on a business trip, leaving Hale in his place. In the interim I had learned that J. Aron traded oil, sugar, coffee, metals, and the world's currencies—which even under Hale's hawklike stare made me feel more comfortable than the world of bond options. At least I knew what coffee was.

Hale leaned forward on his desk to study my résumé. He did so intently, as if it were some contested bill of lading. Every so often he would look up and over my shoulder, through the glass wall behind me, to the J. Aron trading floor, a group of carrels that looked no more imposing than a computer lab. Meanwhile he asked me some very sharp questions, one after another. Why had I done this? Why had I done that? What was that like? He kept his eyes fixed on me as I answered. I fixed mine back, figuring he'd appreciate that. Then he reached the part of my résumé that dealt with mathematics.

I had known, when drawing up my résumé, that whether trading bonds, options, aluminum, or yen, quantitative skills are very important. And since I had taken some advanced math in college, and since I had worked at the nation's code-breaking agency, my quantitative credentials figured prominently on my résumé. The paper, however, hid a deeper truth. I hadn't done any real math since my sophomore year in college. In fact, after turning from numbers to writing, my long-time hobby, my mathematical abilities had dimmed considerably. It wasn't just the ability to do calculus either, which dims in the best of us; it was the ability to do relatively simple calculations in my head. I simply didn't think that way anymore. So while my résumé implied I was a Pentium processor, the truth was that I was closer to a vacuum tube.

"You've done a lot of math, huh?" Hale said to me, his eyes boring into my head. I nodded.

"Quantitative skills are very important in this business. I've found over the years that the people who succeed usually have a knack with numbers."

I emphatically agreed.

Hale looked out at the trading floor, returned his eyes to me. "We have a guy here who does a little test on people like you. It helps me evaluate their numerical skills."

I have heard of heart attacks occurring in young men, but until that moment I didn't realize one could suffer a brain attack as well. After hearing this unexpected news, my cerebrum began to fibrillate. I had a clear vision of Hale staring at me with his powder-keg expression while some quant with a nasal voice said: "Now, Mr. Stiles, if a chicken and a half lays an egg and a half in a day and a half, how many eggs does a single chicken lay in one day?" (Answer: "I'm a vegetarian.")

"That's fine," I said. "But it's been a while since I did integral calculus."

Hale looked at me strangely, as if in anticipation of something I could not imagine. "That's okay—the questions are simple."

I waited in the quiet room, listening to the clock tick while Hale searched the trading floor for his ruthless interrogator. One egg, I thought. No—two thirds.

The door opened behind me and Hale slid behind his desk. "Couldn't find him."

I breathed out, releasing my death grip on the chair. "Maybe later, then."


By late afternoon I had had three more interviews, including one with the head bond trader, and my energy was lagging. One can stay at the peak of concentration for only so long, and I had been at it nearly six hours. Thankfully the market had closed and it was time to go home.

On the way out I caught Silver at his computer.

"I'm busy now," he said. "How did it go?"

I told him in so many words that I had found all areas of Goldman equally interesting.

"Unh," he grunted.

I thanked him for all his help.

"Not a problem."

I waited, but Silver didn't add anything.

"Do you want me to call you?"

He immediately glanced up. "Yes. If you want."

"Okay, I'll call you in a few days."

"Good! Thanks for coming by."

I turned and waited. The electronic door clicked open on its own.

"You're learning," Silver said.


I called Jim the next day.

"So how did it go?" he asked.

"I have no idea. I really don't." I filled him in on the details and asked what to do next.

"Call them, of course. They're not going to call *you*, certainly."

"They all seem so busy."

"They are. But don't worry, they love this stuff. It's the closest thing they've got to the soaps."

Jim promised to see what he could find out, and I left a message with Silver's secretary, asking him to call me. To my surprise, he did.

"So how do things look?" I asked.

"Well, everyone liked you," he said. "No problem there."

*They liked me.* This was undeniably a positive sign and cause for some celebration, but all I could think of was Lynn Margulis and the note she had sent me in sixth grade: "Paul. I like you. Do you like me? Please check a box. Yes. No. Maybe."

"Well, *that's* good," I replied. "What's next?"

"Yes, what's next."

The light went on. "Next I come back," I said.

"Good!" Silver then gave me the number of the head emerging markets trader and told me to give him a call.

I hung up, wondering what this meant. I liked the emerging markets, but what about bond options? I called Hale and left two messages. He never returned my calls. What did that mean for commodities? I called Jim in Tokyo to solicit some advice.

"I just got an E-mail from Silver," he said. "He said you did all right—but options is out."

"Damn." I paused a moment to digest this.

"It doesn't mean he didn't like you. He just doesn't think you're right for the options desk."

"He's right," I admitted. "I just wish it wasn't that obvious."

"Keep at it," Jim advised. "Let me know."


The days that followed were full of bad news. After the Harvard job fair I had sent résumés to the human resources departments of all the major investment banks, seeking interviews. In return I received an equal pile of rejection letters: J. P. Morgan, CS First Boston, Salomon Brothers, S. G. Warburg, no, no, no. They all seemed to have colluded on the wording: "We're sorry but we have no positions open at the present time." This was a ridiculous assertion. Wall Street was booming and people were hiring like crazy. Didn't they think I read the *Journal?* I had visions of Ms. Winthrop laughing in her attic.

In the meantime, I called the head of emerging markets trading at Goldman, but he was in London for a few weeks. I tried the Harvard family jewels too, but for all their apparent luster they turned out to be cubic zirconium. And Jim, my only friend on the Street, had done what he could. As the days wore on in the cottage, the trail grew cold and Wall Street became a distant memory. I felt very much back at the beginning.

I had, however, learned some important lessons about the Street and vowed to put them to good use. The first was that Human Resources should be avoided. The real hiring power lay with the trading desks, not with a bunch of bureaucratic functionaries sifting through résumés according to a narrow set of rules. I should therefore approach the emerging markets groups directly. The question was, how?

This brought me to the second lesson I had learned: trading desks operate at breakneck speed, putting great time demands on their personnel. On the negative side, this made it tough to get in touch with someone or to keep their attention for long. But on the positive side, an organization too busy to pay attention to you is one easily outmaneuvered. It was time to get creative.

"Morgan Stanley," a voice said rapidly.

"I'm looking for Mike Kowalsky. Is he in?"

"You got him."

"Mike, this is Paul Stiles. I was wondering what you thought of my résumé."

A moment of silence followed. A shuffling of papers. Kowalsky, head of emerging markets trading, was perplexed. And understandably so. I had never sent him my résumé.

"Sorry," he said, "I can't find it. There's crap all over my desk. Can you hold on?" Kowalsky took another call, returned. "Listen, can you fax it to me? Here's my number."

I sent it off immediately.

"Did you get it?" I asked an hour later.

"Yeah . . . it's here somewhere. I've got it." A pause as he read. "Looks good. We're interviewing next week. Are you on the schedule?"

"Not yet. Can you put me on?"

"Call my secretary, will you? I gotta run."

And so it was done.

## 5

The rails were clacking beneath me, the Atlantic barely visible through the thin trees and the houses sweeping past. Once again I was on my way to New York.

In the past month I had become a regular on Amtrak and at Goldman Sachs, where I finally made contact with their emerging markets group. The subsequent interviews all went fine, leading to the next step: more interviews. The Goldman philosophy, it seemed, was to interview people until there was only one person left standing. Well, if that's what it took. Meanwhile I had also gone through my first round of interviews at Morgan Stanley, which went even better than I had hoped. I met with their head emerging markets trader, Mike Kowalsky, and his boss, the head of Morgan's junk bond desk (emerging markets bonds were considered junk bonds because of their high yield.) Morgan, the fourth largest firm on the Street, was expanding abroad, they said, and hiring. Neither man was too concerned with my lack of experience, stressing that it was the "intangibles" that mattered most. And within a week Kowalsky had called to invite me back. We're thinking of you for a sales job in London, he said. Are you interested?

The news electrified me. A sales job—in London! I had no idea what that meant exactly but it sure sounded good.

Sarah was happy too. She had been following my travails, and our dwindling bank account, with silent frustration. I would disappear to New York and return with some interesting stories, but never the tale either of us wanted to hear. Now after more than two months of effort, and unemployment, the end seemed near. And a good end it was, if things worked out. Not only could I work in the emerging markets, but we could skip New York and go directly abroad. For once the future looked bright.

The change in my fortunes also changed my attitude. In my previous trips north I had always felt a twinge of resignation I couldn't shake. It was a very deep, strangely satisfying melancholy, separating me from the passengers, distancing the clacking of the rails, and turning the miles into a blurry tunnel of green. While the world rushed by I traveled inward to a private spot, one I clung to with the force of self-preservation. And part of me always remained there even during my interviews: I would look back from a distance, watching a young man facing the partner of some great Wall Street firm, and wonder how he had ended up there and where he might possibly be going. But now I was no longer dragging myself north in futility—I was a real *prospect,* for a *sales job*—in London! My thoughts were on Piccadilly Circus and stiff upper lips, the articles I had read and reread on bonds and the emerging markets, the lessons of my previous interviews, and how Sarah would react when I told her the good news. I had the *Journal* spread out on my lap; I had finally bought a subscription. Short speeches—why Wall Street, why bonds, why the emerging markets—were playing over and over in my head. And as the train hurtled on, I no longer saw, nor wanted to see, the path to my private place. There were only the rusty tracks, leading me forward; the gray twisted trees that lined them, shorn of their leaves; and a fading memory of the previous summer.

• • •

Morgan Stanley was abuzz when I entered their midtown offices later that day. There were people rushing back and forth down the halls, their jaws firmly set, calling after someone, running to the bathroom—as if there were a fire down the hall and they were trying to put it out. In the past, this frantic motion had always intimidated me. It produced the feeling that one did not belong; or worse, that you were in the way. But now I had a chance to be a part of it all, not merely observe it. I was one step closer to the market.

Kowalsky came out to the front desk and pulled me into a room. Quickly he told me that I was going to meet a number of people from the desk, one after the other. Then they would make the decision. That surprised me—just like that?—raising some anxiety, but then determination rose to squash it and I welcomed the chance to bring this entire process to a swift end. Okay, I thought, just a few more interviews and that's it.

Kowalsky stroked his boyish face thoughtfully as he worked up a piece of advice. "Just be yourself, buddy. You'll do fine." Then he left me in a small conference room crowded with chairs. I sat near the end of the central table, listening to the sound of voices passing by outside.

The door opened and in stepped my first interviewer, a curly-haired, outgoing young bond salesman named Greg. He had a huge smile, big hands, and a strong Boston accent. He looked over my résumé, which he pronounced "very cool," and we went on to discuss everything but the market. We had a few things in common, Boston being one of them. I relaxed, happy to have started off in this informal way and to get along with my first interviewer.

Suddenly the door flew open and a red-faced young man with his tie askew charged in and threw himself down on a chair against the wall. He looked about twenty-five. Greg eyed him silently, then asked me another question.

"The National Security Agency?" the new arrival interrupted. I turned: he was looking at my résumé in dismay, his lower lip trembling. "I don't know that firm. What do they trade?"

"A different kind of security," I said, smiling. "It's an intell—"

"Do you have any fixed income background?"

"That's why I'm here."

He shot from his seat and departed, tossing my résumé on the table with a grunt.

Greg shook his head in embarrassment. "Can you believe that guy? Jesus, these people—" Then he caught himself and changed the subject, but the atmosphere never recovered. He departed a few minutes later, wishing me luck.

My second interviewer, a shorter, squatter young man with a crew cut, was from the trading desk, a fact he was proud to tell me. He was also intent on approaching this business of interviewing as shrewdly as possible.

"So you started there when?" he would say, checking the dates on my résumé.

"And why did you leave?" All the time he kept his eyes leveled on me as if rooting out deception. By the time he reached the end of my résumé I had had enough.

"So why did you leave the navy again?" he asked suspiciously.

"The Cold War is over," I said. "We won."

My third interviewer, or my fourth, depending on how you counted, was Sharon, an attractive young woman my age, with black shoulder-length hair, a halfhearted smile, and a red business suit. She carried herself uncomfortably into the room, knocking into the end of the table, sat down opposite me, and clasped her hands formally in front of her as if trained in How to Influence People. She began by introducing herself very precisely, informed me that she was the head of marketing, and that she was looking for someone in London. If I got the job, I would be working for her.

"I thought it was a sales position," I asked, although the fine print didn't matter much. Sales or marketing—what was the difference?

Sharon shut her eyes and shook her head impatiently—not with me, I thought, but with her own organization. Then she looked over my résumé. I felt a tingle of anxiety. There was no glint of recognition, or appreciation, in her eye. She went on to ask me a few questions, looking uncomfortable the entire time. With me? Herself? Or what?

"Well, thank you for coming," she said and departed, grazing the table again.

Kowalsky came in last. "Okay, that's it, buddy. I'll know by the end of the day. Give me a call tomorrow, will ya?"


In the weeks leading up to my interviews at Morgan Stanley, Sarah and I had decided to take a vacation. This was a financially irresponsible thing to do. Thanks to me our savings account had slid into a low four figures and was sinking fast. But the pressures of unemployment and the ups and downs of my forays into Wall Street had come to a head at last and needed to be released. We had consequently rented an efficiency apartment on Culebra, a small, undeveloped island off Puerto Rico, chiefly because it appeared to be the cheapest vacation in the Caribbean. We departed the morning after I returned from Morgan Stanley. It wasn't easy; I sorely wanted to know the outcome of my interviews. What a perfect ending it would be, I thought: flying off to the Caribbean, knowing that we were moving to London upon our return. But the risk of failure was there as well. Some of my interviews had gone well, while others had raised questions in my mind. So to play it safe, I decided not to call Kowalsky until I returned. There was no use spoiling a perfectly good and well-needed vacation.

We had barely lifted off when I noticed the phone. It was set into the seat in front of me, staring me in the face. I couldn't believe it. Airplane phones had just been introduced and this was my first one. What timing.

"Did you see this?"

Sarah looked at the phone, then at me. "Don't."

"I have to call them sometime."

"You said you'd wait."

"What if they try and get in touch with me? They might give the job to someone else." I stared at the phone. It stared back, mocking my indecision. "I wonder how it works."

Sarah sighed in exasperation and lay back tensely in her seat, her eyes closed.

I carefully pulled the receiver free. It made a loud click but she didn't move. My conscience stirred, a guilty unease I sought to quell. Why should I wait? Am I a child? If I don't make it, I don't make it, that's all. I read through the directions and slowly slid my credit card through the slot. The Touch-Tones beeped . . .

Sarah opened one eye.

"Morgan Stanley."

It was Kowalsky, I could tell by his voice. Staring blindly forward, I said hello and asked him how things had worked out. My world narrowed to the scratchy sound of his reply.

"Oh hi, thanks for calling. Listen . . . we talked it over and decided the fit wasn't right."

*The fit wasn't right.* A roaring echo in my ears. *The fit wasn't right.* The flip side of *We like you,* the Wall Street euphemism for rejection.

"That's too bad," I said flatly.

"Sorry it didn't work out, buddy. If there's anything else I can do for you, let me know."

I barely heard him. A distant voice mumbled some thanks and I replaced the phone. Suddenly Kowalsky was gone, Morgan Stanley was gone, and Wall Street was gone. There was only the cramped cabin of an airliner and the persistent wail of its engines.

I felt a hand slide over my forearm and squeeze. "It's okay," she said.

"The fit wasn't right. He said the fit wasn't right."

"It's okay."

"Dammit. I really thought—"

"It's okay."

I felt my throat tighten and looked out the window, heard the steady whine of the engine, watched the passing clouds, and found myself retreating to a quiet place beyond the reach of my emotions. It was still there, thank God.

## 6

**M**organ Stanley was just the beginning of the bad news.

We had left on our vacation looking forward to celebrating two events: my twenty-ninth birthday and Thanksgiving, both of which fell during the same week. This posed a challenge to our traditions, since we were going to a remote island; but if the Pilgrims could feast in a New World, we decided, so could we. We had consequently packed a large suitcase full of all the holiday trimmings, including a frozen turkey, confident that we would arrive before the thaw, and have a true Thanksgiving in the Caribbean.

Naturally, this didn't happen. Instead we arrived in San Juan without our luggage. And over the next few days, our bird became the first migratory turkey ever tracked down the eastern seaboard. There were sightings in Washington and Miami—where it sat in the sweltering heat of a warehouse for two days—San Juan, and finally Culebra, where we picked it up at the local tar-strip airport. By then the case had the scarred visage of an old steamer trunk and left an oily trail in its wake. Inside we discovered a jumble of crushed cans, burst packages, and a pile of rancid meat. The perfect metaphor for the past few months, I thought, as I surveyed the damage back in our room. How could I screw up Thanksgiving dinner, and an entire vacation, with such effortlessness?

Determined to make the best of it, I pinched off a piece of graying meat, grabbed my fishing rod, and headed across the street to the island's long bay. I have long been of the opinion that the best kind of therapy is fishing, particularly when it is done alone and in a quiet, scenic spot. It also helps if the fish are biting, which they were. Within minutes of impaling the turkey on my hook, my line zinged out and I reeled in a nice red snapper—only to have it cut in two by the barracuda that lived beneath the dock.

I stared at the lifeless remains hanging from my hook, wondering how long a losing streak like this could last. Wall Street, the airlines, and now even Mother Nature—the entire world was arrayed against me. The thought stirred a deep-seated sense of injustice. It was time to strike back!

The next day, strengthened by a strong wire leader, I caught the barracuda.

"What is *that*?" asked an awed young boy standing beside me on the dock.

"That," I said, holding the dripping, snapping fish by the gills, "is Merrill Lynch."

●　●　●

I knew nothing about Merrill Lynch the day I called the New York City operator—just the name and the corporate bull charging through all those television commercials. I wasn't even sure it was the right kind of bank to call. Judging by the ads, Merrill Lynch had offices all over America, while a place like Goldman Sachs did not. Were they even in the same business? But at the time I felt a strong need, as they say on the Street, to diversify my portfolio; and having just landed my first interview at Morgan Stanley, my confidence was running high. This was an important factor. When you're trying to mount a frontal assault, confidence is everything.

The New York City operator connected me with the Merrill Lynch operator, who found a listing for "International Emerging Markets." I dialed the number.

"Merrill Lynch," a feminine voice answered. Noise filled the background.

"Hi. I'm supposed to send a fax to your head trader but I don't have his fax number." She gave it to me. "How do you spell his name?" She told me. "He is the head emerging markets trader, isn't he?" She assured me he was. "Thank you!"

I sat back down and gave a great deal of thought to the fax. Creativity was at a premium—Morgan Stanley had taught me that. And I would need to be direct, since I was dealing with a fast-moving trading desk. After reworking the cover letter to my résumé a number of times, it went out like this:

```
Dear Mr. Forte:

I will be in New York next week interviewing for positions in
the emerging markets, and was hoping to get on your schedule as
well. I can be reached at the number below. Thank you.
```

A few hours later I was reading a book in the quiet of the cottage when the phone rang. I rose hopefully from my chair and listened with excitement to a feminine voice rising above the noise of a far-off trading floor.

"Mr. Stiles? I'm calling for Miguel Forte at Merrill Lynch . . ."

I didn't know it yet, but I was approaching Merrill Lynch at an interesting time. Nineteen-ninety three would be the most profitable year in the firm's history, the fruit of strategic changes that had turned a mom-and-pop retail brokerage into a Wall Street titan.

Merrill Lynch began its life in 1914, when Charles Merrill opened up a small merchant bank for retailers. Prior to the crash of 1929, Merrill sold much of the firm to E. A. Pierce, the nation's largest brokerage firm, forming the core business that has survived to the present: retail stock and bond sales. Merrill then returned to the firm in the forties, having spent the interim managing one of his former clients, the Safeway food chain, an experience that helped him develop Merrill's retail capability. In the ensuing years Merrill Lynch opened offices across the United States, earning itself the nickname "the Post Office of the Street," a term that came to describe not only its wide distribution network but also a reputation for being bloated and poorly managed.

In the late seventies, however, the firm began to change. First, recognizing that its plain vanilla brokerage business limited its involvement in the increasingly profitable institutional arena—underwriting, trading, and fund management— Merrill purchased an investment bank, White Weld, in 1978 and began expanding its potential in that arena. Second, perceiving the increasingly global nature of finance, the firm went international, opening offices in numerous countries and pursuing business in both private banking and the global capital markets. These twin strategies, both timely adaptations to a changing banking environment, propelled the firm through the eighties, aided by a booming market, management reforms, and cost-control measures. By the time the decade was over, Merrill had become so broad and deep that there was no single word to adequately describe it. It was a financial management and advisory firm, an investment bank, a retail brokerage firm, and a major trading house in all markets worldwide and for all types of clients, from the small-time investor to the world's largest corporations. It was a financial powerhouse.

Today Merrill Lynch dominates almost all major areas of the securities industry. With 49,000 employees, $6 billion in capital, and $700 billion under management—a figure projected to grow to $1 trillion by the year 2000—it is the largest firm on Wall Street.* It is the largest retail brokerage firm as well, with 13,000 financial consultants spread across the country. It is the top underwriter of both stocks and bonds in the world and has been since 1988. In 1994, Merrill finally unseated Goldman Sachs to become the top-earning firm on the Street after its second consecutive year of billion-plus profits, a position it retained in 1995 when *Euromoney* named it the top investment bank in the world. Such successes have brought the firm international recognition and a multinational personality. With offices in forty-nine countries, Merrill Lynch now earns a third of its revenues abroad, a figure the company predicts will soon climb to a half. From New York to Shanghai, the Merrill Lynch bull has become one of the most visible financial symbols in the world—an emblem of a new *global* capitalism rather than a strictly American brand.

But these are just superficial statistics, fodder for the annual report. The real Merrill Lynch remains an enigma. The history of the firm and the markets it participates in, the people who built them and their significance for society all fade

* The merger of Morgan Stanley and Dean Witter, announced as this book was nearing publication, will create an investment bank even larger, in many respects, than Merrill.

as you submerge beneath the macro level, into the belly of the bull. I discovered, for instance, that there was no book on Merrill Lynch—surprising, for the world's top securities firm. The annual report didn't even reveal who Mr. Merrill was or when the firm was founded. Likewise, information on the emerging markets was dominated by current market news, the charting of ups and downs. I had to draw my own conclusions on the global implications of the business by reading between the lines. It is the same all over Wall Street: markets, and the firms that run them, are too complicated, too specialized, too technical, too diverse, and too rapidly changing to be of much interest to historians, aside from the pull of scandal. Similarly, the banks at all levels, from the business units to the trading desks and the individual broker, have no interest in anything that won't make them money today. History is about tradition, about values, about forming bonds with the past and other people. Wall Street isn't.

The cab swayed from side to side as it hurtled down the West Side Highway. The Hudson River was passing on my right, a sight that normally would have attracted my attention, but now all I could think of was the challenge ahead. I was still riding high from my first visit to Morgan Stanley and hoped I could keep up the momentum at Merrill. The men at Morgan were right: it was the intangibles that mattered most, and the intangibles on a trading desk, I had learned, were aggressiveness, speed, intensity, the presence of mind to make rapid decisions, and a very thick skin. This was the mold into which I would try to fit myself.

The towers of the World Financial Center loomed ahead, straight from CNN. How strange that name had sounded, coming from my lips for the first time: World Financial Center, please. As if there was one world and we were printing its currency up the road. And across the street was the World Trade Center—all the economic bases covered in just a few acres. You gotta love New York. The cab braked to a quick halt by the side entrance to the North Tower and I hurried inside. The traffic had been heavy and I was late. I shot up the escalators, paused at the reception desk, which called ahead, and boarded the elevator, telling myself to relax.

The sixteenth floor was empty when I emerged. I followed a narrow hallway to an open doorway, entering a large, rectangular, noisy room about the size of a tennis court. The room was dominated by a figure-eight of people, computers, and screens at its center: a small trading desk, some twenty-five seats in all. The walls were lined with numerous filing cabinets stacked with so many boxes and papers that the walls themselves were barely visible. It was as if a bomb had gone off in the center, blowing everything loose to the perimeter. On one end the debris had been kept down to waist level, exposing a line of large plate glass windows and a panoramic view to the south: Battery Park, the Hudson, the New Jersey shoreline.

The adjacent wall, opposite me, looked into a thicket of skyscrapers. There was a small office with a glass front at one end, and a large conference room next to it, its door ajar. Apart from a row of offices around the corner, which housed the investment bankers, this was IEM.

I stood at the entrance surveying the scene, feeling out of place in my heavy navy pea coat. Forte's secretary, a thin, attractive blonde, approached and told me he was in a meeting. She returned to her chair, glancing into the corner office. There were two men in there. A few minutes later the door opened and they shook hands. One of them passed me on his way out, a résumé in his hand. We smiled knowingly at each other.

Miguel Forte emerged a few moments later to greet me. He was a thin, swarthy Panamanian in his mid-thirties, with a bright smile, buoyant black hair parted down the middle, and a soft-spoken, upper-class charm worthy of a diplomat, an air underscored by his Latin accent, the gold links on his French cuffs, and his shiny tasseled loafers. To this was mated the alacrity bred on a trading desk, which lent his walk a distinct spring, and a sphinxlike reserve, a product of the same.

He invited me back to his office and sat down behind his desk. He had been reading my résumé, which lay in front of him, and turned to it in silence, then proceeded to ask me a number of questions. After each answer he would glance back at the résumé, pause, and phrase another question. He was in no visible rush and was not discomforted by spaces in conversation, which he bridged while sipping on a carton of fruit juice. We got along well. Forte liked my background, especially the intelligence aspect; he found that interesting.

In the middle of our talk the door opened and a young man stuck his head in to ask Forte a question. He was thin, mid-twenties, with unkempt wavy brown hair, slipperlike loafers, and a narrow tie with a tiny knot so tightly tied around his thin neck that it seemed to bulge his eyes. I stared at him a moment. "Kenny?"

He looked at me in surprise. "Paul Stiles—what are you doing here?"

I stood to shake his hand. Kenny Breen and I had gone to college together, though we hadn't known each other very well. He was a friend of my roommate and had stopped by our apartment occasionally. I knew he had gone on to work at Bankers Trust but had lost track of him since. Now here he was, working for IEM. Good news?

We chatted a moment, laughing at our surprise meeting, and got caught up. "Make sure you see me before you leave," Breen said, then departed, leaving me with Forte.

"So you know Kenny," Forte stated with a curious smile.

We went on to discuss trading, and here Forte was more loquacious. In his view trading was primarily psychology, the mind of the market: if you could read that, you would be a success. Others were driven by technical analysis, projections of the future based on past market movements, but to him the numbers played only a supporting role. It was a matter of taste. The most common psychological error, in his experience, was taking profits too soon and cutting losses too late. People were prone to take the money and run or hold on too long, hoping a bad situation would turn around. Instead one should try to ride the winners as long as possible and drop the losers right away. And this wasn't just a philosophy of trading, Forte stressed: it was a philosophy of life.

He bared a bright white smile. "You know, you go out on a date and you say to yourself, I don't think I'll ever marry this woman. So why waste your time anymore? Cut your losses. When you come upon a situation you don't like, just cut your losses." He sliced the air with his hand.

After we were through, Forte grabbed a few other people off the desk and sent them in to see me. They were all young, midtwenties to early thirties, and didn't seem especially put off by the fact that I had no financial experience, although, as one of them admitted, "We all have to agree here. One thumb down and that's it." Then Forte returned, sounding upbeat, and asked me to call him later.

On the way out I looked for Breen but couldn't find him. By this time it was late and the panoramic view had changed. Darkness had fallen on southern Manhattan, bringing thousands of lights to life. New York always looks good at night.



Like Merrill Lynch, IEM was booming in December of '93, the result not only of a soaring bond market but of the profound changes that had wrought the emerging markets phenomenon.*

The history of the emerging markets stems from a rash period of international lending that began in the early seventies. At the time the world's oil-rich nations, mostly in the Middle East, were enjoying a cash surplus, which they transferred to American and European banks. In turn, the banks lent the money to the emerging markets, principally the "Big Four" Latin American economies: Argentina, Brazil, Mexico, and Venezuela. For their part these countries, which were facing increasing budget deficits, borrowed all they could. This created a risky situation, one masked by the rapid growth of Latin American economies at the time, and the prevailing financial wisdom, as summarized by the chairman of Citibank, that "countries can't go bankrupt." The debt of Latin countries consequently soared,

* Though "emerging markets" refers to both the stock and bond markets of developing countries, I will use it strictly to refer to the bond business. There are other confusing usages. "Emerging bond markets" refers to bond markets in developing countries. "Emerging markets bonds" refers to the bonds of developing countries. "Emerging markets *debt*" includes both bonds and loans. Depending on context, "emerging markets" can be taken to mean any of these things.

from $23 billion in 1970 to $223 billion in 1980, 86 percent of it owed to international private banks.

Then in the early eighties two things happened that popped the investment bubble. The prices of commodities, the principal Latin export, fell, bringing down revenues with them; and interest rates rose, causing debt payments to increase. Suddenly Latin countries found it increasingly difficult to pay their bills. Instead of cutting back on spending, however, they continued to try to borrow their way to solvency, adding another $100 billion to their debt between 1980 and 1982 alone. Sensing danger, international lenders finally pulled back, but by then it was too late. With its funding cut off, Latin America plunged into financial crisis.

The Latin Debt Crisis, as it came to be called, began in August 1982 when the Mexican Finance Secretary informed the U.S. government that without immediate aid his country would default on $80 billion in foreign debt owed to commercial banks. This was a staggering sum all by itself. But over the next few years, as attempts at aiding Mexico failed and other emerging markets teetered on the edge of collapse, the full magnitude of the problem became apparent. By 1985 international private banks held $300 billion in outstanding loans to developing countries, 75 percent of them to the Big Four alone. U.S. banks had an unprecedented exposure to the region—$120 billion—much of it held by the biggest names in banking; Citibank had a whopping $12 billion exposure all by itself. The prospect of a financial collapse in the developing world thus threatened not only the entire U.S. commercial banking system but, because of its interrelated nature, the world financial system as well. It was, as the vice chairman of Citicorp stated, "an international financial crisis without precedent in modern history."

The situation didn't improve until 1989 when, after years of negotiations, reschedulings, restructurings, and more loans, U.S. Treasury Secretary Nicholas Brady announced a two-part program aimed at resolving the crisis once and for all. The first part of the Brady initiative was a series of economic reforms, monitored by the International Monetary Fund, aimed at strengthening Latin economies. The second part was the securitization of debt, whereby banks would tear up their old loans and, in return, debtor nations would issue them new bonds. These bonds, quickly termed "Brady bonds," came in many different flavors, but they all involved some kind of debt relief and lengthened payment schedules, lessening financial pressures. In 1990, Mexico became the first country to issue Brady bonds, followed by Venezuela later that same year and Argentina in 1993—a total of $80 billion in new bonds. Meanwhile Nigeria, Costa Rica, Uruguay, and the Philippines instituted smaller Brady programs, adding another $8 billion to the total and expanding the Brady program beyond Latin America. By the end of 1993 Brazil, Poland, Bulgaria, Ecuador, and the Dominican Republic were all at some point in the Brady pipeline.

The appearance of these Brady bonds formed an entirely new market. For the previous few years a handful of Wall Street firms had specialized in trading the distressed loans of emerging nations, a technical and cumbersome business open only to highly sophisticated investors. But as the Brady initiative unfolded, these loans turned into billions of dollars worth of easily tradable bonds registered on major exchanges. Brady bonds were also attractive investments: denominated in dollars, partially backed by U.S. Treasury bonds, and offering high returns—especially when compared with low domestic interest rates. Investors were drawn accordingly.

The Brady market was dominated in the beginning by the commercial banks, which suddenly had billions of Brady bonds on the books; Latin investors in the U.S. holding "flight capital," especially in Miami and Texas; and speculative investment funds, known as hedge funds. Their involvement brought rising trading volume and liquidity to the marketplace: investors grew confident that they could exit the market if they wished, and, hence, did not hesitate to enter it. Then with the maturation of the market in 1991–92, the big institutional players jumped in—the mammoth U.S. mutual funds, junk bond funds, insurance companies, and pension funds—and the boom was on. Trading volume of emerging markets debt, which had been $225 billion in 1991, more than doubled in 1992, then tripled in 1993, reaching $1.5 *trillion.* Prices climbed steadily and profits mounted. In 1993 the annual return on Brady bonds was nearly 50 percent, while the return on loans, which continued to be traded, grew at a fantastic rate: Peruvian debt climbed a total of 260 percent, Russia 209 percent, Bulgaria 172 percent, and the Ivory Coast 157 percent. Moreover, with the kickoff of the NAFTA agreement on January 1, 1994, it seemed like the emerging markets were just beginning their ascent.

Along with this growth, of course, came the increased participation of the banks. Emerging markets groups sprung up all over the Street, and midtown as well, as the profit potential of the new market became evident: Citibank, Salomon Brothers, Chemical, Chase Manhattan, J. P. Morgan, Morgan Stanley, Bankers Trust, and Goldman Sachs all became important players. Their efforts were fueled not only by the core Brady market but by the growing demand for other emerging markets financial instruments—corporate bonds, certificates of deposit, foreign Treasury bonds, derivatives—and, as the legacy of the debt crisis faded and Latin issuers rose from the dead, the opportunity to earn hefty underwriting fees. These groups were heavily staffed, as one might expect, by Latin bankers, many of whom had been on restructuring committees or worked for foreign banks in Latin America. Hired for their connections and their knowledge of local markets, they arrived in New York at a time when information was scarce and, in turn, hired more of their own.

From the very beginning, Merrill Lynch was a major force in this evolution. In 1985, a group of Latin bankers assembled at the firm to establish an LDC loan trading business. Merrill Lynch International Emerging Markets, as it came to be called (with some redundancy), grew on its success and expanded with the market. In 1989, IEM added underwriting to its credit by successfully placing the first Latin bond issue in eight years, a major coup that effectively signaled the end to the debt crisis. It also became a major trader, first in the nascent Brady market, where it was one of a handful of "market makers" committed to both buying and selling the same bond at any time, and then expanding into other instruments, such as corporate bonds (the fruit of its underwriting efforts), derivatives, CDs, and Mexican Treasury instruments. Meanwhile its sales effort garnered some of the biggest institutional clients in the business: Fidelity, Scudder, Steinhardt, Quantum. Profits rose accordingly and the group expanded, hiring an international staff, placing salespeople in Chicago, Dallas, and San Francisco, and opening offices in Tokyo and London. By the end of 1993, IEM was the top underwriter of emerging markets bonds in the world and a major profit engine for Merrill Lynch, netting nearly $100 million that year with only forty-two professional staff members.

And they were hiring.

## 7

The World Financial Center was a lot larger than I had expected. In my previous visits I had entered its North Tower directly from the street, seeing nothing but the elevator. Now, as I wandered the full length of its cavernous interior, I was surprised at every turn by more hallway, another building. It never seemed to end. Its spaciousness was magnified by the lavish use of glass, revealing on one side the World Trade Center, its foundation holed by a terrorist's bomb, and a marina on the other, empty this late December day, which opened on the Hudson River. There were two overhead walkways as well, great tubes of aluminum, lined with portholes, spanning the West Side Highway and connecting Finance with Trade—a marriage of obvious abundance, as reflected in the fine polished marble of rosy hues clicking beneath my feet, the shiny brass rails fit to trim the *Titanic* lining the way, the uniformed maintenance and security crews manning their positions every few yards, and the corporate nameplates, torn from the Rolodex of Finance, that were riveted beneath the various towers: American Express, Oppenheimer, Lehman Brothers, Nomura, Merrill Lynch. The hub of the complex was a massive atrium known as the Winter Garden, a huge hangar of metal and glass fit to house the *Hindenburg* that harbored instead a square oasis of perfectly straight palm trees, like a valued source of oxygen in someone's biosphere. By the time I reached this oddity I wasn't in an office complex at all, but in an immense spacecraft, hovering over southern Manhattan and Hoovering it for profits.

It was the World Headquarters of Merrill Lynch: two granite towers, South and North, full of the Bull.

The entrance to the North Tower was guarded by a phalanx of gold turnstiles and more security. I skirted these obstacles with the aid of the reception desk, turned the corner, and stopped cold, face-to-face with the Merrill Lynch Principles. They formed an immense gold plaque on the wall, five commandments found throughout the firm—and the world—on napkins, coffee cups, and stationery, in elevators, hallways, and corporate speeches, in letters to investors, magazine advertisements, and commercials on network television:

CLIENT FOCUS

RESPECT FOR THE INDIVIDUAL

TEAMWORK

RESPONSIBLE CITIZENSHIP

INTEGRITY

An involuntary shudder wriggled up my spine. If I had learned anything in the government, it was to beware of organizations that put their principles on the wall.

I pressed on, head down. Money, think money.

The elevator took me to the seventh floor and a boisterous hallway. Midway to the end the roar of the market reached my ears. It drew me through an open pair of doors into the largest room I had ever seen. It was two stories tall, a football field long, and took up almost an entire floor of the building, with low windows all around. People looked small on either end. It was the main Merrill Lynch bond trading floor, known throughout the firm simply as Seven: a vast field of computers furrowed by humanity.

I looked about in awe and consternation. How I was supposed to find the Syndicate desk in all this mess was beyond me. Then I spotted Breen just inside the entrance, as he had indicated. He was sitting at the end of a long row of shouting, gesticulating men on the telephone, a receiver pressed to either ear. I went over and put my hand on his shoulder but he didn't move.

I took off my heavy pea coat, slung it over my arm, and waited. Like my other trips to Wall Street, I didn't know what to expect except a long day. In the past two weeks, while still interviewing at Goldman and revisiting Forte, I had kept after Breen, hoping that he would lobby IEM on my behalf. He had eventually informed me that there was a job opening up on the Syndicate desk, where he was IEM's representative, and that they were thinking of me for it. This prompted some consistent pressure on my behalf, which yielded only frustration. Breen was cagey and not very responsive: just busy? Finally one day he called me out of the blue, all apologetic, and told me to come up to New York to see Tim Ridley, the head of the desk. After another fruitless round of calls, I was finally given a date during

Christmas week. That was all I knew—except that in the wake of my failure at Morgan Stanley, and my perpetual interviews at Goldman, I had to make this work.

The biggest question mark of all was Breen himself, whom I didn't know very well. He had seemed likable enough in college. But Breen had been known for sliding by, and had also told classmates of run-ins with the Harvard disciplinary board, one of which had threatened his graduation. Had he changed? Now, according to my interviewers at Goldman, Breen was a rising Wall Street star. Funny how that worked.

Breen hung up the phone and turned around. "Well, look who's here," he said with a wide and syrupy smile. "Drag up a chair." He turned back and hit another line.

I hung my coat over an empty chair and sat down, looking over all the high technology on Breen's desk. It looked as formidable as ever. Then I turned my gaze on the room. I had taken an early train and the market had just opened. The line of seats to either side of us, a good fifty yards in length, was full, and the continuous desktop awash with paper, some of which had fallen, spotting the floor. On the wall ahead, an electronic billboard worthy of a sports stadium—and known accordingly as the scoreboard—was reeling off a continuous series of news stories, dominated by closing prices in Tokyo and trading in London. From the roof hung a series of flags adorned with the familiar snorting bull and the glories of past achievements:

TOP DEBT UNDERWRITER, 1992.
TOP GLOBAL BOND UNDERWRITER, 1992.

And so on, back to the early eighties. A voice suddenly barked some economic statistic over a loudspeaker and a clamor arose in the center of the floor as a small crowd assembled. The announcement ceased, the crowd dispersed amid scattered shouting, and the noise settled down to the room's constant muted roar, the sound of surf heard at a distance.

"Pretty impressive, huh?" Breen said by my side.

"It's *huge*."

"It's the biggest trading floor in the world."

"Really?"

"Well . . . it's *got* to be—though I doubt they keep statistics on such things." He looked off in the distance. "Every year they bring the summer interns down here and see if someone can throw a football from one end to the other. I don't think anyone ever has. And there's another room just like it for stocks down on Five." He gestured to a few seats around him. "So this is the Syndicate desk. Over there"—he pointed across the room—"you have Corporate Bonds. In the back is

Non-dollar and International. Mortgages are in the corner. That's the Preferred desk—preferred stock. And that's the Government desk, way down there, where they trade Treasuries. They say every seat in this room costs the firm a million bucks a year in overhead."

"A million bucks!"

"Something like that."

I looked across the cavernous room. There were a lot of seats. "Why isn't IEM down here?"

Breen laughed inscrutably. "You don't know the Latin Mafia."

Avoiding further explanation, he went on to explain some of the technology on his desk, including the vast information available on his Bloomberg monitor, a special financial database. Then he briefly described his job. The Syndicate desk priced new bond issues and organized the vast Merrill sales force and other firms into a selling syndicate, which placed the bonds with clients. Once the bonds were issued, desks like IEM traded them in the secondary market. Merrill had the capability to place bonds through both its institutional salespeople and its worldwide network of retail offices, a power no other firm could match. It had made the firm the top bond underwriter in the world. The Syndicate desk was the central nervous system of this network. Breen had recently come down from IEM to fill a new position there necessitated by the boom in emerging markets underwriting. He was still learning the ropes, he said.

He picked up the phone and called Tim Ridley, the head of the desk, but he wasn't in. Ridley wasn't feeling well, his secretary said, but would be in later. In the meantime I had one interview after another with people on or connected with the Syndicate desk, each time returning to find that Ridley had not arrived.

The last of these was with Ron Sewell, the managing director of Preferred Stock, whom I met in Ridley's office. Sitting behind the desk, Sewell looked like the oldest man I had met so far, perhaps in his forties, maybe even his fifties, but it was hard to tell how much of his worn, elongated visage was the product of age or experience. His hair was raked back over his head in classic Wall Street fashion, and he spoke with a gravelly voice as he asked me about my past.

"So how did you like the government?"

The idea was appealing, I said, but the bureaucracy was not.

"Yeah," he agreed, "I was in the army for a while. . . . How long were you in?"

His tone put me on guard. Like a chef, I thought, asking how long I had boiled the pasta.

"Four years," I said.

"Four?" He paused. "I guess that's okay. Any more than that—" He brushed the air aside with a laugh. "If I had a guy come in here with ten years in the government, forget it."

I knew what he meant and had to agree. And since this was common ground I played to the audience. "The problem is, if you give people a set pay scale, take away their incentive, and keep them immune from market pressures, you get a bloated, inefficient bureaucracy that squeezes the life out of them. It's the closest thing we have to communism, actually."

Sewell smiled appreciatively, his yellow teeth sealed in a familiar clench; one was gold. It was an advanced version of Breen's smile, the curling at the hind quarters of the divide that spoke of inside information, superior knowledge. But I was happy he was happy. The interview was going well.

"So now you're at the other end of the spectrum," he said amusedly, "the cutting edge of capitalism."

"That's what I want. At least no one is masquerading as something they're not. I mean, you know what this place is about. No one says they're doing it for the country."

"No, we operate on a different principle," Sewell admitted. "We just do what we can get away with."

His smile reappeared, stretching all the way back to the last filling in his molars. I tried to smile back, but I guess I wasn't convincing enough. Suddenly his expression vanished, replaced by a sharpness that cut whatever common sentiment had joined us. In that moment the room seemed to widen and we were left a great distance apart.

"If you're done, I am," he said a few minutes later.


"Unfortunately, it looks like Ridley won't be in today," Breen told me upon my return to the Syndicate desk. He had the unease born of helplessness. "Hopefully, he'll be in tomorrow."

I didn't say anything. I was tired of unknowns—Was Ridley really sick? What was going on with IEM? What did Breen think of all this?—but mustered only an expression of great tiredness.

"I would suggest staying over," Breen said. "I don't know what your plans are, but it doesn't make sense to go home and come all the way back. You can crash at my place if you'd like."

I agreed, hoping to have all my questions answered in a more casual setting.


At the end of the day the great trading hall cleared, leaving only the paper scattered across the floor to remind you of the day's activity. Breen was one of the last to leave, taking his laptop with him. We hopped in a taxi and proceeded to the Upper West Side of Manhattan, where he lived with his fiancée, Patty, a student of massage therapy. Considering the responsibilities of his new position, and the fact that he had been on Wall Street a few years now, I expected to arrive in a spacious flat with new furniture and a sparkling appearance, the bounty of his efforts. What I found was a small garden apartment that looked more like a college dorm room, with one bedroom, low ceilings, an antiquated kitchen, and a small living area sporting a couch long past its prime: my bed. It was my first inkling that life on Wall Street was not as profitable as I had imagined—not at first, anyway, and not when those profits had to be spent on life in New York.

"I'm just curious," I said, wondering whether Breen had suffered some financial calamity. "What does a place like this go for?"

"We got a good deal," he said. "Only fifteen hundred a month."

"Plus utilities," Patty chimed in.

I raised my eyebrows. I hadn't given the economics of New York a second thought until now, thinking that a Wall Street job would make up for any increase in the cost of living. But fifteen hundred bucks was more than twice what we paid for the cottage; it was a *mortgage payment*!

"Welcome to New York," Breen said, seeing my incredulity. "Actually, this place has a lot of advantages. We have a small patio out back. And Central Park is only a few blocks away. You wouldn't *believe* how important that gets."

By now it was close to nine o'clock. Since Patty had already eaten, as was her norm, Breen and I walked around the corner to a Thai restaurant. It was bitterly cold. The wind was gusting down the street and biting at my face. We took off our coats at the entrance and spied an empty table in back. Breen led the way through the seated patrons. He had a different walk than he had in college, I noticed. It was more of a glide, a slippery stroll in which his shoulders never moved but stayed an even height from the ground, his open palms paddled by his side, and his jaw stayed firmly up, keeping his eyes above and beyond the crowd.

". . . must be the power suit," I heard a man whisper as we passed his table.

We sat down and ordered some beer and Breen began to smoke. I was reminded of college, when Breen would come over to see my roommate, sucking on a cigarette, and we would all sit around, drink beer, and swap stories. Only now the market sat with us as well. It showed in his hands, which trembled as he lifted his glass; in his attention, which wandered away from our conversation, then snapped back; and in his suit, now in its fourteenth hour of use, which trailed threads in spots and was stained in others. It was the suit of a man with no time for tailors, a twenty-seven-year-old whose sole focus in life was on keeping his head above water. And how did he do it? The trading floor was much tougher than a campus, the market much harder to beat than the Harvard administration. It was already taking its toll, forcing its compromises. Here I was, hoping Breen would help me, yet having misgivings about Breen myself. Somewhere inside him was an intelligent and likable young man, but the market had brought out the worst in him. As we talked, my feelings about him were torn in different directions: gratitude to an old acquaintance, annoyance with his new persona, respect for his success, disdain for how he achieved it, sympathy at the pressure he was under, unwillingness to accept that excuse. All these things bound us and broke us as I sought his help in getting a job.

We began, after the meal arrived, with some of the basics of the business. I had been struggling to learn about bonds, but my self-instruction had its limits. This was especially true of the concept of yield, which Breen outlined on the back of a napkin. "Simple, isn't it?" he said when he was through. "If people knew how simple it really was, we'd all be out of a job."

This was pure baloney—bonds are as complicated as you want to make them— but I let it pass. It was just another way for Breen to show me how natural the business came to him: one of many mirages he had constructed on the road to getting ahead. By now they were a way of life. His laugh was often artifice, his words well filtered, his delivery too smooth to be natural. It made you want to scream "Cut it out!" after a while. Did he even realize it?

"So how did I do today?" I asked.

"Good!" Breen said cheerily. "The desk liked you." He looked down, adding in discomfort, "The only bad news I heard was from Ron Sewell."

I tensed. "What did he say?"

"Oh, I don't know, something about the government, he didn't like that, I don't know." He quickly changed the subject. "Ready for another beer?"

"Sure."

He waved for the waiter.

"Will Sewell matter?" I asked, hiding my disappointment.

Breen shrugged. "I wouldn't worry about it. Ridley is the important man. You'd be working for him."

I sat back in my chair, frustrated. Just one syrupy smile and Sewell would have loved me. "So what's Ridley like?"

Breen smiled widely and knowingly. "Ahhh, Timmy Ridley. Ridley is Napoleon. He's about five-five and thinks he's God. The Syndicate desk is his private empire. He runs it worldwide. But the firm loves him. I think he made five million last year."

"Whew!"

Breen beamed at me.

"Do you like working for him?"

He cleared his throat, casting me a loaded stare. "Well, you know where you stand. I like that."

I raised my eyebrows but he indicated that he had said enough—as much for effect as anything else. My fortunes in Syndicate having dipped some, I turned to IEM. "Have you heard anything from Forte?"

"I heard it went well," Breen said carefully.

"He seemed to like my résumé."

"Oh, you know these Latins. They think the CIA controls the world."

"He really thinks—" My forehead fell into my open palm and I shook in laughter. The whole job-hunting process—indeed, everything that had led me here—suddenly seemed absolutely hysterical. Maybe it was just the beer.

"What's the pay like, anyway?" I asked, raising my head.

"It depends. You'd be coming on as an associate, right? Like people from business school?"

"I guess so. Where would that put me?"

Breen frowned thoughtfully. "Oh, your salary would come in somewhere between sixty-five and seventy-five a year. Plus your bonus, which depends on how well you and the group do. They guarantee those too, sometimes. If I had to guess, I'd say you'd gross about . . . one-twenty your first year, something like that."

One-twenty! "Can't complain about *that*," I said with a laugh. Breen kept smiling. "What about a training program?"

"That wouldn't apply to you. The training programs run in the summer. You'd be a direct hire. They'd train you right on the desk."

"Is that good or bad?"

"Depends. I think you could handle it. But hey, you know how this works. You don't always have a choice, right?"

"I suppose not."

But who cares? One-twenty! The warm glow of that number continued to infuse me. It was so close I could almost . . . deposit it.

"Who else do I need to see?"

Breen shrugged. "I think you've met everyone you need to see."

"What about the head of the group? I still haven't met him." This had struck me as odd in such a small group as IEM.

"Lisardo?" Breen smiled. "You don't want to meet him."

"Why not?"

"You're not Latin."

"Oh." What do you say to that?

My surprise must have showed. "There's some people we have to stay away from," Breen counseled, "if you want to make this work."

Soon our meal was over and we were back out in the cold. I wanted to get a good night's sleep before meeting Ridley—hopefully—but Breen insisted on dropping by a bar across the street. There I watched him gulp his beer and finish a pack of cigarettes while we traded college stories. We had become, to some known degree, coconspirators in a game whose rules were only vaguely known to me, one that repelled as well as attracted. The lure of winning, of the number at the end of the rainbow—one-twenty!—was undeniable. But it obviously didn't come easy.

● ● ●

The next morning we left Breen's apartment late. It was nine-thirty when we entered the trading floor, the day before Christmas Eve. And Ridley was in.

"But he can't see you now," Breen said quickly, three phone lines blinking on his touchscreen. "Syndicate!"

Stymied again, I paid a quick visit to Miguel Forte in IEM, just to show the flag, and returned to sit with Breen. I sat there the next five hours watching Breen come and go and trying to decipher bondspeak, my hopes for an interview fading. The market was almost closed when Breen returned from one of his forays and tapped me on the back.

"Ridley's ready."

I hopped to my feet with nervous energy, collected myself, and made my way back to Ridley's office. It was one of many off the trading floor, each guarded by a secretary and used by a senior manager when he needed to get away from the commotion. Finding it empty, I sat in the chair facing his desk, my résumé on my knee. Except for the hiss of the market down the hall, it was suddenly disturbingly quiet.

I leaned back and looked through the glass wall behind me, down the long row of secretarial desks. No ambling martinet was visible. There was only Ridley's secretary, a woman in her fifties, looking at me like a concerned parent. I turned back to inspect the small room, hoping to dampen a rapidly growing case of nerves. It was filled with the bric-a-brac of past bond deals. Official announcements of new issues, known as tombstones for their appearance, were framed on the wall. Others, printed on various curios, decorated Ridley's desk: little globes, pen sets, small Lucite headstones. Behind his swivel chair was a poster of Vince Lombardi entitled *The Winner*. "The winner," said the caption beneath it, "is someone who—"

A body brushed past me and swaggered to the desk. Ridley sat down without a glance in my direction and began searching his in-box. He was very short, as Breen had said—his feet barely touched the ground—but, as if in compensation, his face bore the menacing glare of a junkyard dog, supported by a square, clenched jaw. It was an expression in startling contrast with the white collar clasped together by a gold pin, which sat atop his dark blue shirt like a cleric's band. The modern Inquisition?

I coughed to make him aware of my presence.

"My secretary," he said, as if we were in the middle of a conversation, "saves me this stuff for a week at a time." He spread a stack of mail across his desk and began sorting rapidly through it, forming two piles, one of which he dumped in the trash.

I made a polite comment. In reply Ridley began opening and slamming his desk drawers in succession. "I can never find anything in here . . ." He finally produced a metal letter opener in triumph, sliced open the first envelope, and began perusing the contents.

"So you're a friend of Kenny's," he said while reading.

"Yes."

"I like Kenny." Ridley's eyes darted around his desk. He lifted his mail and looked beneath it. Then he hit the intercom button. "Are those FedEx packages ready?"

*"I'll bring them right in!"*

The knife returned to the mail.

"Would you like a résumé?" I asked, proffering my sheet.

Ridley's eyes flickered upward a moment. "I've read it."

I dropped it back to my knee.

"So you want to work on Wall Street," he said.

"Yes."

"Why?"

I let go the usual spiel.

"Not to mention the money," he laughed when I was through.

I smiled awkwardly. "The money wouldn't hurt."

The secretary arrived with a stack of mailing envelopes, each with a different letter clipped to it. Ridley took them from her, adding, "Those posters need to go out too." He pointed to a stack of framed pictures in the corner, each of the same familiar face and with a note card attached: "London," "Tokyo," "Sydney," "Frankfurt" . . .

"You know who that is?" Ridley asked me.

"Looks like Vince Lombardi," I said.

"A great man. I'm sending one out to all my guys worldwide. Just a little Christmas present from their Uncle Timmy."

The secretary hauled them away. Ridley began looking through the correspondence she had left behind, signing each letter when he was through. "So are you still working for the CIA?" he asked without lifting his head.

"No."

"That's good. I'm not sure how the Chinese would react to *that*," he grunted, half laughing. The thought suddenly reminded him of something. "Hold on a minute." He grabbed his phone and hit a memory button but nothing happened. "Dammit!" he flared, slamming down the receiver. He slapped the intercom. "Get me another phone!"

He stared at me, shaking his head as if beset by idiots, then searched his computer for a phone number and used it. "Jack, it's Timmy," he said to a distant machine. "Need to talk to you about the China deal." He hung up, stared at the phone a moment, made another call. "It's Timmy . . . Yeah, right . . . I know it. Listen, it's a billion plus, and the first, so let's quit fucking around . . . I'm going to Beijing next week . . . Right . . . Later."

Ridley dropped the phone. "You didn't hear that" he said, his face serious, then laughed softly to himself. "Yeah, right."

The door suddenly opened behind me, raising the hair on my neck. Ron Sewell came in, wearing a long winter coat.

"Just wanted to pick this up," he said to Ridley, grabbing a shopping bag by the wall. He turned to me on his way out, his Cheshire grin in full bloom. "Happy Holidays."

Ridley finally focused on me. "So have you got any questions?"

"I just—"

"We run the top Syndicate desk in the world from here. Merrill is number one. And we're only going to get better. It's taken me a while but everyone finally knows what they're supposed to do." Ridley reflected on this a moment with visible satisfaction, his jaw jutting out as if clamped on a heavy bone. "Kenny is going to need an assistant, I guess you know that. But we're not sure what kind yet. So keep in touch."

With that, Timmy Ridley picked up his mail, left the room, and my two-day wait ended.


January 26, 1994, was another grim day. It had been four months since I began my Wall Street journey. I was now a fifty-interview veteran. Yet I didn't seem to be any closer to reaching my goal than when I started. At Goldman Sachs I was in interview Twilight Zone. I would go up on the train, meet a few people in the emerging markets group, and hear the old "Thanks for coming by," but no one ever made a decision either way—except for their commodities traders, whom I had stopped calling, receiving a nice rejection letter in return.

"That's normal," my friend Jim advised me. "It's common for people to be interviewed fifty times at Goldman."

Fifty times! I thought. I would be broke before I ever got a job.

"Why don't they just tell me the scoop?" I asked.

"Because they're Goldman." Jim laughed. "They do what they want."

My fortunes at Merrill Lynch didn't seem to be any brighter. I called Breen and Forte the next few weeks and they both pushed me off. The market is booming, Breen explained, and IEM needs more people, but everyone just got back from Christmas and no decisions have been made yet. I asked him about the Syndicate job and he said, "Same story," though less convincingly. Was I out of the running? I wasn't sure I cared. I needed a job more desperately every day, but the thought of working with Breen and Ridley, or *for* Breen and Ridley, left me with as much apprehension as joy. To quote a phrase, the fit wasn't right. I therefore focused on

IEM proper and Breen seemed more eager to help there, offering to show my résumé to the head of IEM Sales, a man named Raoul Savegre. At the same time I kept talking with Forte, who would always ask how things were going with Syndicate. Forte, Savegre, Breen, Ridley—I wasn't sure who was thinking of hiring me, if anyone. The whole process seemed completely disjointed, an adjunct affair to the market and more a function of luck than anything else. To top everything off, I finally received a reply from Merrill Lynch Human Resources, whom I had sent a résumé after the Harvard Job Fair four months before: "We regret to inform you that we have no positions open . . ." the letter began. Perfect.

Then Breen called out of nowhere to invite me back for another round of interviews at IEM and the roller coaster began inching back toward the summit. "I don't think it's a question of *if* they're going to hire you but *where* they're going to put you," he said, inspiring a great deal of excitement on my end of the line. This was the most positive news I had heard to date.

When I arrived in IEM two days later, however, everything had changed. Forte, the head trader, and Mickey Gurevich, the top salesman, had just announced that they were leaving the firm to found their own company.

I was crushed. Forte, I suspected, was my chief supporter. No wonder he had been so preoccupied. Since he was involved in "intense meetings" all day, I was shepherded into the IEM conference room and left there alone. No one even knew that I was coming. Finally a heavy-lidded, stocky, red-faced Venezuelan named Diego Barbero came in, lit up a cigarette, told me that he was going to be the new head trader, and asked me what my name was.

My patience reached its end. "Look," I said, "it was *fucking hard* getting here."

Barbero's cigarette paused in midair and he smirked—oddly enough, in appreciation, I thought. He left the room without further comment.

All these events kept running through my head as I paced the cottage alone. I had reached that point in the jobless cycle when one stops shaving and walks around in sweatpants all day teetering on the edge of depression. Life was perfectly unfair. I had done my best for months yet here I was alone in this cramped, confining room, in this unbearable quiet, with nothing to show for it and no idea what to do next. Where had I gone wrong? Had I been wrong to shoot so high after all? Was that old hen Ms. Winthrop right?

Sometime in the midst of this self-flagellation the phone rang. I lifted the receiver with contempt. "Yes?"

The sound of a distant trading floor rose to my ears, filling the entire cottage. It was Forte. He was sorry he had missed me, he said, but everything was back to normal. He had decided to stay at the firm after all. And he hoped that I was still coming.

Still coming!

"How much are you looking for?" he asked.

I paused; I hadn't expected that. "The standard associate salary," I said, not wanting to sound too greedy.

"Okay, that will work," he said abruptly. "I'll talk to you soon."

A few hours later after wandering ceaselessly throughout the house, I heard the phone ring again. This time it was a fax. I pulled the paper off the machine and glanced at the prancing bull at the top:

```
Dear Mr. Stiles:

I am pleased to confirm Merrill Lynch's offer to you as an In-
ternational Retail Trader for the International Emerging Mar-
kets Group of the Global Debt Financing Division. If you accept
this offer, your salary will be at an annual rate of $55,000.
In addition, you will be eligible for a bonus this year payable
in February 1995 . . .
```

I held the paper over my head in triumph and joy, flipped on some ear-shattering music, and danced around the cottage, so scaring Tugger, my loyal companion for all these months, that she fled downstairs in a clatter of little paws. The whole house shook to my celebrations. I had just scaled Everest—without a single piton!

It was a while before I had cooled down sufficiently to actually study the offer. Obviously, the salary was lower than expected, and there was no bonus guarantee either. Forte had taught me my first lesson in the market: never let a trader set your price. In the blink of an eye, I had lost ten thousand dollars at least. Nor was I in a position to make a counteroffer. But the important thing was, I had a job! And a good one too. Fifty-five thousand dollars was more than my father made after teaching high school for thirty-six years. That figure didn't include my bonus either, which could double it. The gross injustice of that didn't even strike me, so carried away was I by my newfound wealth and the position I had been hired to fill: *International Retail Trader.* I didn't know what that meant—but trading was in the title!

Suddenly life seemed grand. The losing streak that had plagued me was over. My unemployment ended. My bank account rescued from oblivion. I could hold my head up now. And the future seemed limitless. We could buy a decent house and send our future children to good schools. I could fulfill my fiscal responsibilities to one and all. I was going to be a bond trader!

I went downstairs to shave and to change from my sweats into nicer clothes, my head spinning with thoughts of telling Sarah, a magnificent dinner, and a fine bottle of champagne. A tremendous challenge still lay ahead, I knew, but I was confident the worst was behind me.

Nine days later the Federal Reserve raised interest rates, sparking the worst bond market since the Great Depression.

# *2*

C O M P R E S S I O N

## *8*

The first thing you notice when you go to New York, unless you're a New Yorker, is the decay. It's everywhere—in the gutter, in vacant lots, blown against fences, in your nose and eyes, sprayed on the buildings, cratering the road, staring at you from the corner of the subway. "It's so *dirty* here!" the tourists say, in between *Cats* and *Phantom*. Even the spans of once-noble bridges seem to sag beneath the weight of it. But there are two times when New York looks pristine: when it's snowing and when it's dark. It was both when I arrived in Brooklyn.

It was early February and midweek. With Sarah working, I had driven up from Maryland to scout around myself. I knew next to nothing about the New York metropolitan area, so I had drawn a rough arc around the World Financial Center based on commuting distances. Within that boundary were a few places friends had mentioned to me and others I thought might fit our criteria. I knew that I was entering a far different world than Annapolis, naturally, but I wanted to retain the most important elements of our experience there: a sense of history and some quiet, private space, even if it was the small patio off a garden apartment. Most of all, I wanted to live on the water. Annapolis had spoiled us in this regard, but with New York City equally blessed by miles of rivers and bay, not to mention history, I didn't think it was asking too much.

I focused first on the Hudson River, which divides the Empire State from New Jersey. The Hudson is one of the most spectacular waterways in the United States, a wide, deep current cutting through dramatic cliffs, bordered at its mouth by the tremendous skyline of Manhattan. The winter adds a special quality to the river, for it fills with floes of rapidly moving ice, a fierce white current that races the cars down the West Side Highway. I began on the Jersey side, thinking that it would be quieter and less expensive than Manhattan, while offering the better view. I soon found, however, that almost no one lived on the water. Instead, from the mouth of the river to the George Washington Bridge, the Jersey waterfront is a run-down littoral of docks, warehouses, and vacant lots. An example is Hoboken, which sits beneath the cliffs on a spit of land facing the World Financial Center. I had heard this town was an up-and-coming spot full of young people and just a ten-minute ferry ride to work. But while Hoboken has undoubtedly made great strides since its industrial age, it has not quite left it yet. The city still focuses inward on an uninspiring strip of shops rather than outward on one of the finest views in the country. It is like driving to the Grand Canyon and staring at the parking lot.

Crossing the George Washington Bridge, I found a similar situation on the other side of the water. I chose Hastings-on-Hudson because of its prime riverfront location, far enough from Manhattan to be reasonably priced, and because of that wonderful name straight from the Cotswolds. Here again, however, the prime waterfront property had been sacrificed to commerce: a commuter railroad that stretched down into Manhattan, eating up the shoreline. I had also underestimated the commute: an hour and a half to the World Trade Center.

I looked over the map. Manhattan was the next obvious choice, but the thought of tackling that megacity bred more intimidation than hope, as well as thoughts of Breen's expensive one-bedroom. I decided instead to swing away to Larchmont and test the waters of Long Island Sound, arriving in late afternoon. Larchmont, I discovered, had some nice homes on the water—if you had a million bucks to spend. Maybe in a few years.

Frustrated by this string of failures, I headed back toward the city, still convinced there had to be at least one reasonably priced apartment on the waters around New York. What I didn't understand was the fundamental dynamic limiting such opportunities: New York is not focused outward on its bountiful natural resources, but inward, on itself. The water has been abandoned to commerce. To the average New Yorker the Hudson is a road for ships, a blue highway over which barges pass on their way to the dumping grounds and tankers steam up from the Narrows. Words like *harbor, river,* and *canal* are practically industrial terms, with attendant connotations of sludge, slicks, and dead fish—even though local waters are cleaner than ever and the bulk of the shipping industry has moved to Newark.

This has bred a curious situation, especially to an Annapolitan: in a city with hundreds of years of nautical history, millions of people, numerous waterways, and three seasons of good weather, there are hardly any marinas. There is the yacht basin at the World Financial Center, built to showcase the toys of financiers; some dock space at South Street Seaport, most of it taken up by floating museums; and the sparsely inhabited Seventy-ninth Street boat basin; but for the most part Manhattan is ringed by miles and miles of empty piers, bulwarks, and seawalls. Some claim the cost of slippage is to blame, others the risk of leaving a high-value item unattended, or even the chance of bumping into a barge. But I suspect a deeper truth is at work. On a casual sail one floats at the mercy of the wind, blessed with hours to contemplate wave, sun, and sky, the beauty of the day, the power of the elements, and, set against that vast expanse, one's own incredible smallness. This is the antithesis of Manhattan, where, in the perpetual, high-speed pursuit of one's largeness, via the dollar, there is little time to contemplate the Great Outdoors or the perspective it demands. Indeed, since contemplation—of one's mortality, say—can cause a man to pause or even come to a shuddering halt, it is practically a threat to the city's constitution.

I arrived at my final destination, Brooklyn Heights, as dusk fell. It had begun to snow as well, limiting the range of my vision. Exiting off the Brooklyn-Queens Expressway, I turned down an attractive lane of shops and restaurants called Montague Street and headed toward the water to take a look around, finding parking on a narrow side street. I stepped from the car into the crisp evening air buoyed by what I saw: long rows of brownstones, black wrought-iron fences, elegant streetlamps, lines of slumbering trees, and even a few carriage houses, all brushed with freshly fallen snow, and hushed by it. It was a postcard of old New York, straight out of *The Age of Innocence*. Squinting through the drifting flakes and editing out the cars, I imagined myself back in the nineteenth century. Now this was more like it.

I headed toward the water to look around. I soon found myself on the Brooklyn Heights Promenade, a wide, sweeping walkway that edges the neighborhood. The view of Manhattan, a wide panorama stretching from the Brooklyn Bridge to Battery Park, sparkled through the snow and held me fixed to the rail. Down below, beyond the BQE, lay the waterfront. Once again, I was disappointed to find only shipping piers, in this case the empty warehouses of the Brooklyn Marine Terminal, but in the lateness of the hour, with other charms at hand, I finally conceded this point, hoping to find an apartment that bordered the Promenade and make Brooklyn Heights our home.

The next day I arose early and went looking for an apartment. I figured that I would simply look in the newspaper, but as I sat in a Heights café leafing through the *Times* and *The Brooklyn Paper* I was surprised to find hardly any ads for apartments in Brooklyn Heights.

"Why is that?" I asked the waiter.

"No one advertises anymore," he sniffed. "You never know who might show up!"

"So how do I find—"

"Everyone uses brokers."

"Real estate brokers?"

"Apartment brokers!" He cast me an impatient look. "You're new around here, aren't you?"

There were a number of apartment brokers on Montague Street, I soon discovered. The sidewalk was littered with their placards, announcing the latest bargain: "Sunny one-bedroom with eat-in kitchen! Walk-in closets! Don't miss it!" One of them, Homes on the Heights, caught my attention, and I ducked inside. It was little more than a closet, a narrow hallway that led back from the street, past a column of old school desks, their inkwells stuffed with pencils. At the end I found a heavyset, over-rouged, middle-aged woman named Darleen sifting through a pile of index cards.

"Oh!" she exclaimed. "I can help ya with that . . . let's see . . . just a minute here, let me clean this up . . . okay . . . just a minute now . . . okay . . . now what can I do for ya?"

"I'm looking for an apartment," I repeated.

"What kind?"

"A two—"

"Wait a minute, hold on, there's somethin' we gotta do first." She lifted the lid of her desk, extracted a legal document, and slid it in front of me. "Here ya go, it's just a formality."

"What is it?"

"Just the usual agreement. Ya sign at the bottom."

I looked over the contract. It stipulated that if I rented any apartment that Homes on the Heights showed me I was obligated to pay them a fee equivalent to the first month's rent.

"Just sign on the bottom there," Darleen urged, snapping her gum nervously. "It's just a formality."

"Am I reading this right—*I* pay you, not the owner?"

"*Shew*-ah!" she confirmed, brandishing her Brooklyn twang.

"So you get something like . . . fifteen hundred bucks, just for showing an apartment?"

Darleen smiled uncomfortably. "We all work this way."

"Let me think about it."

I left laughing. Imagine, fifteen hundred bucks—for opening a few doors! But by the time the afternoon had rolled around, I had exhausted all my alternatives. Doormen knew of no empty apartments, and wondered why I was asking. Property managers told me to go through a broker. "We work with them," one said, "not you."

Resigned to my fate, I finally crawled back to Darleen. "OHH-ohh!" she sirened knowingly, her false eyebrows fluttering at me. "Still lookin' for an apartment?" I sagged into the seat in front of her and a legal agreement slid in front of me. "Just sign at the bottom."

I signed.

"Now what can I do for ya?"

I told her my requirements: two bedrooms, some charm, and a view, hopefully from the Promenade.

"And how much do ya want to spend?"

"Twelve, thirteen hundred," I replied, thinking hard about the fee.

Darleen pursed her lips in pity. "That's gonna be a problem. A nice apartment in the Heights is gonna run ya fifteen hundred at least."

I sat back in my chair. "What about a one-bedroom then?"

"I'm talkin' 'bout a one-bedroom."

"Oh."

She let me think this over before adding, "I do *have* some though, if ya wanna see 'em."

"But nothing below fifteen hundred?"

"Shew-ah! If ya wanna studio. Ya wanna studio?"

Thoughts of marital discord flashed through my mind. "No, let's go look at the one-bedrooms."

Darleen pulled a few index cards from her stack. "Now, there's only a handful in your range," she warned. "The market's tight right now. But let's see what we can find."

She donned a long winter coat and a floppy red hat and we began traipsing around the Heights. It was a beautiful day with a winter-blue sky, and the snow had just begun to turn gray as we slogged through it. We stopped at a number of decent-looking buildings, each harboring a vacant apartment. Darleen was on a first-name basis with all the resident building superintendents—"supers," she called them—who provided her with the keys and looked at me, if they did so at all, with the deadpan expressions of those keeping their thoughts to themselves—

or worse, knowing smiles. I assumed this was because of the apartments, not my agent: all of them turned out to be unrenovated, or claustrophobic, or facing a brick wall, or some combination of flaws: the Unrentables.

"Like I said," Darleen explained, "the market's tight."

Parking was another issue. I had already decided to put my car in storage, the victim of doubled insurance rates and a convertible top, which made it easy to break into. Sarah, however, needed her car; her company had offered her a job in its New Haven office, necessitating that she commute up I-95 two weeks per month. Where would she park?

"In the street," Darleen replied. "Don't worry, everyone does it. Ya just have to be careful 'bout the street cleanin'. They're very strict here. On Mondays, I think it is, ya have to move your car to the right side of the street, between eight and ten. Then on Wednesdays ya move it to the left side of the street. On Fridays, ya move it back—or is it Saturdays? Wait a minute—Mondays, the left side . . . Tuesdays and Thursdays—oh, I dunno, it's on the signs. I can show ya downstairs."

"How do we manage that when we're at work?"

"Ya just pay someone to do it for ya, that's all. Everyone does. Or ya rent a space somewhere. That's what I'd do. Don't worry, there's a place right around the corner. It's only two hundred a month, tops."

I returned with Darleen to Homes on the Heights, growing increasingly alarmed. I was already hemorrhaging cash and hadn't even moved in yet. Nor was there a decent apartment in sight. Perhaps, I thought, I should use another broker.

Darleen must have read my mind. "Have ya looked at Cobble Hill yet?" she suddenly asked. I admitted I hadn't. "Oh, ya'd *like it* down there! It's just like the Heights. A bit farther from the subway, maybe, but the parking's not as strict. I know that's important for ya."

"Is it expensive?"

"Cheaper than the Heights. Ya might even find a two-bedroom down there in your range. Ya know, I might even *have* one . . ." She rummaged through her index cards. "Oh *good*, I got a *few* nice ones. Do ya wanna take a look?"

Of course I did! And off we went. Fifteen minutes later we entered Cobble Hill, an area similar to the Heights in architecture, though not in maintenance. "It's up-and-comin'," Darleen said. "Soon it'll be just like the Heights." Our destination was the Cobble Hill School, a former Catholic girls' school that had been turned into condominiums. This offered us a rare advantage, Darleen explained. Most apartment buildings in New York were cooperatives, known as co-ops, where residents owned a share in the whole building rather than their own apartment. This caused havoc among renters, who had to be approved by the local co-op board rather than a single landlord, a time-consuming and annoying process. A condo rental, on the other hand, was subject only to the approval of the owner's agent. I doubted Darleen would lodge any objections.

We approached the Cobble Hill School from the rear—a wise choice from a sales standpoint. The back of the long, five-story building was a relatively attractive red brick and faced a quiet, pleasant side street named Cheever Place; the front was painted a sickly yellow and bordered the whines and rumbles of the Brooklyn-Queens Expressway, a highway consistently voted Worst in America by the people who should know: truckers.

"What's that noise?" I asked as we neared the back door.

Darleen looked about in puzzlement. "Oh, that! That's just the BQE. Don't worry, the apartment's not on that side of the building." She glanced hopefully at me. "Though the rent *is* cheaper over there, if you're interested."

She located the super and took me upstairs. The history of the building was evident in its large hallways, the wide stairwells, the wire mesh in the windows, and the waxed floor—everything but the Flying Nun. We reached number 404, which Darleen opened with difficulty—she wasn't good with keys—and went inside. The apartment immediately struck me with its brightness and space. One large classroom had been divided into two voluminous whitewashed cubes: the first, in which we stood, with polished hardwood floors reminiscent of my elementary school gym, the other with wall-to-wall carpeting in dire need of cleaning. They both had tall rectangular windows that began at chin level and provided a nice view of the antennae of Brooklyn. A renovated kitchen completed the picture.

Darleen looked around and cleared her throat. "Like I said, this may not be—"

"This is nice . . ." It was by far the best apartment I had seen.

"Isn't it? I *love* the view!"

I stood by the window. There was a gated parking lot below, through which we had just entered, that opened onto Cheever Place—the remains of the former recess area. "Does it come with parking?"

"Ummm—hold on." Darleen checked her index card, her eyes widening. "Oh, it *does*! Ya get one space *free* with the apartment." She clucked, "Well, ya can't beat *that*, can ya?" She led me toward the other room, her energy on the rise. "Oh and look at this! Wouldn't *this* make a nice bedroom? It even has a *balcony*!"

There was indeed a door off the bedroom, which led out to a ledge, the remains of the former fire escape, but whether this qualified as a balcony was open to debate.

"Ya'd pay an extra hundred and twenty-five for that in Manhattan," Darleen confided.

"What's the rent like?" I asked warily.

She checked her card. "Only thirteen fifty! I can probably get that down to thirteen twenty-five too."

I paused to think this over. Darleen looked out the window, pulling absently on her felt hat. "This is one of the safest precincts in the whole city," she mused. "I bet your wife would appreciate that."

"Is it?"

"Third safest, I think. Somethin' like that."

I took a last look around. "Okay, I like it. But I need to show it to my wife."

"Shew-ah! How about tomorrow?"

Sarah returned with me that weekend. Before taking us to the Cobble Hill School, Darleen whipped Sarah through the Unrentables just to put things in perspective. Sarah came away with a forlorn look, bordering on shock, which I earnestly sought to relieve: "Just wait 'til you see the school!" Meanwhile I wondered if I meant what I was saying. In the past few days the snow in Brooklyn had melted like running makeup and now, in the sober light of day, I felt myself uncomfortably linked to last night's pretty face.

"I think you'll find there's a lot ya can do with this place," Darleen told Sarah as she led us into the schoolroom.

I held my breath.

"Oh, this is a lot better!" Sarah said relievedly.

"There's a decent view too," I quickly added, sounding uncomfortably like Darleen.

We walked around, our voices echoing in the empty interior. The high ceilings reminded Sarah of my old loft apartment in Annapolis, causing her to pull me aside at the first opportunity. "Do you remember how much the heat cost in your old place?" she whispered.

I did indeed. Four hundred dollars in one cold February. Darleen, however, assured me that the heat was included in the rent. "That's the way it works in New York," she said. "All these old places are like that. All ya pay is electric and phone."

"Why isn't there a thermostat?" I asked.

"They heat the building as a whole." Darleen loosened her jacket. "Nice and warm too, isn't it? Now, did ya see this great kitchen?"

By the time we left we had made up our minds to take the apartment and returned to Homes on the Heights to sign the lease. I read it over carefully, but everything appeared to be in order. There was even a clause that stipulated "Landlord will supply heat as required by law."

"See?" Darleen said, pointing it out to me, "there ya go. Now, 'bout the fee—we don't take personal checks, only cash or cashier's checks."

"I only have my checkbook—"

"There's a bank across the street. Don't worry, you can use your credit card."

I returned presently with a cashier's check, which I placed in the hands of a smiling Darleen. "It seems like a lot now," she said, tucking it in her drawer, "but ya got a nice apartment. And I'm sure it's nothin', with you at Merrill Lynch and all."

She handed me the keys to our new home. In that moment we became New Yorkers—at least according to the tax authorities—though we didn't think of ourselves that way. We were just happy to have found suitable housing, having surmounted all the obstacles in the process. In fact, so relieved were we that we didn't even question the wisdom of trading a quiet, two-bedroom riverside cottage on three acres in Annapolis for a one-bedroom apartment in a renovated Catholic girls' school perched on a major highway in Brooklyn at an additional cost of ten thousand dollars the first year. It had a parking space!

We moved the seventeenth of February. Thankfully, after some prodding on my part, IEM had consented to pay for the move: after the broker's fees, the first month's rent, the security deposit, and utility start-up costs, our combined net worth had fallen to $1,400, all of it in one checking account. I felt like a man whose parachute has opened moments from earth.

We arrived in Cobble Hill just before noon, when we were scheduled to meet the movers. There was a strange new hole in our apartment door—the upper lock was missing. And the key wouldn't open the lower one. "Divine intervention," Sarah laughed. Then the movers arrived and devised a solution. They began unpacking in the hall.

I imposed on the woman next door, who was from England. "I'm so glad we have a new neighbor," she said as she handed me the phone. "The last one was horrible. Loud music all the time—he even put his motorcycle on the elevator."

"Homes on the Heights."

"Darleen!" I said in relief. "You gave me the wrong key!"

"What? Oh, ya *kiddin*' . . ." I assured her I wasn't. "Well hold on, let me take a look . . . no, that's not it . . . I dunno *where* it is . . ."

"One of the locks is missing too. There's a big hole in the door."

"Huh? Oh, that's just the tenant lock. You buy that yourself and take it with you wherever you go. That's the way it works here." She continued her search but came up empty-handed. "I'm gonna have to call a locksmith. Stay right there!"

"We're not moving."

An hour later a red-faced, rotund man in blue work clothes came puffing up the stairs carrying a box of tools. "The elevator was full of boxes," he explained, squeezing past a similar pile in the hallway. "Gee, they're everywhere."

I pointed to the lock. "Now you know why."

He glanced at our door, twitched his bristle-brush mustache, and knelt down with some picking tools. Ten seconds later the lock sprung open.

"It's *that* easy?" I said, dumbfounded.

He struggled to his feet with a gasp. "Sure," he said proudly. "That's why ya need a good tenant lock. I can get ya one too if you're interested. Only sixty bucks." I told him I'd think about it. He glanced at his watch, which was nearing the two-minute mark. "That's eighty-five bucks."

I eyed him. Nature's aesthetics may have been absent in New York, but its logic was woefully omnipresent. "The woman said it was an emergency," he added hastily. "I came right away."

I sighed. "Will you take a check?"

"No—but I take credit cards." He whipped out an imprint machine from the small of his back, ran my card through, and handed me the slip with a "thanks." Then he disappeared down the stairwell as quickly as he had arrived, his walkie-talkie squawking another eighty-five-dollar emergency.

We went inside with relief, the movers following us with loaded arms. A set of keys was lying on the counter: Darleen had left them behind. That mystery solved, another immediately presented itself: the apartment was freezing cold. I checked the heaters, which weren't working. "That's strange," I said. "I thought the building was heated as a whole."

Puzzled, I roused our British neighbor, Rebecca, who came over to take a look. "All you have to do," she said, as she flipped up a hidden panel, "is set this knob right here. But don't put it too high—we had a big bill last month."

I stared at the knob in disbelief. "Doesn't the landlord pay for heat?"

"No, it goes on your electric bill."

"What!" Sarah exclaimed.

"Don't worry," I said firmly, "the lease is clear on this point."

I used Rebecca's phone again: Darleen wasn't in. So I left a message and returned to unpack. I found Sarah in the kitchen staring at the dishwasher. "Have you seen this?" she asked. The empty racks were covered by a greasy black film.

I took a closer look. "Motor oil," I pronounced.

"Motor oil! What's that doing in the dishwasher?"

"Looks like someone cleaned their engine parts in there."

Sarah sagged against the counter. "This isn't going very well."

My marital warning detector chiming, I offered to clean the racks, and Sarah went into the bedroom to unpack. Meanwhile the movers continued to bring in furniture and boxes, their efforts slowed by the need to leave a man at the truck. "Once I went downstairs and somebody had run off with a whole table," the head mover said. "Can ya believe that? A whole table. Gone. Like that. But that's New York for ya, huh?"

A few pieces of furniture later we were interrupted by a loud buzz in our entryway. Moving some boxes aside, I found an intercom and pressed TALK.

"Yes?"

"Yeah, Mr. Coyle?" a gruff voice said.

"No."

"Is Mr. Coyle there?"

"No."

"Ya sure?"

"He doesn't live here anymore."

A pause. "Mind if we come up? It's the Brooklyn police."

I stared at the intercom in disbelief, then buzzed them in. "Hey Hon!" I called into the next room. "We have nothing to worry about anymore. I've called the Brooklyn police and they're on their way!"

Sarah emerged from the bedroom. "I'd like to call them!" she said angrily. "I'd send them straight to Homes on the Heights!"

A heavy knock sounded on the door.

"Here they are!"

I swung open the door. To Sarah's amazement, three large uniformed police officers entered our living room. They stood in a cluster, hands clasped together, looking around at the mess.

"We're moving in," I explained.

"I see," said a plump lieutenant with a frown. He took off his cap and ran his hands through his black hair. "Any idea where the previous tenant is?"

"No idea. I don't even know who he was."

He kept his eyes on me. They all did. "His name was Coyle, Mike Coyle. Also Mike Carlyle. Also Larry Davidson. Any of those names ring a bell?"

"No. What's he done?"

The cops glanced at each other. "Nothing much," the lieutenant said slowly. "We just want to talk with him."

"Well he's not an *ax murderer* or anything, is he?" Sarah asked.

"Nah," the lieutenant grinned, "nothing like that. Anyways, we'll let you go."

I followed the procession to the door. "There's nothing we need to worry about, is there?" I whispered. "You don't expect him to come back or anything . . ."

"Nah, he's long gone." The lieutenant stuck a finger through the hole in our door. "You need a lock though."

Soon thereafter the movers followed the cops out the door, their mission complete, leaving us facing a mountain of boxes in the living room.

"Where did we get all this stuff?" Sarah asked.

"It's not a lot of stuff," I said. "It's just in a smaller area."

We had barely put a dent in it when another knock sounded on our door. Sarah and I glanced warily at each other.

"Mike Carlyle?"

"Larry Davidson?"

I crept to the fish-eye and stared cautiously through it. Rebecca was standing outside. We had a phone call.

"Darleen," I said coolly into the receiver. "Things have not been going very well here."

"I'm sorry to hear that."

"You told us the heat came with the rent. It doesn't. It's on our electric bill."

A pause. "Did I say that?"

"Yes."

"I don't remember sayin' that. I think I said there was a heat pump or somethin'—"

"*No,* and it's in our lease. You specifically pointed out the clause."

"Well I'm sorry then, there's been a misunderstandin'. Why don't ya talk to the landlord?"

I sighed. "Because we've never met him. And I'd rather not under these circumstances."

"But it's between you an' him—"

"You're his agent."

"If he wants to pay for it, then fine, otherwise . . ."

I kept arguing my point but Darleen wasn't budging. The conversation grew heated. "We paid you a lot of money for a service we didn't get!" I finally exclaimed, the frustrations of the day pouring out. "You locked the keys in the apartment, the movers had to unload in the hall, the apartment was freezing cold, there's oil in the dishwasher, the former tenant is wanted by the police, and now I've got to pay for a year's worth of heat—with fifteen-foot ceilings!"

"Lemme talk to my boss," Darleen said hurriedly. "I'll call ya right back."

She never did. Two days later I called the bank that had issued me the cashier's check and asked if there was any way to stop payment. "If the check was registered," I was told. I unfolded a crumpled receipt, read off a number, and waited, fingers crossed. "Yes, that *was* a registered check," a beautiful voice said. "Do you want to stop payment?"

I gripped the phone in triumph. "Shew-ah!"


Once we were unpacked, our first priority was buying a new couch, our old one having seen better days. This apparently simple task proved to be far more formidable than it seemed. We knew next to nothing about New York City and no one in it. Where should we shop?

The first step, I figured, was to locate the stores nearest us in Brooklyn, both because of their convenience and, I suspected, their economy. This I did using the Yellow Pages and a map of our new borough, on which I marked a few likely prospects. Sarah and I stood silently looking at these, neither one of us admitting what was on our mind: safety. For as everyone knew, there were parts of New York that *you just didn't go to.* But which ones were they? The map didn't say.

"I don't know . . ." Sarah said. "How are we going to find these places?"

"Drive, I guess. Use the map."

"But we don't know anything about these areas . . ."

"Why don't we just take a look? If we don't like what we see, we'll come back, that's all."

Sarah reluctantly agreed, and we blocked Tugger in the kitchen. The Little Beast was not taking well to apartment life, and had resorted to intestinal protests.

We left behind an apartment now protected by a shiny new tenant lock, one of the impregnable kind common to New York, which added a thick metal plate to the outside of our door. This and our other lines of defense had brought my key chain to a record membership, which were arranged in order of use so I could keep them all straight: aside from the car keys, there was the key to the outer gate, then the key to the building, the mailbox key, the upper tenant lock key, and the lower apartment lock key (the route to the storage closet—three more keys—I kept on a separate chain). Sarah's key ring was even more impressive. She had a pressurized canister of pepper spray that could knock a man down ten feet away and a whistle worthy of a traffic cop. The final addition to the arsenal, even in our gated parking lot, was that perennial favorite of the New York City car owner, The Club, which not only immobilized our steering wheel but provided us with yet another key. We had stopped short of buying The Door Club, however, even though every billboard in the city seemed to demand it. The Door Club was a T-shaped piece of metal that fit into the floor behind your door, preventing it from opening. In other words, assuming some intruder got past all your locks plus the safety chain by guile, picking tools, or crowbars, you could still be reasonably confident in making a last stand on your threshold. Judging by the billboards, they were selling pretty well.

I drove while Sarah navigated, using our newly purchased Five Borough Street Map of New York City. It made Brooklyn look like one of those magnified images of a computer chip, a mass of interconnected lines that reveal their logic only to an engineer. In this way we finally emerged from Cobble Hill, which was a maze of one-way streets, and headed down Atlantic Avenue, a broad commercial thoroughfare slicing through the heart of Brooklyn. We followed it as far as Flatbush Avenue, where we turned and began scanning for street numbers.

Meanwhile the city declined before our eyes. Paint faded, peeled, and dropped off, leaving mottled patches on the facades of buildings; once-elegant cornices cracked and lost their dentils; shutters drooped, fell, and weren't replaced; windows clouded with cataracts of grime and filled with plywood or bits of cardboard. Then whole townhouses disappeared, leaving cavities filled with rusty cars, burnt-out oil drums, chain-link fences and razor wire; the trees withered and vanished; and the gutters overflowed with refuse—paper plates, beer cans, newspapers, all glued together by a gray paste that stuck to the curb. Above all, there was the graffiti. It was everywhere—on lightposts, on automobiles, on billboards, on sidewalks and the street itself, on the front steps of buildings and the water towers on the roofs.

The car fell silent and our tension rose. The urban devastation stirred a primeval sense of danger, like a forest suddenly gone quiet, stealing the words from your mouth and the warmth from your body. On top of that I felt guilty for having brought us to the edge of this horror. I hadn't seen squalor like this since traveling in Jakarta during a port call. So, searching for some means of accommodation, I seized on the same feeling I had there, and other developing countries, regardless of their reality. New York was an adventure, I decided. That was the only way to look at it. The difference, of course, was that this wasn't Indonesia, and we lived a mile away.

I glanced at Sarah. She was sitting stiffly, looking straight ahead, and unusually quiet, typical signs of discomfort for her. But there was nothing I could do. We're here now, I thought; we have to live with this. So I drove on, acting unperturbed, hoping that conditions would soon improve and we could breathe again.

"Look!" she said, pointing to the oncoming lane. A vehicle was raging toward us completely covered in brilliant, multicolored graffiti. Engine sputtering, driver hunched over the wheel, it sped back toward Manhattan like an emissary from hell, its tangled hair ablaze.

"Let's just go back," Sarah said. "This is too far."

I felt an immediate resistance. "We're almost there."

She groaned. "We're not going to find what we want out here."

"We've come this far, haven't we?"

There was silence until, a few minutes later, I pulled over. "That's it."

Sarah looked out the window. "You've got to be kidding me."

The Furniture Emporium was not an encouraging sight. A hand-painted sign canted outward hung by chains from a precarious brick building. There were two large display windows in front and four stories of windows above them, each of them revealing a jumbled array of chairs, couches, lamps, and tables. It was as if someone had pulled off the roof and dumped a load of furniture inside.

I instinctively checked the rearview mirror. There were noticeably few cars on the street behind us, which was dominated by a group of youths lounging on the broken stoop of a nearby hollow row house. Sarah saw them too; the electric locks buzzed shut.

"Let's just *go*," she said.

"We might as well take a look around."

"And leave our car here?"

"That's what this is for." I brandished The Club.

"I'm not enjoying this."

"Where's your sense of adventure?"

"Give me a break."

We locked the car, lifted the handles to double-check, and went inside. There were two hefty bouncers at the entrance who looked us over suspiciously, then curiously. The cement floor was a tangle of furniture with narrow pathways of no particular logic leading through it. The only common thread was the owner's taste, which ran to leopard skin, black velvet, and luminescent floral patterns—including the couches.

Sarah took one look and headed for the exit, her face itching to scream I-told-you-so. She doesn't understand, I thought. You can't let this get to you. This is an adventure, that's all. It has no meaning except for that.

Back in the car, I looked for our next destination on the map. "It's not that far away."

"Come on, it's not going to be any different."

"How do you know?"

"Paul, just look at this place!"

"It can't *all* be like this."

Sarah groaned and slumped in her seat. "Let's just go home. This is too hard. We should've called ahead."

"And what, asked what the neighborhood was like?" She didn't reply. "If the next place is no good, we'll go back. I promise. But we live here now. We need to know what this place is like—not hide in Cobble Hill!"

I pulled out into the traffic, my marital radar chiming a loud warning signal. Maybe I shouldn't push it, I thought. But I didn't want to give in to New York. I wanted to deal with it *right now,* not slink back home defeated. And I wanted furniture, dammit! Was that too much to ask? Meanwhile Flatbush Avenue passed by, a parade of ugliness unmatched in my memory, bringing a funereal silence to the car. Sarah sat with her head resting against the passenger window, looking dully at the gray skies and the first drops of rain.

The light ahead turned red and we paused at a major five-way intersection. On our left was the well-known landmark of the Williamsburg Savings Bank building, an enormous middle finger thrusting at the sky. The rest was more urban desolation. On Sarah's side a triangular island speared the intersection, full of dirt, drifting trash, and the glint of broken glass, through which hopped a three-legged dog. Flanking the road on my side was a broken, rusty chain-link fence with three homeless men, spaced apart, leaning against it. One of them lurched to his feet and approached our car with his cup: a face burned, toothless, whiskered, its eyes vacant, caught through slapping wipers, then passing from view. In front of us was a van, separated by the space I had purposefully left between us just in case we needed to make a hasty exit. A door opened and the driver appeared. He walked around to the far side, pulled his penis from his pants, and began urinating on his rear tire.

"Paul," Sarah said, stressing each word, "let's—go—home. *Now!*"

"All right, all right." I pulled an illegal U-turn and headed back toward Cobble Hill, taking a familiar street. Minutes later we came to an orange-striped barrier, a blinking yellow light, and a pile of old mattresses and burst trash bags, their contents scattered across the end of the road. There was no bridge over the Gowanus Canal.

"I don't believe this," Sarah muttered.

"Help me navigate," I asked, handing her the map with more urgency than I wished.

Suddenly she screamed. "Would you look at this place! It's *disgusting*! What are we *doing* here!?"

We continued our journey in silence. It took us through a neighborhood eerily reminiscent of Cobble Hill—the same rows of brownstones and brick town houses, the elaborate moldings, the tall four-paned windows, the carved wooden porticos, the short connecting streets known as Places—only this one was overwhelmed by atrophy and disrepair, a long-lost twin that had led a harder life. Then the buildings improved, a familiar street appeared, and we began breathing easier.

We arrived back in the apartment exhausted, our senses shaken, having been gone barely an hour. I didn't know what to feel. I was relieved at our return, frustrated by our fruitless search, depressed by what we had seen, sorry for having put Sarah through it, and happy about living in Cobble Hill. For the first time Cobble Hill looked *great*.

"It's hard to believe," I said, looking out our window at the distant Williamsburg Savings Bank, "the difference between here and there."

"Or Annapolis," Sarah said.

## 9

I awoke early and watched the room slowly fill with light, the walls fading from black to white through scales of gray. Safely wrapped in the warmth of a down comforter, I felt no great desire to bound from bed and end these final moments of my previous life but to stretch them out as long as possible. I eyed the clock with one eye, my mind working in reverse: in-processing began at eight o'clock. The commute, which I had tested the day before, would take forty-five minutes door-to-door. Breakfast could be gobbled in fifteen. Dressing took five. A shower ten. Add another fifteen for safety and I had to get up at . . . six-thirty.

Five more minutes.

My eyes moved inexorably to the back of the bedroom door. A new suit hung there, one of five I now owned, one for every day of the week. It was charcoal with a light gray pinstripe—no one could complain about that—and halved by the slanting morning light. A new white shirt hung next to it, straight from the Lands' End catalog, freshly pressed, along with the red silk tie Sarah had bought me. Too bad she wouldn't see it on; she was at a conference in Atlantic City. On the floor were my new shoes, black Italian wing tips, smooth, like stones in a stream, soft leather, felt great. Three hundred dollars worth of discount armor ready to be put to the test.

Six-thirty.

I hauled myself with a groan from the warmth of my empty cocoon. Half an hour later, draped in my finery, I blocked Tugger in the kitchen, turned off the lights, and paused to take a last look around, unwilling to admit there was nothing left to do. The apartment was gray, quiet, empty. Oh, how odd it was to turn those locks behind me, walk down the empty hall, descend alone in the elevator, and walk out into the bracing, snow-lined streets of Brooklyn! There was no doubt about it any longer: this was our new home. And this was the first day of a new routine, stretching as far ahead as I could see.

Ducking into a bodega, I emerged with that champion of the market, *The Wall Street Journal,* and tucked it under my arm in the approved fashion. Ahead of me a few others filed from their buildings in their winter coats, briefcases in hand, and fell into line. We all trudged silently toward the distant subway station in Brooklyn Heights—the bane of Cobble Hill life—each of us taking his favorite route, separating us here, rejoining us there; there were many different ways to follow the grid.

Once at the Court Street subway station in the Heights, I held my breath at the entrance—having learned that painful lesson yesterday—and hurried past the homeless, descending into a gloomy cavern awash in yellow light. I was already armed with subway tokens, which took me through the turnstiles, cranking like slot machines in the morning rush. Then came a long, dingy tunnel lined with movie posters—Terminators, Robocops—and an elevator that took me down two more stories to the platform where the N and R trains ran. There I leaned against a metal beam layered with decades of sloppy paint and unfurled the *Journal* with a yawn.

The subway car screeched out of its hole and rushed by to a breezy, lengthy halt. I stood in the first car watching the tunnel unfold ahead: bright beams on shiny, well-worn rails, metal pillars covered with decades of grime, a rat. The rails peaked like the verge of a roller coaster and plunged us beneath the East River. Turning around, I blinked at the brightly lit tube behind me. The passengers, all bundled against the winter cold and more tightly packed because of it, were doing their best not to look at one another. Above them was a colorful row of advertisements: the picture of a smiling young man in his graduation cap with the caption "I'd ask you to keep guns off the street, but I'm dead"; the usual shot of The Door

Club, sparkling gold; the equally omnipresent Dr. Zizmor, the city's most well known dermatologist, offering his wart-removal services; and New York City's own toll-free number for downed police officers, 1-800-COP-SHOT, an advertisement noted for its prominent bloodstain and its reward money: ten grand went to the first witness who called. Then there was the latest Poetry in Motion, an attempt to brighten the city's mass transportation with verse, this one from Allen Ginsberg:

> *Let some sad trumpeter stand*
> *on the empty streets at dawn*
> *and blow a silver chorus to the*
> *buildings of Times Square.*

I tried contemplating the meaning of this, but the lurches of the car and the painful screech of the brakes, the waves of new passengers spreading through the car at every stop, the stroboscopic effect of dark tunnels, bright platforms, and flickering interior lights, and the impending drama of my first day on Wall Street all turned the journey into a sensuous blur where coherent thought was impossible. Like skipping through channels on television.

Cortlandt Street finally appeared, and I ascended with the crowd to daylight. Across the road was the World Trade Center, its vertical shafts disappearing into the clouds, so tall they seemed more like silver bolts coming down from heaven than buildings rising up. Behind them was the north causeway to the World Financial Center, an aluminum tube lined with portholes that stretched across the West Side Highway. Crossing over, I was momentarily suspended above the city and isolated from it—the masses of people pouring from the mouths of the subway, the cabs slithering on river bottoms, the angled plane of the river beyond, and the distant cliffs. Was this really happening? I wondered what the future would bring. Then I was on the other side, in the hands of Finance. The Winter Garden was full of men just like me, coated, briefcased, passing back and forth on their way to the elevator. I walked briskly toward the North Tower, happy to be among them—I was back to work!

It wasn't until I actually saw the golden turnstiles that the challenge ahead struck me with full force. Absurdly, I had been so focused on *getting* a job on Wall Street that I had never considered actually *doing* one. Now that practice was imminent, I was seized by apprehension. Had I succeeded too much? Was I in over my head? Don't be silly, I told myself. Look at this place: it's full of people who started out just like you: clueless. Besides, this is a pretty nice suit.

After the usual in-processing—fingerprints, benefits, drug test—I received a magnetic security pass with my picture on it. This unlocked the golden turnstiles in the same manner one entered the National Security Agency. Then it was on to IEM, an official Merrill Lynch employee. I sensed a change the minute I arrived.

Gone was the hectic exuberance of before; now the same motion was charged with tension. Serious faces sat contemplating their screens, hands rubbing tight jaws. People I recognized passed by without so much as a nod. I went straight to Forte's office and greeted him with good cheer. He looked up from his paperwork as if surprised to see me, his expression barely rising above the flat. "I'll be with you in a minute." His head fell back to his work.

I turned to the bagel cart, which stood at the end of the room, and poured myself a cup of coffee. Definitely an anticlimax. Forte emerged presently and apologized for keeping me waiting. "There have been a few changes since I spoke to you last," he said. "You have a new job. Actually, you've had a couple of new jobs lately." He smiled, brilliant white. "You're going to be working for Raoul now."

"Okay," I replied, not knowing what else to say.

Forte backpedaled toward his office. "Have a seat in the conference room. He'll be with you in a minute." He shut his door behind him.

The IEM conference room was adjacent to Forte's office. It had a long rectangular table with a speakerphone in the middle, ten chairs, and nothing else. Outside stood the trunks of skyscrapers, checkered with windows, each one a square, silent, backlit drama. I sat down and considered my own little story, which was unfolding by the minute. My sudden shift in bosses surprised me: what did it mean? I was sorry to lose Forte, but perhaps his replacement would work out. Raoul, I knew, meant Raoul Savegre, the head of Sales and the man who had hired Kenny Breen. Breen spoke highly of him; Savegre sounded like his mentor. And look at the job Breen had after working for Savegre only a year!

Twenty minutes later, with my cup drained and my mind absorbed in silence, Savegre walked in. He took a seat across the broad table from me with a quick nod, a how-are-you, and the concerned frown of a man preoccupied with weighty matters. He was short and wiry, like one of those action toys that can assume any shape, and appeared too small for his clothes. His suit pants were crimped at the waist, his shoes were too long, and his dark blue shirt, with its mandatory French cuffs—de rigueur for management—made his shoulders look like a hanger. What held my attention most was his head, a bald and tannic oval with a wrinkled brow, eyes of opaque brown, a wavering furrow of a mouth, and tobacco-stained teeth, which seemed to have shrunk a size as well—like a grape, well on its way to becoming a raisin.

Savegre took a pack of unfiltered Camels from his pocket, knocked one into his palm, lit up, and leaned back in his chair, taking in a pleasurable lungful of smoke. His glassy eyes were fixed on the ceiling, his face laundered free of expression, his cigarette held off at a lazy angle, uncoiling smoke.

"So, do you have any questions for me?"

His eyes fell to mine and his head dropped to a curious angle, part forced humility, part subtle challenge. The question came as a surprise—of course I had questions!—but I suspected it was supposed to. In Savegre's manner there was not the slightest hint of common ground, of mutual discussion, of cooperation, of openness; there was only a deep, profound sense of unknown, captured in the opacity of his eyes and the unyielding line of his mouth. Here, in the opening of a game I did not understand, this was the initial joust, its purpose to elicit some reaction.

"Nope."

He lifted his eyebrows—enjoyment or irritation?—took another deep drag and looked away without comment. My response was a gamble: if jousting was his game, he would appreciate a parry. It appeared to work.

"I suppose Miguel told you: you'll be working for me now."

"Yes."

"I'm very pleased about that." He spoke so flatly I wondered if I had heard him correctly. Only his knitted eyebrows hinted at satisfaction. The cigarette moved coolly to his lips, then away. "You'll be starting in Marketing."

Marketing! The word speared me. I was supposed to be a trader!

"Marketing and Sales both report to me."

I tried not to let my disappointment show. "What happened to the International Retail position?"

Savegre's eyelids fluttered. "I think," he reflected with firm control, "Miguel said that just to get you in the door, more or less. Past management." He shrugged with a grunt of humor. "Well here you are. It worked."

I felt a pang of gloom, which must have showed.

"I wouldn't worry about it. Marketing is an important function. It's a good place to learn the business." Savegre overturned a palm like a playing card. "Kenny used to work in Marketing."

"No, sounds great," I quickly assured him.

"And frankly, with everything going on right now, we haven't had time to think about anything else."

He glanced at me as if this were self-evident. It wasn't. I had no idea what was going on. And although a new voice of warning was telling me not to ask, it wasn't loud enough yet.

"What's going on?"

Savegre stared coldly at me. "The Fed raised interest rates a few weeks ago."

"Oh, right."

"When rates go up, prices go down."

"Right. Of course."

"We've had the worst drop in prices since"—he struggled for words—"since our market *began.*"

"I see."

His eyelids fluttered down and he frowned concernedly at his cigarette—not just because of my ignorance, I suspected, but because I had so willingly shown it.

I sought to defuse the situation with some humor. "So now we're in the *submerging* markets."

Savegre quickly inhaled up and away, his glance passing through me without the slightest trace of a smile, just a strained call for patience. Looking out the window, he brought his cigarette to his mouth, wrapped his lips around it, and took a very, very long drag, the longest I had ever sat through. The air seemed to kindle from the briefly glowing ember, burning all the available oxygen in the room. Meanwhile his face remained a model of cold statuary, stealing whatever warmth was produced. There was nothing funny about the market, I learned then. Humor was for kids.

I waited uncomfortably, wanting to say something, anything to lighten the mood, but afraid to do so and not sure how. Savegre was a different breed than I was used to. I wasn't sure how to communicate with him or even what "him" was. Then, as sometimes happens in such overcharged moments, the pressure gave way to feelings of unreality, separating me from this humorless man, this sleek tower, and the city that supported it. There was only the shining glass window behind him, and the distant arm of the Statue of Liberty holding up a cloud.

"Anyway," Savegre finally said, interrupting my thoughts, "you'll be working with Claire. Have you met her yet?"

"I think she interviewed me."

"It'll be just the two of you plus an analyst on rotation." He studied the table; Savegre rarely kept his eyes on you long. I wondered what was coming next.

"Well," he said, sliding smoothly into a new, at-your-service manner, "where should we start?"

"I better leave that up to you," I smiled.

"I see." He pondered the options painfully.

"Whatever you—"

"Okay then." He popped to his feet with impatient alacrity. "Why don't we talk about Brady bonds."

Savegre moved to the end of the table, pulling an ashtray with him, and perched his cigarette on the rim. He stood by the marker board a moment, pen in hand, then drew the cash flows of a bond, a diagram resembling a ladder with a missing side. I copied it in my notebook.

He pointed to the tines. "This is your average Par bond. You get one coupon payment every six months for thirty years. Now, you can think of this bond as having three parts because of the collateral involved. First you have the principal, which is collateralized with U.S. Treasury zero coupon bonds. If the country goes under, you get the collateral at maturity. Then there are two or three interest payments that are collateralized, depending on the bond, this time with corporate bonds rated AA or better. If there is a default, you get this collateral in lieu of the next two or three coupon payments. Finally, there is this long series of coupon payments that has no collateral at all." He circled it. "This is pure country risk."

Savegre's delivery was extremely smooth, so smooth it bred its own sincerity. I imagined him giving the same speech to people with a lot more money than I and receiving checks at the end. Meanwhile I wrote furiously, reminding myself to purchase a financial dictionary. "Is this explained in writing anywhere?" I asked.

"No. If you want a good book on bonds get Fabozzi, *The Handbook of Fixed Income Securities.*" He warmed up at the thought. "In fact, go get it and expense it. There's a bookstore in the atrium."

Savegre's eyes were drawn to the door, which was bordered by glass. He motioned someone inside.

"Now," he went on as the shoeshine man bent over his feet, "how do we compare the risk in this bond with some other bond that has no collateral? We strip out the collateralized portions and calculate the yield on the remainder. This special yield is called a stripped yield. You only find it in the emerging markets. The more stripped yield, the more country risk investors think it has. There's a sheet we put out called the BBYA that calculates all the stripped yields for our bonds, among other things. It goes out every day. You'll see it later."

He fielded a few questions from me and lifted another wing tip to the shoeshine man, a thin Latino like himself. "We might as well talk about Merrill Lynch while we're here," he added with interest. Savegre was a man of little ego but he liked to stand up and talk. He erased his diagram and began creating another, looking back at me and explaining as he went. "There are two basic legal entities in the firm, even though we own scores," his arms flung open, "probably *hundreds* of businesses. The first is Merrill Lynch and Company, which is the banking side of the firm . . . and the second is Merrill Lynch, Pierce, Fenner, and Smith, which is the brokerage arm."

Savegre went on to explain as best he could the legal structure of the firm, mixed in with organizational details, often smoothly correcting himself when he talked his way into a contradiction, as if he had done so on purpose. Like most people at the firm, he knew very little beyond his area of specialization; but as a managing director, he knew how to fill in the gaps.

He picked the cigarette up from the edge of the ashtray and took a drag while the shoeshine man collected his polish and rags. Flipping open his wallet, he handed the man a few rumpled bills, turning toward me in the process.

"Want one?"

"No thanks." I glanced down at my shoes. "They're new."

The shoeshine man scurried off, leaving Savegre to finish his explanation. He was obviously very clever, and not to be underestimated, but his focus was scattered among competing thoughts, diverting his attention, sending him sinking into reflection, then leaping forward impulsively, keeping him checking his watch and looking at the door. You could hear the market chanting in his ear.

"Well," he finally announced, "anything else?"

It wasn't a real question. Savegre put the marker down and quickly erased the board while he said it.

I closed my notebook. "No, that was very helpful, thanks. I wish we could do it more often." Already I was getting the feeling that information was going to be gold.

"All right," Savegre promised, "why don't we meet like this, say, an hour a day until you get up to speed? Just do me one favor: put it on my schedule."

He offered to introduce me to his secretary and we left, walking along the edge of the trading floor. Savegre's position was located at the top of the Sales loop, overlooking the four salesmen within. His secretary, Dawn, a tall redhead from Staten Island, sat next to him. He gave her a few instructions: "He needs to get into the computer system . . . and the phones . . . and get on the research list. He'll need a computer too. Tell Habib to get him a Sun—no, buy him a laptop, one of those new ones the bankers have. He may be traveling." Savegre looked up from the floor. "I guess that's it."

"Where will I be sitting?" I asked.

"Good question!" Dawn exclaimed.

"We're a little pressed for seats right now," Savegre said. "Hopefully something will open up soon." He turned to Dawn. "Have you seen Claire?"

"Not lately."

Savegre frowned and led me inside the Sales loop, where he stood looking around the room. "Well, she sits here . . . but I don't see her. Anyway, this is how the phone works." He gave me a few quick instructions on the touchscreen: outside lines, inside lines, forwarding, pages of numbers. "All right?"

My head was spinning. "Okay."

Savegre walked off, leaving me standing alone in the middle of the Sales loop. I looked around. One of the salesmen was chattering on the phone next to me, his finger stuck in his uncovered ear; another was gesticulating toward a trader across the divide, arguing about a price; one was listening to a report coming over his squawk box; another was sitting back with his arms crossed, staring at the screens. Other people were passing by and around me, delivering papers, passing on information. Everybody was busy, everyone had something to do, and all their voices hummed in my head. What should I do next? Where should I begin? With the bonds? The countries? The economics? The market? Where should I even sit? One of the salesmen turned and I quickly looked away—what if he asked me to do something? I suppressed a moment of panic and quickly sat down in Claire's seat, hoping that she would provide me some formal training, and blessedly unaware that I had just received my last.

Claire Mundt. I looked over her interior section of the loop, which was utter chaos. Books, notebooks, pamphlets, all intermixed with a pile of paper inches thick. So this was Marketing. I had met Mundt once in a distant interview but remembered little of her peculiarities. Mundt was Swiss and looked like a thin blond elf, with the pointy, low-cut shoes of Santa's helpers, the white-stockinged legs of a ballerina, and bloomers off a Beefeater bottle. She had a strange accent, a lilting, high-pitched drawl that turned a hall into a *haaaal,* and her own sense of humor, causing sudden bursts of shrill laughter for reasons difficult to fathom. When walking the halls, she was often seen with her head cocked at a curious angle, wearing a lost expression that took moments to clear away.

"Paaaal?"

I turned, barely recognizing her. Mundt was holding a stack of pamphlets to her chest, which she dropped on her desk. A thin young man accompanied her, bouncing nervously up and down on his toes.

"Welcome baaaack. You've come at a good time! Ha!"

I said hello and loitered next to her while she looked over her desk.

"Are you here to see me?" she finally asked.

"Yes."

"Oh! Okayyy. Well, if you can hold on just a minute—how much time do you have?"

"All day." Puzzled, I finally realized she had no idea what was going on. "I'm starting today," I explained.

"Where?"

"Here. In IEM."

"Oh! Where?"

I laughed. "With *you.* Didn't Raoul tell you?"

Mundt leaned forward on her desk with both hands and broke into a high-pitched laugh, immediately followed by her associate, who chuckled artificially.

"I take it he didn't," I said.

She wound down like a dying siren. "Sorry—you'd have to know Raoul! Anyway . . . welcome—I suppose!" She burst into another fit of laughter. "What are you supposed to do anyway?"

"I have no idea."

She slumped into her seat, her hands held over her eyes. "Oh, Raoul, Raoul! Well—this is Marketing. And this is Peter Goth. He'll be with us a few months."

The young man's face grew serious. "Hello."

Mundt threw up her hands. "What else is there?"

"Not too much," Goth snorted.

"We'll have to wait and see what Raoul wants to do with you," Mundt said, searching the room. "I don't see him right now."

I drew up an empty seat and they returned to work. Goth pulled out a pair of half-lensed reading glasses, adding another ten years to his twenty-four, and sat down in front of a large monitor with a display of authority.

"What are you doing?" I asked, looking over his spreadsheet.

"The BBYA. Don't worry, you'll find out about it soon enough." He chortled, inspiring the same reaction in Mundt.

"Have you ever used Lotus?" she asked.

"No."

Goth's hands froze on the keyboard.

"But if it's Windows based," I said, "I can figure it out."

"It isn't," Goth snapped, eyes forward. "Not this version."

"Don't worry," Mundt said, "it's not that hard to learn." She stood up and collected her pamphlets, handing me one entitled *Mexican Eurobonds:* "Here, you might want to read this." Then she sashayed around to all the salesmen, dropping off the rest with little purrs of explanation, and returned to rummage through the papers on her desk.

I rolled my chair next to hers. "So what's a Eurobond?"

She paused, her head cocked in her palm. "A Eurobond is . . . a bond traded in Europe, that's all."

I thought this over a minute. "But aren't they traded here too?"

"Yeeees, but they *mainly* trade in Europe; in London mostly."

"I see." I kept reading the report. "And the issuers, they're all in—"

Mundt dropped her hands on her desk. "We're *not* going to answer all your questions!"

My face reddened. Goth's keyboard ceased clacking.

"Okay," I said flatly.

She spun around. "Did Raoul say you were going to get any training?"

"I'm meeting with him an hour a day, that's all I know."

"Just you and him?" Mundt threw her head back in a scream of laughter, joined by Goth's supporting chortles. "Sorry! Good luck!"

"You don't think he'll do it?"

She held up her hands. "Who knows? Maybe. But if he does, it will be a first, let's just say that." She looked over Goth's shoulder. "Are you done yet?"

"Almost."

"Noooo! *Peter,* what are you *doing?*"

"You wanted a BBYA update."

"*No*-oh, I want a *Eurobond* update!" Mundt rose, shaking her head with a tight smile. "I have to go back to Research. Make sure you get that out as soon as possible."

"I will."

She breezed past me, her head cocked to one side.

I moved closer to Goth. "Where is Research?"

"Hold on, I really have to get this out. The traders need it."

I glanced back over the report. A few minutes later Goth stripped his work from the printer and entered the adjoining loop at a near run, delivering his update to the traders with all the gravity of battlefield intelligence. They promptly confined it to their in-boxes.

He returned with a voice of authority. "You want to do some lunch?"

"Ah—sure."

"Hold on then, let me just sign off here."

"Goth!" a voice called out. Goth jumped to his feet; a trader was standing across the divide. "I need a new yield on the BNCE global! It's down half a point!"

"Okay, give me five minutes!"

Goth slammed back into his chair, his back stiff, his face taut. Quickly recalling his program, he typed in a new figure and started recalculation. "Come on," he urged, impatiently strumming his fingers on the desktop. He snapped his head toward the trader, then back to his computer, his face charged with the importance of his work. "It's always like this!"

Tearing the sheet from the printer, he strode back to the traders' circle and handed it over with the utmost deference. Then he was back, grinning like a man relieved of a great responsibility and offering lunch again.

We descended in the elevator. One of the perks of working on a Merrill Lynch trading desk was free lunch in the employee cafeteria, an upscale operation with Mexican, Italian, and Chinese sections, a grill, a deli, and a sushi bar. The rationale behind this policy, it was said, was to save the firm money by shortening the time it took employees to eat. Instead of leaving the building you would fill up a cardboard carton on the third floor and head back to your desk. In reality, however, the free lunch did more to define the office class system than it did to preserve capital: none of the top echelons accepted it. If you were anybody worth anything on Wall Street, you certainly didn't need a free lunch. So instead all the salesmen and traders, and those who wished to emulate them, ordered takeout from one of the World Financial Center's many restaurants and had one of the analysts go down and fetch it.

Goth had performed this service enough times to know the value of takeout. "You don't want to eat *there*," he snickered as we passed the cafeteria. He took me to a sandwich shop instead, where we bought the daily special. Meanwhile he acted like a man who had slugged down twenty cups of coffee. His hands were always in motion, massaging his arms, wiping imaginary specks from his eyes, rubbing a perpetually itchy nose. He walked with an unnatural, uncomfortable motion as if thinking about each footstep and talked constantly, rapidly, with brief bursts of nervous laughter, uncomfortable with any silences. In the brief moments when I actually spoke, he focused on his next comment rather than listening. He steered me toward the Winter Garden as if to a scheduled meeting, where we climbed the marble steps to the top of the atrium. Below, in front of the ordered grove of palm trees, a brass band was playing.

I had barely sat down when Goth commenced his life's tale. He told me how he had grown up in a small town in Iowa, the son of chemists who had instilled in him a love of mathematics; how he had decided in junior high, in some revelatory moment, that he wanted to be an investment banker; how he had recently graduated with a master's degree in statistics from the University of New Mexico a year ahead of time; how he had written his thesis on a new statistical method he had devised to beat the stock market (one too complicated to explain right now, he demurred); how one of his professors had been a consultant for Merrill Lynch; how he had been one of a handful of people accepted into Merrill's elite Global Financial Analyst program, which would allow him to rotate on various desks worldwide for periods of six months over the next two years; how this program was the brainchild of Edson—meaning Edson Mitchell, cohead of the firm's stock and bond trading operations; and how he could practically write his own ticket anywhere on Wall Street now: repo trading at Nomura perhaps, mortgage trading at Bear Stearns, derivatives trading at Merrill, maybe even IEM. It all poured forth with the fluidity of a story told a thousand times, supported by a number of glances confirming that I was following it. I was. By the time I had taken three bites of my chicken sandwich there was no question that I was in the presence of a financial wunderkind.

"So what did *you* do before you came here?" he asked.

"I was a naval officer."

He snorted. "Wow! *That's* weird. How did you end up *here*?"

"It wasn't easy."

"Did you know somebody?"

"Well—I know Kenny Breen."

"Oh, I get it."

"It's not that simple."

"So he introduced you to Raoul?"

"No, that was a surprise."

"Then why is he giving you special instruction?"

I paused. "I need it."

Goth snorted. "They didn't give *me* any."

"You're on rotation."

"Still—"

"How long have you been here so far?" I said quickly.

"About two months."

"Do you like it?"

"It's all right." Goth shrugged. "I get to help the traders—that's what I want to do, trading. But working with *Claire*"—he snickered, looking at me with an all-knowing glance—"you'll see." He held himself briefly in check, then burst out, "She doesn't know *anything*. I mean, *I* have to explain things to her sometimes. You have to check on everything she says." He laughed self-consciously. "I'm just warning you."

"Sure."

"And she has big problems in the office," he whispered. "I mean, the traders *hate* her."

"Why is that?" I asked warily, unsure how much of this was fact, how much exaggeration.

"They just do," he said. "Don't get me wrong, I don't have anything against her—except when she gets in the way of my job."

I crumpled my wrappers and stuck them in the bag. "Ready to go?"

"Yeah, I have to get back. I almost never eat down here. You never know when the traders might need something."



Mundt was still absent when we returned to IEM, leaving me wondering what to do next. Sitting there in her seat, I watched Goth, out of the corner of my eye, reach into a file drawer, covertly withdraw a toothbrush and toothpaste, and retreat to the bathroom. It was a habit of his, oft repeated during market hours. To him, personal hygiene was a matter of diligent sanitation. This included throwing an arm over his head at times as if stretching, and sniffing beneath it. He was not alone in this regard either: Savegre was also seen frequenting the men's room, where he washed his hands until the skin cracked white. But the hands-down winner in the hygiene sweepstakes had to be the young Indian man down the hall who was known for his fastidiousness in front of the urinal. Standing next to him, one had a hard time deciding whether it was cleanliness he was after or pleasure.

"Hey, hombre! Pick up one of those lines!"

I turned around: Carlos Espinosa, the only salesman present, was talking to me with his bandolero's banter, his headset strapped on. He turned back to his call, raking his fingers through his slicked-back hair.

I stared at the touchscreen: three lines were blinking, then four. I touched one and grabbed the receiver—nothing. I hit another—nothing. I hit another—then saw the other receiver lying on the desk. There were two at every station. I had just cut off two people.

"Hello, is Juan there?" the third voice said.

"Just a minute." I turned to Espinosa, interrupting his conversation. "Do we have a Juan here?"

"Do we have a Juan? This is the emerging markets, hombre! We got more Juans than they got Chins in China."

I uncovered the phone. "Juan who?"

"Juan Fuentes," said the voice. "Is he there? It's important. I must speak with him."

I covered the mouthpiece. "Who's Juan Fuentes?" I asked Espinosa.

"I'm on the line, kemosabe!"

Frustrated, I stood up, raising the phone above my head. "Juan Fuentes!"

Fuentes popped up across the divide. "Who is it?"

I uncovered the mouthpiece. "Who is it?"

"Tell him it's Victor," an impatient voice said. "It's important!"

"It's Victor!" I announced. "It's important!"

"What line?" Fuentes asked, quickly searching his touchscreen.

"Ahhh . . ." I looked over the screen—numbers blinking, steady, lit, unlit.

"What page are you on?" Fuentes demanded.

Page? I searched for some telltale number, lifted my hands helplessly.

Fuentes exclaimed something in Spanish—it wasn't *buenos días*—and began jumping into all the open lines searching for Victor. But Victor was gone. He threw down his receiver and glared at me.

I sat down feeling like a complete fool. I couldn't even answer the phone! But what did they expect?

A voice laughed lightly on the other side of my position. "Let me show you how to use that." It was Savegre's secretary, Dawn, her head barely visible between two notebooks.

I moved sheepishly to her side and received a more thorough instruction in the complex office phone system. "Thanks," I said gratefully.

"No problem. So you're going to be working for the Queen, huh?"

I looked puzzled.

"That's what we call Claire: the Queen."

"Oh. *With* her, I hope."

"Good luck. I heard her snap at you this morning. She's got a lot of nerve. You just started."

I shrugged. "What can you do?"

"Don't put up with it. You're an associate, same as her. You don't have to take that."

"Maybe she's had a bad day."

"Nah, she's always like that. She tries to speak down to me all the time. Just ignore her. Otherwise you'll end up her slave, like Goth. But you have to be careful: the salesmen love her."

Mundt finally returned and set to work. I sat next to her, not knowing what to do next. I didn't feel inclined to ask her any questions. Nor did I feel like speaking with Goth. Since returning from lunch, his openness toward me, however unwanted, had disappeared, replaced by a sharpness similar to that which Mundt displayed toward him. Every time I asked him something I ended up feeling reminded of my ignorance. In his mind, the office hierarchy had been established.

"So do you know what you're going to do yet?" Mundt asked me.

"No. I guess I'll speak with Raoul tomorrow."

"Must be nice," Goth quipped, "having a managing director on your side."

I put myself on Savegre's schedule for the next morning and went downstairs into the atrium. It was time to take things into my own hands. In the Rizzoli bookstore, I located a copy of the Good Book of bonds, *The Handbook of Fixed Income Securities* by Frank Fabozzi, a dense, eighty-five-dollar tome that could easily break a toe if you weren't careful. Over the next few weeks, Mr. Fabozzi and I would become close friends. Back in IEM I staked out a spot on the lunch table in the corner of the room. It was here that the operations people, the blue-collar support staff who did the legwork on trades, unfurled their brown bags at noon. I stayed there for the rest of the day communing with Fabozzi. At five, while contemplating the features of bonds, I raised my head to the disquieting sound of quiet as the market finally closed. By six-thirty I was on to the time value of money and half the room was empty. By eight only a handful of diehards remained and I could concentrate on bond pricing more easily. At nine my scrambled brain was the only one left in the room. I put Fabozzi, appropriately, in a banker's box, which I carefully hid on the windowsill. It was my first piece of IEM real estate. Then I reached another Wall Street watershed: I called a car service. Anyone who worked past seven-thirty at Merrill was entitled to a free ride home, courtesy of the firm. The rationale was similar to the free lunch: if you didn't have to worry about moving around New York at night, you would be more inclined to work late. There were various car services to choose from, the largest of which, TWR, sounded more like an airline. Another had the audacity to call itself Love. The cars were large American sedans—Lincoln Town Cars and Chrysler New Yorkers were common—which lined up outside the entrance to the North Tower summoned by roving dispatchers with walkie-talkies. In this way my chariot arrived and whisked me away.

I sat in the backseat watching the lights of the city go by, feeling exhausted and numb and strangely relaxed. This moment, this priceless few minutes between work and my apartment, I grew to enjoy like a hot bath after a long walk in the snow. I would leave the market behind and sink into fifteen minutes of soothing quiet. The lights of the Brooklyn Bridge would pass by like a runway at night. The streets of the Heights and Cobble Hill would turn this way and that directed by an unseen hand. Then I was back out in the cold, running through my key chain, listening to the whines of a hidden expressway, and walking the empty halls of the Cobble Hill School.

The phone rang soon after I entered the apartment. "Well, how'd it go?" Sarah asked from Atlantic City.

I wasn't sure where to begin. With the people? The job? The environment? The thousands of thoughts that had flashed through my head throughout the day?

"Fine," I said. "How about you?"

## 10

My first few weeks in IEM were spent wandering around observing the office and trying to make sense of the bizarre new world that I had entered, in all its diverse facets. This was not the result of a directive from management but of its absence: I was simply left alone without any explanation. My own wandering thus became one of the many mysteries I sought to unravel in my efforts to understand my group, a process that would take many months. There was a lot standing between me and the truth: a fogged pair of cultural goggles, the many intricacies of the market, and the secrecy of the Latin Mafia. But as time went on, a clear picture began to form.

Each day in IEM officially began with the morning call, a global conference call connecting the entire group. This daily ritual began around quarter to eight when people would begin filtering in from home. After shedding their suit coats—no one wore a jacket on the trading floor—they would swarm around the bagel cart, stripping it like a breakdown on the BQE, and carry off their loot to the conference room. There they would assemble around the long central table, the first few taking the available seats, the rest lining the walls, tightly packed.

All told, the gathering was normally some thirty strong, mostly male, and noticeably international. Due to the globalization of finance, all the major Wall Street banks had gone international, turning themselves into gated communities within the global village; but in the emerging markets, where the employees were as diverse as the bonds, this was especially true. In IEM there were people from Mexico, Brazil, Argentina, Venezuela, Colombia, Iran, India, Uruguay, Chile, Panama, Peru, Lebanon, Spain, Russia, Poland, Japan, Great Britain, Canada, and Switzerland. This league of nations turned the conference room into a multilingual, predominantly Latin place, where Spanish was as common as English, especially among management.

Another striking characteristic of the group was its youth: the average age appeared to hover near twenty-eight. The reason for this, however, was less obvious. Where were the old hands?

At precisely eight o'clock the mobile speakerphone in the center of the table would ring, announcing the presence of the operator. The chairman of the call, usually Savegre or Forte, would answer and confirm the names of all those who had dialed in—only IEM employees were allowed to participate. Once this security measure was complete, all the participants would be connected: IEM offices in London, Tokyo, and Hong Kong; IEM salespeople in Dallas and Chicago; the Syndicate desk on Seven; Research on Twenty-one; and any traveling members of the office, wherever they might be. To the first-time visitor, this global conferencing looked impressive, but it was not without its problems. Oftentimes the sounds of a distant trading floor could be heard, followed by the command "Employ your mute button!" People who were caught in traffic would sometimes call in on their car phones, adding horns, sirens, and the static of a fading zone. In one memorable instance, the call was interrupted by a recording demanding another quarter. In another, a participant put his office phone on hold, filling the conference room with the strains of "Rocky Mountain High." John Denver on Wall Street—who would have thought?

The purpose of the call was to pass on timely, relevant market information, a policy that was strictly upheld. Prompted by the chairman, IEM London would go first, its traders and salespeople recapping the morning's price action in the Eurobond and Brady markets, what the Europeans were saying, and any significant trades they had done. New York Trading would follow, each man relating what he had seen the previous day, what his trade ideas were, and what he thought of the market news. Sales came next, sounding noticeably more polished. Like Washington pundits, they would spout the latest buzzword, replay news stories, give their view, and generally sound insightful. Then came a sleepy representative or two from IEM Tokyo, talking about the Asian market, ongoing business with Japanese banks, and price levels of Philippine Brady bonds. Finally, Research would pipe up to give their read on the market, ready to quote a study or two or provide some statistics. Their greatest gift was describing the direction of the market without ever saying "up" or "down"—the dollar is strengthening, there is pressure on the peso, there should be some positive movement, upward slope, curve inversion, reversal in the trend, downward spike—it was an unequaled exercise in linguistic legerdemain. Sometimes you even wondered if they were talking about money.

When the call was over, the conference room would clear out and everyone would return to their positions in anticipation of the market opening at nine. The position, as each seat on the desk was known, was the cockpit of the market. It was here that one received information, analyzed it, communicated with the outside world, and took action. In IEM the average position consisted of a large computer, a stack of smaller broker screens, two phones (one for either ear), the elaborate touchscreen phone system, and a Bloomberg machine. This impressive console of technology was further tailored to the user's specific needs. The virtual buttons of the phone system provided instant communication with scores of personal contacts. The Bloomberg, a small orange monitor, was coded to pull up bonds of consistent interest with a few keystrokes. The large SUN monitor was typically divided up into numerous multicolored windows, chosen from the hundreds of live news pages available from Reuters or Dow Jones, including regional news pages (Latin America and Eastern Europe were popular), country news pages (the major emerging markets each had a page), and market news pages (such as the emerging markets, U.S. Treasury market, Latin equities, various foreign currencies, bond market news, and recent auction prices). In this way the position became one's interface with that nebulous entity known as the market.

The positions in IEM lined the figure-eight trading desk both inside and out. The southern loop, near the windows, comprised Sales (which included Marketing) and the northern, Trading: two circles of interest, clipped by entrances at either end, facing each other across a divide of computers. Sales had four primary positions, each with its own focus: mutual funds, hedge funds, insurance companies, and Latin accounts. In Trading, the primary positions were defined by instrument. There were two Brady positions—the heart of the desk—one for Argentine and Brazilian Bradys, the other for Mexico and Venezuela, and various others positions for Eurobonds, exotic bonds, Mexican Treasury instruments, repurchase agreements, options and derivatives. Trading also had a subdesk known as International Retail, which took orders from Merrill's global Private Client network. The rest of the figure eight was taken up by various support positions: trading assistants, sales assistants, operations specialists, and the odd roving associate, his brain aflutter.

These positions, in turn, were all parts in the operation of a powerful, two-cylinder engine, the Trading desk. In simple terms, the traders operated like grocers. They owned a product—bonds—which were on a shelf in the computer. The prices of these bonds constantly fluctuated. It was the traders' responsibility to buy them low and sell them high and pocket the difference. They did this by setting prices that correctly anticipated market movements and managing their inventory accordingly. Their counterparties—the customers they traded with—fell into two different categories. There was the inside market, a monopoly made up exclusively of other broker-dealers, which posted its prices on the so-called broker screens and was an important source of liquidity; and there was the outside market, the firm's clients, a diverse array of institutions and private individuals yielding the bulk of the profits. The Private Client business was handled by Merrill Lynch brokers located in offices all around the world who called Trading directly for prices. The institutional business, the greatest source of profits for the desk, was funneled through IEM Sales. Sales attracted clients by providing consistently good information and analyses of the market based on Merrill Lynch research, the flows they were seeing, contacts, and market news. They were market specialists: major institutions relied on them for information, advice, and execution.

The mechanics of the Sales & Trading engine centered around the act of trading a bond. Having sold a client on a trade idea or merely taken an order, a salesman would put his client on hold, stand up, and call across the divide to the appropriate trader requesting a price: "Juan, can you give me a bid on five million Argy discounts?" The trader would then check the current price on the broker screens, consider his position in that bond and his view on the direction of the market, and set his price accordingly—"make a market" in industry parlance. "I'll buy five million at seventy-five." The salesman would then confer with his client and announce either, "Okay, you're done at five million" or "Nothing done." If the trade went through, the trader would mark it on his blotter and adjust his position accordingly, ready for the next trade.

This trading activity went on from the market opening at nine until the close at five, a time of intense concentration, broken only by a hastily gobbled lunch, short and infrequent meetings, a rare investor visit, and a few brave questions. There were no offices to hide in: with the exception of the group's investment bankers, who had a string of offices down the hall, and Forte's cubbyhole, everyone sat side by side at their positions inside and outside the figure eight. This made for some tight, noisy working conditions in which all phone conversations were overheard by someone, producing a constant, unrelenting stress. The market was the blast furnace of the economy: the difference between home and office was equal to that between office and trading floor. Throughout the day the market was a tangible presence in the room, driving people forward. There was no better metaphor for it than the bull, the symbol of Merrill Lynch and Wall Street alike. It was a brawny, straining, sweating, muscular creature, pulling from without and driving from within, restrained only by the bridle of regulation and the lash of the law. At the same time the identity of the market was a mystery. It consisted of all those active buyers and sellers of emerging markets debt clamoring over the wires but had no fixed location. It was omnipotent yet ethereal, everywhere and nowhere all at once.

Once the market closed, people would typically linger awhile to take care of administrative matters, then depart. Only the lower echelons worked long hours, staying until nine or ten at night. For the rest the hours on a trading desk were not as long as investment banking or law but equally grueling: a sprint rather than a marathon.


Once I had a basic understanding of how the desk operated, the hidden dynamics of the morning call became apparent. While the purpose of the call was, ostensibly, to pass on information to other members of the group, this goal was consistently undermined by the mistrust that permeated IEM.

Our London office was a case in point. IEM London had less than ten people, none of whom thought the home office cared about them. And for the most part this was true. Like all of IEM's satellites, IEM London was generally ignored. Support was shoddy, communication infrequent. The reason was simple: few people served to benefit from it. Why take precious time to help those who added nothing to your bottom line? This caused IEM London to question the intentions of IEM New York and to worry about them. IEM New York was larger, stronger, and in the center of the market—Would they use that to their advantage? Could they be trusted to safeguard London's interests? Would they withhold information, betray clients, move the market against them? In the silence, anything seemed possible. Consequently, information flow from London was guarded, often from paranoia or sheer spite, and, as the market continued to fall, increasingly so. The problem was epitomized by the speakerphone itself, which was barely audible across the Atlantic. Hardly a morning call went by without some frustrated English voice pleading, "WOULD YOU SPEAK UP, PLEASE?!"

Mistrust raged between Sales & Trading as well, which had a relationship at once both symbiotic and adversarial. Trading needed Sales for clients and Sales needed Trading for bonds, but the two represented opposed interests. When trading with the firm's clients, a trader naturally wished to profit because that is how he was paid. At the end of every day he printed out a profit and loss sheet, known as a P&L, which revealed in stark terms how well he had done. At the end of the year his bonus was directly tied to his net profits. A salesman, on the other hand, was paid based on the trades he brought to the desk, whether those trades turned out to be profitable or not. It was in his best interest, therefore, to get the lowest price he could from the trader so that his client would do the trade and earn him his commission. This bred competition between the two halves of the Sales & Trading equation, one reinforced by an organizational separation: while physically part of the desk, IEM Sales reported to Institutional Sales, an entirely different Merrill Lynch entity. This freed Sales to act in the best interest of clients, and itself, rather than be held accountable to the Trading desk. It also created a situation much like having squatters in your living room.

Information flow suffered accordingly. The most important cards the traders held were the position of the desk, long or short, the market, and their intentions: a big trade from IEM could move the whole market. Hence, knowing about such a trade ahead of time could make a client a lot of money. Could Sales be trusted to keep such information to themselves when they were so intent on winning client business? If they didn't, the rationale for the trade could well evaporate. Similarly, Sales talked to important clients all day long, big institutions like Fidelity whose billions of dollars committed one way or the other could move the market too. In the process, they often divined the positions of their clients, their views and intentions, and pitched them trade ideas. Could they trust the traders with such information when they could profit from it—at their clients' expense? Would they raise prices on them knowing a client's interest in buying or selling? Or would they do a trade themselves, moving the market against the client?

It was such concerns that diluted the content of the call. As a matter of policy Sales wouldn't even mention the names of clients out of fear they would be attached to some market rumor. In turn, the traders stuck to run-of-the-mill trade ideas, or proposed trades that would help their position if leaked, while keeping the most valuable cards to themselves.

Research had its own unique problems on the call. Emerging Markets Fixed Income Research, part of the firm's Global Securities Research and Economics Group, was responsible for analyzing the entire market—countries, issuers, instruments, political and economic events—and publishing its findings in various reports, which were used to attract investors. Like Sales, it had an alternate reporting line to ensure its objectivity, and was even resident on a different floor, Twenty-one. In practice, however, Research did not enjoy the insulation of Sales, since it was not a direct source of profits. Instead, it fell noticeably under the thumb of IEM management—particularly Savegre's thumb—which rated its performance and expected it to toe the line. This created a perpetual conflict that played itself out not only on the morning call but in various publications, meetings, and investor visits as well: should Research say what they believed or what Sales wanted to tell investors? Should they support the Trading desk's position or state their own? Just prior to my arrival, this conflict had resulted in the noisy departure of the outspoken head of IEM Research, who had refused to bend. He left behind a demoralized department, the stuffing pulled from its morning commentary.


Unlike the Sales & Trading engine, the culture of IEM was an enigma difficult to unravel. Its main elements were apparent during any morning call: a triad of Wall Street culture, Latin culture, and the unique environment of the emerging markets boom. But each of these elements had a great deal in common with the others, making it difficult to identify the root causes of surface effects.

Viewed on its own, Wall Street culture wasn't difficult to fathom. It was the purest product of market forces, applied, and strengthened, over many years. In the broadest sense, the culture of the Street wasn't even unique, just cutting edge, the modern product of an old capitalist recipe: technology, efficiency, speed, and competition, all cooked under very high pressure. You might even call it a leading social indicator: the changes that have occurred there are only too familiar.

Wall Street has always had its share of sharks, for instance, but there was a time, in the not-so-distant past, when the Street also enjoyed strong bonds between employee and firm. This yielded distinct corporate identities, some strengthened by ethnicity, which encouraged a sense of belonging. Thanks to their smaller size, even entire markets enjoyed a sense of community. Before the boom years of the eighties the U.S. Government market, the big daddy of them all, comprised only a hundred and fifty traders, all of whom knew one another, forming an extended family in which entrance was gained through nepotism or friendship. Each year the entire *market* had a party for the holidays. Such small, closed, and entirely domestic groups were facilitated by a relatively low level of technology and its resultant effects: low competitive pressures and a slower pace of life. Traders came into work at nine-thirty, got going around ten, started wrapping up at three-thirty, and left at four. If things got slow, they played cards. The line of demarcation was clearly the firm: people cooperated within, and competed without.

Such an approach did not maximize efficiency, however. Personnel couldn't move to other firms, where they might be needed, while, within a firm, groups were sheltered from competition. So over time, thanks to technology and increased competitive pressures, the market broke its traditional loyalties, and a new culture emerged. The team players of yesterday gave way to free agents and mercenaries to whom firms were nothing more than uniforms worn at a price; collections of electronics whose history and culture were irrelevant. Instead of making an investment in people and promoting from within, management became a matter of hiring superstars from the free-agent pool and keeping them happy. Employees became contractual commodities purchased or discarded as the market demanded and only as good as their last trade. Like professional athletes, the life span of these market people depended on their continued ability to compete against the rookies; unlike them, they spent their careers playing on a team of one. Efficiency was maximized when each man had to look out for himself—when there was risk on his head and nowhere to hide. The best were greatly rewarded for it; the rest weren't.

The herald of this new era was the stock market crash of 1987. In its wake, Wall Street employees were fired by the thousands; by the end of 1990 the securities industry had cut 20 percent of its employees. At Merrill Lynch people who had come up through the ranks and served at the firm twenty-five years suddenly found themselves out in the street. High-salaried people in their forties and fifties were thrown out in favor of cheaper bodies in their twenties. Meanwhile Merrill executives continued to take home $3 million to $8 million pay packages. Company loyalty was never the same again.

By the time of the emerging markets boom this new Wall Street had blossomed, killing the old society. Organizations were run by a few insiders taking home immense pay packages. Wealth was not something to be built through a joint effort but obtained at the expense of others. Loyalty was dead: people jumped ship on a whim and were hired and fired as necessary. Firms seized on short-term business opportunities and moved on, building nothing to last. It was a world managed by the market and fertile ground for the Latin Mafia.


The emerging markets boom was a mostly Latin phenomenon and IEM reflected that. All its senior managers and many of its employees were Latin. They had typically been raised in Latin countries, then emigrated to the United States to study—business or economics were popular—or had come to the States to further a banking career begun at home. This created an office culture more imported than domestic, a factor strongly influencing how the group was run.

In Latin America, as elsewhere in the developing world, the power structure is highly polarized. There are tremendous disparities between rich and poor, and a thin middle class, creating, in effect, a divided culture: a few insiders at the top and everyone else. This unbalanced concentration of wealth places society on a more defensive, distrustful stance rather than an open, cooperative, mutually beneficial one, affecting how business is run. To maintain their power those at the top form cabals, small defensive groups based on trust. These often take the natural form of families, which rule the largest Latin corporations; drug gangs, such as the Calí and Medellín cartels; or *grupos,* coteries that manage diverse business interests—all of which wield tremendous political influence. It is a winner-take-all system, with the many excesses that produces.

IEM was not immune from these influences. It was, in some ways, as if a Latin corporation had arisen within the walls of America's most powerful investment bank. And its management structure reflected it. The group was run by a coterie of insiders known throughout the firm as the Latin Mafia. Although their membership was never expressly defined, it consisted of a Cuban-Venezuelan, Lisardo Escobar, founder and head of the group; a Mexican, Ricardo Micó, the head of the investment banking wing; an Argentine, Mikhail Gurevich, the top-producing salesman; and a Panamanian, Miguel Forte, the head trader. (Savegre was noticeably excluded. Though he was head of Sales, and of Cuban descent, they didn't know what to make of him.) There were allegiances within the Latin Mafia as well, which shifted over time, but with the partial exception of Forte, their policies toward the outsiders remained consistent. There seemed to be little interest in sharing the wealth, developing talent, and building a lasting business. To the Latin Mafia, IEM was a tremendous opportunity for getting rich. They had little apparent allegiance to the rest of the firm, which they viewed with suspicion, nor to most of their employees, whom they held at a distance. Inside the office, they seemed to be less interested in you the further from the top you were and the less Spanish you spoke. Communication was limited to their inner circle and, on occasion, a few budding acolytes. Meetings were held in private and never discussed with the rest of the group; policy changes that resulted were not explained. The group was often left in the dark about what was going on. One would enter a conference room filled with the smoke of unfiltered Camels and hear the conversation suddenly switch to Spanish.

IEM also had its share of gringo bankers, of course, whose values were strikingly similar to the Latin Mafia. The marriage of Latin culture and Wall Street was thus mutually reinforcing at times, especially when it came to management. Market management, in which the P&L is all-important, suited the Latin Mafia just fine. Their culture required that the campesinos be left struggling in the dark on their own. If they survived, fine; if they didn't, there were plenty of others to take their place. The result was a hands-off management style so pronounced it bordered on amputation. "Delay and avoid" was the maxim of the moment and pursued as an art form. Ask a Mafioso for a decision and you were bound to witness a well-executed tango. Problems were addressed only when they reached critical mass.*

The most striking example of this was the leadership of the Trading desk itself. In January 1994, Miguel Forte and Mickey Gurevich announced that they were leaving IEM to start their own investment company, a fact which nearly nixed my hiring. The head of the group, Lisardo Escobar, then named our stocky Venezuelan trader, Diego Barbero, to replace Forte. Meanwhile Escobar was negotiating with Forte and Gurevich to return—and finally succeeded, with a promise from Merrill to fund their venture in another year. The problem then became how to fit Forte back into the trading desk, a politically difficult question. So in classic IEM style, Escobar avoided the tough call and made Forte and Barbero co–head traders. The desk was never the same again. Who was in charge? Escobar, Forte, and Barbero were all known to dispense their own trading advice. In one noted case a trader was told to go long, go short, and stay flat all at the same time.

Such confusion permeated the group. Without strong leadership, IEM became a perpetual *carnaval* where people ran around more or less at will reacting to whatever crisis arose, a problem that grew with its size. Office society devolved into a state of nature, a truly free market ruled by Darwin's invisible hand. Thus my own hiring: the mixed signals, the sudden reversals, the enigma of who was in charge, or what my job would be, were all classic symptoms of market management.


The final leg in IEM's cultural triad was the boom. The dramatic rise of the emerging markets created a rare environment, one in which the normal pressures of Sales

---

* It is instructive to note that a debate has recently sprung up in Mexican newspapers on the need to coin a new word in Spanish, one that specifically means "accountability."

& Trading were distorted. The flow of trades, a balanced number of buys and sells in a stable market, turned into a lopsided buying spree, much of it from people who knew nothing about the emerging markets at all. The Latin Mafia responded in character by shifting the focus of business away from creating demand in a professional fashion to meeting it however possible. The group expanded rapidly. Young and inexperienced people were hired at low salaries. Training was negligible. This created, amid the rising tide of the market, a constant pressure to keep your head above water, intensifying office competition. People tried to go as far as possible with as little knowledge as possible, encouraging others to do the same until doing so became the status quo. True competence remained what you knew, but success became a matter of how far you could stretch it. To some degree, such pressures are always present in the market, where the daily deluge of financial information soon teaches you to study only what you absolutely need and to wing the rest—a corner cutting that occasionally shows.* But the emerging markets gold rush magnified such tendencies to the breaking point. It was a boomtown culture all its own.

The dangerous part of this culture was that it hid the very problems it caused. During the boom, it was nearly impossible not to make money—a great deal of money—on an emerging markets trading desk. Almost any bond held on the books overnight was worth more the next day. This created a situation in which everyone looked good no matter what they knew, or didn't know, allowing any corner cutting to go unnoticed, or at least be ignored—a cloaking action that extended to the Latin Mafia themselves, who looked good no matter what decisions they made or didn't make. While their absentee management bred a number of vexing problems, no one noticed or cared with profits so high. The invisible hand grew arthritic, crippling the force of change. Problems festered accordingly.

The attitudes and policies of the Latin Mafia were further cemented in place by the effect of the boom on their self-image. They had all enjoyed the extreme good luck of getting in on the ground floor of a tremendous bull market, one that had made them young millionaires. A few of them were even capable bankers; others were purely mediocre. But over time the role of luck grew dim in their minds, supplanted by their own skill and foresight. Their success was no freak of nature: it was something they had *earned*, something they *deserved*—it was their *right*. They were in power for a *reason*, a reason supported by their seven-figure bonuses, the group that had risen around them, and the free rein granted them by their firm, which was enjoying their run of profits. Consequently, if an outsider brought a problem to their attention, it was dismissed; if an error occurred, it was not their fault. Their power simply put them above reproach or accountability. They were the junta of Merrill's Latin boomtown.

* One common market term, for instance, the *tenure* of a bond, has somehow become its *tenor*—as if Pavarotti were a fixed income investment.

## 11

My first few days at work I stuck around after the morning call and tried to corner Savegre. He had, after all, promised to provide me instruction on a daily basis, the chortles of the Marketing Department notwithstanding. I soon found, however, that this was an exercise in pin the tail on the donkey. Savegre had more blow-off lines than the market had reversals. "I'll be with you in a minute." "I need to go next door for one second." "Go to my desk, I'll be right there." "Let me just finish this first." "Have you read this? Talk to me when you're done." "Can you copy this first? Thanks." He seemed completely incapable of simply saying, "Sorry, I don't have time"—if that were even the case. Meanwhile I had to fend off Goth's probing wit: "Learn anything from Raoul today?"

Naturally, I wondered why this was happening. Had Savegre changed his mind about me? Or had the Marketing Department changed it for him? So I turned finding out into a private game, determined to get Savegre either to keep an appointment or to admit that he was never going to meet with me.

I never won. The denouement occurred at the end of my second week. After sitting in the conference room for ten minutes waiting for Savegre to arrive, I walked to the door and noticed him scurrying across the trading floor, heading for the exit. Aha! Leaping forward, I intercepted him in the hall.

"Oh, I thought you were coming to the conference room," I said innocently.

Savegre frowned concernedly. "I am . . . I just have to go to the men's room first."

I knew better. "Oh. So am I."

I followed a pace behind him until he turned. "Come to think of it, why don't you go find Breen? He was the one who promised to train you."

While still pursuing Savegre, I found myself fleeing from Mundt. Though we were both nominal associates in the firm, Mundt and I were not on the same level in the food chain: she had a job. This made me fair game for any of the larger fish, especially in the same department. I had learned this by watching Goth, who was consumed in this manner many times a day. His knowledge of spreadsheets and statistics had proved valuable to the traders, who utilized him in modeling various bonds. Once word got out, he was seen working ever later at night, until Mundt, who used him to put out marketing products for herself, began to complain. Stiles, however—now there was a puzzle. But it didn't take her long to find a solution. She had a lot of copying to be done.

The first time she asked I took it as a matter of urgency. She was pressed for time, I would help her out. The next time I was walking in that direction anyway, so I agreed. Certainly she didn't think that at twenty-nine and $55,000 a year, plus bonus, I was going to be her copyboy? Then she invited me to go upstairs to the Graphics Department, where I was instructed in the art of filling out forms to get slides made, and to the Word Processing Department, where long documents were picked up, and everything became clear to me. That's exactly what she thought.

What should I do? I wondered. I didn't want to make waves, not my first week. I imagined what people would say: so he doesn't want to pay his dues, does he? But I've already paid my dues, I wanted to shout; that's why you hired me, isn't it? I'm not a kid anymore. If I wanted to do copying, I would have been an investment banker. Now train me!

But of course I didn't say these things, I just hid from Mundt. What else could I do? She had the upper hand and we both knew it. Mundt had seen it all before, the new man in the fast world of trading buckling under the first loud voice—I didn't want that to happen to me. If I fell into the black hole of the first-year analyst, I might never emerge. I needed the chance to put my five years of "real world" to good use. So, wedged between Savegre's indifference and the copying machine, for reasons yet unknown, I decided to find myself a job.


I stood at the entrance to the traders' circle. I had decided on Trading not from any strong preference—although it did have a lingering aura—but because it was the best place to hide from Mundt, who sat with Sales. As the stealth associate, my objective was clear. I needed to make myself valuable, and soon, by finding some real work—anything but copying.

I looked around the circle, which was busy as usual. I knew nothing about the various positions, but to the right of me was an eddy of bodies, sheltered by the height of the desk and a tower of broker screens that fit my more pressing requirements. Now I only needed a seat. This was no small challenge in Trading, however. The loop always had more bodies than seats, spawning a perpetual game of musical chairs—a dangerous game if you were a small fish. But I couldn't stand up all day either: aside from the physical strain, I had my visibility to think about.

All the seats looked the same, I noticed: typical black office chairs on rollers. No one would ever track me down. I hovered by the printer, looking busy, confident that with all the available coffee there had to be at least one strained bladder in the crowd. Sure enough, one of the trading assistants soon lifted himself from his perch and passed me on his way out of the loop. As soon as his back was turned, I zeroed in on my target and led it noiselessly away.

No one had noticed a thing. The screens were my ally, keeping everyone look-ing in the wrong direction. I sat down and looked silently on. Two men were sit-ting in front of me closely watching a tower of screens, which were blinking and moving with prices and news. The phone lines were blinking too, keeping them hitting the touchscreen—"Merrill!"—and filling the air with a strange lexicon—hits and lifts, spreads, average life—the peculiar names of particular bonds—Argy Global, BNCE '04, Molinos, Banco Rio Nines of Ninety-seven, the Colombia Yankee—and proper trading procedures—"I sell you five hundred thousand Ba-namex floaters at ninety-five." The air bled tension, springing from the upright postures, the quick movements of head and hand, the sharp voices, the red faces, and the cramped bodies sitting elbow to elbow trying to concentrate amid the noise. Callers piled up on hold, phones slammed down, money was made and lost. The pressure gave rise to sudden, colorful outbursts: "The son of a bitch lifted me!" "God*dammit*, Nafinsa is down half a point!" "Where's my fucking blotter?" Right away I knew it was going to be difficult to learn anything, never mind *do* anything. These people didn't want to be bothered with my questions—they didn't even want to *see* me.

I had ended up at the Eurobond trading position. Unlike the larger and more so-phisticated Brady market, which was driven by institutional trading, the Eu-robond market was primarily a retail business in which small quantities of bonds were sold to large numbers of private investors, predominantly in Latin America. The desk was run by Colin McCarthy, a ruddy, gregarious Irish American with long years in the market and a raging personality. He had started out as a teenager working for Chapdelaine, one of the broker screens he stared at, ended up in Mer-rill's corporate bond division, then transferred to IEM when the boom began. Now in his early thirties, he had a wealth of trading experience, a fact apparent during the morning call when he spoke with an authority no one else could match.

This experience had come at a tremendous expense to McCarthy, however. After many years of pressured, full-tilt days, followed by long nights to blow off the steam, his nerves had begun to fray. "Pick up the fucking phone!" he would scream at the other traders, "we're running a business here!" In the next second, he would be telling a joke. Then, just as suddenly, he would explode again. "Dumb bitch, get off my line!" Sensing a problem, McCarthy had taken to running the desk from IEM London, where the pace was slower, then swung the other way, coming in late, taking two-hour pub lunches, going on long vacations and re-maining incommunicado. Now he was back in New York, a place he associated with all his problems and vehemently hated because of it. Not only was the pres-sure more intense here, but his cultural credentials excluded him from the Latin Mafia—a difficult adjustment from London, where he was the senior man in the office. This did not sit well with someone from a work-hard, party-hard, talk-straight ilk—none of it did. So during the week the partying had increased until it began to show in the morning. He also lapsed into self-destructive behavior. While chairing a small lunchtime meeting for new people in the conference room, a place not known for its conviviality, he commenced the proceedings by pulling a six-pack of Budweiser from a paper bag and handing me one. Another time, when the group was assembled at an outdoor cocktail party at the World Financial Center marina, McCarthy approached the crowd by walking through the shallow reflecting pool in his suit. On the weekends he would go skiing to release the pressure, often arriving Monday morning with goggles imprinted on his wind-burned face. But like many market people, he only turned the sport into an extension of the desk: the slopes opened, you went up and down all day, then to the lodge to sleep off your exhaustion, then back the next morning. It was no different than a weekend in Manhattan: you spent your whole time in motion without ever pausing to reflect. But it *was* easier to go back to work that way.

"So what have they got you doing?" McCarthy asked me while typing something into his Bloomberg.

"I don't think that's been determined yet."

"So what—they just hired you to float around?"

"Looks that way."

"Ha! That's typical. When are those clowns going to figure out you have to train somebody? You can't run an office this way." He took a call. "Half a buck? Right, you're done there. 'Bye." He hung up. "Well, don't let it bother you, something will come along. Just don't do anything stupid, like that idiot Goth. Did you hear about that?"

"No."

McCarthy laughed. "Someone called looking for Miguel. It was Goth's first day. So he stands up and says, 'Is there a Miguel here?' Then Forte walks over and says, 'That's for me.' So Goth, the idiot, says, 'There's a bunch of Miguels around here. Which one are you?' Ha! Ha! Ha! 'I'm the one that's the head trader,' Miguel says. Ha! Ha! Ha!" McCarthy erupted in laughter.

"So do you know what a Eurobond is?" he asked me.

I repeated what I had heard earlier.

"Ha! Who told you *that*?"

". . . Claire Mundt."

"That's typical! You can't believe her. She's a dope. A Eurobond is any bond issued outside the issuer's domestic market. Any bond, anywhere. To us that means mostly Latin sovereign and corporate bonds."

"Sovereign bonds—"

"From a government. Like Mexico. UMS eight and a half of oh-two. That's

United Mexican States, eight-and-a-half-percent coupon, due in two thousand and two—"

"Colin! I need an offer on a million BNCE floaters!" one of the traders yelled.

So Mundt had given me some bad information, I thought. But she was far from a dope. And some of what Savegre had taught me had turned out to be wrong as well. What was going on here?

"Two million BNCE floaters at one-oh-one," McCarthy said.

I spent another hour on the desk. McCarthy kept watching the screens, taking calls, giving bids and offers to the retail traders, and sometimes sharp advice, all the while fielding my questions when he could. Unlike the other traders, he didn't want to be known just for his P&L. He wanted to make a connection, pass on his experience, place himself in a larger picture. He wanted his life to make sense.

Then the desk got busy.

"Sorry," he said, "I can't train you right now. Come back later."


Sitting next to McCarthy was Judd Weaver, one of the Street's top exotic bond traders. The exotics were the *emerging* emerging markets, countries like Panama, Peru, Poland, the Ivory Coast, Bulgaria, Ecuador, and Russia. Once the last frontier of the market, they had been mainstreamed during the boom. Trading them was highly risky but, in 1993, had proved immensely profitable. Propelled by a soaring loan market, the value of IEM's exotics book had risen at a dizzying pace, posting a $30 million profit. Judd Weaver had benefited accordingly. In his early thirties, he drove a Ferrari, had a large apartment on Gramercy Park, and owned a waterfront home in Amagansett, Long Island. A number of women seemed to appreciate such things, for they were always calling the desk. Weaver was also a strident individual, something facilitated by making the firm millions. He had shoulder-length hair, quite unlike your average banker; he wore designer jeans on casual day, contrary to the firm's policy, avoided meetings he didn't want to attend, and in general kept to himself as much as possible. He understood well the Wall Street dictum, stolen from Truman's Washington, that if you wanted a friend in the market, you'd better buy a dog. So he had. Its picture was in his wallet.

"Judd?"

Weaver turned around. I introduced myself, explaining that I was interested in learning about the exotics.

Weaver had a tremendously expressive face. In a moment the subtle shifts in his visage spoke far more than he ever did.

"We can talk about that," he said with a wry smile. Then he turned back around and stared at his screens.

• • •

As I continued to drift around the office, asking questions, I was constantly struck by the limits of people's knowledge. The inaccuracies I'd been hearing, it turned out, were but symptoms of a broader epidemic exposed by frequent contradiction and confirmed by Fabozzi. People in IEM were quite capable of carrying out their daily responsibilities, but the theory behind them and their broader meaning, not to mention the responsibilities of others, were shrouded in a fog of guesses, assumptions, and errors. This was especially true when it came to basic terminology: ask a trader to define a security, for instance, and you would end up with a stream of blather. Like physicists, they operated quite well with certain assumptions, but the meaning of energy or mass left them scratching their heads.

At the same time few would admit what they didn't know, especially to someone below them. Oh sure, it was all right for *me* to go around asking questions—no one expected me to know anything. But *they* had a position to uphold. With so many sharks in the water, who would be stupid enough to say they didn't know? Everyone *else* was saying they knew! In fact, saying you didn't know was such a faux pas it risked sounding that death knell of Wall Street: the . . . fit . . . wasn't . . . right.

This gave my innocent questions a power far beyond my practical intentions. What if you asked someone a question and they didn't know the answer? Would they admit the truth—or not? In this way, my wanderings became a kind of social experiment charting the character of IEM—and a dangerous one at that. Not everyone appreciated being put to the test, even if it was an inadvertent one. I wasn't firing illuminating flares, I realized, but potentially explosive rounds! Still, by aiming carefully, I did manage to conduct a lengthy survey—attendant to learning the bond business of course—that yielded some interesting results.

IEM, the survey showed, had three distinct breeds of people. The first, a rare one, was those who would admit they didn't know something. This wasn't easy, since it came at their personal expense, but there were still a few heroes in the office. Miguel Forte was one. Forte was the one exception to the inner circle, a man with both feet in—for the money—and his heart out. Having helped build the group, he felt responsible for it. If you asked him a question he couldn't answer, he would typically admit it and direct you to someone else. This may have been facilitated by being the head trader, but position was no assurance of immunity, as Forte later discovered.

McCarthy was also heroic in this sense, though with one caveat. He would tell you the truth but never allow it to be held against him.

"Are you sure?" I asked him one day after puzzling over a term he had defined for me.

"That's what it means to me."

I cracked open Fabozzi. "But it says here—"

"I *said*," McCarthy fumed, *"that's what it means to me."*

The second breed, and by far the most common, was the waffler. Wafflers tried to have it both ways. In response to a question they couldn't answer, they would give you some halfhearted response while letting you know it wasn't reliable, as in:

Q: *Are all bonds securities?*
W: *Sure—aren't they?*

This strategy let the waffler off the hook. You knew he didn't know but he didn't have to admit it. At other times wafflers would listen to the question, then duck it. "Sorry," they would suddenly announce, "it's getting busy."

The final breed, and the carnivore of the lot, was the slick. If a slick were asked a question he couldn't answer, he would simply make something up as if he knew. To them the office environment was an open invitation to fly by the seat of your pants without the slightest compunction. You only had to be convincing. And almost all of them were. The ability to fabricate went hand in hand with the ability to avoid getting caught. Ask a slick a question and you always received a reasonable-sounding answer. It required legwork, or Fabozzi, to prove otherwise, and even then one was never quite sure. Just an honest error? Or deceit? Ironically, the only thing that consistently betrayed a slick was his own body. There was the Wall Street smile, lips curling over clamped teeth; the artificial laugh, exposing the incisors; the power glide, slipping across the floor; and the fast talk, an effort to overwhelm, all provoking a sense of unease in the audience—a sure sign a slick was around.

Naturally, this office paradigm had application far beyond the province of the question. Slicks applied the same methodology to everything they did, such as making appointments (they never intended to keep), briefing investors (they always had the answers), and, in general, issuing promises and statements of all kinds, each with the substance and staying power of the average soap bubble. This drove the heroes crazy. To them, a man should advance by the merit of his hard work alone. But to the slicks, the heroes were fools. Any man was a fool who didn't understand how the market worked. It was purely a function of profit and loss, man to man. To the heroes, this was preposterous. Right and wrong, and profit and loss, were two very different things. But to the slicks, they were synonymous.

The wafflers couldn't decide who was right. On the one hand, they respected the heroes, but on the other hand, the trophies often went to the slicks. Free of all restraint, the slicks could do what was necessary to succeed. They even formed an alternative culture, smiling with knowing appreciation, even reverence, at one anothers' slick acts and promoting the best among them. Some of the wafflers, and the young, were swayed accordingly. Most just stood by and watched, cowed by a raw fascination. For in the market that dominated everyone's life, the slicks were perfection: they were totally focused on making money. Their efficiency was un-hindered by any restraint. Their actions were purely selfish. Their methods were manipulative. Their motives were ulterior. Their friendships were convenient. Nothing but the law stood in their way and there were always ways around it. Consequently, most slicks were rich and successful. How could you not admire that?

On the morning of March 24, 1994, I arrived at 7:30 to find the traders and salesmen already in their seats fielding calls. They had been there for hours. Overnight, Luis Donaldo Colosio, the front-runner in the Mexican presidential campaign, had been shot dead during a campaign stop in Tijuana.

The assassination was a major blow to a market already reeling. Since February 3, the bond market had been continuously rocked by a series of Federal Reserve interest rate hikes that had depressed the value of bond portfolios across the board. In order to cover their losses, major institutions had taken profits in emerging markets debt, driving down the prices of Brady bonds and Eurobonds and sending the risky exotics into a tailspin. At the same time Mexico, the flag-ship country of the emerging markets, had been plagued by an armed uprising in the southeastern state of Chiapas, in which rebels had seized several towns, and the kidnapping of the chairman of Banamex, the country's largest financial group, raising concerns about the country's political stability.

These concerns had been mitigated by the choice of Colosio as the ruling-party candidate in the upcoming elections. The handpicked successor to President Salinas, Colosio had been expected to win, provide a smooth transition of power, and maintain the free-market policies of his predecessor. But now his violent death, the first assassination of a major Mexican political candidate since the twenties, had thrown the outcome of the elections, and the political stability of the country, into doubt, a doubt magnified by questions over who was behind it.

The market reacted accordingly. Mexican financial markets were closed follow-ing the assassination, but in New York the price of Mexican bonds plunged 5 per-cent in early trading, bringing the rest of the emerging markets down with them. To assuage fears of a run on the peso, the Mexican government quickly reiterated its support for the Pacto, the centerpiece of Mexican economic policy. Unknown to foreign investors, however, the Mexican Central Bank was buying billions of pesos in the market to prop up their price, draining its reserves. Equally un-known, the cause was Mexican investors, who, having seen all this before, were quietly bailing out.

The evening assassination naturally dominated discussion on the next morn-ing's call. Everyone was trying to figure out what it would mean for the market, due to open in less than an hour. By coincidence Carlos Espinosa, the salesman who covered Latin accounts, had been in Mexico City meeting with some of his clients and dialed in to give a firsthand report. A Mexican himself, he sounded abnormally somber, his heavy voice filling the quiet conference room: "It's a sad day for Mexico, no?"

"It's an even sadder day for Colosio," a young trader piped up, rocking the room with laughter.

## 12

We eventually managed to furnish our apartment. After giving up on the wilds of Brooklyn and being lured to Macy's on false pretenses ("Sure, we have that model in stock!"), we ended up finding our couches at a store in the Heights. It had been within walking distance the whole time. Most of our new decor, however, came from an even closer source: the street. With uncanny regularity, trash day began producing just what we needed. First it was the slatted frame of a folding futon couch, spotted on Cheever Place, which when separated into its major components yielded a headboard and a railing dividing the living room from the dining room. A wooden pedestal for a platform bed appeared next, replacing ours, which had broken in the move. When Sarah's new job loaded her down with technical manuals, *presto!* there was the bookshelf to hold them. My favorite piece of all was a brass coach lamp in classic gaslight style that I noticed poking out of a box on the sidewalk while coming home from work one day. I took it home for restoration. These artifacts were all in good condition, lending our apartment a humorous, castaway character known only to us and which felt appropriate. They also saved us from going shopping—an advantage in more ways than one.

In the process of establishing ourselves, we also became acquainted with our new neighborhood. Cobble Hill was a rectangle comprising some twenty blocks. The BQE formed the western boundary, beyond which were some run-down streets, vacant lots, and the long blue warehouses of the Brooklyn Marine Terminal jutting out into the water. Atlantic Avenue was the northern limit, a major commercial route stretching all the way to JFK airport and bordering Brooklyn Heights. DeGraw Street defined the southern end, beyond which lay Carroll Gardens, a neighborhood similar to Cobble Hill but offering small front yards. And Court Street was the eastern edge, another commercial roadway, with its shops, movie theater, and restaurants but with a neighborhood feel, our version of Montague Street in the Heights. Inside this mostly commercial perimeter was a residential neighborhood with a few bodegas and delis mixed in. Cobble Hill was home to a mixed population of Italian Americans, mostly working-class families that had lived there for generations, and numerous Arab Americans, including a large contingent of Yemenis: a cultural mix that blended quite smoothly, yielding some excellent restaurants, veils, men's clubs, clotheslines of laundry, and relative stability, the latter enforced by a quiet force, rarely mentioned, that emerged most noticeably from our neighbor's car horn. It played the theme from *The Godfather.*

Cobble Hill was also a designated historic district, as evinced by the signs hung throughout the area. Many of these were obscured by graffiti—no mean feat since one had to shinny up a light pole to accomplish it—but an unblemished one finally revealed that the area had been developed in the 1870s as the city's early working-class housing; that it was home to fine examples of various architectural styles; and that it was the birthplace of Winston Churchill's mother, Jenny Jerome, whose house stood a block from our apartment. The sign concluded with an economic statistic: when constructed, the average home had rented for $1.94 per week.

The character of the area was the product of its working-class roots. Cobble Hill had a plucky, defiant, scrappy air, as if it could handle anything the city could dish out, along with a somewhat worldly visage. This stood in contrast to its wealthier neighbor, Brooklyn Heights, a long-standing bedroom of Wall Street, whose frequent face-lifts afforded a more elegant facade. In the Heights, if either cleanliness, renovation, or security were found wanting, they were purchased immediately. Not surprisingly, Cobble Hill also had more of a neighborhood feel than the Heights, where a certain coolness dampened the warmth of the common struggle. Before the movie started in the Cobble Hill Theater, you would swear you were standing in someone's living room. And at the Café-on-Clinton, you could always count on Ron to dispense wisdom as well as Guinness. In the Heights, he would have served Merlot.

These demographics were slowly changing, however, breeding a Cobble Hill somewhere midway between its former self and its northern neighbor. Fleeing the crime, congestion, and expense found in other parts of the city, middle-class people of all stripes were increasingly seeking refuge in the relatively subdued streets of our neighborhood, often in old brownstones ripe for renovation. And the occasional old school, of course.

Our new life in Cobble Hill required considerable adjustment, different as it was from our previous existence. There were the little things, like the fumes of the BQE, which stung your eyes and left them feeling scratched. And there were the larger things, chief among them the crime and the sense of danger it induced. More than anything else, it was the omnipresent sense of danger that regulated life in New York City.

The genesis of this feeling was hard to identify. Like everyone else, I knew that New York was a dangerous place long before I arrived. But after living there awhile one moves beyond merely knowing about the danger to feeling its presence. There is a subtle transition from understanding to sensation. Undoubtedly this is due in part to being constantly bombarded with reminders of the city's crime problem. You read about crime in the morning newspaper, hear about it at work, and see it on the nightly news. The neighbors warn you about it, as do perfect strangers. You take precautions against it and watch others take theirs. You see areas that obviously breed crime and people who look capable of committing it. You come across evidence of it—cars with their windows smashed, yellow tape sealing an entire house—POLICE LINE DO NOT CROSS—and even witness crime itself. But the air of violence in the city also enters the mind at the level of sensation. It is in the crowding, the decay, the sharp attitudes, the high velocity, the winners and losers placed side by side. After a while, such general perceptions fuse with one's conscious knowledge, forming a gut-level sense of danger, rising and falling with the location, the circumstances, and the time of day, and immune to the statistics, criminal or otherwise. Why people join the rush for a big lottery jackpot in New York City, for instance, is a mystery. By the laws of probability you are far more likely to be murdered before you win.

For the green New Yorker the sense of danger quickly compels you to adopt various defensive countermeasures. The first and most intrusive of these is to define where you can and cannot go in the city. Our boundaries emerged from all sorts of sources: a view from a highway, an overheard conversation, maps, the news, other people, and our own personal standards. Places we knew nothing about—and there were many—were immediately placed off-limits; Flatbush Avenue had taught us that. In this way, we created a mental map of New York in which Manhattan was carved up into various green and red zones and whole boroughs were completely outlawed.

In our own backyard, our borders emerged through experience. We ultimately formed a mental free state three and a half miles long and half a mile wide encompassing all of Brooklyn Heights, Cobble Hill, and Carroll Gardens. The northern border of this region was the Brooklyn Bridge. The eastern boundary was Court Street, beyond which the grunge factor climbed, graffiti were more prevalent, and the occasional crack vial or syringe was found on the sidewalk; we crossed Court Street only to reach the F train. Our southern and western boundaries were both defined by the BQE. The Cobble Hill School looked westward across the highway at a run-down industrial area by the waterfront; from the apartment across the hall, you could see the local junkies shooting up in a vacant lot. One regular was noted for pulling down his pants and using his thigh. The highway then curved beneath Carroll Gardens, marking the southern limit of our territory with an overpass and separating us from the notorious area of Brooklyn known as Red Hook. Red Hook's reputation was so bad that people didn't even want to mention it. It was something you just sensed, a way in which the place "down there" was mentioned and the sobering effect it had on people's faces. Don't go to Red Hook was the clear message. Don't even think about it. The magnitude of the problem wasn't even clear to us until, months after moving in, I turned on the television and saw Red Hook featured in "The Killing Fields," a national television special on gang violence. As it turned out, one of the most dangerous areas in the United States was a short walk down the road.

In addition to limiting your freedom, the sense of danger in New York also determined your behavior in public, where the threat was greatest. Since you never knew who might be prone to violence, you avoided looking anyone in the eye for fear of provoking them. Anonymity was the rule. This was especially true on the subway, where the sense of danger was always magnified, but also on the street, where everyone walked around looking at no one. Ironically, this universal anonymity, while lessening the danger in one sense, only increased it in another. If something did happen, who would come to your rescue?

Another common defensive measure was looking over your shoulder at the sound of footsteps. This practice, which was quite unnerving to witness at first, extended to all people, from large men to frail old women. Women were the most alert, though, turning yards away while clutching their handbags. More unnerving still, they wouldn't relax their grip even when they saw a young man in his suit walking too fast and clutching his Fabozzi (a weapon?). Eventually, feeling like a social nuisance, I learned to maintain a fair distance and wear leather soles. But I never slowed down—no one was sneaking up on me.

In private, one's sense of danger naturally lessened but did not dissipate. There were still the locks on the door to remind you that home was not a sanctuary. At night a sudden noise in the hallway, a shout rising up from the parking lot, or the wail of a nearby siren would awaken your slumbering instincts. Descending alone into the darkened laundry room in the basement would as well. The car was no refuge either. With all the red spots on the mental map, it seemed more like a vehicle for getting *into* trouble than out of it. And what about carjackings? They didn't call it The Club for nothing.

Finally nightfall changed the rules everywhere. As the sun fell, the sense of danger increased, shrinking the areas in which you could go and the ways in which you could get there. Central Park became a big red zone. Cabs became preferable to walking or the subway. Travel in groups was recommended. Even walking the familiar streets of Cobble Hill became a hackles raiser, the jaws of the Little Beast notwithstanding.

Eventually the sense of danger became a daily, gnawing worry, fluctuating in degree but omnipresent, spurring you to act. It was then that one entered the second phase of reaction to the city's crime problem: shielding yourself not only from the danger but from the sense of it as well. In this phase, your urban countermeasures expanded from physical self-protection to mental health.

One method was simply reducing the reminders of the problem. One day while leafing through the local Cobble Hill rag I came upon the crime blotter. It detailed the crimes that had occurred in my neighborhood over the past week on the streets I walked every day. I couldn't believe how many there were. A man held up at gunpoint on Henry Street? At eight-thirty at night? I walked home then. Two houses broken into on Cheever Place? A woman mugged on Congress Street? These were all a block or two away from my apartment. I never read that paper again.

One could not remain completely immune from the news, of course, so the next filter you developed was a mental one. You saw or read the news but it made no impression on you. Another crime, another murder, another statistic. Who cares? At the same time positive news was welcomed. When the nation's murder capital was announced and it was *not* New York, it was cause for rejoicing. See, there were worse places to live! You could be in Gary, Indiana!

Another way to deny the sense of danger was to blame crime on the victims rather than the criminals. If your car was broken into, you had left it on the wrong street. If you were mugged, you must have been walking in the wrong area. If your apartment was broken into, you didn't have a proper security system. The advantage of this strategy was clear: if you took the proper steps, you would never be a victim. So you didn't have to worry about anything.

The capstone in one's urban bulwarks was not only to adopt these measures oneself but to demand that everyone else do so as well, making them the norm. By doing so you not only justified your own actions ("Everyone does it!") but could repel any challenge ("That's the way it is here!"). This created a distinct city culture full of people who had done what it took to accept crime as a normal part of life while refusing to admit the horror of the life they led. If you accused them of lowering their standards, you were vehemently attacked. If you complained of the crime problem itself, you were a whiner. That's the city, they sneered; deal with it or depart. This attitude defined the difference between the old New Yorker and the new. One arrived with his judgment intact; the other had long since neutralized it in order to survive.


There was at least one class of New Yorker that lived free of the worries and restrictions that plagued the rest, however: the dogs. In New York, dogs were king. They pranced down the street, their only worry being the cars. When they met other dogs, they played and kissed. To the dog owner, such behavior warmed the heart, but it also bred envy. Why is it, you wondered, that my dog has it better than me? This was especially true when you met a dog being walked by his owner—or rather an owner being walked by his dog. For in the city the roles were reversed.

This painful truth became apparent during my evening walks of Tugger. Each night after work, the dog owners of Cobble Hill would assemble on the playground of a local elementary school two blocks from my apartment. A large paved space surrounded by a tall chain-link fence, it was the only place in the neighborhood you could let a dog run. Having finally adjusted to apartment life, the Little Beast greatly looked forward to these evening jaunts, speeding around, meeting all the other dogs, sharing her tennis ball. She became quite well known as well. "Oh, look!" I would hear as I approached the crowd of owners, "It's Tugger!" I wouldn't even get a glance. I was merely Tugger's Owner, just as everyone else was known by their dog's name. I was even greeted this way on occasion. "Oh, you're Tugger's Owner, aren't you?" said the dry cleaner. And it was clearly not New York protocol to break with such anonymity. Ask an owner on the playground "And what's *your* name?" and you were liable to inspire a look of panic. "You've blown my cover!" their faces said. "Now I can't be a nameless dog owner—I have to be a person!" If that didn't serve to sanction me, Tugger would eventually stop her running and squat by my side, tail quivering, forcing me in full view of everyone to reach down with a little plastic Baggie stretched over my hand and do my duty per the city ordinance. Yes, we knew who was in charge.

Luckily, I didn't have to put up with such indignities for long. With less diligent dog owners in the neighborhood, and with schoolchildren tracking the results through the halls, the Brooklyn police cracked down, stationing a cruiser by the playground and threatening to ticket anyone walking their dog upon it. Some owners reconvened across the BQE, where a lack of diligence apparently went unnoticed, but that was one of my red zones, especially at night. So instead of relocating, the dog just didn't run anymore.


One of the more striking elements of Cobble Hill was the number of old churches in the area. There was practically one on every street corner. Obviously, religion had once played an important role in the life of the neighborhood, but, judging by the condition of these old buildings, those days were over. Many were in a state of disrepair, one had been turned into condos, and another was closed entirely.

We experienced this firsthand at Easter when we attended a neighborhood service at Christ Church & Holy Family on the corner of Kane and Clinton streets. We entered a dark, cold, and musty building. The rear pews were empty; about twenty parishioners were huddled up front. The dim lighting revealed peeling paint on the ceiling and dark water stains on the walls. Our visit happened to coincide with the last sermon of the departing senior reverend, who was retiring after decades of service. He did not speak with the nostalgia or encouragement expected under the circumstances, however, but like a man torn between such traditions and his own frustrations—a struggle he occasionally lost. They were *way* behind in the fund drive, he said. Without the necessary funds to fix the roof and the "crumbling" exterior, he couldn't say what the future would hold. His superiors had not even named a replacement yet. He had hoped, he concluded, to live out his years on Cape Cod, but a "surprising" pension necessitated his staying in Queens.

Such decay was not restricted to houses of worship, either; according to the local paper (before I ceased reading it) cemeteries were under attack as well. Brooklyn was suffering from a spate of grave robbing, driven by the increased demand for human skulls used in the rituals of at least one progressive faith. A good pair was fetching fifteen hundred bucks. What this said about the state of religion in the former "City of Churches" wasn't explained, but adjacent Manhattan provided a graphic answer. There, one church of note, the former Episcopalian Church of the Holy Communion, had been turned into one of the city's longest-running and most popular nightclubs, known as Limelight. People danced on the altar.

The state of belief in New York was perhaps best encapsulated by a trip to St. Mark's, which I made months after our arrival. St. Mark's is the oldest church in Manhattan and of great historical importance to New York City. The original chapel was built in 1660 by Peter Stuyvesant, the Dutch governor who surrendered New Amsterdam to the English, and later served as his burial vault. Stuyvesant, I discovered, was still at rest there—in body at least. His church, in addition to its services, was now an avant-garde theater. Its entrance was guarded by statues, their faces removed by acid rain. The adjacent cemetery was surrounded by an iron fence with a rusted bike frame locked to the entrance. Outside the fence was the East Village, the city's epicenter of alternative lifestyles, as exemplified by the nearby Hell's Angels National Headquarters. Inside, past the bags of garbage waiting to be collected, were the burial vaults of some of New York's great old families, along with a former vice president of the United States. These were in the form of headstones set flat in the earth, obscured by dry soil, and traversed by the many people who picnic within. Standing there, I was reminded of the motto of the Roxbury Latin School, a quote from Homer: *Mortui Vivos Docent*. The Dead Teach the Living.

Well, they might have been trying, but the local residents weren't listening very hard. Not content with destroying the history of their forefathers, they were literally walking on their graves.


One morning on my way to work I met Mikhail Gurevich, better known as Mickey. I was turning onto Montague Street in the Heights, looking at a straight shot to the subway, when I almost ran into him. There was no avoiding it: we would have to go to work together.

Gurevich was one of the Latin Mafia. A Russian Jew who had grown up in Argentina, he covered the largest hedge funds in the business: George Soros's Quantum Fund, Michael Steinhardt's Falcon Management, and Julian Robertson's

Tiger Management. Through them he had generated millions in sales commissions in 1993, earning himself a seven-figure bonus and making him the number two salesman in all Merrill Lynch, second only to Michael Stamenson, who covered Orange County. His success had not made him an endearing presence, however. He had one of those puffy Russian faces, topped off by a thin layer of stringy hair, mated to the jaws of a Maurice Sendak creature, and had mastered the aloofness of the cabal, which, when combined with his reputation as the smartest guy in the office, became a colder, harder indifference. Not exactly a fountain of companionship in other words.

"Hi, Mickey," I said as our eyes met. "I didn't know you lived here."

He lifted a lazy finger over his shoulder—"Montague and Henry"—nodded toward the subway with a grunt, and resumed walking with his mechanical lope, his jaw set. A few steps later he ducked into a store and returned with both the *Journal* and the unmistakable orange *Financial Times*. He turned toward the subway without a glance at me.

I kept up with him and mentioned something about the market.

"Where are you from?" Gurevich interrupted.

"Annapolis."

"Where's that?"

"Maryland. It's the capital."

He bared his incisors with a little laugh. "Must be a big change. Coming to New York, I mean."

I admitted it was, relating a few of the virtues of my former home until the black mouth of the subway yawned before us. Meanwhile Gurevich grew increasingly amused.

"The only problem," he said as we slipped beneath the street, "is that after you live in New York awhile every place else looks so provincial."

## 13

It finally happened. I was sitting next to McCarthy learning more about Eurobonds, and feeling impregnable because of it, when a shrill voice broke through my concentration, paralyzing my thoughts.

"Paaaal?"

Mundt had found me at last.

"I have a job for you!" she sang.

"I'm kind of busy right now—"

"Raoul wants you to take over the BBYA."

I froze in panic. The BBYA! Was I ready for that? I was just getting comfortable!

"See Goth when you're through."

"Okay."

McCarthy let out a tremendous belch. "Bend over, son. Here it comes again."


The Brady Bond Yield Analysis—BBYA. It was an abbreviation worthy of a military weapon system, inspiring equal warmth. The BBYA was the primary marketing product of IEM, a single sheet of information listing the major Brady bonds and their ever-changing quantitative parameters. Produced daily from a computer program, and distributed worldwide, it was the chief analytical tool of traders and salesmen alike, who made trading decisions based on the information it contained. For that reason you did not want to be the person responsible for a mistake.

Unfortunately, there were years of IEM management standing between me and error-free work. Like the Latin Mafia, Savegre hated to manage. He had a natural aversion to planning, written communication, or formal processes of any kind. He, Mundt, and I never even had a single meeting together. Savegre preferred to be in constant motion, reacting on his own to whatever situations arose, and expected his subordinates to do the same. Everything was done ad hoc as daily conditions required. With a complex, evolving technological product like the BBYA, however, such a scattered approach was deadly.

The BBYA was a three-dimensional spreadsheet arranged in a stack of virtual pages. The top page was the output; the rest were complex mathematical models of each individual Brady bond. These models worked from inputs, such as price, that the user typed in and were constructed to automatically adjust for the passage of time. After calculation, the models would yield values for the various parameters of the bonds, which were then fed back to the output page. That was the theory anyway. In practice it often failed to happen. The BBYA file had evolved with the market, expanding in size and complexity as new bonds were issued. Four different people had had a hand in building it, each with his own programming methods and skill levels. As a result the BBYA program was constantly breaking down, forcing the operator to delve deeply into the models, figure out what was wrong, and apply another Band-Aid. Moreover, while some logic errors were obvious— yields would come out 0000—others were more insidious and only became apparent after weeks of growing inaccuracy—and many trades.

These problems were multiplied by the IEM computer system, which like the BBYA file had suffered from unmanaged growth. In the beginning, the group had purchased SUN computers, connected by an old-fashioned UNIX network, which, contrary to the philosophy of the personal computer, required a full-time system administrator to manage; in the case of IEM, this was a smiling young man named

Habib who sat in the corner of the room typing on his keyboard. Other people preferred IBM PCs, however, and since they had more clout than Habib, management kept procuring them until the two were present in equal numbers, sometimes on the same desk. This filled the office with two incompatible operating systems, which Habib bridged on the network with a conversion program. Few people knew about it, however. There was no formal means of familiarizing new people with the office computer system. So instead they picked a favorite platform or even duplicated their work. Meanwhile the spiraling need for more memory resulted in the continual addition of storage drives, each a letter on your screen, and the movement of files to new locations until it was difficult to remember where you had put things.

The addition of IBM computers also multiplied the available software in the office—much of it unneeded—causing further problems. There was no software training; like everything else, you were on your own. Pressed for time, people chose one of the many word processing or spreadsheet programs available, taught themselves the bare essentials—the manuals were soon lost in the office chaos—and refused to use any other, spawning a multiplicity of standards and preventing file sharing. Before long, people gave up on sharing files anyway. The existence of two different versions of the same program, an old one on the SUNs and a new one on the IBMs, caused a one-way flow of information to the IBMs, since you couldn't convert backward. Some of the PC software was also incompatible with the network, or the conversion software, causing programs to crash if you tried to effect a transfer. In the end, after spending one million dollars on their trading floor, the Latin Mafia had succeeded in creating a technological quagmire ruled by the same principle as the rest of the office. It was every man for himself.

Prior to my appointment, the BBYA had been managed by Goth. I had seen him come in early and produce the spreadsheet, which had to be done by market open, and do updates when necessary, sometimes four or five a day if the market was really moving. Aided by his degree in statistics and years of experience with Lotus, he had met the challenge fairly well, jury-rigging enough solutions to keep the time bomb ticking. When he hadn't, the results had often been messy and public. "Goth!" someone would shout across the trading floor, "This yield is off half a point at least!" At which point Goth would gulp and shrink back to his computer. Having witnessed all this, I approached my new responsibility warily. The BBYA was a field of opportunity, I realized, but seeded with mines.

I found Goth sitting in Mundt's chair. "Don't go away!" he said gleefully. "You're supposed to take over the BBYA!"

"That's why I'm here."

He quickly finished his work and popped from his seat. "Come on, I'll show you how it's done."

We walked hurriedly over to the International Retail desk, my sense of alarm rising. When Goth was happy to see you, something was generally awry.

He plunked himself down in front of a SUN computer. "This one is usually available," he informed me.

A longtime Macintosh owner, I had never used a SUN before and told him so.

"You'll get used to it," he replied.

He brought up Lotus 1-2-3 on the monitor. I told him I had never used that either.

"It's simple," Goth said.

He pulled up the BBYA file and the image of the sheet appeared on the screen. Looking it over, I saw a number of parameters—coupon, bid and offer prices, daily change, yield, stripped yield, current yield, spread over the benchmark U.S. Treasury, implied volatility, duration, stripped duration, average life, principal and interest collateral values—few of which I understood.

"Don't worry about that right now," Goth informed me. "Here's what you do."

There were twelve separate steps involved in putting out the BBYA. The first few involved collecting market data—current price levels, U.S. Treasury bond yields, zero coupon yields, and Eurodollar futures—from Reuters, Bloomberg, and our own traders and manually typing it into the spreadsheet. This process was complicated by the need to memorize where all the sources of information were, how to bring them up on the computer, which numbers you needed out of the available columns, and where to put them in the spreadsheet. Naturally, you also wondered what it all meant.

"Eurodollar futures?" I asked.

"To build the forward curve," Goth said, as if it were obvious.

"Oh," I replied, not wanting to say I didn't know.

The next step was calculation. Due to the unwieldy size of the program and the old model of computer it was on, calculation took half an hour.

"Half an hour!" I exclaimed. "Why don't you put it on a faster computer?"

"You can try," Goth said. "The program is too big to put on a disk."

"Can't you send it over the network?"

Goth snickered. "Have you ever used the network?"

"No."

"Wait and see."

I didn't have to wait long. The last step in the BBYA production process, printing, required two different computers. The unwieldy BBYA program, now held hostage by the SUN, had been built using an early version of Lotus, which had no graphics. A newer version, Lotus for Windows, had graphics but was on an IBM across the room. Therefore, after a half hour of calculation, one had to effect a transfer of the output page across the network, where it could be brought up in Lotus for Windows and printed out. If, however, this was done incorrectly or there was some network problem, as often happened, the transfer would fail and crash the program, forcing you to spend another fifteen minutes retyping all the input data and another half hour waiting for it to calculate.

"So don't make any mistakes," Goth advised, smirking.

"Ah—I'll try not to."

He stood to go.

"Don't you think we should run through it once?"

"I don't have time right now. I've got some stuff to do for the traders." Goth fought back a trembling smile. How *long* had he waited to say that! He didn't have *time* for someone—below him! He was sailing up the food chain! He hurried off to his nook.

Thus began my apprenticeship with the BBYA. I collected my Reuters and Bloomberg printouts and sat down at the foreign computer thinking about everything I had just heard, which I summarized on the back of my notebook. After a few tries, I succeeded in getting output to the screen and went to ask Goth to have a look.

"I'll be with you in a few minutes," he said.

He eventually arrived, sat in front of the computer, and frowned impatiently. "You typed the thirty-year Treasury into the thirty-year zero," he said.

"Oh."

"Recalculate," he said and left.

In my next effort I managed to get the right output but couldn't remember all the steps necessary to print it. This time I turned to Mundt.

"It's been a while since I did it—ask Goth," she replied. "In the meantime, can you take these up to Word Processing?"

Upon my return, I appealed to McCarthy. "Sorry man," he said. "I don't go near these computers unless I have to."

Finally I went back to Goth. "Printing is simple," he quipped as we strode back to my computer. He went rapidly through the steps on the keyboard and sent the document across the room. "See?"

"Let me write it down."

Goth set his jaw impatiently and went through the steps as if tutoring a small child. "Now I've got to go."

Later on, once I was acquainted with production, Mundt offered to show me the last step in the BBYA process: delivery. Since the BBYA was faxed to Merrill Lynch personnel and clients all over the world, our first stop was to my friends in Word Processing, who had fax broadcast equipment. Savegre had bought the same equipment himself but no one knew how to use it; it sat in a box by his desk. A better solution would have been to mail it electronically, but through an oversight of management, the IEM computer system had never been connected to the rest of the firm, including our own Research Department. Thus, within the North Tower the sheet was delivered the old-fashioned way: by hand. Mundt traced the route through the building for me: around IEM, up to Research, then the Executive Suite, down to High Yield, and through the maze of Seven, where she pointed from side to side: "He gets one . . . and he does . . . he gets five . . . so does he . . ." By the time we reached the end all one hundred and twenty-five copies had been delivered. "So you can do it starting tomorrow," she said on our way back to IEM. "It has to be out by nine."

The days that followed were full of frustration. I soon reached the point where I could do all the mechanical steps necessary to produce the BBYA, but if there was a computer problem, I was sunk. If it was a programming problem, I had to go find Goth, who was increasingly reluctant to help. He made it clear that he had more important things to do now and wanted to be approached accordingly. My old "Hey, Peter, can you come over here a minute?" no longer sufficed. Peter Goth didn't come when called—except by the traders. If the problem was with the SUN, I had to track down Habib, our smiling UNIX whiz. He was a lot more responsive than Goth but didn't come in until after the market opened and was often busy thereafter. This turned producing the BBYA into a daily gamble. I would enter the data, hit calculate, and ponder the screen for half an hour praying for results. If I got them, I would pray that the file would successfully transfer across the network. Then I would pray that the sheet would print out. If my prayers weren't answered, I would be left sitting on the edge of a demanding trading floor, the clock ticking, staring at a frozen computer screen or a file that had just been dumped, gritting my teeth and waiting for that chilling call: "Where is the BBYA?"

Ironically, I also benefited from these frustrations. By maintaining a near-constant presence on the International Retail desk, I was finally able to secure myself a seat, under the possession-is-nine-tenths-of-the-law doctrine. In so doing, I had achieved both responsibility and real estate, elevating me an important notch in the food chain, albeit one just a hair from the bottom. I was no longer the peacock flounder hoping to get by on camouflage alone; I was any manner of small-reef fish hiding in the corals and occasionally darting out for a good meal. The BBYA also turned out to be a demanding tutor, its nerve-racking breakdowns providing me the strongest incentive to learn. When I wasn't producing it I was trying to master it, leading me to study Lotus, the science of modeling bonds, and the meaning of the spreadsheet itself—what the bonds were, where they came from, and the meaning of their parameters—providing a well-needed grounding in the fundamentals of our business.

Learning did not come easily on the trading floor, however. IEM was the antithesis of a library: instead of sitting in a quiet carrel, thinking, you sat elbow to elbow, the market—and McCarthy—blaring in your ears. At the same time, one couldn't leave. The floor was the beating heart of the organization. A new man who avoided the action in favor of sitting in an office somewhere, studying, was risking his reputation: was the fit right? This led me to do a great deal of sneaking around. I would maintain my visibility on the trading floor until the right people had seen me, find out which investment banker was traveling, and slip into his office for an hour or two, taking Fabozzi et al. with me. Any further study I confined to nighttime hours.

My new seat also formed a permanent gulf between me and the Marketing Department, which, while welcome in some ways, aggravated our differences over the BBYA and the problems that kept plaguing it. One day, as I labored over another software glitch, Mundt showed up to reprimand me.

"Paul, it's almost *ten!*"

"You don't *understand*," I said. "This whole thing is a mess. You need to be a software expert to fix it."

"Goth used to get it out on time."

"He's used Lotus for years."

"Then learn Lotus."

"I'm trying. But this file isn't for beginners."

"Paaaal!" Mundt exclaimed in a shrill huff. "I don't care how you *do* it. *Just get it out by nine o'clock!*"

She spun around and wheeled back to her desk, her head cocked at a dangerous angle. I watched her sit down and turn to Goth. They both began laughing.

I sat down at the computer. It was just me and it. And across the loop, them.


Such encounters were not easily forgotten. They, and the conditions that caused them, began generating a great deal of internalized emotion, which did not dissipate when the market closed. Instead it often rose higher. I would take a car home, or choose to walk at times, seething at my treatment at the hands of Goth and Mundt or someone else who had refused to lend a helping hand. I took each blow personally, my mind free to dwell on each one. Savegre didn't care, Mundt didn't care—what was wrong with these people? Why did they hire me if they were going to treat me this way? At least in basic training there had been a purpose behind the actions of the drill sergeant.

I unloaded many of these feelings on Sarah. "I don't get it," I said. "Is it just me or am I working for the biggest assholes in the world?"

"Have you tried talking to them about it?"

"Talking to them!" I laughed painfully. "You can't *reason* with them. They'll just step on you."

"Well, you can't keep coming home like this and not sleep. You have to *do something*."

She was right.

Shortly thereafter the BBYA blew up in my face. I went to calculate and all I got was zeros. The whole sheet was zeros. I had never seen an error like that before. Where would I begin to look to fix it? By nine-thirty I had given up trying and went to look for Goth.

I found him getting his shoes shined. He was leaning back in his chair, his hands behind his head, the shoeshine man at his feet. I explained my problem. Have you done this? he asked. Have you done that? I've tried everything, I said.

Goth sighed. "Take another look."

"I've been looking at it for two hours."

Goth inspected his shoes and paid the shoeshine man, who departed with his box of rags. He lifted a wing tip back to his eye. "That guy gets worse every day."

"It's nine-thirty," I said.

"So what do you want me to do?"

He sounded like he was trying out a new line. I felt a now familiar anger rising up, held it back. "I would like some assistance."

Goth smirked and spun around in his chair. "I'll be over when I can."

I went back to the computer. I had begun to hate the computer as much as I hated Goth. My entire fate lay in its cold hands. Without the proper instruction, I was handcuffed to the keyboard. The dense manuals I had managed to find, hundreds of pages of nonsensical instructions, were useless. Even the cursor took an eternity to cross the screen for reasons no one could explain.

I sat there for another hour pointlessly staring at pages of Lotus programming, my mind dulling in the process. The trading floor buzzed around me; inside the Sales loop, a voice shouted, "Goth!"

It was Carlos Espinosa, his headset pulled down around his neck, searching the floor.

Goth popped up in Trading, where he was sitting with his idols.

"I need a BBYA update—fast," Espinosa said. "Argy pars at sixty-five, discounts at seventy-seven."

Goth shrugged carelessly. "Stiles does it now." He pointed in my direction and sat down.

"Stiles!" Espinosa shouted across the floor. "Give me a new BBYA. Argy pars at sixty-five, discounts at seventy-seven."

I stood up. "All right—but the computer is down right now."

"I need it *fast*."

I fell back in my seat and stared at a page of zeros. How could Goth *do* that? I wondered, fists clenched. I looked across the floor. Mundt was nowhere to be seen. Savegre was nowhere to be seen. There was only Goth. Had he forgotten I needed help?

I went over and tapped him on the shoulder. "I still haven't fixed that problem."

He turned around, traders on either side of him, and looked at me like I was interrupting an important discussion. "I'm busy right now." Our eyes remained fixed on each other, mine pools of anger, his cold wells of contempt. "Okay?"

"Sure, pal."

I stalked back to my computer and sat down. The minutes were ticking away. I looked over at Espinosa, then back at my screen of zeros, and decided to take desperate action. I reached behind the computer and pulled the plug. Imph! The BBYA disappeared. Then I brought it back up and did the whole thing over, carefully following my notes, checking my figures, adding the ones Espinosa wanted. I started calculation and waited.

Meanwhile the complaints began to roll in. "Where's the BBYA?" a trader called out. "It's coming!" I said. "Stiles?" Espinosa asked. "How much longer?" "Soon!" I promised. After half an hour, the blinking cursor halted—and numbers appeared. Numbers! I breathed out relievedly. I had never been so happy to see numbers. I sent the file across the room, ran to the IBM, then waited by the printer in Marketing pleading for the familiar whine and scrape.

Nothing. The printer just sat there speechless. How could that *be*?! I wanted to scream, my mind exploding with frustration. The screen had distinctly flashed "printing!"

"*Stiles,*" Espinosa said, "*where is the BBYA?!*"

"It's done!" I said. "I'm just waiting for it to print out."

"I don't *need* a printout. I just need those two yields!"

"Just a minute then." I ran back to my position intending to check the screen of the SUN. But in my hurry, I had forgotten to save the original file; once I had sent it across the room, it had vanished.

I quickly ran back to the IBM; someone else was using it. "There was a file on the screen here," I said hurriedly.

"Did you save it?" the user asked.

"No—I was just printing out."

"Sorry—that's what *I* thought."

I straightened, all the energy draining from my body. The BBYA was gone.

"*Stiles!*" Espinosa said.

I looked up at an angry salesman. "It's gone," I said flatly.

"You said you were printing it out, no?"

"I was, but—"

"*¡Hijole!* Forget it, kemosabe!"

Goth stood up across the divide, glanced at me, fighting a smile, and sat back down with a wisecrack to the traders. I fled back to my desk, enraged at him and this whole insane system, and sat back down to do another BBYA. I was furiously inputting data when Mundt showed up.

"Paaaal! What is the *problem*?"

"You tell me, Claire."

"It's almost *noon*. Carlos tells me he's asked you *three times* for the BBYA!"

"Look, you have no idea what's been going on here."

"I don't *care*! The BBYA is supposed to be out by nine!"

"No kidding!"

"Then do it!"

"How can I when you haven't bothered to teach me how it works?"

"Come *on*, Paaaal," Mundt scoffed, "you've had plenty of time to learn it."

"Don't tell *me* that. You sit here and try to figure out how this thing works."

"I told you, if you're having problems, get someone to help you."

"Like who? Goth? I've asked him twice today already but he keeps blowing me off."

"Then let me talk to him. But it's still your responsibility."

"No, it's *not*. You just can't sit someone down and expect them to do a job without any training."

She shook her head, smiling. "No, Paaaal, *you* are the one—"

"You're not *listening*!"

"You have to figure these things out on your own! Everyone does here."

"That's a stupid way to run an office."

"That's the way it *is*," she laughed.

"Then don't be surprised when things break!"

She rolled her eyes. "It doesn't matter! You still need to fix it!"

"I wasn't hired to be a computer programmer!"

"Paaaal—"

"I was hired to be an International Retail trader, whatever the hell that is."

"Paaaal—"

"And I'm not your copyboy either!"

"Paaaal!" she laughed.

"And would you *stop* being so *goddamn* condescending?" I shouted. "I'm sick of it!"

Mundt's face froze in surprise, then cracked in understanding, my feelings finally penetrating her own. "You don't have to take it so *personally*."

"Wouldn't you?"

"That's just the way it works here." She shook her head uncomfortably. "Let's talk about it later."

"Fine."

She turned on her heel and marched off.

I sat back down in my seat and stared blindly at the computer, head in hands, the noise and heat of the room rushing back in.

A laugh sounded across the desk. "You're learning."

I lifted my head. McCarthy was grinning at me. The tension faded beneath his knowing look. I suddenly felt myself relieved of a tremendous burden and floating happily because of it. Like that pleasant feeling you get from a concussion.

A few minutes later one of the retail traders tapped me on the shoulder—"Is this yours?"—and handed me the BBYA.

"Where did you get *that*?"

"Right here." He pointed to a printer on the file cabinet behind me. "The IBMs print out here now."

The next day I arrived after a night of worry, expecting to deal with the fallout of my confrontation with Mundt. To my surprise she didn't bear the slightest grudge. She came over to my position and mentioned our previous conversation as if it had been a business discussion, promising to make Goth provide more help. After that, she never asked me to do any grunt work again and always treated me as an equal. My animosity toward her subsequently faded, allowing me to see things more clearly. I realized that I had been judging her by the normal rules of society, where her behavior would have been a personal affront. But in IEM it was just business as usual. There the norm wasn't to respect a person's space but to challenge their boundaries; that is how the food chain was defined. Try to be civil and people would be in your face, dictating your actions. Instead you had to constantly draw the line with them, using brute force if necessary. Nice guys finished last. Thereafter I took a new attitude toward my office. I suppressed my openness to people, put my gloves on before walking in the door, thickened my hide to protect myself from the inevitable blows, and focused on winning the fight like everyone else.

Unfortunately, Goth didn't share Mundt's dispassionate view. To him the food chain was a zero-sum game and I had just raised myself a notch at his expense. This became apparent the next time the BBYA broke down. Instead of approaching Goth to help I approached Mundt, taking advantage of our new equality. She immediately told Goth to fix it. He arrived at my computer barely in control of himself. While fixing the program he said the minimum amount necessary, never looked me in the eye, and departed as soon as it was running. I had made my first enemy in the office.

At first this didn't worry me. I was confident that Goth would get what was coming to him. But over time the opposite happened. In the crucible of the market, Goth thrived.

On April 18, Wall Street was rocked by the news of a major trading scandal at Kidder Peabody, one of the Street's oldest firms. A single trader, Joseph Jett, was accused of having booked fictitious trades amounting to a staggering $350 million loss. Jett was a graduate of M.I.T. and the Harvard Business School and the head of Kidder's government bond desk. In the course of his trading he would sell bonds forward—that is, agree to conduct a trade in the future. Since a bond accrues interest over time, the forward price would be greater than the current price. Kidder's flawed computer system registered this difference as a profit. Before the trade ever occurred, Jett would roll it over—extend its life—creating a perpetual stream of such profits. And Kidder's management supposedly never questioned where they came from. Instead they made Joe Jett their star trader, naming him the firm's top employee in 1993 and paying him a $9 million bonus. It took two years for Kidder's accountants to uncover what was really happening. When they finally did, management blamed Jett and fired him. Jett blamed management. Lawsuits followed but the damage was done. Kidder's reputation never recovered. Personnel fled and the firm began losing $25 million a month. By the end of the year venerable Kidder Peabody, a 129-year Wall Street veteran, had been sold to PaineWebber for $670 million, cutting some two thousand jobs.

By all accounts it was a steal.

## 14

I had reached the point where I now saw my position in the office with a cold, clear eye. I was utterly and completely on my own. I had an island of real estate unto myself, I had a unique responsibility, and I had drawn the line with Mundt, escaping from beneath her thumb. My position in the food chain was a precarious one, however. Words, not actions, had won it. Now I had to perform. Like it or not, my future was inextricably bound with that of my wounded charge, the BBYA. I had to make it work. People were watching to see what would happen. Some of them undoubtedly hoped I would fail.

This left me facing the usual obstacles to self-instruction, which were complicated by my new position. In my previous role as wandering associate I had simply asked questions of people when I wanted to know something. While an implicit statement that I didn't know, I was already at the bottom of the food chain: there was nowhere else to fall. But now that I had raised myself a notch, asking questions made me vulnerable if done carelessly. Ask too many questions of the wrong people and I could soon find myself floundering back in the weeds. I therefore entered a more rarefied realm of scraping society where such brute methods were replaced by guile, diplomacy, and skill. I learned as much as possible by osmosis. I asked people only for the basics and figured out the rest on my own. I spread questions around so no one person knew how many I was asking, always choosing the right people—those who wouldn't hold it against me—and the right time. I made them sound like they weren't even questions—"That's right, isn't it?" I would add at the end of a statement, sounding more like a waffler than a flounder.

There were limits to such methods, however. My primary objective was learning the intricacies of bonds and how they were modeled in the BBYA using the Lotus spreadsheet: that was my Achilles' heel. Such specific information was best gleaned from those who had actually worked on the BBYA themselves. This left me choosing among Goth, Breen, Mundt, and a young analyst named Natasha Orlova. In other words, there was no choice. My future had suddenly become inextricably linked to someone I hardly knew.

Natasha Orlova was a small, bespectacled, mousy Russian blonde who had come to Merrill Lynch midway through her training at Moscow University and lived with her parents in Brooklyn. At twenty-two she was one of the youngest people in the office and worked the longest hours of anyone, arriving at seven, leaving at ten or eleven, and coming in on weekends, often without a pressing reason. Her life was spent in front of her computer or asleep.

Aside from her hard work, Orlova's greatest attribute was her quantitative skills, which had promoted her from Operations to the trading desk, where she performed various analytical jobs. These skills were also the dominant element in her personality. She was particularly Russian in that way, a reminder of the old Soviet state, in which math, science, and engineering had filled the gap left by religion, transcending passion or function to become the philosophy of a culture.

This placed us on different sides of the technological fence. I had always looked on the computer as a machine that served me by supplementing my abilities. I had owned various Macintosh computers, accordingly, because they thought the way I did—or appeared to anyway. Orlova (and Goth for that matter) took the opposite view. To her, the computer was rational perfection and man was muddled. *She* wanted to think like *it*. So while I flipped on my Mac and brought forth a happy face, she preferred to see C:/. While I liked a mouse that moved icons in and out of little windows, she preferred to memorize keystrokes and give the computer precise commands. In fact, she *hated* Windows-based software, which she viewed as a concession to human weakness.

The root of our differences lay in the value of numbers. Orlova preferred numbers over concepts because numbers were precise. Numbers had absolute values and absolute relationships. They were either right or wrong. Her computer was a shrine to this digital philosophy. She turned it on or off. All its thinking was comprised of zeros and ones. Each keystroke was a cause yielding an effect. And being part of the market, she had a whole religion to follow centered around the same digital principle: profit or loss. It has a system where moderation was unheard of, where limits were unknown. To a quant, there was no such thing as a happy balance unless it was in the bank.

This difference in opinion led to some conflicts between us, beginning, ironically, with a matter of jealousy. I finally received my laptop computer. The first on the trading floor, it was, in high IEM style, a four-thousand-dollar Toshiba laptop replete with all the latest gadgetry. Orlova was incensed. Here I was, a *Windows person*, getting the latest quant gear ahead of her—after she had practically *built* the BBYA! She immediately went to Savegre to lodge a formal protest; he ordered her one.

My next affront came when I asked her how to translate the entire BBYA file into the new Lotus for Windows program that had come with my computer. This would not only humanize my spreadsheet, it would obviate the need to send the file across the network to be printed, a major cause of BBYA breakdowns. Orlova, who still took pride of authorship in the file, suffered an allergic reaction to the idea. No! she objected in a rare display of emotion. It is technically impossible! You must learn the keystrokes!

Then there were simple problems of communication. Orlova spoke with a heavy accent and did not understand American humor or slang, which sometimes yielded interesting results. In one case, the BBYA had finally calculated correctly after hours of repairs. "Whew!" I exclaimed, looking over her shoulder at the screen. "All right, let's print that baby."

"Paul," Orlova said coldly, "you should not call me baby."

Even Goth laughed at that one.

Our greatest source of conflict, however, was the inevitable struggle over our respective positions in the food chain. In the beginning of our relationship, I let my guard down with Orlova, thinking that at twenty-two she was too young to be dangerous. What did she know about how the office worked? Lulled by this false sense of security, I asked her a lot of questions about the BBYA and allowed myself to depend on her to an extent I never would have otherwise. She seemed so harmless sitting there pecking away at her keyboard, her feet unable to touch the floor. But I made a tragic miscalculation. Orlova was not the hatchling of Darwinism I had expected. She was a full-grown hawk. Over time, she took a growing interest in the BBYA, first making suggestions, then giving instructions. The coworker became the teacher, then the manager. At first I chalked this up to pride of authorship—the BBYA was mostly her creation. By the time I began to sense her true intentions, it was too late: she thought I worked for her. At that point I rarely needed her assistance, having finally figured out more or less how the BBYA worked, but she had me in her clutches. She refused to admit to my progress and continued to try to exercise control over the spreadsheet, having me perform special calculations for her, editing the sheet without telling me, checking it for errors and telling me to fix them. Chafing at this, I finally decided that it was time to draw the line. Once and for all, I would make the BBYA mine.

I had always hated that abbreviation, BBYA. It sounded like another set of keystrokes. Wasn't the sheet a marketing product? Didn't marketing products go to human beings? Then why not give the title some life?

One day after making my delivery rounds, an agitated Orlova arrived at my position, clutching the sheet.

"Paul, what is this?"

"The Brady Sheet," I said.

"No, no, no," she laughed. "You can't do that."

"Why not?"

"Did you ask anyone?"

"I don't have to ask anyone. The Brady Sheet is my responsibility."

She cringed, all laughter gone. "I designed it. I built the code."

"So did Goth. And Breen. Now it's my turn."

Her mouth puckered. "I want you to change the name back!"

"I told you, I like 'the Brady Sheet.' "

"It is *not* a Brady Sheet!" she exclaimed, reddening. "It is a *Brady Bond Yield Analysis*! You must be *precise*!"

"Call it what you want. I'm calling it the Brady Sheet."

"We will see!" Her eyes darted around the trading floor. "I'm going to speak to Raoul."

That surprised me. Bring in Savegre on something like this? I wondered what he would make of this titanic moral conflict—or, given the more likely interpretation, how he would define the food chain. Viewed in that light, the issue was not a small one at all.

I watched Orlova circle the trading floor searching for Savegre, the troublesome Brady Sheet clutched in her hand. He emerged presently from the conference room and she rushed toward him, arriving a second before myself.

"Raoul, could you look at this?" She thrust the sheet breathlessly in front of him. "Paul has changed the name of the BBYA!"

Savegre looked it over, frowning in contemplation. "The Brady Sheet," he said. "That's catchy. I like it."

## 15

In late spring IEM had an informal get-together at Johnny Fish's, a bar and restaurant at the base of the North Tower. In typical IEM fashion it wasn't announced to the group either on the morning call or elsewhere. The insiders told one another and left the rest to nature. I heard about it from an analyst who passed the word among the lower ranks after overhearing a trader mention it—that was typically how things reached my ears and those of many others.

I wasn't too excited at the news. My travails with Mundt, Goth, and Orlova, my developing understanding of how IEM worked, and the armor I donned before going in the door all argued against socializing with anyone. As far as I knew there wasn't even a single friendship on the trading floor—a glaring contrast in a group so young. Just a few years ago most of us had been strolling across some college campus in our jeans, nodding at people we knew, stopping for a moment to shoot the breeze. Since then, however, we had all learned the price of sentiment. We had stared into the wake-up smile, the "you fool" smile, the sneer that said the market doesn't care. And we had strapped on our financial breastplates as a result, making any glimmer of emotion, of humor, of warmth, of sympathy not a ray of light but a chink. Human bonds were a weakness, the market said. Buy a dog. This, we were told, was maturity. And part of this maturation was apparently to pretend none of this had happened—to socialize as if we still meant it.

So I went down to Fish's, curious to see what I would find. About half of the group was present, forming a clump in the middle of the restaurant. The rest were still upstairs, of course, unaware that the office was having a social and wondering why everyone had gone home early. I stood at the bar with a pint of ale in my hand, watching the clump of people slowly divide. It was like the formation of life itself—office life. The mixed group slowly separated into two cells—one Trading, the other Sales—revealing between them a common nucleus of Latin Mafiosi—seated, of course—talking only to themselves. Meanwhile the rest of the group wriggled around the outside trying to penetrate.

Ale in hand, I drifted around the perimeter trying to strike up a few conversations with people I normally avoided. It wasn't easy. I found that whenever I approached a group above me in the food chain, my presence was ignored; and if I spoke, any conversation that resulted was brief. This included a brush with Breen, who was dexterous enough to be an old college acquaintance in private but a representative of the Syndicate desk in public. The reverse was true when I approached a group below me in the food chain (there actually were such animals).

Then I would see a group of bright shining faces eager to expound on the market. Perhaps they were just happy to have someone speak to them.

Given these choices, I found myself, like everyone else, staying more or less with people on my level. But even there relations were defined more by verbal swordplay than discussion, as my peers and I jockeyed for position. The food chain was never static. The conversations I did have—brief, adversarial, or out of sympathy—were limited to the same topics allowed in the office. These were, in general, the market and its emotional analog, sports. So, I heard, did you see that the Knicks traded so-and-so? Did you hear that PaineWebber bought Kidder? Do you think the Yankees will break .500? Do you think the Fed will raise rates? The great reservoir of human discourse—the panoply of the arts, philosophy, religion, politics, history, current events, hobbies, books, ideas, opinions, the human condition—was drained, leaving only those subjects that proved without any doubt your unswerving commitment to the cause. There were even limits to what you could say *about* the market. Being new to Wall Street, I was bursting with various first-time observations on the subject and eager to engage someone in discussing them. But I soon found, in testing the waters, that they received a cold reception. My observations were too general in nature. They smacked of philosophy. And if there was a stick in the eye of the market, philosophy was it. We didn't want to *think about it.* We didn't want to *know what it meant*—or didn't mean. Action, boy, not observation! Don't you know what philosophers are? Flakes? No, worse— poor!

One of these test cases was, unfortunately, Savegre. I had not spoken to him much at all since my first day, many weeks previously, and decided, emboldened by a pint or two, to break the ice. I found him at the nucleus of the Sales cell and filled the chair next to him with a casual hello. I expected he might ask me, the new man, how things were going or what I thought so far. Instead he announced my name like a game-show host, as if I were entering *Family Feud,* and turned back to his salesmen. He seemed to be in a very good mood. He laughed when they laughed—I had never seen him laugh so much—he listened intently whenever they spoke and was, by all appearances, greatly enjoying their company. The IEM salesmen were his producers: their work paid his salary.

"The last few weeks have been very interesting," I said.

Savegre slowly turned his head back to me. "Oh? Good."

I felt a growing nervousness working its way up my spine to my larynx. "Sure— I've never seen a place move so fast. Sometimes I think the office is about to spin out of control."

Which was perfectly true, although in my nervousness a fact blurted out without much thought as to how it might be received.

"Don't worry," Savegre said flatly, "we know what we're doing."

The light went on. "No—I mean—it's really impressive," I quickly added, regretting this drivel the minute it crossed my lips. "Everyone performs to the maximum." Aaah!

Savegre raised his eyebrows, letting me twist in the wind a moment. "It has to be. There's an ax over your head at all times."

I smiled winningly, an arc of pure capitalism. "Sure, but there's a pretty big carrot to match that stick."

Savegre frowned. "It's not a stick—it's an *ax*."

I decided to get another beer.

When I returned to the crowd I sat on the edge this time, determined just to watch. While there were no true friendships in the office, there were numerous alliances based on position and these were very much in evidence. Savegre was still laughing out of character with his salesmen. Breen, his acolyte, was now sitting next to him. Mundt was dutifully looking over Savegre's shoulder, an eager and attentive listener. A couple of Brady traders stood next to me, talking hopefully about a brief market rally in Brazil. Goth was buddying up to them, calling them all repeatedly by their first names. Orlova was listening and learning. McCarthy, in contrast, was standing by himself, his foot up on a chair, downing another beer. Forte was nowhere to be seen. The air was permeated by false conviviality as if this were some brief cease-fire in our continual efforts to unseat the man next to us. Oh, what a game it was! Putting scales on our backs, sharpening our fangs, forking our tongues. The hissing rose in volume, growing so loud I wanted to scream, "Stop it! Stop it! I know what's really going on here—and so do you! So let's cut the bullshit!" Then, while still surveying the crowd, I began to wonder if I was mistaken—whether this smoke screen existed or whether their armor had truly thickened to the core. Maybe, I thought with an unnerving chill, these people weren't pretending anymore.

I left soon thereafter, needing a walk, and decided to take the subway home. The escalator in front of the restaurant took me up to the mezzanine level of the World Financial Center. Rising through its hollow core, I listened to the voices below, hundreds of voices echoing in its innards—a dissonant chorus it was, evoking the image of a trading floor.

The causeway over the West Side Highway bore a few stragglers like myself, working our way through the rush in the opposite direction. I had forgotten that it was Thursday, the opening of the evening market. The bodies marched past me in waves, arms linked, faces painted, nails manicured, hair blown and cut, heels clicking in unison, and voices bubbling nervously, drawn inexorably to the largest concentration of moneyed young men in America—young women from all over the city, bidding for the bankers.

## 16

While still battling with Orlova, Savegre asked me to take the Series 7 exam. The Series 7 is the driver's license of the securities industry. Passing the exam, which requires a score of 70 percent, registers you as a licensed broker, allowing you to give investment advice and trade. Since the exam had almost nothing to do with the emerging markets business, it required a fair amount of preparation, which I began to receive two nights a week at the Securities Training Corporation, near Battery Park. There the greatest challenge was staying awake. After a full-tilt day in IEM the quiet of a classroom was like a cradle rocking your head until it ceased to right itself, broken only by the drone of the instructor, whose talk of capital stock and capital surplus, reserve requirements and registered representatives soon formed the gentle rhythms of a lullaby. After class I would walk back to IEM along the Hudson River and begin production of the Brady Sheet. Savegre had decided to produce the sheet after the market closed. In that way, if there was a problem I would have hours and hours to fix it. This policy change frequently made me the last person to leave IEM, especially on Series 7 nights, something that began to bother me. Why should I suffer for someone else's mismanagement? But I knew the score: I was on my own.

At the same time, doing my job became increasingly difficult. On April 24, Brazil entered the ranks of Brady countries by exchanging a mammoth $34 billion in foreign debt for Brady bonds. This nearly doubled the size of the Brady market overnight—and added even more bonds to my overloaded spreadsheet. Delivery expanded as well. Then Habib, our smiling system administrator, wisely took a job in another group, leaving his seat temporarily vacant. Without his supply of Band-Aids and the knowledge of where to apply them, the network's wounds soon festered into a plague. Monitors froze. Data disappeared from the screen. Files moved to unknown locations. Access was denied for no reason. Strange error messages arose, my favorite being YOUR PASSCODE IS CURRENTLY BEING USED BY H. RODRIGUEZ. We didn't even *have* a Rodriguez.

Faced with such intractable problems, I decided that the only solution was to build an entirely new Brady Sheet—an automated version based on live feeds from the wire services that would be distributed by electronic mail. The proposal went through Savegre to Lisardo Escobar, the head of the group, and was never heard from again. As a last-ditch effort I returned to my previous idea of translating the unwieldy file into Lotus for Windows on my faster laptop in order to spare myself the two greatest headaches, the half-hour calculation time and the need to send the output across the tottering network. I asked Itzhak, the departed Habib's boss in the mysterious System group, if there were any way to do it.

"Sure," he said. "It's simple." Two disks, and five minutes later, it was done. In the first trial run, calculation time fell from half an hour to twenty seconds.

I sat looking at the screen absolutely aghast. "You've got to be *kidding* me. Do you know how many *hours* I've *wasted* on this damn thing?"

"Why didn't you do it before?"

"Orlova said it couldn't be done!"

"I don't know *why*," Itzhak said. "I showed her how to do it myself. She got one of these laptops weeks ago."

Experiences like this eventually worked their way through the tough skin I was trying to develop. Had Itzhak really explained it to Orlova? If so, what did that say about her? It almost didn't matter. All I knew was this: When going to IEM in the morning I felt the same nausea you get before stepping into a boxing ring. During the fight that ensued, I thought of nothing but staying on my feet. When it was over I would collapse in the back of a car or shuffle to the subway, unable to shed the memory of it. The antireason of the office, all the technical problems I was experiencing, the difficulty of scraping for information, the harshness of the work environment, the constant pressure and stress, and the isolation of my existence, of always being kept in the dark, came out at different times as insecurity, paranoia, worry, frustration, and anger, hidden on the job, released at home. I would lie awake thinking about something that had happened in the office and it would pop into my head the next morning. A cycle developed of pressured, full-tilt workdays followed by exhausted weekends. Sundays became the worst day of all. By then I had slowed enough to feel the fatigue and think about it. After digesting *The New York Times,* I would stick in a Jackson Browne disk and stare at the ceiling, not wanting to move.

Meanwhile the bond market continued to decline. In April, Merrill Lynch posted a record $372 million first-quarter profit, but earnings had already begun trailing off, as they had all over Wall Street, precipitated by declining bond prices. By May, the benchmark thirty-year Treasury bond had fallen from January highs over $1,010 to around $840; if you owned any, you had lost 17 percent of their value. The emerging markets came down with them. Brady bonds were particularly sensitive to U.S. rates since they were collateralized by U.S. Treasury bonds. When the value of the collateral fell, the value of the bonds dropped too.

In IEM, Carlos Espinosa became the market's first casualty. Espinosa was a rising star of the Sales desk. A former investment banker, he had joined the office at an elderly thirty-five and quickly made a name for himself as a solid producer. But during the general market plunge, one of his Venezuelan clients, an account handed to him by Savegre, had slipped into bankruptcy. Discrepancies had begun to appear in the back office, where trades were tallied. No money arrived; the client made excuses. Management either didn't notice or didn't deal with it until the loss grew to $4 million, bringing the loss to the attention of the Firm. Someone had to take the fall, and that meant either Espinosa or his boss. "The choice was simple," a trader later told me. "Savegre cut off his head."

In late May Espinosa was pulled aside by Savegre and summarily dismissed. He wasn't offered a few weeks of office space elsewhere in the firm in which to find a new job—a common practice—but told to leave the premises immediately. He couldn't believe it. Neither could anyone else. The Latin Mafia gave no reason for his departure; there was only an empty seat in Sales.


To help alleviate the pressure of the trading floor, I began forcing myself to take a walk every day at lunchtime. This was not as easy as it sounds. The same pressure I needed to release also kept me in my seat all day long. I felt anxious when away from the desk for too long—what was happening in my absence? My sense of security came from being part of the momentum, the action. It was something I had to consciously break away from. Sometimes in the midst of the headlong daily rush I didn't even notice the passage of time. I would look up surprised to find that it was two o'clock when it seemed like ten. This allowed for a mercifully quick workday—or, depending on how you looked at it, an unnaturally short life.

My walks took me along an established route past the World Financial Center marina and down the walkway along the Hudson, all the way to its southern end near Battery Park. Usually I would find myself passing other people and consciously will myself to slow down. When I reached the end I would take a seat beneath the gazebo and eat my lunch while looking out over the water. There were always a few ships to be seen, usually the huge tankers and container ships waiting to pull into Newark or Bayonne. Every so often one of the colorful old vessels of the Circle Line would steam by, lined with tourists, its proud, pug-nosed brow pushing defiantly through the water. Then there was the river itself, which hustled by as if fleeing the scene of a crime. It passed over Manhattan like the cloth of a weary nurse, rubbing it down, leaving dirty. But there was some hope there, at the tip of the island, that salvation lay ahead.

A half hour later, on my way back to the office, I would pause at the marina to study the yachts. It was usually full of them: the World Financial Center marina was not a holding company for penny stocks. They lay thrust out between the docks like so many middle fingers, monstrous in size, displaying their shiny brass, their uniformed crews, their helicopters and cocktail tables and lounging, bathing-suited owners, all locked safely within the granite confines of their exclusive square marina surrounded on three sides by a vast stadium of spectators.

It was a grand reciprocal arrangement: they showed us what we wanted and we gave them what they wanted. For of course they needed to know that we were up there behind the reflective glass just as we needed to know that they were down there in the brilliant sun. They needed to feel the affirming heat of our gaze, the glow of the admiring thousands, standing in cramped and noisy offices, on trading floors and in cubicles, hoping to one day own a yacht, to pay the thousands in docking fees and maintenance costs, to plunk down a seven-figure sum for a boat used thrice yearly. We were the strivers, the wanna-bes, the supporters, the suckers—and they were the winners. Weren't the yachts grand! Made in America, registered in the Cayman Islands, spanning the globe.

Meanwhile the timeless Hudson slid by, mocking us all.

On the Friday commencing Memorial Day weekend, I flew down to New Orleans to meet Sarah for a well-needed break. She had also begun a pressured job, requiring that she travel up and down the East Coast two to three weeks per month giving sales demonstrations of educational software. The rest of her time was spent commuting from Brooklyn to New Haven, Connecticut, where her company's closest office was located. This entailed making a two-hour drive in either direction along the Highway from Hell, I-95, at rush hour. By the time she returned home she was as frazzled as I was.

She met me in the airport, having flown in from a conference in Atlanta, and we checked into a quiet hotel in the French Quarter. By Saturday afternoon we were both so exhausted we decided to take a nap. When we awoke, it was dusk. I dressed for dinner and opened the curtain, surprised by the empty streets below. It was Sunday morning. We had slept fourteen hours.

"We may be in the South," I sighed, "but we're still on the Northeast Habitrail."

The trip back on Monday was marked by silence. As the plane approached JFK airport, I looked down at the incredible sight of the metropolis below. One cannot appreciate the full size of New York City except from the air. You look out at an industrial carpet of concrete and asphalt, rooftops and roads, unrolled in all directions and spanning the water to cover New Jersey. Nature has been smothered, retreating between the crowded banks and the borders of claustrophobic parks. Neighborhood after neighborhood passes beneath the wings, each with its own forgotten history, dramas that will never be heard and people you will never meet, some of whom have never even been to Manhattan. As the plane sinks, you feel like you are shrinking into the world of the microscope. The scale increases, details emerge—cars, pedestrians, aerials, utility poles, water towers—the tires screech and there you are, back amid the pond life.

It was then, my head pressed to the plane window, that I began to seriously question the wisdom of our move from Annapolis. I didn't share such thoughts with Sarah—not after all the uprooting I had caused us—but I did call my friend Jim in Tokyo the next day and tell him about life in IEM.

"I hear you," he said. "The fact is, I don't think I ever would have made it with Goldman if I had stayed in New York. By the time I left for Tokyo I had only been there, like, four months and I was real close to just saying forget it, I'm not this corporate guy, this isn't me. I even had to be *threatening* a couple times. I'm serious. I went head-to-head with a couple guys. One of them even came up to me later and admitted the only reason he left me alone was because he thought I was going to deck him."

After this conversation, I finally decided to have a talk with Savegre. With things as untenable as they were, it seemed to me the only solution was to go abroad as Jim had done—which is what I had always wanted anyway—and Sarah agreed. So I mulled over how to approach the issue and caught Savegre one day as he was leaving the trading floor.

"Raoul," I said. "I was wondering—if I'm able to get the Brady Sheet automated, is there another position—"

"Don't worry about the Brady Sheet," Savegre interrupted. "You're going to have a new job soon—derivatives."

He disappeared down the hall.

## 17

While the decline in attendance in Cobble Hill's churches had precipitated a decline in the buildings themselves, there was another modern American faith, of a kind, which was prospering in Brooklyn and to which we were unwillingly drawn. This one took place in a courthouse, where its primary service, the lawsuit, was conducted.

Darleen had spoken.

Two weeks after canceling payment on my check to Homes on the Heights Realty, I finally received a call back from Darleen. She was in a new mood. Maybe we can work something out, she said sweetly. Forget it, I replied, listing my litany of complaints, chief among which was my heating bill. As before, our conversation went nowhere, only this time I had the upper hand. The money was back in my account. And it stayed there.

Within a week I received a summons to appear in small claims court in Brooklyn.

"Is she crazy?" I asked Sarah. "She doesn't have a case."

"She's trying to get us to settle—no way."

The wheels of injustice turned slowly: our court date wasn't for many weeks. Then it was delayed another six weeks when my star witness, Sarah, had to go on a business trip. But eventually, with all leeway expired, we both left work early one afternoon and made the trek on foot to the courthouse on Livingston Street, near Brooklyn Borough Hall, prepared to plead our case.

We were directed to an enormous room full of crowded pews, a staging point for the evening drama. Though we were twenty minutes early, it was already standing room only. Scores and scores of Brooklynites were sitting quietly in rows waiting to sue one another. They all looked straight ahead, hoping, like us, not to lock eyes with the opposition. It was just like the subway. The pews faced the large, solid judge's bench, which was empty. A uniformed bailiff was sitting at a table in front collecting his papers.

Sarah and I stood against the side wall and surveyed the crowd. Darleen was nowhere to be seen. I hoped she wouldn't show up at all: it looked like it was going to be a long night.

When the big clock on the wall neared seven, the bailiff stood up in front of the room with a computer printout in his hand. He was going to read off the suits in alphabetical order, he boomed. Both parties should say "Here" if they were present. If the defendant didn't show, the plaintiff automatically won. If the plaintiff didn't show, the case was dismissed. If both parties were present, they would approach the bench and decide on either arbitration or a trial.

"Which one do you think is better?" Sarah whispered.

"I don't know." Arbitration was a curveball for me. Like most Americans, everything I knew about small claims came from Judge Wapner. And in *The People's Court*, there had been no arbitrators.

"All rise."

The crowd struggled to its feet as the judge entered, then dropped back down with a collective sigh. After a quick word with the black-robed judge, the bailiff began reading off the lawsuits in alphabetical order. If a problem arose, such as a request for a delay, the judge would step in and settle the matter. Otherwise the evening quickly settled down to a monotonous constancy of names and replies, broken only by the sudden appearance of Darleen, somewhere late in the Fs, betraying her startling familiarity with the system. She stood in back with an acquaintance.

"She brought a lawyer," Sarah whispered.

I nodded, worried that my reliance on *The People's Court* was showing some limitations. Judge Wapner had never dealt with lawyers, only real people. Now someone had changed the rules of the game. Why did I need a lawyer, anyway? I wondered. I had a signed contract explicitly stating that my landlord was supposed to supply the heat for my apartment. Darleen was his representative. Open and shut.

The bailiff kept plowing through the endless roster of names, revealing the presence of a number of other lawyers in the crowd. When their clients' names were called, they would stand up and earn their fee by spouting something impressive like "Of counsel." Only lawyers can speak nonsense like that and get away with it.

"Homes on the Heights Realty—"

I sprang to alertness.

"—versus Meredith, Ronald T., and Meredith, Jacqueline H."

I sagged back against the wall.

"Heights, of counsel," said Darleen's lawyer.

"Meredith," said a young man amid the pews.

The two parties converged on the bailiff's desk. By coincidence Homes on the Heights was suing another couple just like us, a brown-haired guy in a blue suit, his wife in a sundress. Wall Street, I thought with one glance at the man. We definitely stuck out in the crowd.

"Must be a busy week for Darleen," I whispered to Sarah.

"A busy year."

The Meredith family departed and the bailiff boomed, "Homes on the Heights versus Stiles, Paul W."

"Here we go," Sarah sighed.

We walked to the front of the Big Top. Darleen was still standing in front of the bailiff's desk wearing a silly hat and slowly masticating a piece of gum, her over-rouged cheeks moving up and down like the cursor on a sing-along song. She kept her eyes straight ahead. Her young lawyer looked like he was going to skate off into the slick capades. His brown hair, falling in rows of curls to his shoulders, glistened from the liberal application of some synthetic gel. He had a full set of Wall Street choppers too, bulging the clay of his lower face. He turned as we approached and fixed his eyes on me with a deliberate stare, his glossy features teeming with hungry delight. Did they teach them that in law school? I wondered. "And now, class, the art of intimidating the opposition. This is where justice is really served." I raised my eyebrows and he bared more mandible, affecting a carefree aside to Darleen.

"Who's the defendant?" the bailiff asked.

"I guess I am," I said.

"Arbitration or trial?"

"How am I supposed to decide?"

"Arbitration is quicker," the bailiff said mechanically. "We only have one judge tonight. He may not get to you. But it's your decision."

I glanced at Sarah—let's get it over with, her expression said.

"Arbitration," I said.

"Sign here." The bailiff slid a form in front of me. The form said that we had chosen to decide our case by binding arbitration and willingly relinquished our right to a trial. I hesitated—a formality?—and signed. So did Darleen.

The bailiff handed me a carbon copy. "Room Thirty-nine. Go outside the doors, take a right, go up the elevator one floor, bear to your left, and it's the first room on your right."

Darleen's lawyer spun on a well-greased heel and walked off with a grin I didn't like, his manicured curls bouncing on his shoulders, his cowboy boots thumping on the floor. Darleen hurried to keep up with him. We followed, of course, having the same set of directions, and consequently ended up in the same cramped, clanking elevator. Elevators are never comfortable places to stand with others, but they are especially uncomfortable when the occupants are suing each other. I immediately pushed the CLOSE button. All eyes focused on the numbers overhead. I snuck a glance at Sarah, who rolled her eyes. There were some whispers to my other side. Then a smell wafted to my nose, the smell of cheap perfume. My nose twitched like a divining rod seeking direction. It was coming from the lawyer.

The doors opened mercifully and we spilled out into the hallway, looking self-consciously about. Room 39 was no improvement on the elevator. It was a drab, windowless cell with a judge's bench at one end, six rows of mismatched chairs at the other, and walls like the guardrail on a sharp exit ramp—scratches, gouges, scuff marks, dents. From the chairs, I hoped. It was as if some animal had been subdued here at great expense. Overhead two parallel rows of fluorescent lights, of laboratory variety, projected a harsh, artificial glare, exposing every last shadow and generating the prickly sense of an impending interrogation.

As I moved toward a chair, a man was sitting behind the high bench cleaning up some papers on top. "Come here," he said, waving me forward with a big meaty arm like a plump Thanksgiving drumstick. I approached the tall bench, which hid most of his hunched body. I placed him at forty-five, though it was difficult to tell. He had a red-hued, pie-shaped, puffy face, his thin black hair was plastered to his scalp, and he wore a pale blue work shirt with the top buttons undone and the sleeves pushed lazily past his elbows. A maintenance man, obviously.

He scratched a hairy arm. "Who are ya representin'?"

"Myself."

"Oh." He looked surprised. "I thought ya were counsel. Ya can give me that."

I handed him my paperwork. "When will the judge be here?"

"There's no judge. This is arbitration. Ya selected arbitration, Room Thirty-nine?"

"Yes."

"I'm the arbitrator. Have a seat."

I returned to sit with Sarah, passing the lawyer, who tried to hold me with another stare. I snorted back at him. By now the seats were filling up with people from downstairs, making me feel out of place. I had kept my suit on after work, a plain blue single-breasted type, thinking that one should be reasonably well dressed when going to a courthouse. But mine was the only suit in the room—except for Darleen's lawyer, whose double-breasted shapeless model, unbuttoned at the waist, hung from his shoulders like a cheap pair of linen curtains. The rest of the people looked as if they had walked over from the Greyhound terminal after a sleepless night, and leading the parade was the arbitrator, who had just changed the spark plugs on the bus.

"I just want everyone to know," he said after calling the silent room to order, "that we're all volunteers up here. And I've had a hard day, just like everyone else. So keep that in mind." He ruffled his papers. "Bajeen versus Leonard?"

A few people stirred from their seats. One was a tenant whose security deposit had not been refunded. The landlord showed all kinds of photographs showing the disputed damage. Then our case was called.

Sarah and I walked to the front of the room. I still felt uncomfortable, though I saw no reason for it. Should I have lowered my standards to come to this courthouse? Should I feel bad for having a job that required me to wear a suit? I assumed my position before the bench, Sarah to my left, the perfume to my right, Darleen beyond reach of my fist.

The arbitrator was looking over the paperwork. "This is a complex case. Homes on the Heights—that's you," he said to the lawyer, "is suin' Stiles for nonpayment, and Stiles is countersuin' for damages—is that right?"

"A year's worth of heating bills," I said.

"We'll start with the original suit, since it affects the second one. Everyone knows how this works, right?"

"Shew-ah," said the lawyer, sounding exactly like Darleen.

"Could you go over it once?" I asked.

"Shew-ah," said the arbitrator, sounding exactly like the lawyer.

That's when I knew we were in trouble.

"It's simple," the arbitrator said. "He calls his witnesses, then ya go, then we have closin' arguments. Okay?" He edged forward, looking a bit too eager for my tastes, and nodded toward the lawyer. "Go ahead."

The lawyer ruffled though his folder and unfurled a paper with a hundred-dollar-an-hour flourish. "Is this ya signature?" he asked me, pointing to the bottom of the page.

"Yes."

"In this agreement, did ya agree to pay my client a fee for any apartment she rented ya?"

"Only on the condition that the apartment—"

"Just answer the question. It's a yes or no question," the arbitrator said.

"I signed the paper, yes."

"Did my client find ya an apartment?"

"Not the one I wanted."

"Did ya rent an apartment she showed ya at 501 Hicks Street?" the lawyer sneered.

"Yes."

"Have ya paid her a fee?"

"No. She told me that—"

"Wait!" The arbitrator slapped his hand down on the bench. "I've already talked to ya about this. *He's* askin' the questions—not you! Proceed."

"I'm done," said the lawyer with a shrug. "The defendant has admitted to agreein' to pay my client for services rendered."

The arbitrator turned to me. "All right, *now* ya can go."

I opened a folder I was carrying and removed my statement, two pages, single-spaced, describing what had happened the day Darleen rented us our apartment. I cleared my throat. "Your Honor," I began, raising a chuckle from the audience, "on the morning of—"

"Wait a minute, wait wait wait." The arbitrator sprung on me with surprising abruptness. "It doesn't work that way. Ya have to ask questions."

"But I've prepared a statement."

"We don't take statements," he said with tough-guy authority.

I paused, stunned. No statements? This definitely wasn't *The People's Court.* Judge Wapner always read people's statements!

"Do ya have any questions?" the arbitrator asked.

"I didn't prepare any," I said.

"Fine," he said, turning with apparent satisfaction. "Counsel?"

The lawyer, practically overcome, put his head in his hands to calm himself and think. "Aaah, okay." He lifted his shiny curls, and flourished the rental agreement. "Well, all I can do is say again—did ya sign this agreement?"

I felt the blood rushing to my face and told myself to relax. "First of all, let's look at the contract. The contract specifically states—"

"Wait a minute," the arbitrator interrupted. "Ya had your chance. It's his turn now."

The lawyer held out the contract again. I gritted my teeth. "Yes," I said. "Yes, yes, yes."

"Now, do ya have any witnesses?" the arbitrator asked me.

"Yes, my wife," I said, and turned to Sarah. "Did that woman there"—I pointed at Darleen—"show you and me the apartment at 501 Hicks Street?"

"Yes," Sarah replied.

"And did you ask her if the heat came with the rent?"

"Yes. I specifically remember that because we had a problem with it once before, in Annapolis."

"And what did she say?"

"She said the landlord paid for it."

"I never said any such thing—" Darleen clucked, until her lawyer seized her arm. The arbitrator turned his head, but said nothing.

I took out my copy of the contract. "The contract specifically states, under paragraph two, that 'the owner shall supply heat—' "

"Ya supposed to be askin' questions, not makin' statements," the arbitrator said.

"I will—if you will allow me."

"Go ahead," he said indifferently.

I held the contract in front of the lawyer. "The contract specifically states, under paragraph two, that 'the owner shall supply heat as required by law'—does it not?"

The lawyer looked away. "So?"

"Just answer the question," I said.

"I'll say that," the arbitrator said.

"Is the landlord paying for the heat in my apartment?" I asked.

"I have no idea," the lawyer laughed.

"He isn't," I said. I handed the arbitrator our latest heating bill.

He brushed it aside. "Let me see the contract." He gave it a cursory glance. "So what's the problem? The landlord is supplyin' the heat, isn't he? It doesn't say he has to *pay* for it."

Stunned, I exclaimed, "Of course he has to pay for it!"

"No, that's not what this says. It says he'll *supply it*. That's different."

"How can he *supply it* without *paying* for it?"

"Simple. He puts in a heater."

"That's not what *she said*." I pointed an accusing finger at Darleen.

"I never said nothin'," Darleen said. Her lawyer grabbed her again.

"Do ya have any more questions," the arbitrator asked, "or are ya done?"

I took an inward breath. "Did you, Darleen, tell me, and my wife, that the landlord paid for the heat in this apartment?"

"No, no, nuh-unh," she clucked. "I never said that. I might've said that there *was a heat pump* in the buildin' or somethin', but nothin' like that."

"That's not true!" Sarah exclaimed. "I was standing right there."

"Ho ho-o-o-o," the arbitrator exclaimed. "Someone hasn't been *listenin'*. Haven't ya heard what I've been sayin' about people waitin' their *turn*, Miss? Well have ya?"

"I was right there. She *specifically said* that—."

"HEY! Are ya *listenin'* to me? Ya better *listen*."

Laughter sounded in the back of the courtroom, causing the arbitrator's face to twitch.

"Look," I said, "there's no need for that—"

"Ya both better listen! There's certain rules we have to follow here, okay? That's the first thing they teach us here." He glanced at the audience, then glared at us. "This is ya last chance. Are ya ready to proceed?"

"All right," I said.

The arbitrator kept staring at Sarah.

"Fine," she said.

"Go ahead then."

I turned to Sarah. "Were you in the room with us when—"

"Nah, nah, ya can't do that," the arbitrator laughed, "ya already asked her questions."

"So?"

"So ya moved on. Ya can't go back now."

"You didn't explain that!"

The arbitrator held up his hands with a smile. You could almost read his mind: don't you Wall Street big shots know everything?

He turned to the lawyer. "Any more questions for the defendants?"

"No."

"Any more questions for the plaintiff?"

"No."

"How about you, Miss. Any questions?"

Sarah didn't answer.

The arbitrator sat back. "Then it's time for closing arguments."

The lawyer quickly repeated what he said before: contract, signature. I said that Darleen was lying, and tried to bring up the wording of the contract again.

"We've already gone over that," the arbitrator interrupted. "Anythin' else?"

I searched for something to say, but what was the point? The scuff marks were already on the wall. There we were, the well-dressed yuppie couple, definitely out-of-towners, just here to make money, and there they were, three natives, people who knew how this city worked, who had paid their dues, who hadn't been handed a silver spoon, who resented people like us. So we had been a bit roughly handled by this rental agent—so what? We could afford it. What do you expect when you don't know the city? Did we think we could just come in here and demand special treatment? Oh, how good they felt, getting people like us where they always wanted us! Getting *even!*

"No."

"Okay, that's it then, we'll let ya know by mail in a few days."

"Do you want my statement?" I asked.

The arbitrator stared steadily at me. "Keep it. I don't need it."

Sarah and I quickly left the courtroom, saying nothing until we were down on the street. Suddenly she erupted, "That son of a *bitch!* That *bastard!* I have never been so *humiliated* in all my life!" Then her face, crimson with rage, broke into a spasm of grief.

"Hey, whoa!" I exclaimed in shocked surprise. I had never seen her so enraged. "Look, I know this *sucks,* but it's not *that much money.* We're not *broke* anymore!"

"That's not *it*," she said, holding herself as if chilled. "Don't you see? I've been so *naive*. I always thought you could go into a court in this country and get *justice*."

Our experiences with the "justice" system were put in perspective one night after leaving a pizza joint on the Upper East Side. We were headed downtown in a cab when Sarah suddenly realized that she had left her pocketbook back in the restaurant. We immediately asked the cabbie to turn around. After another tense twenty minutes adding up the damage—the credit cards that would have to be canceled, the driver's license that would have to be replaced, the money that had been lost—we arrived to find the pocketbook still hanging from the chair where she had left it.

"You are veddy lucky," our Pakistani driver said. "Veddy lucky indeed. I haf done dis two time, tree time maybe, and only one time was it dere."

This conversation then segued into a general discussion of crime in New York, in which I related our expensive loss in small claims court.

"Ho! You tink dats bat?" the driver said animatedly. "No, no, dats nutting, nutting. Let me tell you what happen to *me* one day. I was driving mittown. It was de meetle o' de day. De meetle o' de day, now! And I see a couple like you, just like you. Your age, dressed fine, nutting wrong looking about dem at all. So I pull over and dey get in and I ask dem where dey want to go and dey gif me some address downtown, far away. So I am driving down Broadway and I look over"—the cabbie turned his head to face us—"and dere is a gun in my face. A big silver gun, dis long. 'Gif me your money,' de woman say. Well, I keep de money in dis container here"—he lifted a Tupperware bowl—"so witout moving my head, I lift eet up like dis an hand it back true de hole. I had just started for de day so dere was only a couple o' bucks in dere already. An de woman takes it and say, 'Dere's only six bucks een here.' She steel has de gun pointed at de back o' my head." The cabbie turned around to demonstrate, causing me to wonder who was driving the car. "She ees very angry," he continued. " 'Hey, dere's only six bucks in ere!' she says to me. Den I hear de man say, 'Shoot heem. Just shoot heem,' he say. So quickly I say, 'Wait wait! I haf a wallet too!' and I reach into my pants and take out my wallet and hand it true de hole. 'You've only got ten bucks in ere!' de woman say. 'Dats all I got!' I say. It ees true! All I got was ten bucks! Den I hear de man say, 'Shoot heem' again. What could I do? I had no more money. So I turn de wheel an I drive de cab straight into de parked cars." The cabbie spins his hands in the air to demonstrate. "An der is a *beeg* crash! De woman hits er head on de metal here and she falls on de floor. De man is fine. He takes de gun and runs, leaving de woman in de car. So I get out and dere is a *beeg* crowd. Some of dem have seen what I haf done. I just drive straight into de parked cars—*boom!* Just like dat. So I tell dese people what has happen and one of dem calls de police. Finally de police show up and what do dey do? Nutting!"

"You're kidding," I snorted.

"Ya! Dey don't do *anyting*! 'What can we do?' dey tell me. 'Nutting happen. Dere is no gun. It is only a car acci-*dent*.' 'What do you mean, nutting happen?' I tell dem. 'Dey were going to *keel* me! I had to crash de cab into dese parked cars!' Den de crowd starts screaming at de police—by now it ees *very beeg*: 'Arrest her! Arrest her!' dey are screaming. Finally another cop, a patrol super-*visor*, stops in a car—you know, dese cars wit no markings. He was just driving by and sees de crowd. And he ees de one who finally decides to arrest her. So dey take her away in de back of his car."

"Good!" Sarah exclaimed.

"So wait! Next I had to go to court. Dey call me in and I had to go and answer all dese questions. So I tell dem dis whole story, just like I am telling you, how she put de gun to my head and all dat. But when it ees all over, all dey do is give her de *sus-pen-ded* sentence! Six months! No jail, no *anyting*!"

"That's not surprising," I sighed.

"So wait! Dat's not eet. I hear de judge say dis and I stand up—I was sitting in de courtroom, right een front of heem—and I shout at heem, 'You don't understand! She was going to *keel me*. She was going to *keel me*!' " The cabbie flings the air away from him. "So what does dis judge do? He fines *me!* He hits de hammer on de desk. 'Five hundred dollars!' he say. *Five hundred dollars.* Me! A cab *driver!*"

"You're kidding!"

"But wait, wait—dat's not it eeder! De next ting, a guard comes over to take me out of de court. A guard in hees uniform. He takes me to de back room. He ees supposed to gif me de fine. Instead he say look, just get out of here, I saw de whole ting. And he lets me out de back door!" The cabbie was laughing hysterically. "De whole ting is rotten! Top to bottom! It ees no better dan Pak-ee-stan!"

## 18

Derivatives. Now there was a word to curdle the soul of any fledgling associate. And many investors too. Derivatives, of course, are the most quantitative of investments, so much so that relatively few people actually know how they work. By definition a derivative is a financial contract whose value is derived from the performance of an underlying stock, bond, commodity, or index. An option on a bond, for instance. This second tier of finance acts like an equation in which the first tier provides the variables, making derivatives inherently flexible and allowing you to tailor them to perform a variety of financial tasks. The danger of derivatives lies in the abuse or misuse of this power and their complexity. The more complicated a derivative is, the higher the probability that the computer model behind it is flawed or, more commonly, that the salesman who sells it or the investor who buys it don't fully understand how it works—problems magnified by market pressures.

Such ticking problems erupted in 1994, turning it into the Year of the Derivative. In January, shortly before my arrival at Merrill, a massive German engineering and metals conglomerate, Metallgesellschaft, nearly collapsed after a massive $1.34 billion loss in oil futures, a type of derivative. In February, Chile's enormous state-owned copper company, Codelco, suffered a $207 million loss on copper futures at the hands of a single trader. In March, three hedge funds managed by David Askin, a mortgage derivatives investor, collapsed in the face of rising rates, handing his wealthy investors a $450 million loss. In April, Kashima Oil Co. in Japan announced a staggering $1.45 billion loss on foreign exchange forward contracts. The most publicized debacle involved Bankers Trust, a leading innovator in derivatives, and a number of its clients, all stung by derivatives losses. After one of them, Procter & Gamble, suffered a $157 million loss in highly complex interest rate swaps, it filed a $196 million lawsuit against its broker, alleging fraud. This claim was supported by tapes from the Bankers Trust trading floor in which one salesman explained his derivatives sales strategy: "Funny business, you know? Lure people into that calm and just totally fuck 'em."*

These developments naturally attracted the interest of the SEC (and virtually every other regulatory body of note), which by summer had launched an investigation into the entire derivatives industry. Its focus was not only on the danger derivatives posed to Wall Street clients but to the world financial system itself. The size of the derivatives industry is estimated to be a mammoth $35 trillion, more than the total value of stocks and bonds in the world and seven times the GDP of the United States. Yet it is highly unregulated. No one knows where most of the derivatives are, what kind they all are, or what role they would play in a crisis, nor do people agree on how they should be controlled.

The reason for the spread of derivatives, of course, is that they are useful and profitable. Prior to all the negative publicity, and the rise in interest rates, the derivatives market was exploding. And one of the leading growth areas was emerging markets derivatives, fueled by twin booms. In IEM the trading desk added a num-

---

* Banker's Trust later settled with Procter & Gamble, agreeing to pay as much as $150 million of P&G's loss (depending on the ultimate valuation of the derivatives). Gary Missner, a former BT managing director, was jointly fined $100,000 by the SEC and Federal Reserve and barred from the securities industry for five years. An independent counsel concluded, "In short, BT's derivatives business was not well managed or controlled in certain important respects and certain individuals exploited these weaknesses for their own purposes.

ber of derivatives trading positions to capitalize on it. But the more arcane derivatives, the ones that were manufactured for a specific purpose or client, were not generic enough to be actively traded. They required a production and sales focus instead, more like manufacturing. So it was that, in early 1994, Savegre decided to establish his own derivatives effort focused on an esoteric instrument known as structured product. He subsequently hired a young banker from Bankers Trust, Charles Post, to run this effort, and asked me to assist him. The idea, Savegre explained during our one five-minute meeting on the matter, was to have Post and me run our own small, entrepreneurial effort. Post would explain the rest when he arrived at the firm.

All this sounded great to me. I didn't know structured product from ruptured produce, but I assumed that Post would teach me everything I needed to know—he had to, didn't he? Instruction at last! Teamwork! Even more exciting, I saw the end of my days with the Brady Sheet—liberty! And the Structured Product Group was a small, cutting-edge enterprise, a chance to use initiative, to build. Opportunity! As a result, I looked forward to the imminent arrival of Post, whom I had never met, like the coming of spring.

In the meantime I had to get rid of the Brady Sheet. At first I held the naive belief that Savegre would give it to someone else, but after forcing him to dip into his repertoire of blow-off lines I finally saw that it was I, not he, who would have to pass it on in accordance with the laws of the office—that is, by sticking someone else with it. Luckily, with the commencement of summer there were plenty of stuckees to be found. Summer is the season of the M.B.A. intern, when a handful of shining faces from the top business schools, having survived a rigorous interview process, descend on the Street for a little summer fun. One of ours was Luis Sanchez, a Venezuelan from the Harvard Business School who arrived eager to take part in the romance of the Street. "Hey!" he announced to his cohorts one day. "I just played a wicked game of Liar's Poker down on Seven!" Unable to resist such enthusiasm, I handed him my troubled charge, only to be disappointed. Within days the Brady Sheet had imploded. Seeing her chance, Orlova seized control and promptly changed the name back to BBYA, but even this couldn't revive it. Savegre finally had to give the whole program to Research, which built a new one from scratch. Someone, I think, had had that idea once . . .

If you could say anything for market management, it was that it didn't play favorites. The Latin Mafia aside, Wall Street was a place where performance, not pedigree, mattered most. Money mattered most. So it was that Charles Post, when he arrived, became a social anomaly in our group. Post came from solid WASP stock. He had a trust fund, a mocking smile, prominent "aaahs" in his locution, and a manner like his Brooks Brothers shirts—full of starch. When his father, the

CEO of a Fortune 500 company, or another of the Connecticut Posts would call the crowded desk, the conversation would generally revolve around the market, the latest board meeting, trust funds, prenuptial agreements, alimony, and the next Post family get-together—which sounded more like the board meetings. Post's silver spoon had not been wedged in his mouth without chipping a few teeth, however. During his difficult adolescence he had developed a marijuana habit, which had led to his expulsion from two prestigious New England prep schools. His alarmed parents—Post Sr. and latest wife—had shipped him off for a year of rehabilitative sailing in the Caribbean, where he had apparently found himself, or at least righted his listing vessel enough to return and graduate from Bucknell. Since then he had spent his time pursuing the Grateful Dead, whom he had seen in concert some sixty times, and working on Wall Street, where he viewed himself as a congenital member of the ruling class. The fact that there no longer was one was something he found difficult to admit.

After a few days wandering around without a seat—"checking out the firm" as he called it—Post finally settled into the position next to mine and got to work. Our first structured product, he told me, would be a senior subordinated structure. This comprised an offshore holding company, or trust, typically formed in the Cayman Islands, which held a portfolio of bonds. These bonds were then cut up into two different notes and sold to investors. Creating one of these structures required building a model portfolio on the computer, cutting up the cash stream into the notes, and making sure they were an attractive investment. That was the end of the discussion. There was no talk of our new joint venture—where we were headed, how we were supposed to get there, how we would work together. Instead, over the next few days I watched Post disappear to meetings and return later on without knowing where he had been or what was going on. Other times he would politely ask me to do things without explanation, as if we had been working together for months. What had happened to the Structured Product Group? I wondered. All I saw were two structured individuals, only one of whom had a clue.

Eventually I determined from the empirical evidence that Post wanted me to model the structures on the computer while he would market them—a dangerous proposition. Putting me in charge of manufacturing senior subordinated derivatives was like taking a kid out of driver's ed and putting him in an Indy car—and a clear call for industry regulation if there ever was one. Wall Street must be one of the few places on earth where an utter novice can create a highly risky multimillion-dollar product without being subject to any regulatory control—as opposed to the lower-rent areas of Brooklyn, where you can't fix a toilet without a plumber's license. And, not surprisingly, I proceeded to crash the financial vehicle at every turn. None of my models worked. Post seemed surprised by this— Savegre had left him with a different impression of my technical abilities—but I was surprised too: Savegre had left me with the impression that Post would teach me everything I needed to know. For a long time Post ended up doing the modeling himself while I took to dissecting his work in an attempt to figure out what it all meant, feeling increasingly on edge. Post was no dummy—he was very bright, in fact. Although a throwback in many ways, he knew quite well how the new Wall Street worked, and he lived by its rules. Already I could see the trader's analysis going on in his mind: should I invest any more time in this guy—or cut my losses?

By this time both Post and I had new seats. After some office restructuring, an island of new positions arose next to the plate glass windows overlooking southern Manhattan, becoming the new home of the Structured Products Group. I called it Operations Island because it was mostly inhabited by IEM's Operations staff, the people who did all the trading paperwork. Various analysts and interns also washed up there, fleeing their harsh reception on the desk and forever stealing your chair.

Life among the castaways was a lot better than it had been—quieter, more relaxed, even fun sometimes. Left to themselves, the lowest-paid people in the office seemed to be the happiest. But to my neighbor, Charles Post, our new home was a warning sign. He was a vice president of the firm charged with starting our new effort. Now he was not only physically isolated from the Trading desk but had been cast adrift amongst the proletarian hordes. In some act of mischief, or social justice, he had even been seated next to Donna Riccatelli, known as the Mouth of the South. A heavyset, large-chested, middle-aged, tan-lamped bleached blonde from Staten Island, Riccatelli motored around the floor like a multiturreted armored vehicle firing off explosive volleys. From inside the conference room, with the door shut and the speakerphone on, the shrill wail of one of her incoming rounds would whistle through the walls: "Hey Ralphie! Where's that fuckin' blottahhh???!!!!"

Thanks to Post, I had my own Achilles' heel as well. Post had struck up a business relationship with Javier Pip, a freshly minted equity derivatives trader in his very early twenties. Whenever he stopped by, Pip never failed to throw a verbal lance at any target in sight. "Stiles," he would say, "when are you going to add value?" Such methods were, in Pip's mind, a way to solidify his new position in the pecking order. They quickly pecked their way right through my skin.


After a few weeks working with Post I was surprised to discover that we were not the only group at Merrill selling our arcane product. The Investors Strategy Group, the firm's secretive derivatives think tank, was also involved and even had their own Latin American salesman. To avoid conflict, IEM and ISG had signed a treaty calling for mutual cooperation on matters of joint interest, but it had all the substance of a campaign promise. In reality the two groups were constantly operating behind each other's back and competing for the same clients.

Post was just as surprised to hear about this as I was, having been led to believe that he would be Merrill's point man for our product. But given his isolation in IEM—in typical fashion, no one was lending him any support—and my own limitations, he saw ISG as a life preserver rather than a shark. Invoking the IEM-ISG treaty, he approached them and suggested we work together.

This was definitely playing with the devil. ISG was the financial elite, the cutting edge of finance. Carefully selected for their unique environment, its personnel were all young, computer literate, highly quantitative, bilingual, came from the best business schools, and made Goth look like a Good Samaritan; one of their favorite tricks was holding phony job interviews to extract information from unwitting competitors. Their attitude was also cutting edge. In the forefront of finance, at Wall Street's leading firm, they considered themselves part of a rarefied, in-the-know, new-world-order stratum, not only professionally but socially. They were citizens of a new global market: at a moment's notice they could jet off to London, Frankfurt, Tokyo, Sydney, Hong Kong, or Singapore, plug in their headsets and feel right at home. Any concern aside from their P&L was thus held in contempt: that's not the way the new system worked. It was the market that shaped their values, paid their bills, and ruled their lives, and it was the market to which they pledged their allegiance.

Knowing he had to be valuable to ISG, Post sold himself to them as a generator of trade ideas, a marketer, and a skilled salesman. His first idea was a complex new trust aimed at investors with a view on the August Mexican presidential election, which ISG modeled for us. At one point, while I listened from my position, Post was describing the trust to an investor in an attempt to sell a $10 million note:

"Well, aaah, it's a leveraged play on the peso, basically. By all accounts, the peso is expected to rise after the elections—excuse me, can you hold on?" Post tapped a persistent phone line. "Merrill."

It was Post's contact in ISG. "We just took another look at the model. It looks like there's a small inaccuracy."

"How small?"

"Small. I just wanted you to know about it. We need to fix it before you send out any documents."

"Okay—but I've got an investor on the line right now. Aaah, it doesn't affect the structure, does it? It's still a strong play on the peso?"

"What? No! We changed the portfolio, remember? It's *convertibility insurance* if the peso *devalues*."

"Oh right, right. Ahhh—I'll talk to you later." Post returned to the investor. "Sorry about that. I was just checking with my modeler. Anyway, aaaah, as I was saying, *some* people think the peso is going to rise after the elections—but we think it's already overbought. There's, aaah, a lot of overconfidence in the market right now regarding Mexico. So what we've done is put together this structure that acts like an insurance policy, aaah, if the peso devalues, and convertibility becomes a problem . . ."

When Post put down the phone, I was laughing. "What the hell *is* this thing anyway?" I waved a printout of the model in the air.

"It's an insurance policy on the peso," he said flatly, as if it were obvious.

I tapped my headset, which he had overlooked. "So I heard."

Post shrugged nonchalantly, keeping his eyes on me. "Now you know why these things can only be sold to sophisticated investors."

They weren't, however. With both the emerging markets and derivatives in a slump, the market for our product had dried up. Structure after structure failed to find a buyer. Knowing this, Savegre began distancing himself from Post, quietly blaming him for our lack of success. This left Post in limbo. He had originally arrived as the leader of a new effort for Merrill, which then became a new effort for IEM, which then became part of the IEM-ISG joint venture. Finally he told me one day that he saw himself mostly as "an ISG asset"—a feeling ISG had encouraged all along. But after a few weeks of dealing with Post ISG knew the truth: Post was not a threat. His boss had blown him off, he had no clients, his modeler was a Mac person, for Christ's sake. The phone calls from Seven grew less and less frequent.

"Charles," I finally asked Post one day, "in all seriousness—who do we work for?"

Post lifted his hands helplessly. "Aaah—you tell me."

One morning I looked up and saw Post talking to Orlova. He was asking her to build a new model for him. She willingly accepted.

I knew what that meant: I had failed to make the derivatives grade. Deep down I had expected this, although I didn't want to admit it. In the last few weeks the complexities of my task had overwhelmed my efforts at self-instruction. I would sit for hours staring at the Lotus spreadsheet, frustrated by problems I could not fix, until my energy slowly drained away. I had reached my limit. Now, in fine IEM fashion, I was being pushed aside without a word. Natural selection was asserting itself.

In the wake of this development, I felt a mounting sense of vulnerability. I had been in IEM four months now and no longer had a job. Meanwhile the market was still falling. I didn't know how bad the situation was—the Latin Mafia did not discuss the group's P&L—but from the flaring tempers and the whispers of concern, I knew that something was amiss and felt exposed because of it. What should I do? I spent a few aimless days at my position pondering the question. I just needed the right opportunity, I decided, one that required different skills. Meanwhile Post and Orlova worked on their new structure next to me. I had never seen Orlova so happy in my life. First the return of the BBYA—and now this!

During one of these moments of reverie my thoughts were interrupted by Javier Pip, my Achilles' heel, who slapped his hand on my back. "Adding any value yet?"

"Go away."

He walked off with an exaggerated laugh, one out of place even for him. A few moments later I heard some of the interns snickering behind me. "Guys, I'm trying to do some work," I said.

This made them laugh even harder.

"What is so *funny*?"

"Nothing," said Luis Sanchez, my Brady Sheet stuckee. He appeared to be near tears. Catching his line of sight, I reached behind me and pulled a note off my back. *Add Some Value.* Crumpling the note in my hand, I looked across the aisle to the main Trading desk, a sudden anger obliterating all thoughts. Pip was doubled over in laughter.

That was *it.* Without thinking, I burst from my chair and closed the distance between us. It was a timeless interval in which the room rushed by in a blur and all sound seemed to merge into a chaotic roar. Reaching Pip's position, I grabbed the knot of his tie and lifted him out of his chair until my arm was at its fullest extension. Shocked, he hung in the air, choking, while two voices broke into my head, two opposed internal voices, one of them demanding that I put him down, shouting for me to think about my actions, the other urging me to tighten my grip, to shake his body, to hoist him higher, to make him pay for all this senselessness.

I dropped him. He struck his chair and fell to the ground, stunned, and I left the trading floor. The entire incident had taken barely ten seconds. But how long did it take to pull a trigger? Then I was in the men's room, splashing cold water on my face, waking up and looking at the mirror. What the hell was that all about? Are you crazy? Now you've done it. All these months of backbreaking work thrown away in a brief moment of violence. How are you going to explain it to people? Get a hold of yourself! I studied my face, the drops falling off my brows and running down my cheeks. Who was this man? He looked like me, but I couldn't quite place him anymore. Then someone opened the door, breaking our mutual stare, and I busied myself with a paper towel.

A few minutes later I returned to the Trading floor, calmer, back in control, and feeling a relaxation I couldn't fathom. Whatever happened, happened.

Operations Island fell silent as I approached. A few eyes followed me to my position, making me feel self-conscious. For once my chair was empty; no intern ever sat in it again. And no one ever mentioned the incident either—except Pip, who sent me a profuse apology via electronic mail. Instead I noticed people treating me with a new respect. I had, quite inadvertently, discovered a secret to the way the office operated, and took steps to make sure I never forgot it.

The next day I arrived at work with a curio I had picked up years before in Florida. It was a varnished baby alligator head. I placed it on top of my computer, where it faced the Trading floor, next to the picture of my dog.

## 19

June opened with one of those lifelong sources of angst and expectation, a parental visit. This involved, as it always does, a great deal of cleaning, activity planning, and, in general, the usual hopes of approval, which refuse to wane with age. When the impending visit is to your first apartment in New York, you also have some additional concerns to worry about. There is the question of where your parents are going to sleep, for instance, when you live in a one-bedroom palace. We solved that one with the sofa bed. For some reason it didn't seem right to have my parents drive all the way down from Boston to Cobble Hill only to stay at a hotel in the Heights. Then there is the question of how your parents find your building, especially if they are driving. This one caused me more anxiety. I had visions of my father calling me from a pay phone: "Paul! We're down here on . . . Flatbush Avenue!"

Thankfully that didn't happen. Instead, after coming home a little early from work that Friday, Sarah and I stood at our apartment window watching a familiar beige station wagon pull up in front of the Cobble Hill School. We descended and let them in the gate.

My parents are exuberant travelers. They like nothing better than tasting a new area, even one relatively close to home. They jumped from the car ready to take on the Big Apple. "Hello, Sarah!" my mother exclaimed. A round of embraces followed.

"How was your trip?" I asked.

"Fine! Just fine," my father said. He was wearing his favorite sweater, a somewhat worn model obtained, I suspect, prior to my birth, but which he refused to part with. He and my mother buzzed around the car a moment, collecting luggage and various trinkets from under seats, and we went inside.

Once in the elevator my father began to whistle, a lifelong habit of his which I have come to recognize as the sign of a very happy man.

"Curt!" my mother said, laughing. "He's been whistling the whole way down. And *that sweater*!" She rolled her eyes. "But he won't listen to me."

"What's wrong with this sweater?"

We entered the living room and dropped the bags.

"Your bedroom," I announced, like a servant at court.

"Oh, look at this!" my mother said, sounding as enthusiastic as possible. "Curt, isn't this wonderful?"

"Hmmm, yesss," my father said, sounding vaguely mysterious as he looked around the spacious cube.

"You have a nice view too." My mother looked down at the parking lot below. "Oh, I think this would be *fun*, living in New York!"

"It has its moments," I said.

We led them on a quick tour—very quick—pointing out the finer points of the apartment, and settled back in the living room with a few glasses of red wine.

"So, are you *enjoying* yourselves?" my mother asked, with that little wobble in her voice that betrays a pointed question.

"I have sworn," I said, "not to discuss this city, or any of its residents, for the duration of your stay."

"A sound policy," my father said.

"Curt!" my mother objected. "We have to know if they *like it* here."

"We have all weekend to find out."

My mother feigned irritation. "So what have you been doing? For fun, I mean."

Sarah and I met eyes and avoided a direct answer. The fact was, between our two jobs, we hadn't done much, certainly less than my parents could do in a long weekend. We had been to a lot of restaurants, because that took no planning aside from the Zagat guide, and we had managed a trip to the Cloisters, a wonderful replica of a medieval monastery where I considered renting a room, but aside from that, we had spent most of our free time trying to get away from the city.

"Well," my mother pronounced with a wave, "you have lots of time. Have you met anyone interesting?"

"Our neighbor is from London," Sarah said. Silence followed.

"Why don't we go see the neighborhood," I suggested, "before it gets too dark?"

My father vaulted from his chair. "Sounds good to me."

"Curt," my mother said, motioning toward his sweater, "don't you think you should *change* first?"


Cobble Hill was a new environment for my parents and me to be in together. I grew up in Needham, Massachusetts, a suburb bordering Boston, and lived in the same house until I left for college. It was a three-bedroom house with an attached garage located on a quiet hillside street with quarter-acre lots, well-tended lawns, and a healthy number of trees, from which you could view the skyline ten miles distant. It was an altogether typical suburban existence—uniform, stable, and predictable. My parents were happily married. They were both employed as teachers except for the years my mother took off to raise my brother, my two sisters, and me. This meant that we had the same schedule: whenever I was home, they were home. During the school year, life was a constant cycle of school and sports—soccer and lacrosse. Then in the summer we would go to Cape Cod, where my parents owned a cottage in Orleans. On the Cape life revolved around fishing and various other outdoor pursuits, at least until I was a teenager, when it revolved around a job at the beach and girls.

What struck me as we walked around Cobble Hill, however, was that we as a family could never lead that life today. No two teachers could afford to buy my parents' house, have four kids, sacrifice one income for fifteen years, and buy a cottage on the Cape to boot, without winning the lottery first. I was also struck by the hidden danger in the life I had led, something I had reflected upon more than once since leaving college—the twin danger of heightened expectations wrapped inside a perfect American childhood.

"Oh, this isn't *bad!*" my mother said, taking in the whole neighborhood. I smiled. My mother was the live wire of the family, a running source of opinion that kept us all on our toes. This time, however, I suspected that her enthusiasm was driven as much by hope as energy. My parents had not wanted us to move to New York. "Find something in Annapolis!" they had urged. But now that we were here, they greatly wanted things to work out for us and were hoping for the best.

"It's not a bad neighborhood at all," I said, surprising even myself. Cobble Hill was definitely growing on me. "It's got some real history to it. There's a lot of great brownstones—like those."

"I would have *loved* to do this when I was your age," my mother said. "Curt, why didn't *we* ever move to New York?!"

"You never wanted to," my father said.

We reached Court Street, one of our mental borders, and the conversation died down. Some of Court Street is a funky, lively blend of shops. The rest is more run-down, with toeholds of graffiti in spots. My mother walked along, head down, through these areas, her energy returning once we reached the Heights. "Well," she said, "there were a few *rough spots* back there—I mean, I don't like *those*—but otherwise I think it's nice, don't you?"

"Sure," I said, pausing to consider what she had said. The fact was, I hadn't even noticed. Four months ago, one walk down Court Street had turned it into a boundary line. Now the streets were all merging together—here, there, it was all New York.

"So how do *you* like it, Sarah?" my mother asked as we walked.

"Well—I'm getting used to it, I guess. It was a little much at first, but now I'm getting in the swing of things. I really like the outdoor markets—there's one in the Heights every weekend. We went to another one down in the Village last weekend, that was really good."

"How about the restaurants? I saw a bunch back there."

"They're good too. There's a Moroccan place we like back there, the Moroccan

Star. And a Middle Eastern place I *love* just off Atlantic Avenue. It's called Fatoosh."

"*Good.*"

"It's good for *now*," Sarah laughed, "but we're *not* looking to buy."

"Oh no, this is just *temporary*," my mother said with a wave. "But at least you're enjoying yourselves."

"It took some getting used to. There's a lot of little things that are different—like grocery shopping. Everybody uses their own cart here. A lot of people don't have cars, of course, but there's no parking at the store either. So you wheel little carts around. Which means you can only pick up a few things at a time. So you have to shop all the time, every few days. Then there's so little space in the aisles—the aisles are only this wide. You can barely squeeze by people. So there are only certain times you can shop. But we can only shop when we get home from work, which is when everyone else does it. So that's a hassle.

"You always have to be careful too," Sarah added.

"Of course," my mother emphatically agreed.

"One thing I didn't realize was how many illegal cabs there are. They're called gypsy cabs. I found out all about them last week. I was flying into La Guardia after three days in Atlanta and this man approached me in the terminal and said, 'Taxi, ma'am?' I was really tired, so I thought—great. He waited about twenty minutes for my bags to arrive. Then we went outside, and I was walking along, not really thinking—it was pouring rain—and he stopped by an unmarked Lincoln Continental. I was putting my bags in the backseat when I thought, wait a minute, this doesn't look like a cab. So I said, How much does this cost? and he said, Just get in. This is when I started to get nervous. I said, No, how much will it cost to Cobble Hill? Just get in the car, he said. I grabbed my bag, pulled it out of the car, and said No, I'm not going anywhere unless I know what it costs. Maybe forty, he said. I said No way, it's fifteen at the most. So I started to walk back to the terminal, and he started following me. Just leave me alone, I said. Come on, come on, we can make a deal. No! I shouted. He kept following me all the way back to the terminal—meanwhile I'm dragging this heavy bag behind me. And this guy is big, too, over six feet. He gave me the creeps. Finally I reached the entrance and he said, 'Bitch,' and left."

"Did you call the police?" my mother asked.

"Mom," I laughed, "be serious. There's thousands of these people."

"I still think you should tell the police."

"I did tell the guard inside the terminal," Sarah added. "He said, 'The yellow cabs are to the right.' That's it. The other day I told one of the women I work with about it and she couldn't believe how stupid I had been. It was my fault for believing a guy who said he had a taxi."

"At least you know now," my father joked.

"You have to learn all kinds of things like that here. You have to stay on your toes all the time. It wouldn't be so bad by itself, I suppose, but when you add it to my job, it's too much sometimes. The last thing I want after a three-day business trip is some hassle getting to my own front door."

"How is your job going?" my mother said.

"Why don't we go back?" I said, giving Sarah the wave-off glance.

My mother intercepted it. She had a knack for deciphering any kind of secret communication. "Is it going *well*?" she asked.

I turned around and led the way with my father, who began to whistle.

"I'm doing fine, but the company isn't doing very well," Sarah said. "We just had a big round of layoffs. Two hundred and seventy-five people got cut."

"Oh no! How many people are in the company?"

"Eighteen hundred to start."

"I thought it was the top educational software company?"

"It was, but then we got fat—anyway, that's a long story. The company then swung to the other side and called in this really slick business guy to clean house. He wasn't an educator like everyone else. He didn't even *value* education. They just told him to turn the stock price around. It was so cold—they called everyone into a large room and told them they were being laid off. Many of the people had been with the company from the start. They only had a half hour to pack up and leave. When they went back to their desks, their hard disks were gone—memos, résumés, everything, all gone. I hear there's going to be another round of cuts in Atlanta too. Next week."

"Do you have anything to worry about?"

"I don't think so. I'm the only person doing my job in the Northeast." Sarah laughed. "The funny thing about this man, the one they brought in—I met him once—he had on a pastel tie with Roman ruins on it. Fallen columns. Everyone laughed about it."

"Sounds like a Caesar," my father said.

"But that's the way business is now," Sarah said. "I guess you just have to live with it."

By now we were moving down the brownstone valley of Clinton Street. We overshot our turn to stop by the local bodega, then headed home, passing a row of houses that were unique in our neighborhood—not any more or less expensive, just different, with a lighter architecture, more glass, a first-floor garage, and balconies. I often thought they belonged by the ocean, a little seaside community, its toes in the sand. They also had a family look about them—a few toys on the balcony, bikes out front, kids playing in the street. My father, having mostly nodded with my mother's enthusiasm up to this point, remarked on the toys, his face pinching into a wince. "I don't know how people live their lives in places like this," he added. Then he caught himself. "I mean, an *apartment* is one thing. But your *whole life . . .*"

"You get used to it, I suppose."

• • •

After arriving home we changed for dinner. My parents had made the tragic mistake of offering to take us out wherever we wanted to go. We soon found ourselves at the base of the Brooklyn Bridge and seated inside the River Café, one of the best, and dearest, restaurants in all of New York. Located on a barge on the East River, its elegant interior looks like the wardroom of a stately ocean liner and affords a magnificent view of southern Manhattan, with the graceful span of the bridge arcing overhead. Our dinners were tremendous, too, topped off by dessert, a delicate miniature of the bridge in chocolate. By the time it arrived the sun was setting, filling the room with a warm orange light. At that moment one of the harbor fireboats pulled up in front of the windows and shot off all its jets, forming the proudest river peacock ever to grace the city. It was, we all agreed, a dining experience unsurpassed in our memory.

Afterward we drove up to the nearby Brooklyn Heights Promenade, where I had first stepped foot just five months previously. The sun was down by now and the city had made its rapid transition from the rowed monuments of day to the ordered constellations of night. The skyline looked as beautiful as ever, a shimmering mirage just beyond reach. Could it be real? Was this whole experience of mine an exception to the rule, an errant data point, as the quants would say, along the probability curve? The evening, the wonderful evening we had had so far, fought with so many other memories in the search for the truth. New York was a continuous series of disparities, incongruities, contradictions, and ups and downs, an alternating current of seductive glances and slaps in the face. One minute you were standing in old Greenwich Village looking at a beautifully restored town house from the eighteenth century and the next you noticed the homeless person camped out beneath the steps. You stood in the Executive Dining Room of the World Financial Center, looking out over the whole metropolis and feeling lifted into the clouds, then you realized you were staring at Red Hook. You emerged from an exhibition at the Metropolitan Museum of Art, one of the great museums of the world, then walked up the street to the Guggenheim Museum, where you saw a pile of Tootsie Rolls on the floor labeled "Edible Sculpture." Then you emerged from there, shortly, wondering if it was too late to walk through Central Park. Then, looking lost, you were approached by someone generously offering to walk you to the nearest subway; seconds later you were both almost run down by a cab. After a while such events sharpened your instincts, like those of the savvy old hands of the market. Whenever you found yourself enjoying the boom, you wondered what bust was lying just around the corner.

"There it is," I said, "the bar graph of capitalism."

"Wow, what a *gorgeous view*," my father said.

"Oh!" my mother exclaimed. "It's beautiful!"

"Too bad you couldn't live up here."

"We tried," I said. "It's a bit expensive."

"Do you come up here a lot?" my mother asked.

"All the time. It's a great walk."

"Is it?" She looped her arm around Sarah's. "Come on, Sarah. Let's go!" And off they went, into the dark.

I stood with my hands on the rail, wondering what to say to my father. I had a few months of turmoil, boiling inside me and was afraid to let any of it out. I didn't want to spoil the mood. Nor was I sure how he would respond. My father had never been through any turmoil, as far as I knew. He was the antimarket, a force of almost perfect stability. Everything he did seemed to last forever. He had been happily married for thirty-six years. He had lived in the same house since I was one. After graduating from the Harvard School of Education, he had taught high school history in nearby Wellesley and was now the oldest serving teacher in the entire school system. To help make ends meet, he had taken a weekend job as a movie projectionist back in 1966, a job he still held. During our summers on Cape Cod, he had worked as a bartender at a restaurant in Chatham for twenty-five years. When it finally closed, he took another position down the street. During the school year, he would leave every morning at six with his tuna sandwich, walk downtown to his carpool, and be home by four. In all that time his values never changed or faltered. He had no sudden swings of mood. I never witnessed a fight between him and my mother. The only time I ever heard him swear was when I backed his new car into a wall. He was reserved in his manner and opinions and always taught by example. Of all the boyhood lessons I ever learned from him I could not remember one that he had ever told me outright—aside from how to catch fish, a hobby he had pursued since his boyhood in Hyannis. He was the stable, even-burning sun around which the rest of the family comets orbited, and I thought he always would be.

The difference between him and me was summarized by an incident that occurred when I was a teenager. I had lost my comb. In the rush to get somewhere, I had left it somewhere else. So I asked to borrow his. He removed from his pocket a frayed piece of black plastic that looked like a fossil. "Dad," I said aghast, "how long have you *had* this?" He considered the question a moment. "Oh . . . about fifteen years."

Now the same son that had filled his father's ears with tales of bureaucratic misery in Washington didn't know what to say about New York. Had times been different for my dad, I wondered? Or were things just different with me? I wished that I could tell him that everything was fine, that the future looked secure, that I loved Merrill Lynch, that Sarah was happy in her job, and that we were happy in Cobble Hill, but none of it was true. Instead there was some profound disturbance, the product of more than just these discrete unhappinesses—a systemic problem of challenged beliefs and expectations, of torn philosophy.

"I look at that skyline," I said, "and I almost forget my life."

He had joined me by the railing. Below us was the hum of the BQE; in the distance, the glitter.

"Is that real?" I asked.

"Is what real?"

"That."

He waited.

"You know what most people think about when they come to New York, Dad? Excitement. The lights, the glamour, the action. They think about the ball dropping in Times Square and Broadway shows and the noisy floor of the Stock Exchange—as if New York is a bunch of skyscrapers in Manhattan. They don't think about the four boroughs of domestic staff keeping them running. Do you think any tourist ever goes out to Staten Island or the Bronx? It's as if those places don't matter. They're not New York, or at least the New York people want to believe in. It's like going to some feudal castle in Europe and saying, Wow, life must have been great back then."

He laughed. "Sure, but there's lots to do here as well. This is one of the great cities of the world. You've got the theater, the museums—"

"Dad—look—all that's great in theory but it's not reality. At least it's not *my* reality. We don't have *time* to do that stuff. And going to the theater adds up. It's not like going to the movies."

"But you two are making a lot of money now."

I groaned. "I *knew* you were going to say that. That's the biggest mirage of all. It doesn't matter how much money you make, it matters what it *buys*. And here a hundred grand doesn't buy much. Taxes take half—the city tax is huge. Our rent has doubled but our living space has been cut in half. Our car insurance doubled—yet we cut back from two cars to one. We work much harder than we ever did and we hardly ever see each other anymore. And when we do, we're so stressed out we don't know what to say." I tried to calm myself. I felt that I was getting to that dangerous spillover point where the dam begins to buckle. "The scary thing is, Dad— I'm a Wall Street banker. Everyone thinks I'm some kind of *rich guy*. What do these people do who make less money than me? How do they live here?"

"Like you said—they adapt."

"It's not just them."

"So what are you going to do?" he asked worriedly.

"I'm going to stick with it. I have an idea I think might work. I just want you to know what this place is like."

He sighed. "Look, you have a great opportunity here. Do you know how many people would like to be in your shoes, working at Merrill Lynch?"

"I know it—it's just—I don't think they realize—I don't think they know—or by the time they figure it out—" I gasped in exasperation. "This is really hard. I mean it's *really hard*. This place is huge, Dad. It seems like it's bigger than any one man. Sometimes I wonder if I'm crazy to fight it."

"Fight what?"

"*I don't know.* Something."

He didn't say anything.

"I know I'm not making sense."

He lifted a vague hand. "You have to be true to yourself."

"Do you think you could live here, and do what I do?"

"I'm not you."

"I know that—come on, I'm serious. Could you do it?"

"Maybe for a short time. I don't know. No, I don't think I could."

"You don't like the city."

He chirped in laughter. "I'm like most people. I like to come to New York for a weekend—but I could never live here. Now Paris—that's another story!"

"Isn't there something wrong with that?"

"Maybe there is. What can *you* do about it?"

I looked away. "We've been thinking about going abroad. Merrill has a lot of offices abroad."

"If it will make you happy."

"Yes." I turned back to him. "Maybe that's the problem."

"You aren't happy."

"What *is* happy?" I circled the air with my hand. "Is this happy?"

He waited.

"Do you know what happy in New York is, Dad? It's being rich. Really, that's the whole idea here."

"It's not just here."

"But it's *louder* here. And emptier because of it. The whole purpose of making money in New York is to rise up in full view of millions of people, to reach the penthouse. It's a very simple philosophy, really. Everybody is piled on top of each other. Success is defined by the numbers. The amount of money you have and the amount of things it buys. You move forward by addition. You get a one-bedroom apartment, then two. You add a parking space. You upgrade your vehicle—more horsepower, more money. You move from Cobble Hill to the Upper East Side. Meanwhile all your achievements are worn like little badges. My God, people say—He has his own parking space! He has a gated lot! He has a balcony! He lives on East Seventy-fifth Street! That's a good number! Instead of confronting the hard stuff, the unknown, the intangibles of life, we've all retreated onto this Monopoly board. We've boiled life down into a few discrete spaces. You get enough money, you live on Park Avenue. If you pass go, you get two hundred dollars. Then you can be happy with yourself. Of course, you never are."

"Like the man said, it's a bonfire of the vanities."

"I suppose I never took that seriously enough."

"But not *everyone* lives that way."

"I'm speaking in general. In general that's how people live here. That's what makes this place go, that's what turns it into the place it is."

"No one says *you* have to live that way though, do they? Your mother and I never did."

"Dad, this *whole place* argues that I live that way. Every day. It screams it from every window. How can you avoid it? Sometimes I don't think anyone ever sits back and asks themselves: Is this right? Is this how I should live? What is the cost? If they do, I don't see it. I don't even think most people realize that there is *life* beyond New York, that anyplace else *matters*. You just get on this train and it takes you in the wrong direction. After a while all your values become relative to this little postage stamp on the east coast of America. It's so ironic—that such a cosmopolitan place could be so provincial!"

"But in the meantime, you and Sarah have a *life* to lead. You can't spend all your time worrying about this city—you have to *enjoy* yourselves. Like your mother always says: this is no dress rehearsal."

"We're trying," I said, "but it hasn't been easy."

And then the floodgates came down. Then I told him about IEM—about Savegre and Mundt, about Goth and Orlova and Post, about how the office worked and how none of it made any sense to me. It all came spilling out against my will amid a rising fear over how he would react. My father knew almost nothing about Wall Street. He had never bought a bond. He did not own a computer. He did not follow the market. He was a history teacher: he knew a great deal about the ancient Egyptians, the Greek and Roman empires, and Western civilization, all those things that people at Merrill Lynch never talked about.

"Did you ever see the movie *Wall Street*?" I asked.

"Sure."

"It's just like that. If you thought that was just Hollywood—it isn't."

"But you knew Wall Street was all about money before you came. *Everyone* knows that."

"But, Dad, that's *all* it's about. Nothing else matters—*nothing*. Maybe you can know that in your head, but when you feel it, right here—"

My father sighed, his shoulders sagging for the first time. He shook his head tiredly. "This is why I never went into business," he admitted.

"You're lucky," I told him. "Do you know how lucky you and Mom have been? You couldn't live your life over today."

"I know it," he said. "We talk about that all the time." He glanced down the Promenade. "Where are they anyway?"

The Promenade was lit by spots of lamplight falling at intervals. My mother and Sarah were nowhere to be seen.

"I don't know," I said. "They should be back soon."

He turned and put his hands on the iron rail. "The thing is, I never cared about money. I remember when I was a senior at Bowdoin I had a few job interviews with major corporations. One was Mobil Oil, I think. These guys would come in in their suits and ask me questions like, Could you fire someone if you had to? I always left feeling empty. I couldn't imagine spending my life that way. So I went into teaching instead and I've never regretted it. Your mother and I didn't make as much money as we could have but we've enjoyed our life together."

"I know," I said, "you're the happiest people I know!"

"I remember in the summers—I admit, I always used to get a kick out of this—I would be standing at the bar and these business groups would come in, you know, for a conference or whatever, and they would sit there talking about how Coke was going to triumph over Pepsi like they were waging the Punic Wars. They would always pretend that they envied me, Joe the bartender, working on Cape Cod the whole summer while they slaved away in their offices, blah, blah, blah. Then they would say something like—So, must be pretty slow around here in the *winter*. You know, as if I were *unemployed* ten months out of the year! So I would say, I don't know, I don't live here in the winter. And they would look at me kind of funny. So where do you live, they would say, and I would explain that I was a teacher up near Boston and only summered on Cape Cod. Boy, I would say, I really love these summers on the Cape! I've been coming down here *twenty-five years!*" He laughed. "You should have seen the reaction *that* got. You could almost see the little gears turning in their heads—wait a minute, this *schoolteacher* gets to spend his *whole summer* on *Cape Cod*—and all I get is one lousy *business trip?* For a moment they actually wondered whether there was more to life than selling soda. Then they walked off to their next meeting, picked up *Fortune* magazine or whatever, and that was it." He laughed again, more sharply this time. "Those people, they never get it. They don't understand what life's all about and what makes you happy."

I waited, but the answer was not forthcoming.

"Why not?" I asked, feigning carelessness.

"Because they have everything backward, like those people in your office. They all think that success makes you happy—but if you're happy, you're a success."

His words struck me like a new idea. Why hadn't *I* ever thought of that? It was so simple. "Then what makes you happy?" I asked tentatively.

I wasn't looking my father in the eye anymore—I couldn't get my head to turn. But I could see out of the corner of my eye that his shoulders drooped, and his eyes closed, and his palm lifted with fatigued wonderment, like the witness of some great and senseless tragedy relating what he had seen.

"The older I get, the more I realize that it's each other we care about."

The tight ball in my throat suddenly parted, releasing a burst of anger. "Dad! What if I *believe* that and I can't put it into action? In my office you would be a *fool* to care about other people. This whole city is about *competition*, about beating out the next guy, about moving as fast as possible. It's not about happiness—

it's about *success*. Success is all that matters here. All we care about in New York is success, money, power, image—and we broadcast that message all over the United States—all over the *world*. You are using reason—reason is a *weakness* here. Reason is for *suckers*."

"Reason is civilization, Paul."

"So what are we going to do about it? Look over there! New York is the avant-garde of society! Wall Street is the cutting edge of capitalism! If you want to see the future—there it is!"

I waited. I wanted desperately to hear the answer, like I had all my life. Dad was the rock, unmoved by anything. He would solve this dilemma for me and I could move on.

"You know," he said tiredly, "you get to a certain age when all you want to do is enjoy the time you have left."

The sound of voices turned both our heads and two bodies drifted out of the gloom. "Well!" my mother said. "What a wonderful walk *we* had, didn't we, Sarah?"

"We sure did!"

"At least *somebody* worked off that dessert."


That night I lay awake listening to the hiss of the BQE coming through our open window and thinking about my father. I had loved him my whole life and yet I wondered if I had ever really thought about who he was. I had always taken for granted that he and everything he stood for would always be there. I had never really considered why he left for school every day—what propelled him on his way and what meaning it had for him. It just *was*. What other assumptions had I accepted, what other dreams had I chased while he had labored right under my nose? And why had I been so blind? I looked at us now, father and son, and the world seemed senseless. I, the roving spreadsheet operator of four months' experience, made more money than he did. While he, over the past thirty-seven years, had taught thousands of young men and women the history and values of our civilization. Where was the logic in that? Where was the justice in that?

The following Monday my parents stopped by the World Financial Center for a final lunch. We went down to a restaurant off the Winter Garden and sat by a window overlooking the yachts in the marina.

"Mr. Stiles?" I heard. "Oh my God, I can't believe you're here!"

It was our waiter, a student at NYU and a former student of my father's. As I listened to them chat, I realized that here was my answer and his final lesson: a man's moral worth, and his net worth, were two very different things.

## P O W E R

### 20

I had reached bottom, and I knew it. Once again I was a roving associate. And I saw no way back up. Then, shortly before my parents' visit, Savegre asked me to lunch. He didn't say why, his secretary said—though I imagined some unpleasant possibilities.

We met at Moran's outdoor café on the edge of the World Financial Center marina. It was a hot day in late June. Savegre was smoking at a table when I arrived and wearing his reflective green glasses, the ones that made him look like The Fly. He looked agitated. His cigarette flicked rapidly in and out of his mouth. Oh shit, I thought, he is going to fire me. Surprisingly, I felt nothing at all after that, just the warmth of the day.

We ordered some sandwiches and chatted about trivialities. Then Savegre's expression turned serious. Whatever was coming, was coming.

"I've got a new job for you," he said. "Actually—three new jobs."

The warmth I had felt before didn't go away. Instead it grew hotter. Savegre explained that he wanted me to provide marketing support to three different groups: our Asian offices in Hong Kong and Tokyo; the Dealer desk on Seven, which traded with regional broker-dealers; and the Middle Markets group, a new sales group aimed at midsized institutions. That was it. After a quick lunch he left.

I wandered back up to IEM feeling no rise in interest, just relief over having not been fired. But over the next few days a number of things came together in my mind, prompted by what Savegre had said. I realized that if I wanted to survive in IEM I had to beat the system, instead of getting kicked around by it. I had to take charge of my destiny and create a world that made sense to *me*, not the Latin Mafia. That meant building my own business, with my own P&L, creating my own power base. And Savegre had given me the opportunity. One of his jobs sounded like just the springboard I needed. The other two were more servitude. So I decided to ditch them in the best IEM manner—by ignoring them—and focus on my own self-interest. It wasn't good for the group—but who cared? They had treated *me* that way and now it was payback time. Time to grab the bull by the horns.

Since the primary focus of Merrill Lynch is selling securities, the firm is cleft by a great divide based on the type of account it handles. On one side you have Private Client, which handles private investors and small corporate accounts; and on the other, Capital Markets, which handles major institutional business. Private Client, known informally as Retail, is primarily a sales organization and the historical core of the firm. Its thirteen thousand domestic financial consultants—the largest brokerage force in the country—are Merrill's most visible element, reaching 4.5 million American households. Capital Markets is a more diverse entity comprising investment banking, sales and trading, and research. It has its own sales element, Institutional Sales, which covers large institutional clients—corporations, mutual funds, commercial banks, insurance companies, state and local governments, broker-dealers, etc.—from offices in major financial centers worldwide. IEM Sales was one of its satellites.

These two organizations attract, and breed, different kinds of people, due primarily to the different natures of their operations. Retail brokers—the financial consultants found in your local Merrill Lynch office—run a low-volume, high-commission, less sophisticated, more entrepreneurial business in which they cover some of their own operating expenses and develop their own accounts, often by cold-calling the local phone book. Only a small percentage survives the first few years. The average résumé is someone who attended a state school, maintained passing grades, played a sport, was an active fraternity member, and somewhere along life's passage showed up at the door of the local brokerage. In contrast, Institutional salespeople work at the heart of the global capital markets, running a high-volume, low-commission business with fewer players and well-established client lists. The typical example is a young M.B.A. product of the academic-financial complex, someone who had his sights on Wall Street for a long time and paid his dues to get there.

These different personalities color how the two organizations view one another. To the Institutional elite, retail brokers are a bunch of used car salesmen hawking a few bucks worth of bonds to Mom and Pop—way, way down in the food chain. The brokers, in turn, either look on Institutional salespeople with grudging respect, envy, even awe, wishing they had taken economics, or—especially the older ones—view them as a bunch of arrogant, impudent little #@%&*!. The irony is, some of the highest-paid people at Merrill are retail brokers, as are most senior managers, though this is changing.

Retail and Institutional Sales have also had a long history of conflict exacerbated by these cultural differences but based primarily on business differences. One of the classic bones of contention has been clients. Since Retail was responsible for covering "small" institutions, and since its brokers had a natural desire to land the largest possible accounts, there was a natural tendency for Retail to cross over onto Institutional turf, especially since Retail had predated Institutional for many years, creating many entrenched relationships. When such coverage conflicts arose, they were typically resolved in an ad hoc fashion based on who knew whom in the firm, how big a producer the broker was, and how much Institutional Sales cared. Coverage policy was thus like the U.S. tax code: driven by special interests, each one demanding an exemption. As a result, Merrill developed a vast tangle of client relationships in that no-man's-land between the firm's two great sales powers, an area known as the middle market. There was no logical, systematic, firmwide means of matching the appropriate salesperson to a client, leading to great holes in coverage, half-baked coverage, and lost revenues.

In early 1994, the senior management of the firm set out to resolve this intractable problem once and for all. After a great deal of bickering and negotiation, Retail and Institutional Sales produced an agreement known as the Treaty, which divided all institutional business in the United States into three market segments—large market, middle market, and small market—based on the size and type of institution involved. The Treaty then assigned these market segments to specific sales organizations. The large market went to Institutional Sales, the small market went to Retail, and the middle market went to an entirely new group, also established by the Treaty, known as Middle Market Sales. Middle Markets, as it quickly came to be known, eventually comprised some two hundred and fifty salespeople, 30 percent taken from Institutional Sales and 70 percent from Retail, organized in twelve main hub offices—Chicago, Minneapolis, St. Louis, Boston, New York City, Philadelphia, Los Angeles, Seattle, Little Rock, Houston, San Diego, and San Francisco, each with its own smaller satellites.

Most important, from a political standpoint, the new group was organized *within* Retail, putting it squarely on one side of the organizational fence. This posed a challenge to the new group, since its brokers would have to source their products from Capital Markets, which ran all the trading desks, causing some to question whether the new effort would even succeed. How much support would Middle Markets get? There were other questions as well: Was there enough business in the middle market to justify their existence? Were the brokers competent enough to handle institutional business? Would retail offices poach their brokers back, having lost some of their top producers? Regardless of how much time and effort management had spent on the new group, its survival would ultimately depend on market forces, both inside and outside the firm.

From my standpoint, Middle Markets was just the opportunity I needed. As IEM's newly designated envoy to the group, I was tasked with helping them sell emerging markets bonds. I had no idea how many midsize institutions would be interested in buying them, but in my mind that wasn't the key issue. My assessment of the opportunity came strictly from my understanding of how IEM operated, particularly the two elements Savegre was responsible for, Sales and Marketing.

IEM Sales had six dedicated emerging markets specialists in the United States—four in our office, one in Chicago, and one in Dallas. As a practical matter six people could cover only so many accounts. Much of their time was spent on just a few big names, the ones that did all the volume trading. The rest of our institutional business came from the extremely spotty involvement of the main Institutional Sales force on Seven, which shied away from the complexities of our business and which we had never aggressively developed, due to the largess of the boom.

The boom had also emasculated our business development capability, a function normally provided by Marketing. With accounts coming through the window, who needed it? Business development was also predicated upon a desire to build *the group.* It required establishing a formal, systematic process for identifying and developing potential clients, the continual management of this process—including plenty of follow-up—and the application of leadership to all those involved. It demanded a proactive effort between Marketing and Sales, a unified, team-oriented approach. In other words, it was anathema to the Latin Mafia. The result was IEM Marketing: a weak and timid organ of Sales used primarily for the production of graphs, briefings, and the Brady Sheet. We had no means of identifying who was entering or leaving the market other than the grapevine. Unlike our major competitors—Chase, Chemical, Salomon—who were frequently seen in industry journals or giving speeches at conferences, IEM didn't even advertise itself.

Consequently, given our limited sales force and our deficient marketing, I figured there had to be a number of potential clients we were missing in both the middle *and* large markets. Indeed, one day I picked up *The Financial Times*, which had a special supplement on the emerging markets, compared its list of advertisers against our client list, and found more holes than matches. I also knew that regardless of how big the opportunity was, management was not about to hire the new salesperson necessary to pursue it. The Latin Mafia's personnel decisions revolved largely around the bonus pool, the pot of profits retained to pay everyone's annual bonus, especially theirs. And with the group's profits down, that pool was already shallow enough without dipping another cup into it. The idea was to wring as much profit as possible from what we had, not grow the group.

This left only one solution in my mind: use the new Middle Markets Group. Middle Markets brokers were free institutional salespeople—we didn't have to pay them a bonus—they were eager to develop new business, and they were used to aggressive cold calling, which was just what we needed. Why not have them cover all those idle emerging markets accounts? Some were even large market accounts, making them especially attractive to them. Sure, they knew nothing about the emerging markets yet; but as we all knew, ignorance meant nothing in Wall Street's Latin boomtown.

The idea expanded from there. If I could put together a team of brokers to sell our product, I would, in effect, have my own sales force. This was exactly what I wanted: a chance to build my own unique business and operate autonomously, unhindered by the office food chain. No one, of course, expected me to achieve anything like this. I was an outsider. No one had even bothered to train me. But it was this very fact that energized me most, the deep feeling that winning would be justice.

Attack, Sun-tzu said of the enemy, where he is unprepared; sally out when he does not expect you.

Once the Middle Markets organization had come together, its head, Joe DePalma, set out to familiarize its brokers with the Capital Markets trading desks. DePalma planned two-week-long seminars in New York in which the various desks were to meet the brokers and give briefings on their products, hopefully sparking some new alliances and smoothing the organizational transition. As part of this effort, Savegre agreed to provide a briefing on the emerging markets. He then asked me to give it.

The news surprised me, stimulating a mild panic. I had recently managed to pass the Series 7, but I was hardly qualified to fill in for Savegre. The Middle Markets required an hour-long briefing covering the full spectrum of our business, with a focus on sales. My experience so far had been limited to the Brady Sheet and one esoteric derivative. Did Savegre know what he was doing? I wondered why he was putting so much confidence in me and if he realized how little I knew. Or was this his way of breaking people in? As usual, there were no answers to such questions. Instead I scrambled to learn everything I needed to know about the emerging markets—and quickly. The seminars were only ten days away.

A period of intense and focused work followed, which lasted until my debut. In that time I created a presentation that covered the history and instruments of the emerging markets, how to get involved, and why. I pitched the middle market as the natural next step in the development of our business, dropped in lures about high commissions and the potential for large accounts, and preached the benefits of high yield, international diversification, liquidity, and dollar denomination. I also put together a questionnaire that would identify those brokers with the greatest potential—a clever suggestion of Savegre's—its cover emblazoned with "IEM Middle Market Group." Hey, you need a name. But when all this work was done, there was still a very real chance I would blow the briefing. My knowledge was dangerously thin, even by IEM standards. One probing question could pierce the facade. This left me with a gnawing anxiety that prevented me from relaxing in my trial runs. It was not just the thought of public humiliation, though that was certainly a factor. It was also the thought of losing my credibility with the Middle Markets. I had to convince some of them to join my team—or there wouldn't be one.

During my preparations I went down to see DePalma, who was organizing the seminars, in search of information. I found him in an office on Seven, just outside the entrance to the trading floor. DePalma was a chubby, middle-aged suit with a rotund, shiny face and a perpetual grin, as if he took no one seriously. He gave me the latest list of all the Middle Markets brokers, indicated a few names to call, and handed me a copy of the Treaty. He didn't seem to take much interest in the emerging markets, becoming even more aloof when I mentioned Savegre's name. Savegre and DePalma had worked together before and disliked each other. Savegre thought DePalma was a control freak; DePalma thought Savegre was Savegre. I was in the middle.

A few days later DePalma called me to see how our preparations were coming. Savegre wasn't returning his calls, he announced, revealing a haughty annoyance. I told him I was almost done with the briefing.

"*You're* doing the briefing?" He paused, his tone hardening. "Raoul told me *he* was doing the briefing."

Poor DePalma. Instead of the promised managing director, his troops were going to be addressed by a mere associate. What a stick in his eye!

"Is Raoul there?" DePalma whined.

I sought out Savegre, who told me to say he was out.

"Have him call me," DePalma said coldly and hung up.

I didn't speak with DePalma again until the day before the briefing, when I called him to confirm the time. "By the way, I finally got hold of Raoul," he told me. "Don't worry, *he's* doing the briefing." He laughed at my expense—silly associate!

More confused than ever, I located Savegre and relayed what I had heard. Savegre smiled craftily, hiding some bright inner amusement. "Did he say that? Well . . . don't worry about him. You're still on."


The first Middle Markets seminar was held July 20 at the Millenium Hotel, an opaque, spotless domino named after the black monolith in *2001: A Space Odyssey.* Leave it to New York: the Empire State Building, the World Trade Center, the World Financial Center, the Millenium, the Big Apple, the Capital of the World, the Monolith of God—sometimes you wonder why they don't just rename the whole island Manhubris. I walked over with Savegre and waited in an empty conference room for the brokers to arrive. They were late from their briefing next door. Never one to stop moving, Savegre popped out into the lobby to incinerate a few Camels and use the phone. The brokers finally arrived, about thirty in all, and began filling in the chairs. I stood in front of the room eyeing them, wondering where Savegre was, and fighting off a major anxiety attack. The entire situation seemed absurd: there I was, ready to stand up and speak about emerging markets bonds, or at least pontificate on what I had taught myself about them, while everyone I was addressing had more experience in the bond business than me—some with twenty years or more. The small, tightly packed gathering made it even worse. I was meeting eyes with virtually everyone. I glanced nervously over the seminar program, hoping to avoid their inspection, and noticed a change in the schedule: DePalma had cut my time in half.

Savegre finally appeared and walked down the center aisle. "Ready?" he asked me.

"They've cut our time—"

He turned and faced the crowd. "If I can have your attention, why don't we begin." He introduced himself and briefly welcomed his audience. "Thank you all for coming. We're all very excited about the Middle Markets effort and we in International Emerging Markets hope that we can be of assistance to you in the upcoming months. Now, since we are running late, let me introduce the speaker . . ."

Savegre nodded to me and sat down in the front row. For a brief moment I felt that this was not really happening, that it was not really me standing here in the Millenium Hotel in New York about to give a talk on bonds, but that I was really back in Annapolis fishing on the Severn River. Then I stepped up in front of the overhead projector and started flipping through my transparencies. I spoke too rapidly, accelerated by tight nerves and a shortened time frame. It caused some minor inconsistencies and lapses of memory that I quickly papered over with spontaneous creativity. Savegre undoubtedly approved.

Fifteen minutes later I had just reached Brady bonds, the core of my presentation, when DePalma showed up. He sat in back, frowning. A few seconds later he interrupted: "I'm sorry, folks, but to keep you on schedule we're going to have to cut this one a little short."

Short! I just *started*!

"Let me quickly hand out these questionnaires then," I said.

"We may not have time for that, ah, Paul," DePalma chortled.

Savegre stood up and loudly cleared his throat. "If you would," he announced to the rising crowd, "please fill out one of these questionnaires before leaving the room. Paul will collect them at the door."

He turned to me with a burning glare of irritation—"See you back at the office"—and walked swiftly down the aisle, his eyes vacuuming the floor. DePalma tried intercepting him at the exit, but holding on to Savegre was like squeezing a wet bar of soap. I heard something about "questionnaires" from DePalma, something about "time" from Savegre, and then the two were separated by a growing space.

Over the next week, relations between DePalma and Savegre worsened. After my presentation, the brokers were scheduled to take a cruise up the Hudson on the *Majestic,* a party boat docked in the World Financial Center marina. DePalma wouldn't let me go, claiming there wasn't enough room. Then DePalma called to inform me that I couldn't hand out questionnaires at the next briefing—he had his own to give out at the end. When Savegre heard that, his patience broke. "Wait here a minute," he said as I stood by his position. He picked up the phone and got DePalma on the line.

Savegre wasn't good at getting mad. He didn't put the fear of God in anyone. His anger was more like that of a perturbed logician. "You know, Joe," he said, "I fail to see the sense in this policy of yours. If you're asking us to help *you* out by giving *your* people a briefing, then at least you could help *us* out by letting *us* hand out a few questionnaires—don't you think?"

The conversation ended abruptly and Savegre slammed down the phone. It was the last time he ever spoke to DePalma about Middle Markets. During my next presentation, which went more smoothly, neither one of them showed up. Afterward I stowed away on the boat cruise and met a number of brokers. DePalma was there and tried to avoid me. I said hello, hoping to separate myself from his conflict with Savegre, but to him I was just another young Institutional guy and inextricably linked to my boss. He granted me a hello-ha-ha in passing and wandered off with a cocktail in his hand. In the following weeks he instituted a weekly conference call for Middle Markets in which the various trading desks of the firm were supposed to participate. IEM's allotted time kept getting moved back due to a perpetual "scheduling conflict." I steered clear of him after that.

Once the seminars were over I focused on building a sales force. I called Middle Market office managers and asked who might be interested; I reviewed the results of my questionnaires; and I began calling specific brokers. I talked frankly about the opportunity the emerging markets presented, trying hard not to sound too much like a salesman—they were well attuned to that—and stressing the personal support I was willing to provide. In this way I built a loose network of people in different parts of the country who were interested in receiving more information. I connected this network to me via electronic mail and proceeded to lend them as much support as possible in order to make them comfortable with the market and me. I sent them daily messages on conference calls, news events, and trades; I put them on distribution lists for research and new issue prospectuses; and I called them regularly, keeping IEM fresh in their minds. After a while some of the brokers began calling me back and asking questions, teaching me as much as I was teaching them.

Meanwhile I began the search for prospective clients—the best way to attract a sales force. This was really an intelligence problem, a matter of defining an information requirement and identifying the resources to meet it. My top priority was building a list of all those institutions that currently invested in the emerging markets. Then I could compare these names against the IEM client list and determine which accounts were uncovered. This was no small task, however. Within the enormous investor universe, there were literally thousands of potential clients of all kinds—corporations, commercial banks, thrifts, credit unions, insurance companies, mortgage companies, universities, endowments, foundations, pension funds, investment advisors, mutual funds, state and local governments, and broker-dealers. Some whole groups I could exclude right away because regulations forbade their investing in risky bonds. But how to sort through the rest? No one in the office knew of any resource listing who invested in the emerging markets other than the grapevine.

I approached the problem from many different angles, with varying degrees of success. Given the chaotic way our office worked, I suspected that some of our clients had drifted away in the boom and searched our computers for old coverage lists. I found a few names this way. I also compared our coverage list with the client list of our investment bankers, who had close relationships with numerous Latin bond issuers, many of them potential trading accounts. Communication in our office was so bad that many of their clients were not being covered by Sales. I also tried to obtain the coverage lists of other desks, namely emerging markets equities and junk bonds. Suspicion prevented me from going through normal channels, but secretaries weren't always so security conscious.

Our office was also full of people who had come from other Wall Street firms, usually from another emerging markets group. Each of them typically had a Rolodex of business cards sitting next to his computer, full of contacts past and present. I asked these people to flip through their files and identify any prospects for me, especially people they had lost contact with since coming to Merrill. I got a weak response from Trading—they were too busy or couldn't be bothered. Sales was even worse: openly suspicious. As a matter of policy, Sales didn't discuss their Rolodexes with anyone and was not in the habit of giving clients away—certainly not to Retail! This made me conscious of an important new dynamic: I was no longer supporting Sales but in competition with them.

Beyond the firm I sought to use whatever commercial resources were available. When I discovered that a book on emerging markets mutual funds was being written, I obtained a manuscript copy. I flipped through newspapers, magazines, and trade pamphlets looking for advertisers or news stories that revealed who invested in our market. When I saw an announcement for an emerging markets seminar, many of which were held in New York, I would call the organizer and get a list of attendees. This was an excellent way of pinpointing investors *thinking* of entering the market. I also tried to identify clients by the information sources *they* used; for instance, by getting a list of subscribers to a Latin American financial news service or magazine. One way to obtain such closely held information was by arranging a swap with your marketing counterpart: my client list for yours.

The most productive resource was corporate bond holdings, which were filed periodically with various regulatory bodies—the Internal Revenue Service, the Securities & Exchange Commission, the National Association of Insurance Commissioners. These were available through a single commercial software package, providing me with a sixty-page list of institutions across the United States that held emerging markets bonds. I was so impressed with the software that I even arranged a demonstration for Savegre. The vendor showed up; Savegre didn't.

Once I had developed a lead, I had to make sure it wasn't covered by another salesperson in the firm. This was a serious matter: Merrill Lynch salespeople were prone to get highly upset if another salesperson called their accounts. At the same time you couldn't pry their coverage lists away from them, making it impossible to check beforehand. The solution was the client database for the entire firm, a well-defended treasure which listed every institution in the United States, who if anyone covered it—sometimes there were multiple salespeople—what product they sold, and how much they had earned the previous year. Once I had secured the security code—a major scraping triumph—I was even able to pull it up from my position. This tremendous resource, which no one in IEM had ever heard of, was the final piece in the marketing puzzle. In addition to my broad antenna for detecting potential new clients, I now had a filter for deciding which ones I could pursue.

I was so excited by the power of this new mechanism that I ignored all my office lessons and wrote down my findings for Savegre. I described all the resources I had uncovered to date and how they formed a very broad, thorough, systematic process for identifying potential new clients. I put it on his desk and never received a reply.

The apex of my research efforts occurred shortly thereafter. One of the traders, whom I had approached about his Rolodex, came over to my position and handed me a floppy disk that had been languishing in his desk drawer. It had some information from his old firm, he said. Check it out. I inserted it in my computer, clicked open a file called "93 List," and stopped breathing. MORGAN STANLEY EMERGING MARKETS CLIENT LIST, said the beautiful screen, followed by a long list of institutions, points of contact, and phone numbers. A warm sense of perfect satisfaction spread across my body. And they had said the fit wasn't right. . . .


While digging up leads I decided to refine my approach to the Middle Markets. I had thrown my net wide, exposing my effort to as many brokers as possible, but since the emerging markets was a specialized business, since I could only support so many people, and since there was, ultimately, a limited number of leads to follow, I decided to split my sales force into two groups, generalists and specialists, much as IEM did. The generalists would be like the Institutional Sales force on Seven: people who sold emerging markets bonds on a part-time, ad hoc basis to clients who had a limited interest in our product. Meanwhile I would focus on developing a few dedicated specialists—like IEM Sales—who would concentrate on the emerging markets, pursue the leads, develop the new accounts, do the bulk of the business, and receive most of my support. Otherwise I would be spreading the business, and my time, too thinly. Over time, three such specialists emerged, each of them in the heart of the market—New York—forming a new Core Group.

The first to step forward was Costas Kerasidis, a Retail broker in Merrill's Rockefeller Center office. Costas had $150 million under management—the size of a small hedge fund. He was a perpetual member of Merrill's "Circle of Excellence," an annual title bestowed upon those Retail brokers who surpassed a million dollars in commissions, earning them a firm-sponsored trip abroad. Two of his clients were Lisardo Escobar, the head of IEM, whom he had met in his apartment building years before, and the head of IEM's investment banking operations in London. Having traded emerging markets bonds for them, Costas had a basic knowledge of our instruments and thought that the expansion of the emerging markets into the middle market was a prime business opportunity. He called me one day out of the blue and stopped by later for a visit.

Costas was a tall, handsome Greek of forty-four with enough old-world charm to disarm the guards at Fort Knox. A former Greek paratrooper who had once run a shipping office in Jeddah, he was worldly and wise, yet without any hardness or pretense. Kind, genteel, soft-spoken, he projected a civility uncommon in the brokerage community. When he walked onto the trading floor with a quiet dignity, his London Fog raincoat strapped firmly around his waist, and extended a warm hand, it was impossible not to like him.

We spoke briefly about Middle Markets.

"I think there's a tremendous opportunity here," I told him. "You would be surprised how many clients are not covered by this office."

"Well, I would like to help you out there, of course, however I can."

"I'm trying to put together an effort to fill in the holes."

"Ah, I see," Costas purred. "Well, it's simple, really. I would be happy to call on some of these accounts and tell them, you know, that I am working with you, in this new venture, here at Merrill Lynch, and ask if they are covered by the firm, for the emerging markets, of course, and if not—well then, I'll tell them, you are covered. It is simple—you are covered now, that is all. In this way you can expand your business, and I can expand mine."

"Sounds good to me."

Costas waited patiently while I took a call, then said, "Paul, my partner and I, Frank Russo, we were wondering, if you had some time, perhaps later this week, if you would like to go out to dinner. It would be an opportunity to talk more about this business, you understand, and I think you would like to meet Frank."

"Sure."

"I will call you then, tomorrow." Costas extended a warm hand. "Thank you very much. It was good to meet you. I will see you soon." He strolled off the floor.

Later that week I met Costas and Russo at Periyali, an elegant Greek restaurant off Fifth Avenue. We sat out on the enclosed brick patio, where Costas chatted amicably with the waiter in his native tongue. He and Russo were regulars there, and decidedly different sorts. An Italian raised in Queens, Russo had slicked-back hair, à la Gordon Gekko, and a brash manner. He lived almost two hours from the city, in Croton-on-Hudson, where he parked his cigarette boat. Holding a fistful of olives, he popped them in his mouth one by one.

In contrast, Costas was a very European epicure. While the waiter stood by our table, he took charge of the menu in a confident, relaxed manner, studying the text closely and speaking in measured, weighted syllables while drawing his fingers together, as if expounding the tenets of a profound philosophy.

"Paul, do you like caviar?"

"I love it."

"Okay then, why don't we begin with some *taramasalata* for an appetizer. It's fine black caviar. Then perhaps . . . some spinach pie. Is that acceptable? And let's see . . . some grilled vegetables?"

"Yeah, get the grilled vegetables," Russo said. "I love that stuff."

"Does that sound reasonable?"

"Sounds great," I said.

"Now, the main course. Anything that interests you? There is a great variety. I know the lamb is very good, and the beef . . . do you like shish kebab?"

"Sure."

"I recommend the lamb shish kebab. It's excellent here."

"All right. I'll do that."

"Is that what you want? I don't want to decide for you."

"No, that's fine. I like lamb."

"Fine. Now, for the wine. I thought we'd try the retsina. This is a Greek wine made with resin. It has a distinct flavor. Not everyone likes it—it is a bit of an acquired taste—but while you are here, well, I thought you might like to try it."

I agreed. Costas turned to the waiter, uncorking a gentle stream of Greek, interspersed with shrugs, entreaties, suggestions, and at last formal thanks.

Then we turned to business. Our discussion focused on the potential of Middle Markets, what my plans were, and how they could participate in them, and lasted throughout a marvelous dinner that arrived in courses and never seemed to end. Russo took the lead, stressing his cold-calling ability in no uncertain terms. He was ready to scour the United States for clients, he said. He loved prospecting. He was the prospecting king. He would call anyone, anywhere. Costas added his support here and there but let Russo handle the brunt of their argument, choosing to smooth over the rough spots. It was clear he didn't do the cold calling himself. Like many Retail partnerships, the two brought different skills to the table.

"My only concern," I told Costas, "is that you're not a Middle Markets broker. You're Retail."

"Not a problem," Russo interrupted. "I'm Middle Markets."

"You are?"

"I will be once they finalize the list."

"You see, Paul," Costas explained, leaning forward, "when we do a trade, Frank will write the ticket. That way it will be counted as Middle Markets. It's a minor administrative matter. For the accountants really."

Our meal concluded with Costas choosing a number of Greek desserts and Metaxa cognac and Russo extracting a promise from me to provide a list of leads as soon as possible. Cognac in one hand, leads in the other—how could I refuse?


The second member of the Core Group was Tim Avery. Tim worked in the South Tower, Merrill's other building in the four-pronged World Financial Center and the home of its largest Middle Markets operation. He came highly recommended by Breen, who had placed a sizable chunk of a new issue through one of Tim's clients. After hearing this, I called Tim up and arranged to meet him after work.

I arrived shortly after market close and quickly got lost. The fourth floor of the

South Tower was a maze of square carrels that easily spun your compass. Each one was a little plot of land tilled by a broker and owned by Merrill Lynch. I passed scores of these fiefs, the brokers eyeing me while talking on the phone, looking defensive. The air was heavy with the tension of a border crossing. Life in the carrels was a daily contest decided at the end of the month by the production statistics posted on the wall. In that battle each broker's precious relationships, their life-giving trading activity, their golden leads were all closely guarded secrets, breeding suspicion and silence. The only thing that ever managed to unify them was their common enemy, Institutional Sales, the account thief. And I was one of its emissaries.

I finally located Tim Avery in his carrel. He was a rugged, soft-spoken midwesterner in his early fifties. Like Costas, he had a partner, Lou Palermo, a short, stocky, mustached Italian from Staten Island who occupied the adjacent cubicle and looked like he could bench press the North Tower. The three of us retreated to a conference room in back. Both men were extremely cautious, saying little to each other or me. Unlike Costas, Tim already had an institutional account buying emerging markets bonds: was I there to take it? I went through the entire seminar briefing receiving little feedback. By the time I finished it was late. I broached the matter of working together, but Tim and Lou were noncommittal. They wanted to talk it over. I left not knowing how I had been received.

The next day, determined more than ever to convince Tim to join my effort, I handed over four leads. Within a few days he had landed a new client and we were going out for drinks. We met at the Hudson River Club, an elegant, well-known, scenic bar and restaurant located at the entrance to the North Tower and brimming with Wall Street. Tim arrived with Lou and bought me a beer; he knew the bartender well. We all stood at the polished wooden bar talking about how we had ended up at Merrill, while darkness fell on the river outside. Tim had spent fifteen years at a midtown commercial bank before making the switch—for the money, he said. He liked the money, but the biggest mistake he ever made had been moving from Maryland to New York: he and his wife had never been able to re-create their circle of friends. Now forty-seven, he lived in Madison, New Jersey, and had two kids. Lou had met him two years before, during their first week at the firm. He had many years in the business, first at Drexel Burnham, the now defunct junk bond palace, then at Dean Witter. They had been close partners ever since.

Like most broker partnerships, Tim and Lou each had his own interests, clients, and skills. According to Lou, Tim was the master of the cold call.

"That's how we work," he joked. "Timmy ropes 'em in and I sell 'em."

"Well, you've landed *one* already," I said.

Tim beseeched me with open hands and a wry grin: "Give me more."

"I've got plenty."

He cocked one eye, regarding me with mock earnestness. "I want 'em."

I explained my goal of establishing a Core Group and Tim seemed interested. He was the one focusing on the emerging markets, he said, having had a long-standing interest in international affairs. I asked if they knew anyone else in the South Tower who might be interested and they both rolled their eyes.

"Yeah, us," Tim said, reaching for a cigarette.

"I'm serious."

"So am I."

"You gotta understand," Lou said. "Those people are the enemy. We don't talk to them, they don't talk to us."

"You have to be careful," Tim said, nodding gravely.

"I've still got to talk to them."

"Sure," Lou said, "we know that—but just don't talk about *us*, know what I'm sayin'?" He laughed, but the point was made. "I learned that the hard way at Dean Witter, didn't I, Tim?"

"He did."

"What happened?" I asked.

"What do you think? They took my best accounts away! There was a big producer in the office and he wanted them and they had to keep him happy, so they took 'em. Boom! just like that. That's how it works."

"Listen to him," Tim said. "I've learned a lot from Lou."

"The one thing I've learned in this business is to keep my mouth shut, know what I'm sayin'? Open your mouth and the next thing you know, boom! there go your accounts."

"Has that happened here?"

"No, not *yet*—I wouldn't be here if it had. But that's not to say it *can't* happen. Believe me, this place is no different than anyplace else."

"It isn't," Tim said.

"The thing to do is just stay away from people."

That sounded so odd it made me laugh.

"I'm *serious*," Lou stressed. "Just stay away from 'em. That's what I do—we both do. I come in, I nod, I say hello, and that's it."

"He's even worse on weekends," Tim joked.

"Who, me?" Lou clutched his heart with a theatrical flourish and a chuckle. "It's true," he explained. "When I get out of this place I don't want to see *anybody*. I'm *serious*. On the weekend, just leave me alone. I'd rather sit in my basement."

Tim took a more even-tempered approach, at least on the surface. He always displayed an unbreakable stoicism, one that resisted any emotional tide, high or low. No change in the market, the firm, or his fortunes ever appeared to move him.

After Lou left for home, Tim invited me to dinner. We took a table in the dining room overlooking the World Financial Center marina, where he revealed some of his philosophy. "You can't let this place get to you," he said, lighting yet another cigarette. "If you take it home, it's a mess. You've got to learn to blow off steam." He lifted his third martini. "Cheers."


The final member of the Core Group was Lee Sullivan. Lee worked in the newly designated Middle Markets office on Fifth Avenue. He was fairly new to the brokerage side of the firm, having spent most of his five years at Merrill doing marketing work for the Money Markets desk on Seven. But five years in Lee's life was fifty to the average man.

Lee rushed into my life one morning on the trading floor—and I do mean rushed. Lee never did less. He moved at the speed of Lee, something just short of light. He was without par: the fastest-talking, fastest-moving broker on the Street—and that's saying something. Lee would enter the trading floor, pat someone on the back, shake three hands, make five comments, pick up research, make two phone calls, and be gone all in the space of three minutes, as if timed by an Olympic judge. He did more in one day than anyone else I have ever known—shooting uptown, buzzing downtown, meeting clients and salespeople, visiting all floors of the North Tower. He covered all markets, all the time, read all the latest research, listened to all the conference calls, knew all the people involved, and always had the inside scoop—on Merrill Lynch, the market, and New York too. He never paused, not even for a moment. His hands were always adjusting his glasses, running through his hair, shaking your hand. Just being near him made you tired. What propelled him on his way was a mystery, however. Lee had a fastidious attraction to the game—there was always something new to do, to learn, keeping him moving—but there was such urgency to his motion, you wondered whether he was chasing something, or fleeing from it.

We went down to the atrium for coffee and talked business for an hour—the opportunity Middle Markets presented, how to get business going, my Core Group idea, how it would work. Lee was interested in joining the effort. Like Tim, he had an interest in international markets and needed to build his client list, having recently made the switch to Middle Markets. As a former marketing person on Seven, he gave me a few valuable pointers on how to proceed—politically as well as organizationally. Lee had worked with Savegre in Money Markets; he knew how he operated.

Once I got past Lee's nonstop delivery, I saw that there was more to him than velocity. Lee was forty-one, married, had two kids, and lived in the Village. He was on his second career, having come to Merrill from a prestigious New York law firm, was very bright, with an insightful intelligence, and had a big heart, no doubt aided by the perspective of a midcareer change. He may have been fast moving but he thought about people along the way.

Luckily, Lee was drinking decaf. By the end of our sojourn he had relaxed enough to contemplate the summer, which shimmered through the window. "God, it's great out, isn't it? Sometimes I think I'll just kick this whole racket, send the kids off to school, and live in a studio in the Village. I dream about that. Really."

I offered to give Lee some client leads and we returned to IEM. Together with Costas and Tim, I had the Core Group I wanted. Now it was time to do some business.

While I was building the Middle Markets Group, one of the premier emerging markets, Venezuela, was in the process of falling apart. Problems had first come to light back in January when Banco Latino, the country's second largest bank, collapsed beneath the weight of its own corruption. Latino had been run by some of the most powerful men in Venezuela, a tight web of insiders with high political connections. The brother of the Venezuelan president, Carlos Andres Perez, had sat on the board. The president of the bank had married the daughter of one of the major shareholders and also worked on the political campaign of his predecessor, a man who had left to run the Central Bank—thanks to President Perez. Some of the Latino board meetings were even *held* at the Central Bank—the equivalent of Merrill's Executive Committee holding court at the U.S. Treasury.

Latino's directors led lavish, *Miami Vice* lifestyles, replete with fast cars, corporate jets, and luxurious homes, some of them in Miami itself. They also pursued brash business practices, which alienated other parts of the Venezuelan banking industry and went unquestioned by regulators. Their simultaneous looting and mismanagement of the bank became so well known in Caracas, however, that it eventually caused a run on deposits, leading to the bank's failure. Shortly thereafter, amid allegations of criminal misconduct—payoffs to politicians, pilfering of assets, business schemes to enrich the directors—arrest warrants were issued for the bank's top managers, most of whom had already fled to Miami after destroying the bank's records. Their chief ally, former President Perez, could no longer protect them: he had been impeached for embezzling $17 million in public funds.

The new Venezuelan president, Rafael Caldera, was left to deal with the mess. Caldera tried to paint Latino as an isolated case, but public confidence was shaken—over 20 percent of the country's savings was frozen in Latino—causing a run on other banks, which needed a continuous cash infusion from the government to stay open. By June $3.5 billion had left Venezuela for safer foreign climes and $2.8 billion had been spent propping up the banks, decreasing foreign currency reserves to worrisome levels and bringing in the regulators. On June 14, the Venezuelan government seized control of eight failing banks, freezing over half the country's bank accounts and triggering a social crisis. With unemployment high, inflation high, and a devaluing currency, rioting broke out throughout the country. The mood darkened when arrest warrants were issued for top officials of two of the seized banks—the money used to prop them up could not be accounted for. President Caldera then suspended many of the constitutional rights of Venezuelan citizens, allegedly to better deal with the crisis. Rumors of military plots circled the capital—the military's retirement and employment benefits were still frozen in Banco Latino. And a crime wave struck Caracas. In 1994, the city's four million people suffered two hundred killings a month, most of them perpetrated by armed young men in the slums ringing the capital. Shootouts with rival drug gangs were common. People were killed for their sneakers.

In the market, the crisis was viewed as an isolated incident rather than a general warning. The price of Venezuela plunged; the price of Mexico did not.


## 21

Our new jobs in New York quickly changed how Sarah and I conducted our marriage. Much of the time, we never saw each other because Sarah was traveling two to three weeks a month. We communicated by phone instead: she would place a nightly call from the road. When she was working out of New Haven we didn't have a great deal of time together either. During the week, we would both arrive home around seven-thirty and be asleep by ten-thirty. This gave us three hours in which to cook, eat, do the dishes, walk the dog, do some errands—like going to the dry cleaners—and prepare for work the next day. If we had any free time we generally collapsed on the couch, put our feet up, and tried not to think or talk. Television was perfect for that. Then it was up at six to repeat the cycle. By the time Friday rolled around we were exhausted. Our Friday ritual became coming home and going to sleep early. Then, on the weekend, one day was typically dedicated to those errands we had put off during the week, like getting the car fixed or food shopping. This left us with one day a week to ourselves, usually Saturday.

During our first few months in New York we consistently spent our free day trying to escape the city. To us New York represented everything that made our new lives so hectic and chaotic. We were in its grip, Monday through Friday. So when our day of freedom arrived we reflexively sought to break its hold and rediscover that peace of mind we had once known. These escape trips were almost always spontaneously conducted since there was no time for planning during the week. We would wake up Saturday morning, feel a sudden desire to flee, put the dog in the car, open a map, and take off. Some journeys were pure sight-seeing; the environs of the New York megalopolis were new to us. We would follow the Hudson north in search of views, space, good air, and fewer people. On other trips, we decided to check out real estate, indulging our fantasy of moving from Brooklyn. We drove into New Jersey—Summit, Madison, Chatham, Harding, Fort Lee, and

Alpine. We explored Bronxville, Riverdale, and Larchmont, New York. We made the mandatory pilgrimage to Greenwich, a Wall Street stronghold, and went as far as Stamford. We saw some beautiful homes. But in the end these trips just made things worse. We were searching for something we never found, a serenity we could not achieve. There was always the nagging feeling that we were kidding ourselves, that when the fun was over we were going back to Brooklyn. Sure, we could buy a house—in a few years. In a moderately priced area. If the emerging markets didn't collapse in the meantime. If Sarah didn't get laid off. If we wanted to make a major financial commitment, tying us to a life we questioned, in a place we were escaping to rather than drawn to, for reasons that were no longer clear. Instead of looking forward to the future, we wondered where it had gone. It had somehow slipped from our hands without our noticing. Now, instead of shaping it, we were being shaped ourselves, by a force beyond our control.

And that force lay in New York. I began to identify the city with it: it was a vise and we were in it. No matter where we went, I could not erase its presence from my mind. Walking in the far woods of Harding, New Jersey, I knew that the megalopolis was over there somewhere, a great rusty engine thrusting its gears in the air, clanking, roaring, spitting, calling us back. A mass of millions warping the fabric of space and pulling us into its orbit. The hand of its gravity was long and strong: you could not escape it.

Some of these feelings I broached with Sarah. Others I didn't. They were, like the city, a constant presence with both of us but a sore point we didn't want to recognize. It was the weekend—we wanted to enjoy these few moments together. There was so little time! If such feelings did emerge, they were prone to cause an argument as we unleashed our pent-up emotions on each other. So we tried not to mention them, or the jobs that caused them, hoping for a respite from the market.

The return home was usually silent. We would stay away until the last possible moment and come back in the dark. The contrast in moods was stark: that morning our trip had been cause for hope; by evening it had tightened the screws.


By June we had both decided that these day trips weren't working. We were returning to work on Monday feeling no better than Friday. So at the end of the month, prompted by Sarah's twenty-seventh birthday, we decided to go away overnight, hoping that a longer period of absence would allow us to shake off the city and relax.

A country inn seemed like just the thing. I bought a book on the subject and found the perfect place: a bed-and-breakfast located on a farm two hours west of the city. Not only did it sound attractive, but the owner bred Jack Russell terriers—Tugger could come too. I took this as a positive omen and made a reservation.

We drove up early Saturday morning propelled by visions of rustic charm, nature trails, and freshly baked bread. Our anticipation grew as we exited from the highway and started following our handwritten directions. The countryside looked a bit rough—a lot of rural shacks dotted the roadside—but these things can change quickly enough. Then we reached one of our directional landmarks, Wanda's Restaurant, which turned out to be a strip bar in a hayfield. The inn was a half mile down the road.

We rolled up to the foot of the driveway and paused. "Oh *no* . . ." Sarah groaned. The "inn," a term of liberal usage, was poised on the brink of collapse. It had a sagging roof, peeling paint, and was seemingly held together by a net of dead ivy. Surrounding it were various outbuildings of a mass-produced variety, creating the impression of a small mobile home park. We didn't even bother to knock—the inn was definitely out.

"Don't worry," I said, trying to sound upbeat, "it's early. It's only . . . eleven. There's bound to be another place around."

"Did you bring the inn book?" Sarah asked.

I froze, staring straight ahead. "I thought you did . . ."

And so the great inn search began. It stretched clear across New York, from the Pennsylvania line to Cornwall-on-Hudson, and from there all the way across to Southport, Connecticut, interspersed with various stops at local chambers of commerce, visitors' information booths, and police stations, motivated by interesting map coordinates, and ultimately landing us on the doorstep of various innkeepers, all of whom said the same thing: no dogs, no vacancies, or, most often, both. By the time we finally gave up after eight hours of driving we were facing a night at a Holiday Inn on Route 1, somewhere south of Greenwich.

"You know," I finally suggested, "let's just go home."

And we did.


From that disastrous foray we learned a lesson about the local demographics. If you wanted to move about the New York megalopolis, you had to outplan the masses and sneak in the dog. But that defeated part of the purpose of escaping. One of life's simple pleasures is the ability to be spontaneous and move about at will. It's a matter of liberty. So rather than deny ourselves that liberty, we decided to outrun the problem. The very next weekend we departed on a spontaneous trip to the Catskill Mountains. Looking at this large green splotch on the map, I didn't see how the megalopolis could defeat us there. The Catskills were a hundred miles away. There were lots of inns and bed-and-breakfasts, and if all else failed, motels. The rest of it—the vast majority—was woods, national park, the Great Outdoors. It sounded like just what we needed and a far more fitting birthday present than a Holiday Inn on Route 1.

It was also the Fourth of July weekend. The traffic crawling upstate was the first clue that my theory was deficient and the reach of the mighty megalopolis stretched farther than expected, but by then, of course, it was too late. Armed with our book of inns, we drove from town to town at a leisurely pace, expecting to see the Catskills and find a hotel at the same time. We saw a lot of the Catskills; we never found an inn. The dog wasn't even an issue this time: there were no vacancies anywhere.

Stymied, we paused in one hillside town to rethink the situation.

"This is beginning to feel awfully familiar," Sarah said as we sat on the curb.

"I know."

"I'm beginning to think you're a bad date."

"So am I."

Then the obvious solution appeared—why not go camping? We were, after all, in the wilderness. I suggested this to Sarah and she quickly warmed up to the idea: "That's great! Why didn't we think of that before?"

"I don't know," I admitted. "All we need is a tent and some food!"

Our spirits rising, we set off in search of provisions. It turned out to be more difficult than we thought to find a two-man tent in the Catskills, but after hopping through a few towns we finally located one in a sporting goods store, bought a cooler, and filled it up with ice and food. Back in the car we broke out the map and had a look. The Catskills cover a huge area. It was early afternoon. We had plenty of time to wander about and find a camping space. "At least we don't have to worry about a vacancy," I said. "There must be a million acres around here!"

We started driving. We stayed off the main roads in favor of the thinnest lines on the map, then took the ones that weren't even *on* the map, looking for some out-of-the-way place to park the car and hike in twenty yards. There weren't any. No matter how deep into the woods we went, how small a dirt road we traveled on, or how far away from civilization we found ourselves, every single roadside parking space in the Catskills Mountains, every small indentation where you could park anything larger than a bike—literally *every single one*—had a big fat NO PARKING sign on it. And every property boundary—every single one we saw—was delineated with highly visible NO TRESPASSING signs spaced evenly and well within visual range of each other. It was a perimeter defense worthy of a federal correctional institution. Hour after hour we drove, road after winding road, but we could not find one single place in the thousands of acres we traversed to legally park our car.

"This is absolutely unbelievable," I said, finally giving vent to our unspoken emotions. "Can you believe this? Now they're legislating the woods."

At one point, needing to take a break, we stopped by the side of the road to fish an adjacent pond. I had brought my rod, hoping to find some fish, and now threw out a lure in search of psychological relief. There was only one house on this pond, at the other end from where we were. I didn't give it much notice until I was reaching back for my second cast and a car pulled up next to us.

A woman with a turkey's wattle stuck her head out the window. "This is a private pond."

"There's no sign," I said.

"It's private. Move it or I'll call the police." The car sped away and turned into the distant driveway.

"What is *wrong* with some people?" Sarah asked. "We're in the middle of *nowhere*."

We moved on, increasingly frustrated and unwilling to mention the reason: New York. Even in the valleys of verdant pine, amid the gurgle of running streams, you could feel the megalopolis a hundred miles away. Millions upon millions of people stacked up in the stifling heat, street after street of concrete bunk beds—how many of them would it take to overwhelm this place? To tick off the neighbors? To leave too much trash? To make too much noise? To add too much traffic? To start fires? A few thousand? A mere fraction of a percent.

Then suddenly it didn't matter. I didn't care about the damn population statistics or their effect on society. Camping was a God-given right in the Great Outdoors, we had come here to camp—and camping we were going to do!

I turned the car around with sudden force.

"Where are you going?" Sarah asked.

"Back to one of those streams."

"Wasn't there a sign?"

"Who cares!" I exploded. "You just get to a certain point where you're sick of all this *bullshit*. There's just too many people in the world. There's too many rules, too many signs, too many fucking lawyers! All I want is a goddamn piece of ground to pitch my tent!"

"Then let's find one!"

The stream I had chosen ran by the main road awhile before heading off into the woods. It was a beautiful sight, a straightaway of white water rushing over stones, leading into tall, majestic green pines. There was a side road that followed it with the usual NO TRESPASSING sign at the entrance, but I noticed some fine print at the bottom: PER ORDER BOY SCOUTS OF AMERICA.

"Them I can handle," I snorted.

We followed the road to a deserted camping area about a half mile upstream where we hid the car beneath the bough of a huge pine tree. We stepped outside in relief, our mood changing immediately. The scene was worthy of a painter's oil: blue sky and clouds, white rocks and pure, clear water, an impenetrable dark wall of pines on the opposite bank. There wasn't a sound but a light wind, a few birds, and the rush of the stream. We collected our equipment, walked upriver until we found a flat spot, and set up our complicated tent. Before too long, the hot sun and the usual exhaustion overcame us and we retreated inside.

The next thing I knew, Sarah was shaking me awake. "Paul, get up! There's somebody outside!"

I emerged from the tent bleary-eyed and looked into the not-so-happy face of a park ranger. He was a young blond man with a long flashlight and big wad of chewing tobacco wedged inside his lower lip.

"You folks got a permit for this tent?"

"Ah—no."

He didn't look pleased, but rather on the verge of writing us a large ticket. This is private property, he said, and found a nearby sign to prove it—you knew there had to be one. Then he told us that someone had seen our tent and filed a complaint, adding that the owner could sue us for trespass. I had a vision of myself going to small claims court in the Catskills. Well, at least I knew to hire a lawyer.

I replied by drawing on all the storytelling abilities at my disposal, crafting such a tale of urban woe that by the time I was done, Ranger Rick was inclined to cede me the whole forest. Or at least another space down the road. "If you leave now and go to a *designated* site, I'll talk to the owner," he said. "There's a public campground not far from here." He whipped out his walkie-talkie and called headquarters for information. Unfortunately, headquarters said, all the nearby sites were full. There was, however, one site left in Campground 2, about ten miles away. "Site number thirty-nine," Ranger Rick said. After giving us a complicated set of directions, he urged us to move quickly, as it was getting dark.

We packed up our campsite and did as he suggested. Naturally, we soon got lost. There may be a lot of NO TRESPASSING signs in the Catskills, and certainly an excess of NO PARKING signs, but street signs are scarce. Our wanderings took us first through a town—a few buildings actually—with the uncanny name of Sundown, then fifteen minutes later the sign for Sundown appeared again. Finally, we took another road and ended up in—

"Sundown!" Sarah exclaimed in disbelief.

"Is this the Twilight Zone?"

Finally, with the last glow of daylight disappearing and a heavy rain falling, we happened upon the public campground whose dogleg entrance had twice slipped past unnoticed. In the parking area was a map that listed the location of the ersatz campsites. I studied it with my new flashlight, then descended a muddy hillside path in the dark, searching for site number 39. The path was flanked by closely spaced clearings, like little golf course greens, each one occupied by a tent. In the dark and the rain I couldn't find any numbers anywhere. Finally, a long way from the parking lot, I came upon an empty site and returned to the car to fetch our gear. It took a number of trips and some frantic antics with the tent but eventually husband, wife, and dripping dog were all safely at rest.

Or so we thought.

Amid our city in the woods we could see five other tents. The one closest to us was occupied by four young men from the Bronx whose vision of the Great Outdoors included an Everest of beer cans on their doorstep, a boom box half the size of their tent, and the unrelenting wail of AC/DC—the complete collection—reverberating within. Their unzipped box was like a great big speaker pointed in our direction, a nylon woofer drowning the sound of the rain and our voices.

Within an hour of moving in we also attracted an uninvited guest. Ranger Rick was back.

"You folks made it, huh?" he said, flashing his light inside our tent. The glow caught the chewing tobacco dribbling across his lip. Tugger gave him an appropriate growl.

"Sure did," I said.

"Problem is, this isn't the right site. This is a four-man-tent site. You need at least three people to use this site."

"Doesn't the dog count?"

"You need to move it," he said. "Site number thirty-nine. Up the path on the right." He pulled his hood back over his head and disappeared into the rain.

Speechless, we listened to the downpour slapping our tent, and the primal screams of *Highway to Hell* reaching over from the Bronx.

I put my arm around Sarah. "Hon, it's about time I said this."

She tensed. "What now?"

"Happy Birthday."


## 22

With summer in full swing, IEM experienced a brief rise in spirit. Nineteen ninety-four was the year America hosted its first World Cup soccer tournament, an event of religious importance in the emerging markets and the only thing that ever took precedence over business in IEM. The salesmen and traders bought a large-screen television to watch the various matches, which they put in the conference room and ultimately gave away to the person who best predicted the outcomes of the tournament. During an important game, more people could be found watching television than at their positions, especially when "GOOOAAAALLLLLL!!!" was heard, commencing a stampede toward the conference room. Remarkably, the World Cup even managed to affect the market itself. When Brazil triumphed over Italy in the final, it kicked up the price of Brazilian bonds.

The office mood was soon darkened, however, by the longer trend, a market now in its sixth straight month of decline. In the last week of July, I was reading the latest news from the wire services when a new headline appeared: TOP EXOTICS

TRADER LET GO AT MERRILL. I looked across the trading floor: Judd Weaver's seat was empty.

I turned to Post, who was reading a new issue prospectus. "They fired Weaver?"

He glanced up. "Did they?"

"It says so on Reuters."

"Huh. I guess they did." He dropped his head.

As in the case of Carlos Espinosa, no explanation was given for Weaver's dismissal, which was carried out in true IEM fashion. One night Weaver got a call from a friend in the office who had overheard the Latin Mafia talking about firing him. The reason was the bonus pool, which was getting dangerously low. There wasn't enough money to make everyone happy; someone had to go. Since Weaver—a gringo—was outside the inner circle, and since the moribund exotics book was down $5 million, he was a natural target. The next day Weaver approached Diego Barbero, who confirmed the rumor. None of the Latin Mafia ever spoke to him directly. Weaver departed immediately, and is still suing Merrill Lynch.

Two weeks later I saw Colin McCarthy's understudy, Rob O'Leary, trading Eurobonds—or trying to. He barely knew what he was doing.

"Where's McCarthy?" I asked him.

"He's moved on."

"To London?"

"No—just *on.*"

McCarthy was gone, too. His departure gave the Latin Mafia another opportunity to prop up the bonus pool while deflecting the attention and criticism of senior management. A lot of IEM's undisclosed losses were in McCarthy's Eurobond book. IEM had underwritten some major Latin bond issues that had done worse than expected—especially an Argentine utility named Sodigas—leaving the firm holding million of dollars in unwanted bonds. McCarthy was then put in the unenviable position of trying to support the price of these bonds by buying them back—which, as the market continued to decline, had only led to further losses. Now he was the scapegoat for bad decisions made by the Latin Mafia. The last thing I heard, he was in Thailand, where he owned a bar on the beach.

A more subtle change took place at the top of Trading. IEM could not afford the confusion of having co–head traders any longer. So Miguel Forte was quietly pushed aside in favor of the rougher Diego Barbero, who had worked his way up from the bottom. Barbero was put in charge of the "front book"—all the trading books used in customer trading—while Forte was placed in charge of the less active "back book," IEM's proprietary trading book, where the group took out long-term positions for its own bottom line. To fill in the slack, Forte was also given a face-saving role as the group's "global ambassador." He began to travel a great deal, trying to drum up business and collect information—an odd hybrid of trading and marketing that never panned out, and succeeded only in diverting his attention from the back book at a time when he could least afford it.

Throughout August our numbers continued to dwindle. In London, our sole remaining trader quit to join Chase Manhattan's emerging markets group, citing disagreements with how IEM was being run. He was followed by the head of our syndicate operations there, who had had a public disagreement with Lisardo Escobar, the head of IEM, and was fired. To fill the gap, the trading desk began shuttling one trader to London for a week at a time. In New York, the office computer wizard was let go, with predictable results on the network, followed by one of our investment bankers. Meanwhile there was a palpable increase in office tension brought on by our mounting losses and exacerbated by the question hanging over everyone's head: Who was next?

Throughout the firm, and Wall Street as a whole, a lot of people were asking the same question. Since February, the drop in bond prices, precipitated by rising interest rates, had continued, cutting underwriting activity in half and causing havoc on the Street. During the second quarter, Salomon Brothers had lost a record $204 million, thanks primarily to depressed bond portfolios, Morgan Stanley was down 45 percent from the previous year, and Lehman Brothers' earnings had plunged 79 percent. A wave of layoffs followed—Paine Webber, Smith Barney, and Prudential fired hundreds—and there was no sign of improvement.

The situation was somewhat better at Merrill Lynch. Unlike most other Wall Street banks, which were driven by institutional business, Merrill's earnings were stabilized by steady profits from Retail, much of it fee based. Moreover, while second quarter earnings were down 25 percent over the previous year, such figures had to be taken in context. Nineteen ninety-three had been the most profitable year in the history of the firm and in the history of Wall Street as well. So while institutional business was suffering and overall earnings were down, Merrill as a whole was still posting steady and sizable profits.

Neither of these facts saved the firm from layoffs, however. The first week in August Merrill Lynch fired 4 percent of its fixed income department, a total of ninety people. The firm's senior management also implemented some cost-cutting measures, limiting the hours at which car services could be used and wiping out forever that time-honored tradition, the free lunch. This courageous move, which made *The Wall Street Journal,* affected only the lowest rungs of the food chain, those hundreds of people who had no status to uphold, saving the firm the equivalent of one executive's annual bonus. In effect, facing a periodic budgetary decline, the rich had levied a tax on the poor. But they did prove that there really was no such thing as a free lunch, even in the most powerful investment bank on the Street.

In IEM the decline of the market also brought us the Undertaker, himself the product of the worst disaster in the firm's history. In 1987 Merrill suffered a staggering $377 million loss at the hands of a single mortgage trader, Howard Rubin. The firm was forced to sell off some of its World Financial Center real estate to shore up its balance sheet. To prevent such an event from recurring, senior management established a special oversight group known as Risk Management to keep tabs on the firm's trading desks. They set trading limits, monitored exposure, and reported directly to the president of Merrill Lynch. The Undertaker was one of their representatives and another sign of IEM's woes. He was literally from down under—Tasmania, that is—and looked like an owl, with a thick-lensed pair of glasses that magnified his eyes. He was routinely seen looking over the shoulders of the traders and salesmen, unblinking, while tapping a forefinger on his lips. Occasionally he would ask a smooth, soft-spoken question that would shiver in your ears. No one spoke to him otherwise. He was a phantom, popping up where you least expected him, standing his emotionless vigils, searching the floor for the next Joe Jett.

His presence didn't faze Luis Sanchez, our winsome intern from the Harvard Business School, however. One day he rushed by the Undertaker and seized a fellow intern by the arm. "Hey, you'll never guess what I just did! I just sat in Howie Rubin's seat down in mortgages! Wow!"

The Undertaker blinked at that.


Shortly after the Undertaker's arrival—and perhaps because of it—a rumor began to circulate that IEM was moving to Seven. If true, it meant a lot more than a change in scenery.

At Merrill Lynch there was as much competition between groups as there was within them, something the firm encouraged as a matter of policy. It was market management, pure and simple. Whole groups were reorganized, consumed, and broken up in this manner. In its early years, due to its small size and specialized nature, IEM had been relatively immune from external threats simply because no one wanted it. The Latin Mafia lived in their own little world on the sixteenth floor where few people even knew about them. But with the advent of the boom, and the perception that the emerging markets were here to stay, IEM became an attractive target. At some point, people on Seven argued, the emerging markets would truly emerge and join the global marketplace. Then IEM should be integrated with the rest of the fixed income world—folded into another group, say, or broken up by instrument. The Latin Mafia knew quite well what that meant: their power would be usurped by Mother Merrill and they would be out of jobs. Consequently, they were forever locked in a life-or-death struggle with the rest of the firm to retain their unique status on Sixteen—and their fat bonuses, of course—its outcome forever dependent on their bottom line.

The rumor of our move eventually died; the Undertaker remained.

• • •

By early September the situation in IEM had worsened to such a point that the Latin Mafia decided to take drastic action: they called a group meeting. During my tenure we had never had a group meeting. But with people quitting and being fired, profits down, and ugly rumors spreading—"Wall Street Firm Bonuses May Plummet Between 25% and 30%," one chilling Bloomberg report announced—the head of IEM, Lisardo Escobar, decided to break with tradition and assemble the people who worked for him.

Escobar was someone I didn't see too often. His office was off the trading floor in our investment banking corridor, and he rarely left it; or if he did, he rarely visited the desk. Occasionally I would see him standing by the traders, looking over their shoulders like the Undertaker and rubbing his jutting lower jaw. He was an investment banker by training and often wore a dazed expression like he was deep in thought, thoughts which would then come out in a strange burst, leaving you wondering what wavelength he was on. It was difficult to tell because he avoided open communication outside the inner circle. He was always hiding behind his desk or behind the hand on his jaw. In the few times I ever asked him for a decision, he always referred me to someone else. He was the king of *mañana* management: even the other Latin Mafiosi rolled their eyes at his vacillation, his weakness, and his inability to lead.

The meeting was a typical example. In true IEM fashion, it was a spur-of-the-moment decision that wasn't announced to the group. Like an office social, word was just supposed to spread out on its own, beginning with the people that mattered. This time, however, even some of the insiders didn't get the message. Key people could be heard asking the next day—What meeting?

In order to seat more people, the event took place in an executive conference room on the top floor of the North Tower. It was a larger version of our conference room though without any windows. Like the morning call, the group assembled around a long rectangular table with a speakerphone in the center. I stood against the wall. Escobar was seated in the middle of the table, facing me.

He looked around the room trying to decide whether to start. "Where's Kenny? Anyone seen Kenny Breen?" No one answered. "Did anyone tell Breen about this meeting?" No one answered. Escobar looked puzzled. "How about Research?" All of Research was absent. Escobar noted a few other missing faces. "What about Raoul?"

"I'm here," said the speakerphone. Savegre had called in from Merrill's Chicago office where he was visiting our salesperson.

"Okay . . . Well then, I guess we'll start." Escobar looked uncomfortable. "Well, I thought I'd call this meeting to talk about what's been happening lately, tell you how I see things. Then I thought I'd open it up for discussion." He produced a pamphlet. "A little while ago we had this research service do a study for us. They asked investors to rate the six major firms in our business according to ten categories." He listed them—sales support, pricing, research, execution, etc.—and discussed IEM's ranking in each. We were somewhere in the middle overall, which Escobar offered as proof that things weren't as bad as they seemed. A discussion of each category followed but was limited to a few insiders—Gurevich, Escobar, two salesmen, a trader. They carried on their private conversation for a few minutes, mentioning policy decisions no one else knew about and meetings no one else had attended, while the rest of the group watched in silence, wondering what no one was addressing: how bad off were we?

"I think we're looking at this the wrong way," Justo Lamberti piped up. One of the Brady traders, Lamberti was that rare thing in his profession, a soft-spoken gentleman. He never raised his voice and more often chose to watch a debate than participate in it. Now everyone turned to listen to him. "I look at these statistics and I say, why aren't we the best?"

"Good point," someone agreed.

"Wait a minute, that's not it, that's not it," Escobar interrupted, waving his arms with a dopey grin. "The point is, we don't *want* to be the best. We're talking bonuses here, guys, not growing the group. We want to make the *most money per man.* I don't know about *you* guys," he chortled, "but that's what *I* call success. And if you look at it that way, we're doing fine. We've had to reduce head count some," he shrugged helplessly, "but I don't see any need to make any further changes. I'm confident that the group we have at the table now is the group that's going to get paid in January."

This was Escobar's idea of motivating the troops. Unfortunately, it didn't say much for the future prospects of IEM, where his strategy was taking its toll. Instead of diversifying into new markets IEM was shrinking in the face of stiff competition—not from other firms but from other elements of Merrill. Our Hong Kong office was on its last legs, the Tokyo office down to two people. The responsibility for India, a market of tremendous potential, as well as other Asian emerging markets, had been assumed by the firm's Asia-Pacific Group, leaving us with a toehold in Philippine Brady bonds. Meanwhile emerging Eastern European countries like Hungary and the Czech Republic were being covered by a new element of ISG—of all groups—rather than IEM London. Instead of building itself a global emerging markets business, IEM was defaulting to Latin American bonds.

"What about Stuart?" someone piped up, referring to the trader who had recently quit in London. "If he wasn't worried about the bonus pool, why did he leave?"

Escobar shrugged painfully without removing his clueless smile. "What can I say? Stuart made a mistake. He says the opportunity is better at Chase—but I don't think so. Maybe they paid up for him, I don't know. But he made a mistake."

"I'm hearing a lot of people on the Street wondering what's happening over here," another trader asked. "First, we lost Judd, then Colin, then Stuart—what am I supposed to say?"

Escobar threw up his hands with a girlish laugh. "I don't know—tell them it's a reshuffling. Happens all the time."

"How long are we going to be making trips to London?" Lamberti asked.

"We're looking to hire someone now, we just haven't found him yet."

A few groans arose.

"Look, why don't we do this," Escobar said. "Let's just go around the table and let people talk. Say what you think we need to improve." Escobar pointed to the man next to him. "Let's start with you, Justo."

"The problem is we're not seeing the flows," Lamberti said. "If we're not seeing the flows, we can't give good pricing."

"Why aren't you seeing the flows?" asked the speakerphone.

"Because Sales isn't bringing us the business."

Sales erupted in denial. "How can we bring the flows if we're not getting good *pricing*?" Gurevich asked.

"You're getting good pricing," the traders shot back.

"Hold on," Escobar said.

"The problem is *Research*," said Savegre's disembodied voice. As IEM's fortunes had worsened and Sales had come under criticism, Savegre had increasingly found fault with Research, located five floors above us—where they were now. "Would you trade with us if you were a client? Look at the research we're putting out!"

"What about Sales? When was the last time you brought us a new client?" Lamberti asked.

The speakerphone was momentarily silent; Savegre had not expected such a public challenge. "Why do you think I'm here in Chicago?" he asked.

"Good question," someone muttered, to general laughter.

"Hold on a minute," Escobar said. "Raoul, this is an important issue. What have you done lately to increase client business?"

Oh, I *loved* that. How was Savegre going to wriggle out of this one?

"We've been doing a lot!" Savegre said, spouting moral outrage. "Is Paul Stiles there?"

I straightened in surprise. "I'm here."

"Paul, why don't you brief the group on, um, you know, that research you've been doing on finding new clients."

I didn't know whether to laugh or to groan. Just when I thought Savegre had finally been cornered—out he popped!

"Ah—sure," I said. I gave a quick, off-the-cuff synopsis of the report that Savegre had read and ignored.

"That's good, Raoul," Escobar said, "but there still seems to be a consensus here that Sales isn't doing their job—or Marketing isn't."

"Then fire *Research*!" Savegre exploded. "Give me the tools I need!"

Escobar waved dismissively at the speakerphone. "Okay, let's move on."

We kept circling the room, everyone giving their comments. There was no real consensus about anything, just a bunch of individual opinions that came out and died on the table. The most marked thing was what *wasn't* said. No one said that we were in a bear market, part of a cycle beyond our control; no one suggested how we might reorganize ourselves to deal with that situation; no one suggested a single follow-up action. By the end of the meeting Escobar had simply decided to maximize our profit by fiat while assuring every man he would get his piece of the pie. He only forgot to explain how.


That same week the emerging markets were dealt another blow when a major financial scandal erupted in Mexico. On September 5, the Mexican government seized control of Grupo Financiero Union–Cremi, the fourth-largest financial group in the country, and ordered the arrest of its leader—named, uncannily, Carlos Cabal—and nine of his cohorts. Cabal, a well-known billionaire, was accused of funneling up to $700 million in fraudulent loans to himself through his $2 billion holding company, Grupo Cabal. Until his escape—he fled to Europe—he had been in the midst of using the stolen funds to purchase a well-known American brand name, Del Monte Foods of San Francisco—partly owned by Merrill Lynch, as fate would have it.

While the details of the scandal remained unclear, it raised a number of important questions. What was the role, if any, of the Mexican ruling party, the PRI, with whom Cabal was well connected? Why hadn't regulators caught Cabal sooner? How healthy was the rest of the Mexican banking system? Was Mexico destined to become another Venezuela? However, aside from the price of Banca Cremi bonds, which plunged, the market reaction was muted. Implicitly, the scandal was seen as the exception, not the rule.

Within a month, Banca Cremi bonds were in default.


## 23

Once the Core Group was established, we began to build a business together. I gave them loads of information on the emerging markets, which they quickly digested, and told them where to find more. I also became their eyes and ears in the office. Whenever I heard of anything that might interest them—a research conference call, an interesting trade idea, a new bond issue, or any timely piece of market information—I passed it on.

Meanwhile the Core began to prospect for clients and develop new relationships. Since their leads were generally the bare minimum, their first task was to locate the right person to talk to, whoever made the investment decisions—no easy task when facing a corporate behemoth. Then they would ask if he was covered by Merrill Lynch (our system wasn't perfect.) If so, they would back off. If not, they would launch into their sales pitch, which stressed the three pillars upon which they stood: their product, their firm, and themselves. Current market conditions made selling the emerging markets a challenge, but not impossible. In the minds of many, the rise of the world's developing countries was like progress itself: an inevitability. Yes, the Core might say, we are experiencing a slight market correction at the moment, but in the longer term the emerging markets are a bullish play and a much smarter place to put your money than the sluggish economies of the industrialized world. And what better firm to trade with than Merrill Lynch? Merrill saw the flows, knew where the market was going, and had access to the best deals. Merrill also offered the Core, who were—ah—emerging markets specialists, part of the firm's institutional sales force. Lowercase letters don't carry over the phone.

The end of all this effort was, hopefully, the establishment of a trading account. Then came the gradual daily working of that account: establishing a relationship with the person, sending him research, promoting ideas relevant to his investment strategy, building credibility, and finally booking trades. Apart from the usual skills of a salesman, the entire process required a great deal of patience, stamina, and a high threshold for rejection. Sometimes the original lead was wrong. Companies had gone out of business, phone numbers had changed, people had moved on. The Core would make a great deal of effort to get in touch with the right contact, only to discover that he was no longer investing in the emerging markets. Other times, people simply weren't interested. Slowly but surely, however, our efforts began to pay off and the phone began to ring on the IEM Trading desk.

Meanwhile, as our effort began to take hold, we ran into one obstacle after another in IEM. The first was office prejudices. The Latin Mafia, Savegre, and the traders and salesmen all viewed Middle Markets through a cultural lens. In their eyes the Core was a bunch of Retail amateurs selling to people who knew even less than they did. This perception, combined with the group's insular attitude and suspicion of the rest of the firm, shaped their attitude toward our effort. On one hand they wanted to do some new business, but on the other they weren't going to bring Middle Markets into the fold, even though they were selling to major institutions. For weeks I had difficulty getting the Brady traders to even pick up the phone.

They weren't used to having retail brokers call them directly, and one or two errant questions only confirmed their prejudices. "Paul, would you tell these jokers to stop calling the desk? I don't have time to explain what a Brady Bond is!" To help bridge this gap, I organized a special seminar dinner for all the Middle Markets brokers in New York City at which various people from IEM were to make formal presentations. It was held in a conference room in the top floor of the North Tower, catered by the firm and chaired by Escobar. About fifteen brokers showed up, a healthy response. At kickoff time, however, most of the IEM participants were missing, including Savegre (who had suggested the idea) and some of the speakers. I had to go down to the office and round people up. Two traders wandered in an hour late, unprepared, and spoke their piece while eating.

Another obstacle was the morning conference call. Although the call was an important source of market information, the office powers came up with all kinds of reasons why the Core shouldn't be allowed to participate in it. They have no experience selling our bonds, Savegre said. How will they get any, I asked, if we don't help them? We can't trust them with sensitive information, Forte said. There're only three of them, I replied, and they would be fools to break our confidence. I lost.

The next major conflict arose over the broker screens. Broker screens were live—they displayed the best bids and offers of the moment—providing the best indication of the current price of a bond and the direction in which prices were moving—a vital competitive edge. They were, accordingly, tightly controlled by the broker-dealer community, which restricted their use to themselves. Everyone else was forced to use passive screens that operated on a time delay, providing the Street a permanent edge over its clients. Naturally, the Core wanted the live screens. All the institutional salespeople on the Street had them, including IEM Sales, making their advice more valuable to their clients. But IEM refused. The trading desk did not trust Retail with the screens, nor did they want to relinquish their trading advantage. Have them call the desk for prices, they said. What good will that do, I asked, when you won't pick up the phone?

My most serious problem was getting approval to pursue the leads I unearthed. In my research I had identified scores of institutions holding emerging markets bonds. Some of these prospects were in Middle Markets territory, as the Treaty defined it, and some were in the large market, making them Institutional Sales accounts. Some were not covered by anyone in Merrill Lynch, and others were covered for products other than ours. Some did a lot of emerging markets business, others did little or none. This created a bewildering tangle of highly sensitive coverage issues. Proceeding carefully, I first submitted a twenty-five-page list of names to Savegre for his approval. I reminded him of it daily but, in typical Savegre fashion, received only some skillful instruction in the art of dodging responsibility. I then adopted a new approach and began asking him about accounts one at a time. The runaround continued: he gave the leads to IEM Sales, who never called them. He referred me to salesmen on Seven who had no interest in emerging markets business—and no interest in giving it away either. Savegre had the power to assign coverage for our product to anyone, but his self-interest was not served by developing my business—not if it meant sorting out coverage conflicts with Institutional Sales.

In one case Costas landed our first big account, Eaton Vance, a mutual fund manager in Boston. But when I told Savegre about it, eager to prove what we could do, he forbade us from doing any business with them.

"It's too big for you," he said.

"We're only interested in their emerging markets fund," I said.

"The Boston office should cover them."

"They don't have an emerging markets specialist."

"I'll talk to them about it."

You know what happened.

I found this difficult to take. Having been subjected to only eight months of Wall Street, I still suffered from a quaint view of a corporation as a different animal. In that view Merrill Lynch existed to make money, IEM and Middle Markets existed to make money for Merrill Lynch, and the Core and I made money for Middle Markets and IEM. We were all at some layer in the corporate wedding cake. How could an organization make sense otherwise? Yet whenever I applied that sense—whenever I went by the book—no business was done! Obviously I would have to throw out the book—a decision that was easy to make by now. If people were going to stand in the way of my business, I was going to get around them.


The first shot of this rebellion began with the morning call, from which the Core was still excluded. It was a simple matter. Each morning when the call ended I would return to my seat and hold my own call, recapping what I had just heard in full color—and in a low tone, of course.

The live screen issue came next. Since I couldn't get the Core approval for the screens, I acted as one myself. Whenever they needed the latest market prices, they would put their client on hold, call me, and I would race to the nearest screen in the office, pick up the phone, and quote them the information they needed. Difficult, but it worked, and on a hectic trading floor no one knew the difference.

Then came the Rolodex issue. I knew there were some hot leads buried in those little boxes, just a few yards from my position, though no one could be bothered to help me dig them out. So one night after the market closed and the trading floor cleared out, I did a little Rolodex surfing on my own, garnering quite a list. Sales never knew the difference.

In other matters my policy became doing first and asking later—or not at all. After our group meeting with Escobar, for instance, Forte came to the conclusion that office communication needed to be improved. He established a policy requiring that salesmen and traders send out electronic messages to the group recapping the day's action, providing valuable, sometimes sensitive market information. Naturally, I assumed I could distribute these internal messages to the Core, creating a daily hemorrhage of IEM secrets.

In order to get the traders to pick up the phone, I also launched a public relations campaign aimed at changing our image. I painted the Core as exceptions to the rule, the best of the lot, three determined specialists working full time on the emerging markets and ripe with business opportunity—the truth, actually. To prove the point, the Core started showing up on the trading desk when the market closed, to chat with the traders. Before long they were on a first-name basis with Trading—a coziness Sales began viewing with suspicion.

My approach to coverage issues also changed. For the most part I just gave all the leads I found to the Core and told them to be discreet: they knew the score. If it was a particularly sensitive client, I would wait for a moment when Savegre was busy—like when he was walking to the bathroom—and spring it on him in passing, hoping that he couldn't be bothered. "You want to take a quick look at these prospects?" I might say, holding a Post-it note with some scribbles on it. He would rip it from my hand, glance it over, hand it back, and charge into the men's room. That was good enough for me. I had unearthed scores of accounts, so many that I could no longer remember all the names, and kept no records of who received what. If a problem should arise, my memory was bound to fail me.

Emboldened by the success of these efforts, I even gathered enough courage to extend my rebellion to my lunch. After the firm had courageously clipped the free lunch from the budget, I had succumbed to the insider urge and ordered takeout; but now, in accordance with my new attitude, I resorted to the brown bag. What a thrill it was walking by the trading desk defiantly clutching that tuna fish sandwich—aaah! Even Post managed to appreciate it. One afternoon, alerted by the crinkle of wax paper, he glanced over at my lunch, raised an eyebrow, and pronounced it "sound financial management."


Our mounting battle with IEM unified the Core and myself against a common enemy and helped weld us into a tight group. At some point the Core even stopped working through me and began calling each other directly. The growth of this fledgling society was something I encouraged, until one day I decided to risk capitalizing on it. In my efforts to uncover new clients, I was being overwhelmed by all the leads I was discovering. Each of them took a while to research on the awkward computer database, and as our effort grew, I had less and less time to spend on them. So instead of doing all the work myself I proposed to the Core that we have a joint "prospecting party."

"Let me understand this, Paul, because it is difficult to believe," Costas said when I told him the news. "You wish to assemble three Merrill Lynch brokers in one room and have them work *together* to find new clients?"

"That's the idea."

"Really, Paul, you are so naive," he sighed. "That is what I like about you."

"Naivete is not knowing," I said. "This is something else."

We assembled on a Saturday, when IEM was empty. Costas came in from Greenwich, Lee from the Village, and Tim from New Jersey. I had a number of computers on Operations Island set up with the firm's Marketing Information System and a long list of prospects waiting for them. I handed out the leads, the coffee, the donuts, and we got to work. In a few hours we had a stack of computer printouts with information on scores of new accounts. Then we all sat around a table and talked about who should pursue what. Costas, Lee, and Tim each had his own preferences. Tim liked working commercial banks since that was his former profession. Costas had done some work with offshore funds. Lee had some Brazilian accounts and wanted more. We allocated as many names as possible that way, then split up the rest equally.

A miracle, I thought: three hardened Merrill Lynch brokers working as a team?

By the end of September our labors had begun to bear fruit. During the last two weeks in the month, Middle Markets did fourteen trades with ten new clients, some of them significant large-market accounts—Bank of Boston, Barings, Citibank—in a variety of instruments. The total face amount sold was $30 million, yielding a notional profit to IEM of approximately $95,000.* This is peanuts on Wall Street, of course, but it was a healthy start, especially when compared with IEM's small initial investment: my annual salary. I broadcast the news to all the Middle Markets brokers and sent a glowing internal message to IEM as well. These messages served their purpose: a few more brokers called and people in the office began paying more attention.

Inevitably, however, we began to receive attention of a different kind. True to his word, Costas's partner, Frank Russo, began a frenzy of prospecting, developing his

---

* Face amount is the amount redeemed at maturity. This is different from the price of a bond, which is what you pay for it. Bond salesmen earn a notional profit because they generate one side of a trade only. The actual profit will not be known until the full transaction is complete. The notional profit in emerging markets is high, due to the risk, with the average commission ranging, in 1994, from .25 percent of face value to a full point. A relatively small face amount can thus be quite profitable.

own leads in addition to mine and expanding his efforts well beyond New York. As a result, one day I looked up to find Savegre standing by my desk looking concerned.

"Paul," he said, "who have these guys of yours been calling?"

I shrugged nonchalantly, inwardly on guard. "All kinds of people, I guess. We're uncovering a lot of leads."

"Well, I just got a call from some guy—I forget his name—he's the head of Institutional Sales in the Midwest. Apparently some guy named Russo at Rockefeller Center has been prospecting out there, saying he's from IEM."

"Really?"

"Do you know him?"

"Um . . . I met him once."

"Well, tell him he'd better stop. What do these guys think, they can prospect all over the United States?"

I immediately called Russo, who promised to be more careful. He was doing nothing but emerging markets cold calling, he said. There was bound to be an occasional glitch.

A few days later an animated Savegre was back looking even less happy than before. "Did one of your guys call AIG?" he asked, referring to a large insurer.

I rustled through my in-box. "It's possible . . ."

"High Yield covers that account. Who said you could call them?"

"I thought you did. Weren't they on that list I showed you last week?"

"Oh . . ." Savegre affected an introspective concern and adopted a more cooperative tone. "Well anyway, AIG is an Institutional Sales account. They're too big for your guys. Tell whoever it is to back off."

As soon as Savegre rushed off, I called Russo. "You guys called AIG, right?"

"Yeah, we're on 'em. They want to do business."

"You've got to back off. It's a High Yield account."

"What? Hold on a minute! I *landed* that account. High Yield wasn't covering it. No one there mentioned High Yield to me."

"It doesn't matter. Savegre's all fired up about it."

"But this is a good account!"

After a short argument, Russo finally agreed to back off. Shortly thereafter, I was summoned to Savegre's position. He was on the phone as usual. He hung up and snapped his head toward me, never a good sign; whenever Savegre was agitated, his movements turned abrupt. "I just got a call from Bud Leonard. Heard of him?"

"No."

"He's the head of Middle Markets."

"What? I thought DePalma was."

"So did I, but DePalma works for him. Leonard's in charge of smoothing over the politics of Middle Markets, making sure it fits into the firm. I guess he's been around for years. He wanted to talk about this guy, Russo. He's not in Middle Markets, you know."

Surprised, I said, "He *is*. He's on my list."

"Not according to Leonard. He wants to come over here and talk about it."

"About what?"

"Russo, and what you're doing."

"Fine, but I know Russo is in Middle Markets."

"He better be," Savegre shot back, running an impatient hand across his bald head. "If these guys keep this up, I'm going to shut them down for good."

"I'll call and ask," I promised, "just to be sure."

"Good—even better, tell me when you've got him on the phone." His head snapped around.

I returned to my position, sensing impending disaster, and called Russo. He put Costas on the line and I apprised them both of the situation.

"I *am* in Middle Markets!" Russo insisted.

"Paul," Costas said, "what does Leonard want?"

"I don't know. Who is he?"

"He's the guy they brought in to enforce the Treaty," Russo said. "He's the biggest asshole in the firm."

"That's saying something," I said.

"He doesn't like me either," Russo said.

"Why?"

"It's a long story."

"Hold on," I said. "Raoul is free."

I shouted to Savegre, who picked up the line. Savegre had never met Russo before and, in contrast with his previous bluster, assumed his usual nonconfrontational tone. "I wanted to talk with you about your prospecting efforts," he began after introducing himself. "I understand from Paul that you are trying to develop some new clients in our market . . ."

Russo, too, suddenly lapsed into a formal cordiality and quickly set out to assure Savegre of his noblest intentions. "Raoul," he said, "I promise that we have not intentionally crossed onto any Institutional Sales territory. We have been tremendously careful in our prospecting efforts. We have no intention of causing you any problems. That would be stupid of us. And we wouldn't do it. I promise you that." Savegre listened quietly to Russo's never-ending speech, throwing in an occasional "I see." When he mentioned the recent call from the Midwest, Russo came right back at him. "That was my mistake. And I take full responsibility for it. I wasn't aware that the account was above the Treaty line at all." He sounded so passionate, you absolutely had to believe him. No wonder he did all the cold calling. "And I absolutely assure you that I am in the Middle Markets. I have it on paper if you would like to see it." Savegre said that wouldn't be necessary.

Costas finally broke in to apply the varnish. "I just want to say, Raoul, that we are extremely happy with the support that you have given us so far and to be able to work with you together on this effort. We think it has a great deal of potential and we hope that we can put this misunderstanding behind us as soon as possible so we can get a move on to developing more new business."

By then the tears were welling in my eyes and I was ready to stand up and cheer. Savegre didn't stand a chance against these guys.

A few days later Bud Leonard arrived, towing his deputy behind him. He was a spry man with a bulbous, red-veined nose, palsied hands, and looked a hundred years old. We sat in the conference room, Savegre and I on one side of the table, Leonard and his deputy on the other.

"My mission," Leonard explained, "is to make Middle Markets happen. Basically, they chose me because I have a reputation for getting things done. You might look on me as the enforcer." He explained that he had been sent to a number of retail offices in his career with the mission of turning them around—and had done so. "Basically, I size everyone up, figure out who should be in, and fire the rest. That's the best way to do it. That's how I operate." Middle Markets, he said, was a similar problem. "Basically, we've put together this Treaty, see, to take care of these coverage issues once and for all. We have to enforce the Treaty. No exceptions. None. We can't have people who are Retail brokers prospecting in Middle Markets territory, just as we can't have Middle Markets brokers prospecting in Institutional Sales territory. See what I mean? It's that simple. So somebody has to come in and break some heads, if that's what we need to do, or else this whole thing will never work, right? So that's my job, to make this whole thing happen." His unsteady hands encircled the air. "And that's how I operate. Now let's talk about this guy, Russo. In order to clarify just who could be in Middle Markets, and who couldn't, I set down a policy saying that no Retail broker can join us unless fifty percent of his accounts are institutional. He has to bring us that much business on his own. Russo only has thirty percent. So that rules him out." He swept the table top with an unsteady hand. "Now I understand he has a partner that you're interested in . . ." Leonard whirled his hand around.

"Costas Kerasidis," I said.

"Right. I'll have to look at his accounts and see if we want him in Middle Markets. But Russo is definitely out."

"Okay," Savegre said compliantly. "Russo's out." When dealing with anyone of power in the firm, Savegre was always a model of circumspection, humility, and cooperation—especially when he couldn't care less.

The meeting ended presently and we all shook hands. "I just wanted to let you know where we stand," Leonard said, and tottered out of the room.

Savegre watched him leave, then turned to me with a wry smile. "Where's Dr. Kevorkian when we need him?"

A few days later, after a bruising battle at the highest levels of Retail, Russo's name was removed from the list of Middle Markets brokers. No one mentioned Costas, however.


On September 28, another blow rained down upon Mexico when Jose Francisco Ruiz Massieu, the second in command of the ruling PRI party and the next Mexican Speaker of the House, was assassinated in his car by a man wielding an automatic weapon.

As in the case of the Colosio assassination, Massieu's death generated a great deal of speculation about who was behind it and what their motive was. Massieu was a moderate reformer in a party torn between its corrupt old guard and a new breed of reform-minded politicians—had the old guard hired a hit man? Others blamed the drug cartels—the machine gun was their weapon of choice and Mr. Ruiz's brother was a top antinarcotics official. Within two weeks investigators had closed in on the ruling party explanation. The Mexican attorney general's office reported that an accomplice to the crime had fingered a number of prominent PRI politicians, one of whom, congressman Manuel Munoz Rocha, promptly disappeared. Even more ominously, the report raised serious questions about a possible link between the Massieu and Colosio assassinations.

The financial community was naturally concerned. Following the August election of Ernesto Zedillo as president of Mexico, and the quiet transfer of power that ensued, investors had been expected to return to the market, confident that Mexico's domestic turmoil was finally at an end. But now, with Mexico beginning to look more like Colombia every day, and evidence mounting of an alarming conspiracy at the highest levels of the Mexican government, the tap began turning in the opposite direction, with predictable results. Instead of an influx of capital, crucial to sustaining growth, the Mexican government found itself in a familiar position: defending the peso.


## 24

In the wake of our camping experience, Sarah and I stopped all spontaneous efforts to get away from our megalopolis. Apart from the long reach of its population, there were simple difficulties in driving. Traffic backed up, especially in the tunnels leading to New Jersey and on the bridges leading anywhere. Many of the roads were jarring, uneven, potholed surfaces, edged with debris. The thought of entry and exit became tiring, unpleasant. Forget it, we said instead—let's just stick around.

This decision created a cyclical imbalance in our lives. If nothing else, escaping the city had kept us in a state of motion seven days a week. Without it, we shuddered to a halt on Saturday, giving us time to think. Instead of waking up and taking off we lay in bed, all the thoughts held at bay by the daily rush suddenly flooding in on us. We became acutely aware of our lives—where we were, what we were doing, and the toll it was taking—and that awareness, combined with the normal end-of-week fatigue of body and mind, produced a frustrating lethargy. Our weekends became an exercise in procrastination, in which we were lucky to get our errands done. We would sit around, watch a movie, read the paper, do nothing. We knew we should be taking advantage of the city but never felt like it. During the week we were too busy to plan ahead. On the weekend we would pick up the paper and look through pages of listings—music, theater, museums, restaurants—wondering which ones we might like. We had no one to ask—or go with. Then we would put the paper down and collapse on the couch. Exhausted as we were, Manhattan seemed to require too much energy. It was too overwhelming. How many hassles lay between here and there? Transportation, expense, risk—it wasn't worth it. So we spent our weekends in Cobble Hill, then dragged ourselves back to the office on Monday.

In this way our lives became a regular manic-depressive episode, five days up, two down. We swung from intense work, motion, and reaction to a sledgehammer of fatigue, contemplation, and immobility. There was no happy balance between work and home, there were no friends or leisure activities to offset the pressures of the Market. How had this happened? We no longer knew. Why were we doing this? Because we had to. What could we do about it? Nothing. There seemed to be no way out. Somehow we had fallen into a life beyond our understanding, one which stole the very time and energy needed to figure it out.

By midsummer the end result of all this—of the pressure and our inability to release it—was a tremendous amount of internalized stress. We didn't even notice it accumulating. It built slowly and steadily, day by day, until it reached a point where it was difficult to control. There was no outlet for it but each other; and the simplest thing could release it.


I was lying on the couch watching television one evening when Sarah arrived home from a business trip. She walked quickly into the apartment and dropped her luggage on the floor with a hello.

"Hi," I said. "How'd it go?"

"Fine." She managed a smile. I was, as usual, wiped out and didn't want to move.

She went into the bedroom and quickly emerged. "You could have made the bed."

"Sorry."

"There's stuff everywhere in there."

"I haven't had time to pick it up." I changed the station. Repeatedly. There was nothing on television.

"Paul, come *on*," she called from the kitchen.

"Now what?"

"Look at these *dishes.*"

"Would you lay off? You just walked in."

"I don't appreciate going away for three days and being greeted by a stack of dishes."

"I've been working late the last three days."

"You could at least put them in the dishwasher."

"All right! I'll do it."

"The bed isn't made, there're clothes all over the floor—"

"I said I'd *do it.*"

"I can't relax if I come home and this place is a disaster. I've been working *sixteen hours a day.*"

"I haven't exactly been sitting around, you know."

"You're lying there watching television!"

"Okay! All right! I'll do the damn dishes!" I flicked off the TV and swung my feet to the floor. "Let's just eat first, okay? I'm starving."

"Are you kidding me?" She stared at me, hands on her hips. "*I'm* not cooking dinner."

"I didn't *ask* you to. Let's just *go out.*"

"I don't want to go out. I've eaten every meal out for the past *three days.*"

"Do you think *I* feel like cooking?"

"Fine—you just do the dishes and *I'll* cook, okay?" She turned her back and began pushing dishes noisily out of the way.

I stood up from the couch. "Sarah, would you just tell me what's wrong? It's not the dishes."

"It *is* the dishes."

"It's not and you know it. Just tell me what's going on."

She dropped a stack of pans with a clang, raising her eyes to the ceiling. "I just don't enjoy this anymore. I hate *traveling.* I hate coming home to *this.* I hate it!"

"Then tell them you don't want to travel as much."

"I *told you,* if I do that I'll have to work in the city schools, and I'm *not* going to do that. I'm not commuting to the Bronx every day to put computers in war zones! You don't *listen!*"

"Then get another job," I said, flicking the TV back on. "Educational software is huge right now."

She came out of the kitchen and at me. "How can I get another job when I'm *never here?*"

"There's thousands of headhunters in this city. Let *them* find you one."

"Paul, do you have any idea what I sacrificed to come here and do this? Do you? I gave up a wonderful job. I had six credits toward my master's degree. Now you've dragged me up here and I can't do anything because I'm traveling all the time."

"Do you want to quit? Is that what you want?"

"I don't *know* what I want. I'm trying to tell you I'm *miserable.* I've been in three different states this week and I don't even have time to read the paper. This isn't *living.* It isn't *worth* it. It's just not *fun* anymore."

"Then quit! Quit! But for God's sake, stop taking it out on me! Don't you think I have enough problems?" I crashed back onto the couch. "Now, are we eating here, or are we going out?"

"Listen to me!"

"Only if you stop whining at me."

"I'm not *whining*! You don't understand the *stress* I'm under, all the time."

"Why don't I? I feel the same thing. I just don't want to deal with it right now, okay? Now do you want me to cook the goddamn dinner or not?"

"Listen to you! Do you know how this job has changed you?"

"*Me?* I'm not the one standing here complaining."

"You're not *listening* either. You never take the time to *listen* anymore. And I have no one else to talk to."

"What do you *mean*—"

"Would you turn that damn *television* off? You *hate* television—why do you watch it all the time?"

"I'm just trying to relax a few minutes, is that all right? You just walked in the door."

"I know—you didn't even get up! You're so absorbed in your job and your work, you never think about me anymore. How long did we talk last night, anyway—five minutes?"

"What do you want me to tell you, how the market's doing?"

"I want you to *listen*!"

I exploded to my feet. "Goddammit, Sarah, I'm doing the best job I can! Don't you think I *know* you hate your job? Don't you think I *know* you want to live in the suburbs instead of this *shitty* neighborhood? That you hate walking around here at night? That you'd rather live in a cottage somewhere? Jesus Christ, haven't we been *through this* already? I didn't have a *choice,* okay? Now, why don't *you* start thinking about *me* and the bullshit *I* have to put up with every day! You think *your* job is hard—you have *no idea* what my job is like. You have *no idea* what I put up with every day. It's *ten* times worse than yours!"

"So what! Leave it at the door!"

I suddenly felt rippling through me a shock wave of uncontrolled anger. Without thinking, I grabbed the nearest object, a small houseplant on the coffee table and hurled it into the kitchen, where it shattered at the base of the wall. "Dammit, you just don't understand, do you?" I yelled. "You just don't understand!"

"I understand! I understand! I'm sick of this!"

Sobbing, she grabbed the howling dog and headed toward the door.

"Where are you going?"

"What do you think? I'm leaving! I can't take this anymore!"

I jumped over the coffee table. "Wait, wait. Just sit down!"

"No—no—I've had it! I can't do this anymore."

"Just wait!"

"Stop it!"

"Hold on—"

"Let me go!"

She broke free, and the door slammed behind her. I heard the elevator open and shut outside, the dog bark somewhere on the way down, and then there were four long hours of silence until the phone rang.

It was my mother, calling from Boston. "Paul! Sarah just got here. She's all upset. Honey—what is going *on* down there?"


## 25

Throughout October the Middle Markets effort continued to grow. We gained experience, refined our methods in many areas, and became more effective. In our prospecting efforts we discovered specific categories of institutions that were more rewarding than others. We learned a great deal about which instruments to push and why. We also began to involve more of the firm in our effort, especially those people disaffected with life in IEM. A frustrated trading assistant brought us some overlooked clients and sold them options on $70 million in Brady bonds. Our neglected Research Department generated trade ideas, which we recommended to specific institutions on the basis of their bond holdings.

I also made an effort to expand the Core, focusing on a broker in Kansas City, three in Houston, two in Los Angeles, and two in the South Tower, with mixed results. In dealing with Merrill Lynch brokers, the most difficult challenge was determining who was telling the truth. It wasn't always clear who was Middle Markets and who was Retail—the notorious list was constantly being updated— and many of the brokers were prone to leave you with the wrong impression if it suited them. In one case a young man called me from Merrill's Chicago office, stridently insisting that he was in their Middle Markets group even though his name was not on my list. He wanted to come to New York, he said, and implored me to meet him. A few hours before his arrival, the office manager in Chicago called to tell me that the man wasn't even a broker but a junior sales assistant on loan from a small retail office in Indiana. He may still be waiting in the lobby.

By the end of October, these expansionary efforts had added to our growing client list. The nascent Middle Markets Group traded with a number of new large market accounts—Banque National de Paris, Union Bank of Switzerland, Commercial Bank of New York, Nikko Capital Management—two small investment firms in Argentina, and, of all things, a grocery wholesaler in Kansas City, proving once and for all that there was fruit in our labors. The most potent addition, both fiscally and politically, was Cargill. The nation's largest privately held company, Cargill was an international commodities trader and sophisticated financial services company with offices all over the globe, including most emerging markets. It was also a former client of IEM Sales, which had broken off relations over a policy dispute months previously. Undaunted, Tim Avery had contacted its emerging markets group and begun a persistent effort to patch up relations, calling them daily, meeting them in person, and finally racking up a string of trades. His success inevitably came to the attention of IEM Sales, who overheard the traders talking on the phone. When a friendly trading assistant informed me of that, I quickly stepped in to preempt any conflict.

"Raoul," I said to Savegre one day, "I want to let you know we've landed a good account—Cargill."

"I know," Savegre said. "We used to cover them."

"So I hear. I guess there were some hard feelings. Anyway, Tim Avery knows some people there and picked up coverage. He's doing pretty well. I met them last week. They like him."

Savegre looked shocked. "Cargill came here? To visit Middle Markets?"

I nodded. "Avery is worried, though." I laughed preposterously. "He thinks you're going to take the account away."

Savegre dismissed the very idea with a wave of his hand. "Tell him he has nothing to worry about. We don't have to take accounts away from *Middle Markets*—I can promise you that!"

I relayed this conversation to Tim. "So relax, he said you have nothing to worry about."

Tim groaned. "I hate when people tell me that."


Inevitably, our success brought us into conflict with IEM Sales. Even though we could never hope to match their output—or even come close—it was the principle of the matter. We were developing major institutional accounts—look at Cargill!—while IEM Sales was stagnant. The traders were only too eager to crow about it too. If the roving associate and a few retail brokers can bring us new business, they chortled across the divide, why can't you guys? Increasingly, Sales no longer dismissed our effort out of hand but viewed it as an annoyance, even a threat, leading to a number of skirmishes.

These were generally spawned by coverage conflicts, which crept closer to home. Lee Sullivan, in scouring the chamber of commerce cocktail circuit, kept coming across Latin accounts covered by Alessandro da Silva, a Brazilian hired to replace Carlos Espinosa. "Da Silva covers their office in São Paulo," Lee would say. "But I'm talking to their New York office."

"An entirely different entity," I said. "As far as I can see."

Eventually, after some of these local accounts had talked to their Latin headquarters, Lee's name filtered back to da Silva. And da Silva came to see me.

"Paul—who is this Lee Sullivan?" he asked. "He's calling my accounts."

In such moments I was the picture of innocence. With Trading I was always a staunch defender of the Core, but with Sales—I just could not believe what they did sometimes!

"He is?" I said, shocked. "Which ones?"

"Icatu, Garantia—"

"He's calling Brazil?"

"No, their New York offices."

"Oh. Well that's different, isn't it?"

"They're still my accounts. Where does this guy work?"

"Don't worry, I'll talk to him."

"No," da Silva said wisely, "*I'll* talk to him. What's his number?"

There was no use hiding the Merrill Lynch phone book. Da Silva went back to his position and picked up the phone. There ensued a loud and abrupt conversation, which terminated with the normally sedate da Silva leaping to his feet, ripping off his headset, throwing it onto his chair, and releasing a torrent of strident Portuguese, the only recognizable phrase being "Middle Markets." Then he went to Savegre. Sullivan lost the battle—Savegre had the final word on most coverage issues, leaving us at a permanent disadvantage—and the sentiment of Sales took a turn for the worse.


Our mutual, tenacious effort to establish a foothold in the emerging markets forged a close relationship between myself and the Core. We talked daily. We shared information that we wouldn't share with others. We laughed about Savegre and Leonard and the way IEM operated. We worked hard, enjoyed our mutual dependence, and made money without any of the adversarial politics that characterized my office. The Core was my link to a more balanced world, a world of sense. I would look across the trading floor at the enemy while speaking to my allies.

Lee Sullivan was the most fun to deal with. His forward momentum was like a steamroller, flattening any obstacle before him. This included Institutional salespeople who were covering one of his leads. Inevitably, Lee would call me with the same tale: "I don't want to say this, *but*—the client is simply *not happy* with their present coverage. I think we can do better."

"Well, I certainly think we should do what's best for the firm, Lee, don't you?"

"Absolutely. Just for emerging markets business, of course."

"Of course."

When Lee went head-to-head with someone in Retail, he showed far less compunction. One unfortunate Retail broker had a client, a commercial bank, that had shown an interest in trading emerging markets bonds. "So I told him, look, all I want to do is cover the client for the emerging markets, and the guy started screaming at me on the phone," Lee told me. "He's crazy—really. That's what I hear. Anyway, he doesn't have a leg to stand on. It's a Middle Markets account."

"So what are you going to do?"

"Me? Nothing. I said my piece. But somehow Bud Leonard heard about it . . ."

I laughed. "Oh no. What did he say?"

" 'I'm going to crush that guy.' Or something like that."

Sometimes Lee did go a little overboard, however. One day Costas called me, as he often did, to brighten up my day with a little story.

"So Paul, I thought you might be interested to hear this. This weekend, Saturday night, I was lying in bed. It was late—I think eleven or so. The kids were asleep. And my wife and I—well, we were involved, shall we say. So right in the middle, the phone rings. I pick it up and it's Lee. 'Costas,' he says, 'sorry to bother you, but are you covering AIG?' "

Costas took a personal interest in my New York education. He had lived in Soho before moving to Greenwich, so he took it upon himself to show me some of his favorite spots. We went out one night and covered a handful of watering holes and restaurants. Another time he generously took Sarah and me out to dinner. Costas loved New York and thought we should too. When he had first arrived in the city, he admitted, it had taken some getting used to, but he distinctly remembered the day when he had been walking down Broadway, the snow was falling, and he looked around and realized that this was the place for him. "What was I going to do, return to Athens? There was nothing for me there," he said over dinner. "I love all the activity here. There is always something going on."

"Then why did you move to Greenwich?" I asked.

"Well—the kids," he said helplessly. "This is a city for adults. It's no place to raise kids."

The majority of my extracurricular activities were spent with Tim Avery. Tim liked to go out after work, eat well, and drink well. It was his way of shedding stress. And often he invited me; his partner Lou and I were the only two people he trusted at the firm. Tim would typically call in the afternoon and ask me to meet him at the Hudson River Club. This was always a starting point, never an end in itself. Invariably, after a few martinis, he would ask if I wanted some dinner, and off we would go. Tim always insisted on paying for everything, including car service to wherever we went—Cal's, the Ivy Club, Dozens. He was a perfectly subdued partier, evincing no change in manner from cubicle to bar. We developed an interesting hybrid relationship, both paternal and fraternal at the same time.

"I'm glad things are working out for you," he told me on one of our outings. "I wish I had come here when I was younger. How old are you?"

"Thirty next month."

Tim lifted a philosophical martini. "You know what they say—if you don't make it by the time you're thirty, you're not going to make it at all."


Having accepted constant struggle as a way of life, I was surprised when the signs of success began to appear in the office. One day as I was looking through my E-mail messages, I found a note from Forte: "You're doing a great job!" I studied it in disbelief. Praise was unheard of in IEM. Then Savegre, overcoming his usual resistance to my effort, began to recognize the potential benefits in it. I was, after all, working for him. One day he came over to my position and invited me to attend a meeting between IEM and Fidelity Investments, one of our largest customers. It was the first time he had invited me to anything. The trading desk also woke up and started picking up the phone. Finally Forte asked me if I wanted to put Middle Markets on the morning call. Now that was progress! The next day the Core called in for the first time, feeling like kings.

Even Post began to look at me differently. Coming back to my position one day, I overheard him telling Orlova that my business was "taking off." Considering what was happening to him, he took the news pretty well. The bottom had completely fallen out of the structured products market, leaving him with nothing to do. On top of his market calamity, Post, Sr., had suddenly died of a massive heart attack. His son's days were now filled with lengthy will-related discussions with family members, faxing his résumé, and taking a host of medicines. More than once I caught him staring reflectively out the window.

After months of bearing down, my success was not quite as I had pictured it. There was no lessening of the pressure, no feeling, as Tim Avery had implied, that I had made it. I may have raised myself a notch or two on the food chain, but there was no noticeable difference in my life. I was still going head-to-head with people every day. No one wanted to recognize my success unless they had to. I still had to rely on the grapevine to know what was going on. Subconsciously, however, I still had faith that better things lay around the corner, just beyond my grasp. I had a recurring vision of opening the door to the conference room and the whole office yelling, "Surprise! You made it!"

The main difference in my life was that I forgot I was living it. My first taste of success released an adrenaline rush that kept me moving and prevented me from reflecting. I had a thousand action items on my plate every day. I wasn't waiting for anyone to tell me what to do nor was I struggling to figure out the basics. I still had much to learn, but for the first time my priority was doing, not learning. I came in early, motivated to do more. I stayed late and came in on weekends. I was beating IEM, and the market, and thinking about nothing else.

It was during this time that I found myself, early one morning, at the Court Street subway station, my daily launching point for Manhattan. Descending the stairs at a fast clip, I brushed past the resident homeless person holding out his cup and came to a halt in an unusual line. A woman was standing at the turnstiles with a clipboard, taking a survey on where people were going. Behind her stood two transit cops in blue winter coats and fur caps with their hands clasped behind their backs, rocking back and forth on their heels and joking with each another. "Destination?" the woman kept asking. People would reply with their next stop and push through.

What a pain in the ass, I thought. This idiot is holding up the line! I unbuttoned my winter coat, letting my double-breasted jacket stick out. I wiped a fleck of mud off my freshly shined shoes. Come on! I don't want to miss the morning call! Finally I arrived at the turnstiles, feeling the flush of the market on my face, and glared at the woman.

"Destination?"

Over her shoulder, one of the transit cops leaned toward the other with a laugh. "Wall Street," he muttered.


## 26

The door opened and Sarah came in. I had been waiting. It took four hours to drive from Boston, and here she was, on time. Without a word she came over and sat down next to me on the couch, hung her arms between her knees and stared at the floor.

I put my arm around her. "We've got to stop doing this to ourselves."

"I know," she whispered.

"We've never had a fight like that."

"I know."

"I feel sick about it."

"I do too."

"All we're doing is taking out all this stress on each other."

"I know, that's what your parents said."

"They did?"

She nodded. "I talked to them for hours. Your poor mother—she didn't get to sleep until three in the morning."

"I know, I talked to her this morning, after you left."

"I don't know what I'd do without them."

I leaned closer. "Sorry about the plant. That was stupid, really."

"Paul—you can't do that again."

"I don't even know how it happened."

She sat upright. "So what are we going to do now?"

"What do you want to do?"

"Go back to school."

I shrugged. "Okay."

"Your parents agree. It's the best thing. Both of us can't be working at the same time, not with the jobs we have—that's the problem. And you're making more money than I am."

"You don't have to convince me, I think it's a great idea. Let's get things back to normal."

"I think it will be easier on us too if I were here once in a while."

"I couldn't agree with you more."

"You don't care about the money?"

"Forget the *money*," I said. "Money is supposed to buy happiness. Is this happiness?"

"We can afford it. I've figured it all out."

"Let's not worry about it. We need to start putting *us* first. I'd rather quit *both* our jobs than go through *this* again."

Sarah released a deep sigh. "I feel better already." Then a smile struggled to her face, flooding me with sudden relief.

"I love you," I said. "Nothing is going to take that away."


Prior to moving from Annapolis, Sarah had applied to graduate school at Columbia University Teachers College, just in case her job didn't transfer. Now, thankfully, we had an acceptance to fall back on.

We visited the campus a week before fall classes began. Columbia is a tremendous school but is disadvantaged by its location adjacent to Harlem: it suffers from high crime levels. The main campus has a high wall around it—in various places, stone, brick, and wrought-iron fence—that is stories tall and stretches for blocks, broken by numerous gates. Over the years most of these gates have been locked up or sealed forever, leaving only a few entry and exit points; if you don't know where you are going, you can walk endlessly in the interior, always finding yourself at a dead end. Like the White House, the once open campus has become a closed fortress.

Not that there aren't good reasons for taking such security measures. During Sarah's tenure at Columbia, one student would be shot in the stairwell of a dorm during a robbery attempt and the Teachers College bookstore would be robbed at gunpoint for the umpteenth time. Unfortunately, the battlements did not protect our car, which was broken into while parked facing the entrance to Teachers College. Someone drove a screwdriver into the driver's door, popped the lock, stole the radio, opened the trunk, and stole the jumper cables, a box of cassettes, and a repair kit. Luckily The Club was on the steering wheel.

Aside from the added risk, Sarah's return to school made an immediate improvement in our lives. Instead of a stressful commute and a life on the road, she spent her time pursuing a master's degree in educational technology, her passion; instead of coming home to an empty apartment, I came home to an excited Internet browser; instead of ordering pizza, we shared cooking and had real dinners together; instead of days of separation, we had a lot of quality time together; instead of a life of total work, we led a more balanced and happy existence. Our marriage was back.

This, in turn, changed the way we related to the city. Instead of trying to escape it all the time, we set out to enjoy it. We explored Manhattan, using our Zagat guide to hunt down good restaurants, and wandered the Village, which was relatively close, enjoying its endless number of cafés. We took in *Miss Saigon* and an off-Broadway show. Sarah also met a lot of people in school, providing us with a new circle of friends. Things were going so well, both at work and at home, that we even decided to recommence our hunt for a house. We located an affordable home in Fort Lee, New Jersey, which faced the water and even looked like a cottage, if you squinted, and seriously considered buying it. It was more than just the fun we were having: we were finally beating the city! We were enjoying ourselves! We were *winning*! By hard-won experience we had finally unearthed the hidden dynamic, the digital nature of New York: you were either surfing the wave or being pounded into the beach; you were either throwing the punches or taking them; you were either riding the bull or being stomped by the bear. There was no in-between. The market, as everyone knew, was never stable for long. So the trick was to beat it. Life in New York was not a stroll in Central Park—it was *war*. And each day was a new offensive. You didn't ever relax: you reaped your joys from *victory*.

Armed with this knowledge, we hit the streets equipped for battle. We adopted a whole new mode of driving, accelerating at the green, braking hard at the red, bearing down on pedestrians until they wisely picked up the pace—damn pedestrians! We leaned on the horn at the slightest excuse—hurry up! It's green! We cut off other drivers, swore at them when they cut us off, didn't let anyone into our lane, passed as many people as possible. We totally blocked out anything we did not like. We no longer saw the trash—that was just the city. We knew where we could and couldn't go and weren't bothered by the question—that was just the city. The crime wasn't even an issue anymore, just another obstacle to avoid. So our car radio had been stolen—who was stupid enough to have a radio in New York? What fools we had been! When two of Sarah's sweaters were stolen from the laundry room, we chastised ourselves—why didn't we keep an eye on them? When a package mailed to me disappeared from the Red Hook post office, I slapped my forehead—why didn't I use Federal Express? We had all our survival skills down pat and laughed at those who paid the price for not using them— dopes! We had lowered our standards and learned to like it. What else could we do when faced with our own decline? Whine? Complain? Speak out? Ha! This was the Big Apple! Deal with it or depart.

In this ongoing, daily struggle, it was Sarah who produced the ultimate victory, and hence, it is she who must always be remembered as the more accomplished New Yorker of the two of us. Her lance was thrown at Macy's flagship store on Thirty-fourth Street, the store which months before had lured us to its couch trading floor with false claims of models in striped blue. Well, he who laughs last . . .

I was sitting in our quiet living room when Sarah burst in to tell the tale. "You're not going to believe it! You're just not going to believe it! Ha! Ha! This is excellent!" She dropped her shopping bags and lifted her arms to the ceiling. "I just totally *screwed* Macy's!"

"You did?" I perked up and dropped the newspaper. This I wanted to hear.

"It was unbelievable!"

"What happened?"

"Oh, this feels *so good*!"

"Tell me!"

"Okay, okay!" She paced excitedly in front of me. "I decided to go to Macy's on the way home. I knew that they were having a sale, so I stopped in to look at some dresses. I needed a cocktail dress. I found a nice one too. Anyway, I'm standing in line to go into the dressing room and there's a woman at the cash register throwing an absolute *fit*. 'Your salesperson told me that I could return these!' she's saying. But they wouldn't give her her money back. They had to call the department manager over. The next thing I know, the girl at the dressing room is saying, 'Miss, would you like to try those on?'—you know, I was so engrossed in watching this scene that I didn't even notice it was my turn to go in! Anyway, I go into the dressing room and I'm trying on the last dress and I hear, right outside the dressing stall, these two saleswomen talking about what's going on outside, the commotion out there. And one of them is *admitting* to the fact that she *screwed* the woman at the cash register! She had lied to her, and now she was hiding in the dressing room! And the other saleswoman says, 'Just go take a coffee break. I'll cover for you.' Meanwhile I can still hear this woman screaming at the manager outside! So I took off the dress—I don't think I've ever undressed so quickly in my life!—and I run out there and it's getting even *nastier*. I can hear the woman saying to the manager, 'Are you calling me a liar? Is that what you're saying? That I'm lying?'" Sarah was briefly overcome with laughter. "So I go right up to the department manager—he's this slick-looking guy about thirty years old—and I say, 'Excuse me, I have no idea what the situation is here, but you have two salespeople in that dressing room who just admitted to *lying* to this woman about your return policy. I think that's disgusting!'"

"You didn't!" I broke into hysterical laughter on the couch. "You're joking!"

"No I'm not! Anyway, when the woman heard me say this, I looked like some kind of saint. And she said, 'That's it! I want the head manager of this store and I want to see him *right now*! I'm not leaving this place until I do!' And by now, there's a crowd of people because she's throwing such a fit. So of course two sales-people swoop in on me almost immediately and ask, 'Would you like to buy those dresses?' and they usher me away to buy that green dress. But as soon as I bought the dress, I went back to the woman to see how things were going. The minute she saw me, she *grabbed me* by the arm. By now she had the head manager of the store there! So she drags me up to him and says, 'This is the woman who finally resolved this issue! Who finally got to the bottom of the matter and exposed the truth! If this woman hadn't heard your two salespeople talking about *lying* to me,' Sarah burst into laughter, 'I would still be in this predicament!' And I said to the man-ager, 'I just think it's a shame that you have salespeople who *lie to your customers* just to make a *sale*!'"

"Ha! Ha! Ha!"

"And I said it in front of this huge crowd!" Sarah joined me in uncontrolled laughter and finally got hold of herself. "So wait, wait, this is the best part. I'm about to leave and the woman—she's so thankful—she turns to me and says, 'You're not from New York, are you?'"

That was it. I fell on the floor in convulsions. I was laughing so hard that Tug-ger came over and started growling at me. "So—ha, ha! So—ha, ha, ha! So what—ha!—so what did you *say*?" I finally asked.

"I said NO!"

"But we are!" I shouted hysterically. "We're New Yorkers!"

*27*

In my continuing efforts to grow the Middle Markets business, I decided to make a trip to Houston and Los Angeles, where I hoped to add a few brokers to the Core. I was accompanied by Eduardo Salvador, our strategist, who had put together an advanced briefing on the technical analysis of our bonds. Eduardo was a Spaniard from the Canary Islands and, while Latin, one of the most visible outsiders in the office. I had seen him take a lot of heat on the trading floor, though I never understood why. On the plane ride down, I finally heard the whole story.

Eduardo's tale was a model of how IEM operated. In June, he had been hired from Citibank, where he had worked for five years as a technical analyst. A week later he arrived for his first day in the office and attended the morning call. As soon as Sales & Trading finished their daily spiels, Savegre pushed the speakerphone toward him: "Research is next." It was then that Eduardo discovered he was not just to be IEM's strategist but the head of our entire research effort.

This was not a position Eduardo was qualified to fill. By normal standards the head of our research effort should have been a Ph.D., with many years' experience in Latin American economics, and be a senior manager. But such people did not come cheap. Their total compensation could amount to over a million dollars a year—another blow to the bonus pool. And in Latin Boomtown, why pay for experience? So instead, with the concurrence of the firm's Global Research Group, IEM hired Eduardo and gave him a promotion his first day on the job.

In the following weeks Eduardo found himself in a difficult situation. Apart from his lack of experience, Research was in a shambles and had been ever since the noisy departure of its former head. Relations with the desk were so bad that the remaining analysts deliberately provided the minimum possible support. They came in at nine, left at five, and didn't pick up the phone in between, tactics aided by their physical separation. Emerging Markets Fixed Income Research was situated on Twenty-one, five floors above us. Weeks went by without seeing a single research analyst on our trading floor.

Eduardo tried to revitalize this staff, and with sufficient help he might have succeeded. But he faced an even larger obstacle as well: Savegre. The research published by an investment bank is supposed to be used by investors to make informed investment decisions, making the integrity of those reports vitally important. But depending on how they were written, they could dissuade readers from making certain investments. Savegre, who was wary of any undue negative effect on Sales, clashed with Eduardo over the reports, and at one point, Savegre took away all Eduardo's responsibilities in IEM. Eduardo had to go to Escobar and his boss in the Global Research Group to have them reinstated, forcing him to publicly defend himself. Meanwhile Savegre began using a research analyst in the junk bonds group, who published findings more in line with what Sales wanted.* Elsewhere Savegre took to disparaging Eduardo, implicitly blaming him for the problems besetting Sales. During the morning call, he would belittle him in front of the group by challenging his findings. "Are you sure that is the way to go, Eduardo?" "Why do you say that?" "On what evidence do you base that finding?" "What makes you so sure about that conclusion?" For his part, Eduardo fought back by being as professional as possible. He also joined our Middle Markets group.

Arriving first in Houston, Eduardo and I went to the well-heeled Galleria, an enormous shopping mall and business complex where Merrill Lynch had its posh offices, noted for their interior balconies. Eduardo's presentation was extremely well received. In the middle of it a secretary arrived with a message for him, which he tucked in his pocket. "Savegre," Eduardo sighed during an intermission. He picked up the nearby phone and called IEM. "No, I said I was bullish on Argentina . . . I'm positive . . . because the fundamentals are there . . . That's not what I said . . . Yes, I'm sure . . . Check with my secretary, I don't have it with me."

Eduardo hung up and said nothing. By the end of our meeting he had another message from Savegre, which turned into another skirmish—Savegre questioning, Eduardo answering; Savegre jabbing, Eduardo parrying; Savegre pressuring, Eduardo trying to maintain his composure. Savegre finally retreated.

"Does he always do this?" I asked.

"*All the time,* man. He's on my back wherever I go."

We laughed about it on the plane to L.A., during which I related some of the travails of the Middle Markets effort. It felt great to finally share my thoughts with a sympathetic voice and to know that my experience was not unique. The attitude in IEM was so senseless, I told Eduardo: wasn't the purpose of business to make money? And yet, instead of helping us achieve that goal, IEM had done everything possible to prevent it!

"They've had it handed to them on a platter for so long, they can't see that," he replied.

"Do you know what we could do if we had some real leadership and worked as a team? We're not a very large organization."

---

* May 13, 1994: "The recent sell-off does not negate the investment merits of international emerging markets debt. Indeed, the declines may have created an exceptional, longer-term opportunity. Typically, in such cases, investors can capitalize on the creation of extraordinary values without taking excessive risks."

"Whoa! Listen to what you're saying!" Eduardo laughed.

"What? I'm serious."

"Man, haven't you ever worked in Latin America before?"

"Not really."

"Believe me, they don't have your gringo attitude down there."

I had no idea what he meant.

"It's this whole Protestant view you have," he explained. "You know—work has a moral value; a corporation is a group effort with a formal hierarchy; employees are a resource, so you distribute profits; the goal is to build, to create wealth. There's none of that with the Latin elite. Down there, power is the right to steal, man. Look at the difference between the haves and the have-nots—it's the biggest spread in the world! They don't care about the long term—they want the profits today, for themselves. It's a gypsy view. You just don't see it because part of the game is keeping everyone else in the dark."

"But Wall Street operates the same way," I said. "What's the difference between the Latin elite and the Financial elite?"

"There *isn't any.* Why do you think the Latin Mafia *exists?* These guys are perfect for Wall Street. This whole emerging markets *bubble* is perfect. Look at what's going on—all these small-time investors go to these huge American firms they think they can trust—and they're just part of the other side, man! They're making a fortune! All these stupid gringos hold out their fistfuls of dollars, they get a happy handshake, the money goes off to Mexico, and then—whack, their hand gets cut off. You wait and see. This entire market was built on the wreckage of the last one, remember?" He snorted in disbelief. "I tell you one thing: they're laughing like hell in Mexico City right now."

"So what—you think this is some big conspiracy?"

"No, it's just the way it works, man! You're not seeing it for the first time. There's this layer of bullshit on top, what everyone *says* they're doing, just to keep all the outsiders happy, to keep the money coming in, and below that is the truth, the way things *really* work. It's all a big game."

"Come on—"

"Look at Savegre," Eduardo said, growing animated, "there's the perfect example. You think he gave you this job so you could build a business and make money for Merrill Lynch? Hell, no! He was just answering the mail, man. The firm came knocking and asked him to get Retail involved in his business, right? You think he wants a couple hundred brokers in his business? Of course not! He's Institutional Sales, he gets nothing out of a retail trade. So what does he do? He gives the job to you! A gringo with a few months' experience. And what are you going to do? You're going to fail! That's what he *wants,* man. He never dreamed you'd actually *pull it off.* And you know, there's very few people in the firm who would fault his logic."

I felt a touch of nausea stirring my stomach. The plane felt smaller, claustrophobic. Was all that true? It was yet another question that had no clear answer.

I released my seat belt. "So what's going to happen to Middle Markets?"

Eduardo shrugged. "We just keep on plowing forward, doing what we can, that's all. They can't argue with success. There are still some rules they have to play by. They're not going to make it easy on us, though. You're like a cancer, man, all this gringo logic."

"Believe me, I know it."

"Hey—I know too," Eduardo said, laughing. He removed a few messages from his shirt pocket. "Want one?"



Our L.A. visit went according to plan. Eduardo gave another great presentation, and I spoke with Rick Daily, the office manager, about some leads I had found on the West Coast. A few weeks prior, I had discovered that IEM had once had a salesman in San Francisco, who had quit the previous year. I unearthed his old coverage list, which yielded a number of idle accounts. Unbeknownst to me, however, Savegre had decided to train a bond salesman on Seven, David Rodriguez, to fill the empty San Francisco position. When Rodriguez learned of my planned trip, he provided me, as a preemptive measure, a list of people he planned to cover, written in longhand on a napkin. I gave the napkin a very narrow reading. If one of my leads was a subsidiary of a napkin name, I kept it. If the scrawl was illegible, I didn't bother to clarify it. The rest of the names I reluctantly removed from my list. I was walking a dangerous line, but Rodriguez wasn't going out to the West Coast for six months: we had plenty of time to plant our flag first.

I couldn't explain all this to Daily, of course. It was difficult to explain IEM politics to anyone. So I told him that our methods of deconfliction weren't foolproof, that we had had some problems in the past, and that we should be discreet.

Daily eyed me suspiciously. "I don't want to do anything that's going to get me in trouble."

I felt the unnerving pucker of conscience, that feeling you get when you're nearing the ethical line. Had I checked the leads diligently enough? Savegre had glanced briefly at the list, and I had reviewed Rodriguez's napkin, but, in a manner reminiscent of my boss, I knew that I was just answering the mail, doing the minimum in the hope of achieving my own purposes. A visceral resolve overrode my concerns: Who cares? Those bastards *deserve it.*

"Don't worry," I told Daily. "I've checked them all out."

As soon as our visit was over, Eduardo and I left for the airport. We checked in at the ticket counter and headed toward the departure gate.

"Mr. Salvador!" the ticket clerk called out. "I forgot—I have a message for you."

• • •

It didn't take long for my actions in L.A. to blow up in my face. After I left, Daily decided to show the leads to his boss, just to make sure. Not wanting to take the risk himself, his boss then called the head of Institutional Sales on the West Coast and read him some of the names on the list. The man grew apoplectic. Who was this guy flying out to the West Coast and handing out Institutional Sales accounts to Middle Markets? he demanded. He called the head of Institutional Sales in New York, who called Savegre, and all three of them had a conference call to discuss the matter—an unpleasant call for Savegre, I suspect, who called me over to the Sales loop soon after it concluded. He was standing with the napkin scribe, David Rodriguez.

To Savegre's credit, he did not immediately explode. Whatever else he was, he was not a hypocrite: he expected no more from anyone else than he did from himself. There had been times when I had found this insulting—the assumption that I was no different from him. Now I felt nothing.

"Paul," he said, adopting his agitated professor tone, "I just had a very disturbing call from the head of Institutional Sales. Did you give out a list of large market accounts to those brokers in L.A.?"

I shrugged. "I gave them a bunch of accounts. I showed you those."

"Do you have the list?"

"I left it in L.A."

"Were any of David's accounts on that list?"

"Not that I know of."

"Yes, there were," Rodriguez said.

"David says he told you to exclude some accounts," Savegre said.

"He gave me some names on a napkin, if that's what you mean."

"Then how did they get on that list out there?"

"They didn't, as far as I know."

"What about Capital International?" Rodriguez said, naming a well-known mutual fund.

"That wasn't on the napkin."

"Yes, it was."

"No, Capital Guardian was on the napkin."

"That's the corporate parent."

I shrugged.

"That wasn't the only one either," Rodriguez said.

"Look—it's simple," Savegre said to me. "The L.A. business is shut down. You're not to give them any more accounts."

Alarmed, I said, "But we have a lot of potential business out there. They've already sold some Bradies and some CDs."

"It doesn't matter."

"That doesn't make sense! I gave them a long list of potential clients. If they don't cover them, who will?"

That's when Savegre lost it. Like most successful people at the firm, Savegre did not like to be challenged. The very fact of his position at the top—of having *won*—made him right, and the constant competition demanded that he *be* right. "It's not your responsibility to decide!" he shouted. A few of the salesmen turned around to watch. "And I want to see that list!"

"Okay," I shrugged, and walked back to my position.

I called L.A. that afternoon to ask for the list. Daily was apologetic for having caused any trouble and quickly grasped the circumstances of my call. "Unfortunately," he said with mock solemnity, "the list has been destroyed."

I never brought up the list again, and Savegre never asked for it. I did notice him looking at me differently, however. It wasn't mistrust I saw, as one might expect, but the respect due a worthy adversary, mixed with a surprising measure of approval—the kind you see in a proud father whose son has finally learned to walk.


One of the benefits of the expansion of the Middle Markets Group was a Merrill Lynch boondoggle of congressional proportions. One of the brokers I dealt with in the Midwest, an avid fly fisherman, invited me to join him on a fishing trip to a remote spot in northern New Mexico. "The San Juan River," he explained. "It's one of the ten best trout streams in the West." The reason, I discovered only too late, was because of the dam. The San Juan River dam has a constant flow of water at its base at the same temperature and pressure all year long. There are no seasonal fluctuations to disturb the organisms on which the trout feed, no unseemly chaos of nature to upset them, allowing them to eat to their heart's content, and to grow. Nature has been improved on, bettered, stripped of its inefficiencies. It was, as our guide called it, a turbocharged trout stream.

A lot of people knew it too. I lost count at forty bodies standing near the concrete mouth, where I witnessed something unique in all my years of fishing: three fly fishermen with their lines crossed. The reason for the crowd, of course, was all the trout swimming by—huge trout, the biggest trout I had ever seen. Every thirty seconds or so someone would catch one and let it go. It was a regulated enterprise: barbless hooks, catch-and-release only, as all the signs on the shore clearly indicated. There were some areas farther down the river where you could keep a limited number of your catch, but no matter: the state kept the river well stocked. Supply always met demand. Between the dam and the Fish and Game Department, man had smoothed out the fluctuations of both the life cycle and the business cycle. The motels nearby were always full.

I sat with my back to the rest of the boat, watching the silent fly fishermen. Apart from the hum of the dam, the only sound was the splash of another fish being caught, which I quickly grew to hate. The fly fishermen would briefly raise their heads, view the size of the catch, and continue bringing in line. Otherwise I was afloat on a river of the dead. They were a uniform crowd, each trying to draw something from the water, yet mindless of why. Somewhere along the way their choice had been lost, mingled with the will of another, a familiar presence, so eerie here, where I least expected it. They had set out to find nature and been herded to this turbocharger. They had been lured to trout fishing by the magazines and catalogs, outfitted with all the designer equipment necessary to land a trout in the San Juan River and a big camera to prove it. And to prove without a doubt that their choice had been the right one—to feel secure about what they were doing with their lives—there was everyone else here doing just what they were doing, wearing just what they were wearing, reaffirming how they were supposed to feel, what they were supposed to do. If all the trout fishermen are here, I must be here. This is what trout fishing is all about. Trout fishing is about catching big trout. If I catch a big trout, I am happy. From the loftiest heights of man, from his need for beauty, for nature, for a spiritual connection, they had stripped themselves to conformity and now stood naked in the stream, naked in their greed for the big fish.

My rod finally twitched and I brought aboard a twenty-three-inch brown trout. It was the largest trout I had ever caught in my life. As I detached the fly from its mouth, I noticed the little red spots on its jaws from the previous hooks—one still bleeding—and suddenly wanted to be anywhere except here, holding this pathetic fish. But before long even it too would be obsolete and we would all throw our lines into the *artificial* artificial San Juan River, a theme park in Orlando where your electric boat took you to the recycled falls for exactly thirty minutes of casting, where fake fish rose to plastic flies, where the guide wore mouse ears and everything was perfectly efficient, safe, sanitary, and, above all, profitable.

I slipped the fish into the water.

"Just like New York, hey, Paul?" my fishing partner joked.

"Yeah," I replied. "A river runs through it."


## 28

In the wake of the L.A. fiasco, there was no longer any doubt about the relationship between the Middle Markets Group and IEM Sales. In the minds of Sales, Middle Markets had been caught red-handed trying to take away Institutional accounts. That was as close as you came to a surprise attack in the bond business. The mood of Sales was also darkened by the marked decline of their revenues, which, as bonus season approached, left them tense and frustrated. So I should not have been surprised when they declared all-out war.

The trouble began when one of our two salesmen in London, Reggie Cowslip, discovered that I had forwarded one of his internal messages to the Core. He called in a huff, ranting about the security of his missives. "I don't want my opinions sent out to thousands of retail brokers!" Naturally I claimed that no one had ever explained the policy to me, which was technically true, and that appeared to satisfy him. But within a few days, through an honest electronic glitch, another note slipped through the cracks, prompting the diligent Cowslip to send out a message to the entire group: THERE IS A RETAIL SPY IN THE OFFICE. I KNOW WHAT MY SOLUTION IS—DO YOU?

The solution, of course, was to drop the spy from your message distribution list. This was easily corrected. Noticing a distinct message shortfall, I went around to various office computers one evening and put myself back on distribution. The long lists hid me well. But the action did nothing to halt my growing isolation.

Within days, the climate worsened. While the Core was allowed into the IEM call, we also had our own daily call to discuss matters of interest to us. I ran this call from the IEM conference room, per a posted schedule, every day at 9:00. It was a brief five- or ten-minute performance. One morning while I was talking into the speakerphone, Mickey Gurevich, top salesman and noted Latin Mafioso, burst into the room and started waving his hands at me. "Paul you'll have to get off, I need the room."

I pointed to the speakerphone and kept talking.

"I *need* the *room*, Paul, *now*!"

All of this was filtering across the airwaves. I held up an open palm—STOP!

Gurevich stormed out, slapping the doorframe.

A few minutes later the call ended and I left for my position. Gurevich was waiting and pounced on me with an acid whine. "Paul, you *can't* use the conference room whenever you want! I have *investors* coming!"

"Mickey, I've been using this conference room for the past month. Look at the schedule on the wall."

"I don't care about the schedule! I have investors coming! I need the room!"

"If you sign up for it—"

"Paul! Paul! You don't get it—"

"Everyone could hear you, you know—"

"Paul! Listen to me! I don't want to hear it!"

"Mickey, you are being ridiculous—"

"I don't want to hear it!"

Gurevich waved me off with both hands, his features twisting in distaste. "Now go away."

I lifted a hopeless hand and returned to my position.

A few minutes later Savegre arrived by my side. His top producer had just lodged a complaint.

"What just happened with Mickey?" he asked.

"Nothing. He's acting like a prima donna." I related what had just occurred.

"Can't you do it at a different time?"

I stared at Savegre in disbelief. "I've been doing it at the same time every day for *months*."

"Then find another room!" He frowned in irritation and sped off. That surprised me. Savegre usually avoided confrontation whenever possible.

The next morning I retreated to a conference room down the hall, hoping that the storm would soon pass and I could return to IEM. Then Sales affected another change in policy: they cut the Core from the morning call.

"I called in as usual," Costas explained, "and the operator said my name was no longer on the access list."

I immediately went to Savegre. "The call has been restricted to Sales and Trading only," he said.

"Why?"

"Security."

"My guys have been on the call for weeks. They're not a security threat."

Savegre snorted. "Who knows who a bunch of Retail brokers are going to talk to?"

"They're *not* a bunch of Retail brokers," I groaned. "They're three guys who have been busting their asses to sell our bonds for months now, and they're *succeeding*. Don't you think someone could have at least explained this to them instead of just pulling the plug?"

Savegre glared briefly at me, then snapped his head back to his position. "It's an institutional call. That's the decision."

I asked Forte to explain Savegre's attitude.

"They're worried about not seeing the flows," he said.

"How is cutting out Middle Markets going to increase the flows?"

"It's not just Middle Markets, it's anyone who's not doing institutional business."

"We *sell* to institutions. That's who our clients *are*."

Forte held up his hands in surrender. "Look, I know, it's stupid. I'm just telling you how they think."

I relayed what I had learned to the Core on our next morning call.

"So now they're blaming *us* for their losses?" Lee exclaimed in exasperation.

"Mysterious leaks sink IEM," Tim joked.

"Paul—what do you want to do?" Costas asked.

"Find a way around it, of course."

Our loophole turned out to be "Fidel." There was a changing code word, the name of some Latin American politician, which allowed ad hoc participants to get on the call. Forte's secretary kept it in the notebook on her desk. The next day this secret key magically fell into the hands of the Core, allowing them to covertly listen in. And what a comfort it was, as I stood in our cramped and tense conference room, listening to the classified comments of the increasingly paranoid Latin Mafia, to look at the speakerphone and know the Core was there. But within a few days, as part of the larger security shake-up, the code word was abolished, leaving us out in the cold once again. There was no alternative but to do what I had done months before: call the Core from my position and repeat the entire morning call to them. It was maddening: as if we were starting all over again, having accomplished nothing. As if the declining health of IEM were the fault of three brokers from Retail.

The final slap occurred shortly thereafter. One morning I entered the packed conference room at the usual time and stood against the wall, sipping my coffee. Within seconds, I was roused from thought by a voice:

"What are you doing here?"

I looked up. Gurevich was staring at me. So was the rest of the room.

"What do you mean?" I said.

"This is an institutional call."

"So?"

"You're Retail. You're not on the list."

"I've been on the list the last nine months."

He flicked his wrist toward the door. "Get out."

There was nothing I could do: Gurevich was a Latin Mafioso. I shook my head in disbelief and left.

Back at my position, I called Costas, extremely agitated. "You won't believe this. Now they've kicked *me* out of the morning call."

"You're not serious!"

"I'm deadly serious. Can you believe it?"

"Have those people lost their minds? You are part of their group!"

"Their *group*? Costas, this is the twenty-first century—there *is* no group!"


As the war with Sales dragged on, Middle Markets continued to experience steady growth in new clients and trading volume. November was a particularly fruitful month, our best to date. The Core traded $83 million in bonds and options on another $74.5 million, statistics which succeeded in turning some heads. Even Escobar came nosing around my position. But while my business survived, the conflict took a heavy toll on me personally. I couldn't detach myself from the struggle; it preoccupied my life. Outnumbered and outranked, I stayed on constant alert all day long wondering when the next attack would come, seeing the heads turn in my direction, catching whispers of conversation, supported only by the Core. "You know, Paul," Costas said one day, "when I was a paratrooper, I once blew off course and came down in a farm in a big pile of—well, shit, actually. I got it all over me. That's what I think of when I think of your job. You are jumping into shit every day."

The insanity of the daily jump was most draining: there was an unbroken tension between my efforts to build a business and the efforts of others to prevent it. It made me wonder what the purpose of my job was. Why was I spending my life in a constant struggle against my own coworkers?

"Oh, you're just dealing with the existential questions," Lee told me. "Don't worry, you'll get over it. We all do."

The uncertainty of my position plagued me even further. Was I committing professional suicide or was this just part of the game?

"There's a light at the end of the tunnel," Tim said. "Hopefully it isn't an oncoming train."

Meanwhile I began to notice some disturbing changes in me that had been brewing for some time. By the end of the day my face now bore the trader's sunburn, the flush of the market. At times I could feel the blood filling my features, pressing on the skin. I had gained about ten pounds too, reaching a record weight, and developed a slight sag beneath my chin. I didn't sleep well anymore, and I had a new sprinkling of gray hair. My patience had dwindled to nothing. I snapped at people in the office and on the phone just as I had once been snapped at. I talked at a faster rate and walked at a faster rate. One morning I accompanied one of my neighbors to the subway and found him having difficulty keeping up with me. Meanwhile I kept up a constant stream of one-way conversation about the market, reminding myself of Lee. On the way home I often found myself dropping into Café-on-Clinton for a Guinness or two. I felt I needed a way station between office and home just to calm me down. And my moral health was suffering. Increasingly I felt I had become part of the problem, no better than Savegre and Breen or any of the others. I wasn't a slick yet, but the better I got at my job, the closer I came to the edge of their slippery slope. Then I started getting headaches and went to see a doctor. He had seen this problem before, he said. A lot of people in the financial industry suffered from it. He prescribed Valium.

That was a shock. Valium? Wasn't that a tranquilizer for people whose lives had slipped out of their control? I tucked the pills in my drawer at work and vowed not to use them. Instead I took longer walks. But once the cold weather set in, the walks ceased and the pressure grew. After a few months on Wall Street I felt my entire constitution—moral, physical, and emotional—under attack.

Finally, one afternoon when everything was about to boil over, I seized on a simple solution, effecting a sudden, pronounced shift in outlook. Everything was a game, I decided, with a great expulsion of breath. Nothing mattered. What I did every day had no meaning. We were all just players here in IEM doing something with no consequences—social, moral, or otherwise—apart from the making of money. My conflict with Sales was nothing personal, just business. Hadn't Mundt taught me that, oh so long ago? There was no use trying to *judge* it, or make any *sense* of it at all. That was the cause of all my problems: expecting my life, my modern life, to be reasonable; thinking that it was susceptible to analysis, to understanding, and ultimately, to my control; thinking that I could plan ahead, invest myself emotionally in a project, expect some security, take charge of my destiny. Well, the market made no sense: you just grabbed it by the horns and rode it. You had no *control,* no expectation of *permanence.* You just tried not to get *thrown.* That was the new meaning of my life: holding on. That was it! And the joke was on me. I had been taking life too seriously. Really, it had no meaning at all.

# 4

## E  X  H  A  U  S  T

### 29

On December 1, I went down to Seven to speak with a trader in Money Markets. As I walked up behind him, I overheard him talking on the phone: "Just sell it as soon as you can. Just my shares in Merrill. Right." The trader spied me by his side and pointed to his Bloomberg monitor: ORANGE COUNTY FUND POSTS $1.5 BILLION LOSS. The largest municipal failure ever had just been announced, plunging Merrill Lynch into the worst scandal in its history. Within the next few days the Orange County treasurer had resigned, the Orange County investment portfolio had declared bankruptcy, and lawsuits began flying, eventually culminating in the county's mammoth $2 billion suit against Merrill, which had sold the fund the bulk of its portfolio. Though culpability had yet to be established, one thing was clear: the lawyers were going to be very happy.

Spurred on by the unfolding scandal, I did some legal research of my own. One of the benefits of the Information Age on Wall Street is the incredible amount of financial information available at your fingertips. This includes all the news on your employer—publicly available news, that is—whether good or bad. By simply punching in M-L-C-N <go> on my Bloomberg machine, for instance, I could view the Merrill Lynch company news for the year, including all the legal and regulatory problems leading up to the Orange County debacle. In this way I discovered that Orange County was not an isolated event at my firm but the latest episode in a pattern of behavior.

The stories began in January, with a growing federal investigation into Merrill's municipal bond underwriting activities. In issuing bonds, municipalities typically use a financial advisor to give them independent advice. The inspector general of Massachusetts had issued a report alleging that Merrill, their underwriter, had had a fee-splitting arrangement with their advisor, Lazard Frères, costing the state millions; Lazard had recommended Merrill for lucrative underwriting deals without disclosing that Merrill was paying them. Subpoenas had been sent out to fifty other states, cities, and banks nationwide. A few stories later, Merrill settled with the U.S. attorney in Massachusetts, the SEC, the Commonwealth of Massachusetts, the attorney general of Massachusetts, and the District of Columbia for a total of $12 million—"without admitting guilt." The controller of New York City also suspended Merrill from lead managing any bond deals there.[1]

Also in January, Edward Scherer, a former Merrill high-yield analyst, was sentenced to six months in prison and two years probation for conspiracy, wire fraud, and bribery. A graduate of Wharton and the UCLA Law School, Scherer had conspired with a Merrill bond trader, Richard Kursman, to buy bonds for their own account at rigged prices, reaping more than a million dollars in profit. Kursman had already pleaded guilt to wire fraud and testified against Scherer.[2]

In February, Merrill's legal efforts to avoid arbitration in the Arvida/JMB limited partnership fiasco finally gave way. In the late 1980s, Arvida, a well-known Florida real estate company, raised over $600 million through the sale of two lim-

---

[1] In December 1996, the former Lazard Frères partner involved with Merrill, Mark Ferber, was convicted of thirty-one counts of mail and wire fraud, sentenced to thirty-three months in federal prison, and fined $1 million. The SEC also fined him $650,000 and barred him from the securities industry for life. Ferber had failed to disclose over $2.6 million in secret payments from Merrill. Ferber's jail sentence was actually considered fairly lenient, in part because the presiding judge, William Young, felt that Merrill and Lazard (which also settled "without admitting guilt") had unfairly escaped criminal prosecution. Referring to Merrill as a "co-conspirator," Judge Young said, "I don't think a $12 million civil settlement caused them much pause on the way to the tennis courts or the yacht club." He also added, "Kickbacks don't just fall out of the sky. People pay them. Merrill Lynch paid them. Merrill Lynch bought its way out here for $12 million. None of them are going to jail. That strikes the court in a very basic equal-justice sense."

[2] Scherer appealed, but his appeal was dismissed by the appeals court in March of 1994.

ited partnerships to private investors. When one of these partnerships, a $234 million fund known as Arvida II, failed, scores of investors sued Merrill Lynch, claiming that they had been misled about the risks. Merrill's legal army responded by filing sixty-eight separate lawsuits in New York aimed at blocking arbitration, but now a Florida judge had finally ordered arbitration to begin in one of those cases, stating that the firm's efforts constituted "a failure, refusal and neglect to arbitrate."[3]

Two former Merrill Lynch personnel also wound up on the wrong side of the law in February. Linda Bustin, a former retail broker in the firm's Burlington, Massachusetts, office, was fined and sentenced to eighteen months in prison and three years of parole for embezzling over $300,000 from twelve of her clients, most of them elderly or infirm, through various schemes involving forged checks and fraudulent accounts. Meanwhile, Nahum Vaskevitch, a former managing director of Merrill Lynch in London, pleaded guilty to insider trading. Prior to his sentencing, he settled a pending civil suit by the SEC for $2.9 million.

In June, Merrill finally settled a five-year-old dispute with Fathallah Sioufi, a Parisian candy merchant who lost $3 million in derivatives trading done at Merrill's Lugano, Switzerland, office, allegedly without his approval. The $5 million settlement came shortly before the New York Stock Exchange arbitration panel ruled on the case, reportedly because Merrill feared punitive damages. It was one of the largest arbitration settlements ever won by an individual against a Big Board firm.

In July, there was a lull in the action, perhaps allowing Merrill's legal army to sneak off to the Hamptons. They returned in August to make a $20-$30 million settlement with 3,500 investors who had purchased failed limited partnerships in ancient art and rare coin funds between 1986 and 1990.

In September, Merrill's self-described "stockbroker to the stars" vanished with her husband, another Merrill financial consultant, after the firm discovered she had fed approximately fifty clients false financial statements. Janie D. Thomas, a broker in Merrill's Las Vegas office and a member of the firm's "Chairman's Club" of top brokers, had promised such luminaries as Paul Anka high returns through sham investments.[4]

Finally, in December came the Orange County bankruptcy. The actual lawsuit against the firm wasn't filed until January 12, beginning a legal battle that will last for many years. By then, more than a third of the top fifty law firms in California were involved, and Merrill had begun assembling its own forty-member legal brigade from six separate law firms (estimated cost: $3 million per month).

[3] Merrill later settled all cases.

[4] Merrill later paid $14 million in restitution to investors. The Thomases have yet to be found.

January did bring at least one sordid legal tussle to a close, however. George Yu, a former stockbroker in Merrill's Fort Lee, New Jersey, office, was sentenced on the twenty-seventh to ten years in prison for attempted murder. Yu had hired a hit man to kill his office manager in order to get his clients. He was arrested when the hit man turned out to be an FBI informant. The sentencing judge called the foiled plot "the most cold-blooded offense of its kind that I have ever seen."

Between this dismal legal record and my own firsthand experience, I began to form a picture of how my firm operated. There was a geometry to Merrill Lynch, composed of two levels. On the surface level, one encountered the theory of capitalism, where the pursuit of profit was restrained by moral principle in all its forms—by the written law, by personal ethics, by regulations, and by social standards. In the glare of the public spotlight, adherence to these rules was a practical matter. But beneath this surface film lay a hidden realm, an underworld known as *the way things really worked,* where market principles operated without restraint, a region below the law where mind met mind and left no evidence behind, and where a man's actions were constrained only by his conscience. The existence of this subterranean reality was never openly discussed or described except with a wink; either you understood it or you didn't. And it formed the natural operating area of the slicks, who were free, on that deeper level, to deceive, to manipulate, and to profit at the expense of others. Here, where the law could not reach them, they found their advantage in the market. And it was here, as the Orange County debacle unfolded, that the truth could be found.

On the surface Orange County looks like this: the Orange County Investment Pool (OCIP) was a $7.4 billion fund in which 187 different municipal bodies—school systems, cities, public agencies, pension funds—invested. The fund was run by the county treasurer, Robert L. Citron, a man highly regarded by his superiors for his consistently high returns; his average of 9.4 percent was a full percentage point higher than the California State fund. Citron's investment strategy included two important elements: leverage (using borrowed money to boost returns) and interest rate risk. Citron leveraged his fund primarily through the use of reverse repurchase agreements, known as "reverse repo." This entailed lending securities from OCIP as collateral for loans, using the loans to buy more securities, and then lending out these securities as well. By repeating this process Citron leveraged his fund to approximately $20 billion, almost three times its size—an extraordinary amount for a municipal fund—greatly enhancing both his potential returns and his downside risk. Citron also bet heavily on interest rates—specifically, that they would stay flat or decrease—always a risky strategy. He did so using a complex derivative called an inverse floater, which responds inversely to changing rates: when rates go up, the instrument pays less. Both of these strategies, involving billions of dollars in securities, were mainly pursued through a single broker, Merrill Lynch.

Citron's troubles began in February, when the Fed began hiking rates, reducing revenues from his inverse floater positions. By the summer OCIP was down 7 percent and in need of cash. To raise money Orange County issued a $600 million taxable note through Merrill. Citron used this money to continue the fund's investment strategy and buy more securities, primarily from Merrill. As rates continued to rise, the fund continued to get hammered. In October, available cash reserves dropped in half, sounding a loud warning chime. It wasn't until December, however, that Orange County was able to price the complex portfolio, revealing a massive $1.5 billion loss (the final tally was $1.7 billion, 23 percent of the fund). Shortly thereafter the county defaulted on its first loans. It still had a chance to weather the crisis with an emergency refinancing, but Wall Street—with the exception of Merrill Lynch—quickly sold off its Orange County collateral, ending Citron's buy-and-hold strategy and driving the county into bankruptcy.

Merrill Lynch was immediately sued by almost everyone involved in the affair: Orange County, all the participants in the pool (cities, schools, agencies), private investors who had money in the pool, county taxpayers, Orange County bondholders, five money market funds managed by Kemper Securities (a major investor in the $600 million taxable note offering), and various Merrill shareholders. At issue were a number of questions surrounding Merrill's relationship with the fund. First, should Merrill have been selling risky securities to Bob Citron? Was he a "sophisticated investor," as securities law demanded? Second, should Merrill have sold risky securities to the fund itself? Did its sales meet fund regulations and California law? Third, did Merrill provide Citron adequate warning about the dangers of his investments?

The questions lead, inevitably, into the underworld. A bond sale is not a computer operation but a human interaction, with all the psychological ramifications that implies. It's a matter not just of what's on paper, what is bought and sold, forming a portfolio, and what statistics change in the meantime, but of what goes on in the minds of the buyer and the seller, how they relate. It is the product of a human relationship, with all its diverse elements.

At the center of the Orange County controversy was a very special relationship. Bob Citron used a number of bond salesmen, but he did an extraordinary amount of business with just one, Michael Stamenson of Merrill Lynch. The two were like Cold War spies tethering together the superpowers: Merrill Lynch, the largest and most powerful investment bank on Wall Street, and Orange County, a municipality whose economic output surpassed that of Israel, Portugal, or Singapore—making it, if it were a nation, the thirtieth-largest economic power in the world.

Through this narrow funnel passed not secret information but securities, generating a flood of profits for Merrill at high pressure. By Orange County's estimate it paid Merrill in 1993 and 1994 alone a staggering $100 million in fees. Yes, Bob Citron was a very important man to the Bull.

When his fund collapsed, the sixty-nine-year-old Citron had been treasurer of Orange County for twenty-one years and married for thirty-nine. He lived in a modest home in Santa Ana and was known for his Californian eccentricities (he wore gaudy pieces of turquoise Indian jewelry), his hard work (he had advanced to his position without a college degree), and his rambling speech. He also had two shortcomings that greatly contributed to his downfall. The first was a lack of technical ability. The inverse floaters Citron purchased from Merrill were built from advanced computer models and notoriously difficult to price. Doing so required skilled quants utilizing partial differential equations—people like the Financial elite. Citron had no such skills. Not many sixty-nine-year-old men with high school educations do. He had begun his career before the term "personal computer" even existed. Nor was anyone in his office an expert in cyberfinance. So while Citron followed a sophisticated *strategy*, he did so without the sophisticated *technology* necessary to manage it. This, in turn, made him unnaturally dependent on his broker. Without Merrill's technical capabilities Citron couldn't price his own portfolio, hedge his risk, or even count his losses. In fact, when OCIP's troubles first became apparent, the county was forced to hire Capital Market Risk Advisors, a high-tech New York consulting firm, to price its own portfolio. It was they who discovered a massive $1.7 billion loss.

According to those who knew him, Citron's other flaw was an inflated ego. He was overly impressed with his long string of investment successes and let everyone know it. He prided himself on his role in liberalizing the state's investment regulations, allowing him to invest in riskier instruments. He liked to associate himself with Wall Street's largest investment banks and to show off his ability to get them on the phone—as if he were one of the boys, a satellite member of the Street. He had also picked up that special breed of arrogance, common to the trading floor, in which all challengers are immediately met with a withering broadside—a defensive strategy, in conjunction with his success, that helped ensure minimal oversight. His comments in his annual reports reveal a tremendous overconfidence. "We have perfected the reverse repo procedure to a new level," he maintained. He called his fund "superior to the vast majority" of others like it. When questioned about his confidence in his interest rate forecast, he remarked, "I am one of the largest investors in America. I know these things."

In cataloging Citron's flaws, however, there is one notable missing element: greed. Ironically, Citron was not someone driven by money. At $100,339 per year, his salary earned him no more than a hard-charging associate. And while he led Orange County into a multibillion-dollar loss, he diverted not one cent to himself.

The second half of the relationship between the great powers was Michael Stamenson. Stamenson, fifty-four, was a salesman in Merrill's San Francisco Institutional Sales office and had been with the firm since 1970. He was an old hand in the California municipal finance business, in which he had a lot of influence. He sat on boards selecting local treasurers—some of whom invested in OCIP—and spoke at various investment conferences. A short, squat man, he was known for his aggressiveness, which sometimes got out of hand. During one treasurer's conference he started a fistfight with a lobbyist over a derivatives disagreement and emerged with a bloody nose. His sales tactics turned off the finance director of San Mateo, who refused to do business with him—"I trust my instincts, and my instincts told me not to be comfortable with Mike." The chief investment officer of San Francisco likewise found Stamenson "very smooth, very calculated" and manipulative. He ended their relationship when one of Stamenson's trades failed to perform as promised.

In retrospect the most remarkable thing about Stamenson was his close involvement in a municipal debacle that was the mirror image of Orange County. In 1984 the city of San Jose lost $60 million after leveraging its portfolio in the repo market and getting hammered by rising interest rates. The city almost went bankrupt. The city attorney claimed that Stamenson was "very instrumental in convincing our people to do this. He convinced us that these very risky transactions were risk-free." San Jose sued thirteen brokerage firms and recovered $24 million. True to form, Merrill settled out of court for $750,000, a fact that came in handy when the Orange County story broke ("There was never any finding or admission of wrongdoing on Merrill Lynch's part," the firm's spokesman said.)

In the rapid-fire, ever-changing world of finance, however, Stamenson's role in the San Jose affair was soon forgotten, while his aggressiveness paid off: his relationship with Orange County blossomed. As manager of the Orange County account, Stamenson's job was to give Bob Citron investment advice, sell him securities, and act as his doorway to the firm. In this role he competed against all the other firms on the Street. Yet thanks to a close relationship with Citron, Stamenson succeeded above and beyond the rest. A whopping 70 percent of the entire OCIP portfolio and fully 95 percent of its derivatives came from him alone—an extraordinary statistic given the size of the account and his fierce competition. In the summer of 1993 Stamenson sold Citron a remarkable $2.7 *billion* in inverse floaters. This was a double coup for Stamenson, since a high-tech instrument like an inverse floater pays a much higher commission than the average bond; and for Merrill as well, which built in a large profit margin.

All this success took Michael Stamenson to the top of his profession and made him a wealthy man. By 1993 he was the top institutional salesman in all of Merrill Lynch, earning three million dollars in compensation. He made more in two weeks than Bob Citron made the whole year—and most of it from Citron. This success bought him a nice life, including a thirteen-room, million-dollar home near San Francisco and a new Mercedes. Not surprisingly, it also made Bob Citron a close personal friend. The two were often seen together in public. Stamenson even contributed $1,000 toward Citron's reelection campaign, as did two other employees in Merrill's San Francisco office (Merrill public statement: "The employees involved were not municipal finance professionals and were not prohibited from making such contributions"). What Stamenson really thought of Citron, however, can only be surmised; to the average bond salesman, if you're managing a multibillion-dollar fund like OCIP and only taking home a hundred grand a year, you sure don't understand the way things work.

From Citron's standpoint, his relationship with Stamenson was principally based on trust. Citron had to deal with someone; the question was who. And like anyone else, the largest institutional investors have to be able to trust their brokers, especially when handing them the lion's share of their business. Whether this trust was misplaced—and if so, why—is another story. But there is little doubt that Citron trusted his broker. Through Stamenson, Citron also placed a great deal of trust in Merrill Lynch, particularly its chief investment strategist, Charles Clough, whose views buttressed Stamenson's investment advice. Citron considered Clough his principal advisor on interest rates. At Stamenson's urging Clough flew out to meet with Citron in person and predicted that rates were going to stay low for years. Even after the Fed began raising rates in February, Clough said that he did not expect the hikes to continue. Citron continued buying inverse floaters.

The result of all this concentrated trust was a booming business for Merrill Lynch. Apart from the millions in fees, Merrill took on a massive amount of interest rate risk in its derivatives sales; if rates did go down, as Citron believed, Merrill would have to pay up. As a broker, however, Merrill typically offset such risk by selling the *opposite* risk to another client, thereby staying market neutral— and by February 1994 there were a lot of clients who wanted exposure to rising rates. Thus Citron's business fueled a mirror business of its own. In addition, Merrill was earning interest on billions in loans to Orange County through all of Citron's leverage transactions and reaping millions in underwriting fees on Orange County bonds, which it sold to investors. The county had become a massive money machine, purchased with taxpayers' dollars, run by Bob Citron and fueled by Michael Stamenson—with a little help from Research.

The Orange County ATM did not spit out cash without a few hiccups, however. Stamenson's success raised concern within Merrill as early as January 1992, sparking an internal battle that lasted up until the time of the bankruptcy. First the Repo desk tried to tack a premium on Citron's borrowing, based on the risk of his inverse floater portfolio. Citron was furious—Merrill had *sold him* the instruments, after all. In a rare move, the head of Risk Management then flew out to Santa Ana and informed Citron that his leverage was too high and that his outstanding loan balance—$1.4 billion—was the limit on what the firm would provide. The Medium-Term Note desk objected, however. They did half their business with Orange County (inverse floaters were derived from medium-term notes) and wanted to do more. The head of the Repo desk countered in a memo that Merrill Lynch was "pushing the high end of a prudent target range with any client." In the end, the loan premium was added, the loan limit subtracted, and sales to Orange County continued.

Risk Management subsequently undertook two studies of OCIP, using the advanced technology at its disposal, and found it highly sensitive to rising rates. The head of Risk Management directed Stamenson to share the results with Citron. Six weeks went by before Stamenson complied. When he did, his letter made no mention of Citron's vulnerability to rising rates at all and no suggestion that he curb his appetite for leverage (Merrill public statement: the letter "fully describes our analysis and conclusions"). Instead, in the following months, Citron *increased* his leverage dramatically—2.6 times by the end of first quarter 1993. Alarmed, the head of ISG, which built the derivatives from medium-term notes, recommended that Merrill buy back $2.8 billion of inverse floaters from Citron and advised that they "employ stronger incentives to encourage Michael Stamenson to continue to strongly urge delevering [*sic*] trades." In March and June, Stamenson made the offer to buy back the derivatives, the latter time in writing. Citron refused, later claiming that he acted in accordance with Charles Clough's economic forecast. Stamenson then proceeded to sell Citron, throughout the summer, another $2.7 billion worth of derivatives, product issued from the Medium-Term Note desk and engineered by ISG. By the summer of 1994 Citron was leveraged to the hilt. He had borrowed almost $13 billion from Merrill—over nine times the limit Risk Management had once tried to impose—nearly tripling the size of his fund. (Merrill later denied that any internal dissension had taken place, claiming that the firm had taken a "teamwork approach" to its Orange County business.)

When OCIP finally melted down, Merrill denied any responsibility, claiming that it had provided Citron sufficient warning about the dangers of his investment strategy. This came as news to the Orange County taxable-note holders, who now owned bonds from a bankrupt municipality. Their lawsuit posed a simple question: if Merrill had warned Citron about the risks of his fund, why hadn't they warned investors before selling them $600 million in Orange County bonds? The firm appeared to be cornered: it was one lawsuit or the other. Merrill's legal challenge deepened when the county's lawyers, skirting the more contentious issues of adequate warning and investor sophistication, claimed that all Merrill's trades had been illegal to begin with based on the stated objectives of OCIP and the laws of the state—an opinion buttressed by the actions of three major Wall Street banks—J. P. Morgan, Goldman Sachs, and Bear Stearns—all of whom had ceased doing business with Orange County for these very reasons.

None of this helped Bob Citron very much. By January he was a broken man, his mental health on the wane. Indicted on a number of counts, he pleaded dementia, as if the bankruptcy had shocked him into sudden self-awareness. "In retrospect," he said, "I was not the sophisticated treasurer I said I was." Few believed him. After all, Bob Citron was an old hand, a man who had been using complex derivatives in a highly leveraged multibillion-dollar fund. And the first to agree with the crowd was Michael Stamenson. In testimony before the California State Senate on January 17, he maintained that Citron knew exactly what he was doing all along and protested his own innocence. "Throughout my career," he stated, "I have conducted myself by the highest ethical and professional standards. I stand by my actions in the case of Orange County. I firmly believe that when the facts are fully understood, all objective observers will reach the same conclusion."

The Orange County debacle generated a continuing series of news stories, which kept pouring into Merrill Lynch as the affair unfolded. Before the morning call, you would read the latest scoop in *The Wall Street Journal.* During the day, the wire service reports would pop up on your computer. Then a secretary would come by, dropping off the latest official statement from Dan Tully, chairman and CEO of the firm. These personal missives to the workforce, elegantly crafted by the Media Relations and Corporate Communications departments, routinely denied any wrongdoing, vowed to fight to the finish, and warned us not to speak to the press (December 7, 1994: "We do not believe we have any legal liability whatsoever, and we would vigorously contest any such action brought against our company"). Meanwhile you could pull up BLOOMBERG BUSINESS NEWS on your monitor and see that all the firm's employees weren't so sanguine, or obedient, especially as time went on ("I assume at some time we settle and pay them to go away"—a Merrill Lynch managing director, January 13).

The principal reaction of people in IEM was to wonder whether the affair would affect their bonuses. It was December: bonus season was just around the corner. Would Merrill have to allocate revenues for the legal battle ahead and whatever settlement occurred? Not this year, was the general consensus. People also showed some interest in being at the center of events. If you were working at Merrill, everyone was asking you what was going on—including your clients. Aside from these passing interests, however, no one really cared about Orange County. That would have required some kind of emotional bond to the firm and a concern for things apart from the making of money. Instead you came to work, the news reports flashed on your screen, and you ignored them. The letters from Tully arrived, you chucked them into the trash, and you took another call. Whatever Merrill Lynch did was no reflection on us.

Meanwhile, on Wall Street at large, most people privately sided with Merrill, seeing their very principles at stake. Orange County was a loss, in their view, and in the market there are always losses. No firm should be held responsible for that. Ultimately the responsibility for a loss must always lie with the investors, no matter what you told them. That was a fundamental principle upon which the market worked: caveat emptor, let the buyer beware. So Michael Stamenson was not responsible. Charles Clough was not responsible. Merrill Lynch was not responsible. Few were willing to state this so openly, however. Most investors, in the view of Wall Street, weren't savvy enough—one might even say *mature* enough—to grasp the true principles of the market. They still lived on that surface level, where you believed the strategists, the salesmen, and the principles on the wall. They didn't understand that there was a dichotomy in the market, a surface world of appearances overlaying an underworld of reality, where compromising your principles gave you a competitive edge. They didn't understand the game we all played, the game of insiders and outsiders, winners and losers, rich and poor—and thankfully so. Their ignorance made it all possible.

Sitting at my position, I found myself contemplating an even greater question. There was no use in maintaining that the actions of the few did not tar the reputation of the whole. Stamenson, Savegre—these were managing directors of the firm. And this judgment was true beyond the firm as well. Wall Street was an integral part of America, as was Orange County, as was the legal system that would decide their fate. These were no rogue entities at work: they were core elements of a society expressing its standards, turning the entire Orange County affair into far more than just a legal trial. It was a test of national character.

In mid-December, one of the operations staff approached my position. "Have you seen the dead guy yet?"

"What?"

He jerked a thumb toward the window with a disbelieving laugh. "There's a dead guy outside. He just blew his head off."

Turning in disbelief, I saw a small group gathered by the window. I joined them and stared down into the courtyard sixteen floors below. There, on the edge of the marina, lay a body in a tan trench coat, facedown in a large red puddle. The toes were stabbing the cement, the heels cocked outward. One of the arms was thrust forward, the other back, like an awkward swimmer. A spot of silver shone by its feet. A number of spectators stood gawking at it, not wanting to get too close. Scores of others were spotting the encircling towers.

A police car pulled up onto the pedestrian area, then another. They dispersed the crowd and I returned to my seat. But I found myself unable to work. There was the persistent sound of voices at the window, and the thought of the body lying outside. Mostly the thought of the body. In its motionless state, it defied everything I knew. There were no dead bodies on Wall Street, there was only a screaming crowd racing after the market. It was the same everywhere. In my entire life, a life spent around millions of others, I had seen only one other dead body, at a wake in my teens. Where did all the dead people go? You could walk around this city for years, thinking that you lived forever.

Drawn back to the window, where a few people were standing, I watched the police go through their crime scene routine. They ringed the body with orange pylons and attached the familiar yellow tape. They took pictures from numerous angles, marked the position of the body, and draped a sheet over it, which quickly grew stained. Then they lined up in a row and walked down the area looking for shell casings.

By now the Mouth of the South had become the office tour guide, a guest on daytime talk shows. "See the gun?" she told her audience. "It's a nine milla-metah."

Then Goth showed up with his usual panache. "Is the dead guy still out there?"

"Sure is," said the Mouth.

"Must be getting cold."

Orlova laughed. *"Peter . . ."*

"Seriously—I hear he was heavily invested in Brady bonds."

*"Peter!"*

The crowd broke into laughter.

"What? It's true!"

"See the gun?" said the Mouth. "It's a nine milla-metah."

Goth craned his neck toward the glass. "I don't know—looks like a forty-five to me."

I spun toward him. "It's sixteen stories down! How the hell do you know what kind of *gun* it is?"

Goth turned away with a shrug. "Relax, man. It's just some dead guy."

A long black hearse finally arrived. The body was lifted onto a stretcher and placed in back by four men. Then the hearse departed, followed by the police cars, leaving only the blood, which was quickly mopped up by the World Financial Center maintenance staff. By the time I left for home, there was only a dark stain on the concrete, and the white chalk outline of what once had been a man.

## 30

As the Orange County saga unfolded, I finally decided to look for another job. There was no specific impetus behind it, just a general desire to change my situation, the culmination of everything that had happened so far. I did not connect my feelings with any issues beyond the office but rather clung to the hope that things would be better elsewhere. And I was encouraged by a recent article in *The Wall Street Journal*—"Emerging Markets Yield New Street Elite"—which noted that people with no more experience than myself were in high demand. With bonus season approaching, the time was right to look around. So I drew up a résumé, called some headhunters, and quietly asked two people in the office for advice. "Good for you!" they replied, as if discovering some long-forgotten hope. Then the bomb fell.

I was in a meeting with Diego Barbero, head of customer trading, and a consultant who was trying to sell us her research services. Barbero told her he wasn't interested. "Our problem isn't research; we're just not seeing the flows. What I really need is another trader to tell me what the Street is doing—and I think I know who." He stabbed a finger at me. "This guy."

It took a week, and daily badgering, before Barbero provided the details. In the decline of our market, the flow of trades, and the information they gave us, had dried up. Barbero wanted me to fill the gap by trading with the Street, the Wall Street broker-dealer community—firms like us. I would sit next to the Brady traders and pass on any intelligence I heard. "You'll have to be careful," Barbero warned, as we sat in the conference room. "You'll be dealing with the sharpest traders in the business. If you don't watch your step, they'll burn you in a second." He gave me a dated list of broker-dealers to work with. IEM had traded with them all once but, with the exception of the major market makers, had stopped doing so during the boom to focus on more profitable client business. "Now listen," he added. "I just want to tell you up front—you'll have to learn this quickly or we'll have to hire from the outside. The market is just too bad. Okay? That's the deal." Then in the next sentence he pushed off my starting date until Christmas week. "The desk is slower then. I can train you better."

I left wondering why he had chosen me. Had Forte heard I was looking around and found me a job, or were they simply trying the cheapest alternative? I even allowed myself to wonder if there was a method to the madness, encouraged by the silence of the Latin Mafia. Had they appreciated the success of Middle Markets after all?

With bond trading dangling in front of me, I gave the organization the benefit of the doubt. I halted all efforts to find another job and decided, as a practical matter, to change my attitude toward IEM. A new year was on the horizon. I had a new job. I was no longer working for Savegre. The battle with Sales was over. And I was finally going to receive some professional training; how could they risk it otherwise? Rather than be weighed down by the past, a clean break was in order.

In IEM, the reaction to my move was typical: there wasn't one. No one had heard about it. To me, my new job was a merit promotion based on a lot of hard work, but to the Latin Mafia, I was just another outsider filling an immediate need: they made no announcement. The only people who knew were the ones I told. And in typical food chain style, their responses were muted. I had just moved up—at their expense. So whatever personal reward a promotion brings in a human sense was completely absent. I didn't let the lack of sentiment darken my new mood, however. I was quite used to it by now. Instead I set out to resolve the future of the Middle Markets Group and free myself to pursue my new opportunity.

Unlike the citizens of IEM, the Core was full of congratulations—they knew the work it had taken. But they were also understandably worried about their business, in which they had invested as much time as myself. What would happen to them? I told them not to worry: unlike the Brady Street, Middle Markets wasn't something I wanted to stick an intern with. I had built it from scratch, it was working, and I felt a responsibility to the Core. I would find an appropriate solution.

I went first to Savegre, since he was still my boss, and framed the problem. He told me to give Middle Markets to International Retail, part of the trading desk. Forte concurred and had me speak with George Navarro, who ran the International Retail operation. "Mañana," Navarro said.

The issue came to a head a few days before I moved to Trading, prompted by a call from Lee Sullivan, who needed some assistance on a long-term project.

I approached Navarro. "Talk to Julio," he said, motioning to a retail trader at the far end of the desk.

I told Julio the situation. "That's news to me," he replied. "Hey, George!" Navarro turned around, the phone pressed to his ear. "What's this about me doing Middle Markets?"

"Talk to Paul," Navarro said, and turned back to his conversation.

The next day I showed Julio how Middle Markets worked, but I could tell he wasn't interested: he had his own business to run. The Core began complaining: they weren't getting the support they needed. Frustrated, I went to see Escobar, who told me to speak to Navarro, who said he'd speak with Julio, who said he never did.

"So what, they're just going to let us die?" Costas asked.

With my new job starting, there was nothing I could do. Death it was.

With bonus season approaching, I began to wonder about my number, as it is called, along with everyone else. Bonuses, of course, are the only reason you go to work on Wall Street, and they can equal or greatly surpass your salary, depending on how high up in the stratosphere you are. Being the object of all eye-gouging, law-bending competition, however, the subject is also generally avoided in polite conversation. This being the case, I wasn't quite sure how the bonus system worked: how my number was generated, when I received it, or, most important, what it was. And since our particular bonus generation system was controlled by the Latin Mafia, there wasn't exactly a profusion of information.

One man who I thought might know, and whom I could approach more easily than the trading floor hierarchy, was our business manager, Jack Plastino. Plastino was, in effect, the group's accountant and personnel officer rolled into one. Our chief bureaucratic functionary, he occupied the office right next to Escobar, a symbol of how important the bottom line really was.

I found Plastino hard at work, crouched over some spreadsheets. He was a very clean-cut, officious M.B.A. in his early thirties, with a useful poker face. As front man for the Latin Mafia, he often kept his cards close and his words ambiguous, a method he had learned from his superiors.

"Jack, got a minute?"

"Sure, Paul, what can I do for you?"

I dropped into the chair across from his desk. "Bonuses. I'm wondering what's going on, how it works."

Plastino clasped his hands together on his desk. "It's simple, really. The group gets a number from the firm's bonus pool, and we cut it up."

"How do I get mine?"

"Basically, it's already been decided. They had the meeting last weekend."

Plastino paused, his eyes fixed on me. It was a reflex action of his, as if he had been through this very moment many times. I had not, although I knew what I wanted to hear next. My goal in life, like all Wall Street people's, was to get a high number, one that would push my total compensation into six figures. All I wanted was to reach that extra decimal place, even if only by a single dollar. What I could buy with that money was important, of course—but the number itself! It was who I was. I was it. We were the same. After a year in this place, that's what it would be—the number me.

"Can you say what it is?" I asked.

"Well tell me this—what were you expecting?"

"Well . . . in my initial conversations with Breen, I was told about one twenty total. But no one else has ever mentioned it since."

"And what's your salary?"

"Fifty-five."

He glanced at his spreadsheet. "You're not far from that."

Euphoria! "No? That's good."

"You're in for fifty. That puts your total comp at one-oh-five right now. But I'll talk to Lisardo about it if you want."

"Oh—well, if you think that will do any good."

Plastino was prone to take a firm moral stand—when the ultimate decision was out of his hands. "Hey, if that's what they promised you, they should stick by it, right?"

"When will I know for sure?"

"End of January."

"Great, thanks." I popped to my feet, not really caring whether Plastino got me more money or not. I had my number—and a damn good number it was!


On Monday, December 19, I spent my first day on the other side of the divide. I arrived in Trading eager to begin—no, euphoric. I hadn't felt so lighthearted in months. With Middle Markets behind me, I had no responsibilities. I was starting afresh, with a new attitude. And with a basic understanding of our business under my belt, I was ready to specialize in a lucrative profession, one that would hold me in good stead for a long time. Marketing was one thing, but trading was the top of the pyramid. I was no longer the roving associate, scraping for information; the spreadsheet operator, fighting for possession of his work; the derivatives modeler, cast aside by Post; or the Middle Markets manager, taking on Sales. No—I was part of the Trading desk now, the heart of the group. I belonged somewhere. And at long last someone was going to train me.

I sat down next to Justo Lamberti, who gave me a cold stare. "You can't sit here."

"I'm starting today. I'm on the desk now."

"I need my space. Sit over there."

He motioned to Judd Weaver's old position, which had remained empty since his firing, and I shifted seats. Oh, well. Just a bad morning for Lamberti. I turned to one of the trading assistants. "Have you seen Barbero?"

"He's out all this week."

"You're kidding! He was supposed to train me."

Strike two.

I took a few more swings in the general vicinity, enough to learn that no one knew I was starting on the desk, or cared. In fact, like the rest of the office, the traders didn't know that a new trading position had even been established. And they didn't seem too excited about the idea either. We had knocked heads a couple of times over their support to Middle Markets, but mostly it was a sign of the times. The traders were completely demoralized. Two of them had been fired, their market had plunged, and their bonuses were in jeopardy. It was the worst year in their careers, leaving them in no mood to train a new man. To them I was just another management error, a quick fix with no follow-up that they would be stuck with. And in Christmas week too! Enough was enough.

This left me with little choice except teaching bond trading to myself. The challenge was depressingly familiar, though I told myself it was only temporary. Once Barbero returned, everything would be straightened out.

I retreated to an empty position on the outside of the traders' loop and sat there awhile contemplating the broker screens. Every so often a price would flicker and disappear. Where to start? I went to Forte for advice, and he suggested I call my potential clients and introduce myself. I returned to my temporary position and looked over the list Barbero had given me, which was two years old. As I read through the names of mighty Wall Street firms, commercial banks, and Latin brokers, I wondered what I would say to them. "Hello, my name is Paul, I work at Merrill Lynch. I have been given a job to do, although I'm not sure what it is. However, it involves you. So I just wanted to call and say hello."

I picked up the phone. Bear Stearns sounded like a good first choice. After all, that was where Howie Rubin had gone after he lost Merrill $377 million. I reached their head trader, but he wasn't interested in doing any business with me. "We're like you guys were—we don't trade with the Street. Just clients." Next I called ING, a large Dutch bank and a major player in the emerging markets. Their head trader knew our whole desk and was more congenial, saying that he looked forward to trading with me. After that I decided to quit while breaking even. In the course of these conversations I had reached that sweat point, well known to me from the Middle Markets seminar briefings, where you appear to be dancing on the edge of a deep gorge of ignorance. I didn't want to fall in on my first day.

I turned to study my bid-offer spreads. The bid-offer spread is simply the difference between the buy and sell price of a bond—the markup, if you will. Since the spread narrows or widens owing to market factors and rises and falls like any price, a trader must be able to adjust it as necessary, immediately. This takes some practice. Flash cards in hand, I sat mumbling my levels like an auctioneer: "Fifty to a quarter, eight to three eighths, quarter-half, three eighths to five eighths, half to three quarters . . ." Then I would change the parameters and have another go, often ending up with peanut butter in my mouth. It wasn't a problem you wanted to have for long: Rob O'Leary, the new Eurobond trader, had recently misquoted a price, costing the desk an instant $90,000.

In the midst of my jabbering, Escobar appeared on the trading floor on one of his rare visits. He stood looking over the shoulder of the Brady traders, clutching his prominent jawbone. Moments later I distinctly heard him say—

"Stiles."

I stood up from behind my computer, wondering what Escobar could possibly want with me.

"Sell the BOTE 10."

I stared at him a moment. I knew the BOTE 10 only by name. It was an obscure Argentine bond so infrequently traded, only one broker screen carried it.

"Ten million," Escobar said.

"At what price?"

"I don't know, just sell it."

I sank back down—is he serious?—and looked over the screens. The sole screen showing the BOTE 10 had no bids or offers posted. What was the price?

I zipped back to Forte's office and asked him.

"You have to call Banco Frances down in Argentina," he said. "They'll know. They trade it in the local market."

I zipped back to my desk. Escobar was still watching the screens. How do you get a phone number in Argentina? Then I remembered: Rolodexes! After Middle Markets, I knew the power of the Rolodex.

I sidled over to Lamberti, the Argentina trader. "Justo," I whispered, "have you got a contact at Banco Frances?"

He handed me his Rolodex without a word. Bingo.

Back at my position, I called Buenos Aires. The secretary who answered spoke English, thank God, and routed me to the trading floor, where I finally reached someone who traded the BOTE 10 and asked him for a price. There was a wide spread on that bond, he told me. Seventy-four to seventy-six was the best he could do.

I hung up, wondering what to do next. The BOTE 10 wasn't traded enough to establish a typical bid-offer spread. I could post a bid to buy at 74 or an offer to sell at 76, like Banco Frances, but that was playing it safe—a two-point spread! The real market values lay somewhere in between, probably with a *half*-point spread. What was it—$74\frac{1}{2}$ to 75? $74\frac{3}{4}$ to $75\frac{1}{4}$? 75 to $75\frac{1}{2}$? I hesitated. I didn't want to screw up my first trade!

"Stiles—where's the BOTE 10?" Escobar called out.

"I'm trying to find out the price."

"What's the spread?"

"Seventy-four to 76."

"Just put it up."

Okay! I lifted the phone and punched a broker button.

"Diego?" a voice asked.

"No, it's Paul."

"Oh, sorry. I thought this was Diego's line."

"It is. He's out this week."

"Oh, okay. This is Mike. What can I do for you, Paul?"

"I want a bid of 74 on the BOTE 10, and an offer of 76."

"How much?"

"Oh—make it five million for now."

"Done. Anything else?"

"That's it."

I hung up, staring at the one screen that held the BOTE 10. It flashed briefly, and a bid and offer appeared. My first bid and offer! I was bond trading! Sort of. I still didn't understand what I was doing. Why was I posting both sides of the trade if I wanted to sell? What if my bid was too high and I bought bonds instead of selling them? I kept watching, but nothing happened.

Keeping one eye on the screen, I opened *The Chase Manhattan Handbook of Emerging Markets Debt,* searching for information on my bond. I discovered that the BOTE 10 (from *Bonos del Tesoro,* Spanish for Treasury bond) was a ten-year bond issued by the Central Bank of Argentina on April 1, 1990, denominated in dollars and amortizing, meaning that along with your periodic coupon payment you got some of your principal back too. A total of $500 million had been issued. It was also a floating rate bond, meaning that instead of paying a fixed rate of interest the coupon floated with prevailing interest rates, in this case LIBOR, the London Inter-Bank Offered Rate, which was the overnight cost of dollars sold between banks in London. Unlike most of our bonds, which cleared through the international clearinghouses, Euroclear and Cedel, the BOTE 10 cleared locally, through Caja de Valores—the Argentine stock exchange. In another twist, it also traded with accrued interest—that is, the price I had just put up on the screen included the interest that had accrued since the last coupon payment, contrary to standard practice. Whew! As a former spreadsheet king, I knew what all that meant. The BOTE 10 was a bond modeler's nightmare. Which made me feel even less confident in what I was doing. As I had learned from the BBYA, a modeler's nightmare is just a trader's nightmare in the making.

"What's the story with the BOTE 10?" Escobar called over.

"Nothing. No action."

"Then change the price. Sell some."

"Okay."

I looked back at the screen. Change the price—how? To what?

"Hey," I asked the nearest trading assistant. "Have you got a model of the BOTE 10?" The BOTE 10 was too obscure to put on the Brady Sheet—oops, the BBYA. But the traders usually had a model of their own for such bonds.

"It's not working," he said.

Forte, who had been standing next to Escobar, appeared by my side. "What are you going to do?"

"I don't know—73¾ to 74¾?"

"Why do you want to do that?"

"Don't I need to move the spread?"

"No—you want to shrink it: 74¼ to 75¾."

He returned to Escobar, leaving me deep in thought. I want to *shrink* it. Why do I want to shrink it?

I called Mike, my friendly broker. "BOTE 10, 74¼ to 75¾."

"Still five million?"

"Nah. Make it ten. What the hell." Then I settled back, arms crossed, and watched my numbers do nothing. They stayed that way for a long time.

"New Prices," Forte called to me an hour or so later. "Move it in." I shrank the spread another quarter point. "Keep it there," he said.

Escobar returned presently, after a sojourn to his office. "What's going on with the BOTE 10?" he asked.

"Nothing," I said. "It's just sitting there."

"C'mon! Sell it!" His volume raised a few eyes on the trading desk. He made a quick aside to Forte, who was standing by his side.

Why so much interest in the BOTE 10? I wondered. And if it were so important, why the hell were they having *me* do it?

Forte came over to my position to check my screen and changed the price again.

"Why is Lisardo so interested in the BOTE 10?" I asked.

"I don't know," he scoffed. "He wants to sell it, for some reason."

The waiting continued. The BOTE 10 remained in suspended animation until well past lunchtime, when, eyes blurring, I decided to go downstairs and get a sandwich. In the excitement of my first day on the Trading desk, I had decided not to bring my lunch anymore, the perennial sign of trying to fit in. On the way out I paused to speak with Forte, who was overlooking the Brady traders. "Can you keep an eye on the BOTE 10? I'm going to grab a bite."

Forte smiled. "Sure."

I left feeling absurd. It was the Structured Products Group all over again. Throw 'em in, don't train 'em. How did these people make any money? Didn't they have the slightest shred of common sense? I caught myself hoping the BOTE 10 was really worth 80. That would fix them.

I returned with my sandwich and sat down at my temporary position. Aaah, sandwich. Then I glanced at the broker screen: the BOTE 10 was blank.

"Miguel," I asked with a ripple of fear. "What happened to the BOTE 10?"

Forte briefly turned his head. "I traded it."

I collapsed back in my chair, crestfallen. My first bond—traded without me! Now *there* was a lesson. The one day I forgot my brown bag . . .


The rest of my first day was spent looking for a trainee phone. After my BOTE 10 experience, I decided that there was no way I could proceed without some basic knowledge of how bond trading worked. And the best way to learn that, I figured, was by listening in on people's conversations while watching them work. In that way I could put two and two together and hopefully discern what the traders were thinking.

By the time I had located such a phone, through various nefarious means,  the market was almost closed. Without an obscure bond to trade, I saw no point in sticking around. After putting on my coat, I said good-bye to Forte's secretary, who had sat next to me all day.

"Paul," she whispered urgently, her face contorted, "I couldn't *believe* that today. That was so unfair! Your first day on the desk, and they expect you to trade without any training? The weirdest bond we have? *Ten million dollars'* worth?" She laughed in disbelief. "What is going *on* around here?"

I shook my head—"I don't know"—not admitting what was really on my mind. When the secretaries start making more sense than the traders, you know you are in trouble.

And we were, though I had no idea how much. The next morning Mexico devalued the peso, plunging the emerging markets into crisis.

## 31

In 1987 the Mexican government instituted a new economic plan, known as the Pacto, in an effort to control the inflation brought on by the Latin American debt crisis. The cornerstone of the plan was a stable currency. The Pacto established a moving trading range for the peso, known as the Band, which increased at a steady 0.04 centavos per day. If the price of the peso (quoted relative to the dollar) rose to the upper limit of the Band—a weak peso—the Central Bank would buy pesos, driving it back down. Likewise, if the peso fell to the bottom of the Band—which happened in January 1994 in the midst of NAFTA euphoria—the Central Bank would sell pesos, driving it back up. This policy was an important lure for foreign investors, because it assured them that they would not suffer the results of a currency devaluation—an assurance that rested, of course, on the credibility of the Mexican government.

Throughout the emerging markets boom, foreign investors had implicitly trusted the Mexican government. By December 1994 they owned 67 percent of the $28 billion Mexican Treasury bills and 26 percent of all Mexican stocks (up from 3 percent in 1989). In turn, Mexico used this capital inflow to finance a mammoth $23 billion current account deficit (their trade deficit, broadly speaking, to include foreign investment). Then came a series of shocks to the system: the uprising in Chiapas in January, the kidnapping of Helu, the assassination of Colosio, the flight of Cabal, and the Massieu assassination. In addition, rising interest rates in the States called capital back home and Mexico had an August election— a time of uncertainty. The cumulative effect of these shocks was to put pressure on the peso—mostly, Mexican pressure. Being closest to the sources of information and with long experience in their country's travails (Mexico had devalued the peso seven times between 1982 and 1987), wealthy Mexican investors began to abandon their country's currency, selling their peso assets and converting them into dollars. This, in turn, drained the dollars from the Central Bank used to stabilize the peso. Between February and November Central Bank reserves fell from $27 billion to $17 billion—most of it following the Colosio assassination.

Obviously, a country cannot follow such a path forever, and in December, Mexico reached its end. First came the inauguration of the new president, Ernesto Zedillo, who not only inherited the problems of the previous president, Carlos Salinas, but inadvertently added to them. Since most devaluations have historically occurred in the beginning of a new administration, investor sentiment worsened and Mexicans flocked to the bank. In the first three weeks of the Zedillo presidency, the Central Bank lost another $2 billion defending the currency. Due to the Band, of course, all traders saw on their screens was a stable peso.

Then on Monday, December 19, the day I began my bond trading career, the year came full circle. Once again there was an uprising in the state of Chiapas as leftist revolutionaries—also known as impoverished Indians—who had vowed to protest against fraud in the local governor's election, broke through army defenses and spread through thirty-eight towns, eleven of which quickly declared themselves loyal to the rebellion. The run on the peso turned into a Mexican sprint.

Rapidly running out of money, the Mexican government decided to devalue. When trading opened on December 20 the peso shot through the Band and kept climbing, stunning the financial markets. While some fund managers suspected that Mexico released fraudulent economic statistics (in fine bureaucratic fashion, an IMF report would later refer to this problem as "information asymmetry"), no one thought the situation had grown that critical. The Mexican finance ministry then steadied the currency, expecting the effects of the devaluation to be temporary—a gross miscalculation. Investors did not view the move as an isolated adjustment to the Band, as the ministry hoped, but a clear repudiation of the Pacto and a serious breach of promise. As recently as the previous Friday, Jaime Serra, the Mexican finance minister, had promised to hold up the Pacto. Now, after seven years spent trying to rebuild their shattered reputation, the Mexicans had undermined their credibility, turning an economic problem into a matter of trust—with devastating results. Instead of lessening pressure on the peso, the devaluation increased it. In the next two days, the Central Bank spent $4 billion trying to defend the new ceiling on the Band, shrinking reserves fell to a dangerously low level—$5 billion. At that point the Mexican government had no choice: they stopped defending the peso and let the market decide what it was worth. In one day, December 22, the value of the new floating peso plunged another 18 percent, blindsiding investors, wiping out billions of dollars in assets, and forcing Mexico to draw on a credit line established with the U.S. government. Even the gods seemed to be angry: forty-five miles from Mexico City, Popocatepetl, the country's second largest volcano, began spewing ash, forcing the evacuation of 75,000 people. It had last erupted in 1921.

Meanwhile emerging markets bonds were getting hammered. As confidence in Mexico plunged, default risk soared, driving down the price of Mexican Brady bonds to their lowest point in three years and dragging down mutual funds with them—an average of 8 percent in the first two days. On December 27, Mexican bonds suffered the largest one-day drop ever, a staggering 9 percent. Other Latin bonds were suffering as well. In the minds of some traders, the emerging markets were viewed as an integral whole, at least initially, sparking what came to be known as the Tequila Effect: Mexico got drunk, and all Latin America suffered the hangover. Argentine, Brazilian, and Venezuelan bonds all plunged.

Once the wrench was thrown into the Mexican economic engine, it continued to sputter. On December 23, Standard and Poor's lowered the rating of peso debt, forcing issuers to pay higher-risk premiums when borrowing money. Many Mexican corporations, some of which had issued bonds through IEM, had their credit ratings downgraded as well: with outstanding bonds to pay in dollars, the devaluation had greatly increased their interest payments. By December 30, Mexican domestic interest rates had risen to 34 percent, stunting growth and raising concerns about the health of the Mexican banking sector: when the economy weakens, companies default on their loans. Even more worrisome was how Mexico was going to pay pay back its *tesobonos,* short-term treasury bonds that paid in dollars and were 80 percent held by foreign investors. Under normal conditions, the Central Bank would have refinanced itself by issuing more *tesobonos,* but now, in the midst of crisis, it was faced with having to pay back more money than it could raise—potentially a lot more money. There was $16.7 billion in *tesobonos* coming due by midyear.

These concerns eased somewhat on January 2, when Mexico received a new $18 billion credit line composed of the existing U.S. credit line (expanded from $6 to $9 billion) and $9 billion more from Canada, commercial banks, and supranational organizations. But the brief uptick this caused reversed itself the next day, when President Zedillo unveiled a weak new economic plan in Mexico City. Three days later the new Mexican finance minister, Guillermo Ortiz (who had hastily replaced Serra the previous week), managed to restore some confidence by going to the heart of the market—New York City—and speaking to a packed room of investors at the Pierre Hotel. By the ninth, however, sentiment had turned ugly again amid concerns that Mexico would impose foreign exchange restrictions and rumors that the Central Bank was printing pesos to pay its debts. To stop the slide, Mexico borrowed $500 million from its credit line and the Federal Reserve stepped in to buy pesos; but their efforts failed, and Mexican bonds reached four-year lows.

The next day, January 10, Mexico failed to sell a fraction of its *tesobono* auction, realizing the worst fears of investors, who stampeded for the door. By noon the Emerging Markets Traders Association had called a special meeting to discuss the plunge and issued a statement urging all its members to continue trading. By the end of the day the peso had dropped 8 percent. Then the tables turned again. Investors decided that the market had overreacted, and Mexican Brady bonds shot up 6 percent, a record one-day gain.

On January 12, the manic three-week-old crisis entered a second stage when President Clinton, having gained the approval of congressional leadership, announced a rescue plan for Mexico. Mexican stocks, bonds, and the peso all rallied, with Brady bonds posting a record one-day gain of 10 percent. Treasury secretary Robert Rubin and Fed chairman Alan Greenspan briefed Congress on the details the next day. The plan called for $40 billion in loan guarantees, which Mexico could use to pay off its *tesobonos* debt, among other things. In return, Mexico would pay the U.S. a loan premium, pledge oil as collateral, and adopt certain economic reform measures. The administration's argument was two-pronged. First, a bankrupt Mexico would cause social and economic problems in the United States. Illegal immigration would increase, and an estimated half-million jobs could be lost. Then there was the chance of global economic catastrophe, an apocalyptic vision in which the implosion of Mexico would destabilize the world financial system (an IMF report later discredited this claim).

For the next five days Congress debated the wisdom of the rescue plan and worked on drafting a bill amid assurances from congressional leadership and the president that it would eventually pass. The markets were relatively stable, and Bradies rose, following a successful *tesobono* auction on the seventeenth. The next day, however, mounting congressional resistance to the plan broke out into the open. Some felt that the administration was bailing out banks and wealthy investors: the rescue plan was of no interest to the middle class. Others said the plan was too risky: if Mexico defaulted, how could we realistically access the oil collateral? Still others used the plan as an opportunity to sponsor tangential legislation, like having Mexico cut off aid to Cuba, or combat illegal immigration, or narrow its domestic wage gaps. There were also calls for more international support and an independent monetary board in Mexico.

On January 19, the proposed vote was delayed in the absence of legislation, though passage was still predicted. The peso fell, aggravated by demonstrators in Mexico's Tabasco state, who set up roadblocks to protest election fraud in their governor's race. For the next six days the market continued to track the latest news from Washington, where politicians were still predicting passage of the rescue plan. On January 26, the International Monetary Fund extended a $7.75 billion loan to Mexico, its largest ever for a single country. Optimism, and Brady bonds, then fell as House Speaker Newt Gingrich, backing away from previous statements, declined to say if the aid bill would be approved, while Senator Bob Dole admitted support had dropped "as far as it can." The American people were speaking through them: according to the polls, 80 percent were against aiding Mexico.

Meanwhile the Mexican Central Bank continued to lose its dollar reserves at an alarming rate. By January 30, reports indicated that reserves were down to $2 billion and Mexico could default on $1.3 billion in *tesobonos* due later in the week. Mexican Brady bonds plunged 7 percent and the peso fell 10 percent, having now dropped 45 percent since the devaluation. Stock markets in Argentina and Brazil fell 5 to 6 percent. The dollar also fell against the yen and the mark and the Dow dropped 26 points amid fears of the impact of the Mexican crisis on the U.S. economy.

On January 31, with the aid plan dying and Mexico on the ropes, President Clinton announced a surprise peso stabilization plan. Using a liberal reading of the Gold Reserve Act of 1934, which established an Exchange Stabilization Fund to defend the U.S. currency, he created a $20 billion credit line for Mexico in the U.S. Treasury, thereby skirting the need for congressional approval. This was the largest chunk of a $52.8 billion package involving various commercial, central, and supranational banks, which brought the peso crisis to a close.

In Mexico, however, the larger economic crisis had just begun. The country was quickly wracked by layoffs and high inflation and entered a deep recession. Having extended themselves on mortgages, car loans, and consumer goods during the boom, it was the country's nascent middle class who suffered most. Three weeks after the devaluation, their incomes had dropped to 75 percent of their 1982 level.

And so the surface picture. In all this talk of money, of trading activity, of economic policy, of currencies and exchange rates, financial instruments, current account deficits, and other economic statistics, one can easily be left with the impression that the Mexican peso crisis was a numbers game, a technical maladjustment imposed on Mexico by acts of God or, at worst, the misguided policies of faceless bureaucrats. But the peso crisis was no power fluctuation in the Mexican economic computer. It was assassination, kidnapping, fraud, and two peasant uprisings that caused it as well as some conspicuous overconsumption, all of it the product of a notoriously corrupt, winner-take-all society. If the crisis shows anything, it is that, in our high-tech age, the chief economic fundamental is still morality.

As if to prove this point, within a month of Clinton's unilateral rescue plan, Mexican politics turned into a tragedy to make Shakespeare blush. First, a second gunman was arrested in the Colosio assassination, belying the previous government finding that a lone gunman was responsible, and pointing to a conspiracy. Then the brother of former president Carlos Salinas, Raul Salinas, a man publicly known as "Mr. Ten Percent" for his standard influence-peddling fee, was arrested for masterminding the assassination of Jose Francisco Ruiz Massieu—who also happened to be his former brother-in-law. Then Mario Ruiz Massieu, Mexico's deputy attorney general, who had been placed in charge of investigating his brother's assassination, was accused of protecting Raul Salinas. Massieu fled to the United States, where he was arrested at the Newark airport prior to boarding a plane to Monaco, a country with no extradition treaty with Mexico. Raul Salinas was then thrown in jail, stimulating great interest in his 1990 book of poetry, *El Secreto* (The Secret), and its revealing moral theme:

*If you steal from them all one hundred percent,*
*This will likely give rise to some moral dissent.*
*Some points gained, other points spent,*
*Morals are a question of such and such percent.*

Meanwhile, to protest his innocence, former Mexican president Carlos Salinas—a Harvard Ph.D. in economics, President Clinton's choice to be the next head of the World Trade Organization, and as fate would have it, a member of the board of Dow Jones and Co., publisher of *The Wall Street Journal*—went on a hunger strike, which barely lasted a day. That having failed, he eventually fled to Cuba, which turned out to be a wise move. By the following December Swiss authorities had arrested Raul Salinas's wife and her brother in Geneva, where Raul had $84 million or so stashed in various accounts. The total estimated sum rose to $120 million when accounts in London and the Cayman Islands were discovered. How did Raul earn all this money? Influence peddling with his brother, *El Presidente,* said an angry mob who filed charges of treason against them both. And where did the money come from? Mexican drug lords, were the whispers. Carlos Salinas denied the charges but few believed him. During his term in office, the Colombian drug cartels, their Caribbean delivery routes severed by American law enforcement efforts, found a new home in Mexico, sparking a drug boom to match the emerging markets boom, one well known to the U.S. government. Today 75 percent of the cocaine reaching America comes through Mexico, where many Salinas appointees are still in power.*

Aside from its moral theme, the peso crisis also signified a change in eras, the shift from a Cold War world dominated by political-military affairs to a new world order run by the market—a shift from the White House to Wall Street. Unlike previous world crises, the White House was not the bottom line in the peso crisis, and the Kremlin wasn't even involved. For weeks the President of the United States was held hostage by a handful of young currency traders deciding the fate of Mexico. And while the President came up with a rescue plan, ultimately it was the market that determined whether or not it was a good one. Implicit in this historic change was a shift in values. American diplomacy is a matter of both power and principle, but the market cares only about profit.

It wasn't an auspicious time to make such a fundamental shift. The day after the

---

* At the time of writing, the body of missing congressman Manuel Munoz Rocha—Raul Salinas's alleged coconspirator in the assassination of Jose Francisco Ruiz Massieu—had just been found buried next to Salinas's tennis court. According to the informant who identified the site, Salinas had beaten Rocha to death with a baseball bat, then had his teeth and fingers removed to prevent identification.

crisis began, news flashed on our screens that a bomb had just exploded in the Fulton Street subway station, which feeds the nearby World Trade Center. One of our trading assistants returned excitedly from the scene with a report of burn victims staggering from a subway entrance and a huge crowd. The perpetrator turned out to be Edward Leary, a former employee of Merrill Lynch, who had brought a crude firebomb onto the subway car, hidden in a knapsack. As the car pulled into Fulton Street, the bomb had unexpectedly exploded in his lap, critically injuring four people and filling the car with thick black smoke. Severely burned himself, Leary fled into the subway system and surfaced in Brooklyn Heights, where he was picked up by police.

Leary had worked as a systems analyst at Merrill for three years, rising to assistant vice president, one step above associate. He also owned three apartments in Brooklyn, where he had lived for many years before moving to New Jersey with his wife. A former army intelligence specialist, he had attended Columbia University, where he studied math and physics—a similar background to Ted Kaczynski. He had been fired from Merrill on January 28—two days after I was hired for sabotaging the firm's computer system. His latest attack had been part of a much larger campaign to extort money from the City of New York by paralyzing the entire subway system. According to the papers, Leary was a volatile man prone to angry outbursts and confrontation. Why he wanted to hold the city hostage was a mystery, however, one deepened by his feelings for his country. When federal agents arrived at his house, they found it decorated with a large American flag.

Three days after the bomb blast—Christmas Day—another disturbing sign arose from the new Capital of the World, this one in *The New York Times,* which reported a rising income gap between the city's rich and poor. The borough of Manhattan was the worst offender. For every dollar made in the top fifth of its households the bottom fifth claimed only three cents—a gap wider than in Guatemala and the second worst in the United States. As the paper found, "Among the nation's counties, the income gap between rich and poor in Manhattan is surpassed only by a group of 70 households near a former leper colony in Hawaii."

These statistics occurred at a time of unprecedented change in the demographics of the human race. According to the United Nations, by the year 2000, 50 percent of all people on earth will live in cities. One billion of these will be classified as urban poor, more than twice as many as in 1990. One hundred million will be homeless. By the year 2025 *two thirds* of people on earth will live in cities. By then the population of the globe will have more than doubled. But no matter—a decent broom closet in Manhattan will cost you only three grand a month.

•  •  •

The news of Raul Salinas's arrest had just flashed over CNN. I flipped off the TV in disgust and collapsed back on the couch.

"What I don't understand," Sarah said, "is why we're in NAFTA when Mexico is so corrupt. Didn't we know that?"

"Sure we knew. The police and judges are rotten, the politicians rig elections, there's drug money everywhere—"

"Then why did we do it?"

"For the money, I guess. And because we weren't thinking. Eduardo was right, you know: we're all such stupid gringos. I'm just starting to see that now."

"What do you mean?"

"Well, look at the propaganda," I sighed. "We're going to sign this nice legal document, the NAFTA Accord! We're going to bring Mexico into the fold, make it a first world nation run by Harvard-trained economists! It's a tremendous joint enterprise, a building enterprise, and everyone is going to make a lot of money—right? Meanwhile the Mexicans are shipping us illegal immigrants by the truckload, and cocaine by the planeload, they're providing phony economic statistics to attract investors, and they're coming to New York to meet all the fund managers. What a slick show! Everyone was impressed with each other. Mexico, America's third-largest trading partner! Mexico, our next-door neighbor! Mexico, a growth enterprise! Look at the numbers, listen to the President of the United States! And look at domestic interest rates—gosh, they're low. Wouldn't you rather invest that money abroad? How Wall Street loved it! Remember, this was a boom fueled by investors, not commercial lending. The banks had learned their lesson the last time. So the fund managers got in bed with the Mexican Finance Secretary—Escobar's former professor, by the way."

"Really?"

"Yup. And *voilà!* The market took off. The mutual funds piled up with money from the American public and all that money was sent to Mexico—once Wall Street took its cut. Prices skyrocketed, everyone was making a fortune, and everyone was happy. Who wants to burst that bubble? Not Wall Street. They said it was going to be a good investment—and it was! So the research reports looked like Mexican financial statistics—caveat emptor, right? What a match it was, the Salinas government and the Street. And the politicians were happy too, let's not forget about them. They were leading the charge across the Rio Grande, flags waving: see what I'm doing for American business? Everybody was slapping each other on the back. The only problem was, we were dealing with a bunch of crooks—and some murderers among them. So the poverty and the election fraud and the injustice took its toll, and the peasants revolted in Chiapas, and the bankers got kidnapped or ran off with suitcases of loot, and the politicians got gunned down in the street, thanks to all the drug money, and the country started to come apart. Meanwhile the Central Bank was losing billions, until one day—

whoomph!—the peso suddenly falls off the screen and the stupid gringos are left holding the bag. But our government can't admit any of this, of course—"

"Did they know?" Sarah asked. "That the peso would fall, I mean?"

"Of course they knew! The U.S. Treasury talks to the Mexican Central Bank *all the time.* They're the only people the Mexicans don't want to piss off. No one in the government ever showed the slightest surprise either. No one ever said, 'I can't believe this! The Mexicans stabbed us in the back!' "

"Then why didn't they let *us* know?"

"Because they don't care! Remember, they had to *save Mexico.* Once they were in bed with these people, they couldn't get out. Can you imagine the president standing up and saying, Hey, I was obviously wrong about NAFTA, let's bag it? No—so instead they come up with a $40 billion rescue plan funded by the American taxpayer! Who are we to complain? The secretary of the treasury, Robert Rubin, even claimed that we were all going to suffer a 'global financial apocalypse' if we didn't go along with it."

"You're kidding!" Sarah laughed.

"I'm serious!"

"He really said that?"

"Yes! Hardly anyone believed him, though. Mexico has devalued the peso *seven times* in the last two decades. No matter what we did, they were going to survive, and so was the Western World. Then he said that we were going to lose 500,000 jobs, all those unfortunate people who sold goods to Mexico. That made no sense either. If you divide $40 billion by 500,000, you get $80,000 per job. So why didn't we just give the loan to *American workers*? Then Rubin said that the drug problem would worsen and illegal immigration would increase if Mexico defaulted. Which makes you wonder—since when does the United States pay people not to engage in criminal activity? I mean, the whole argument was bull! And oh, by the way, Rubin is the former chairman of *Goldman Sachs.* He's spent his whole career on Wall Street. He's worth $100 million. Do you really expect him to make sound judgments for the American people?"

"So what happened? Did we do it?"

"No! Eighty percent of the American public was against it, so Congress backed off. Even the Mexicans complained!"

"Why? What did they have to complain about?!"

"They didn't want to put up their oil as collateral. Yankee imperialism!"

"Oh, *please.*"

"Right. So who solved the problem?"

Sarah threw up her hands.

"The lawyers!" I said. "They found an obscure loophole in the Gold Reserve Act of 1934. The landlord supplies the heat! And the president ran through it with a $20 billion loan for Mexico."

"Without approval from Congress?"

"Right! That was the whole point. But Congress didn't care because they didn't want to vote on such an unpopular bill!"

"No way!"

"I'm serious! So the Mexicans got their money, and they used it to repay people who had invested in *tesobonos,* a kind of treasury bond. Most of these people were currency speculators. How many middle-class people do you know who speculate in Mexican *tesobonos*? So in the end the wealthy Mexicans pulled their money out, causing a financial crisis, and Wall Street got paid anyway, using our tax dollars, and mutual fund investors got hammered. What kills me is, the people in power all think we're so stupid, like we're not going to figure any of this out. Just the other day I called up the full text of the briefing on the rescue plan given to the House Banking Committee, right from my position. The chairman of the Fed, the secretary of state, and the Treasury secretary all talked about the crisis and what caused it. And you know what? The word 'corruption' was not mentioned *once.* Not once! It was as if the entire Mexican financial crisis were a technical malfunction. Can you believe that? Who do these people think they're kidding?"

"You and me."

I crashed back down on the couch. What was the point of ranting and raving? It got you nowhere. Whenever you knocked heads with the system, all you got was a bruise.

"You know what?" I finally said. "I'm really starting to think we're no better than they are."


## 32

Eventually some people reach the breaking point in New York, the point where it is no longer possible to accept the way they live. Oh, they may have tried, they may have walked down the path of adaptation and decline and shed whatever standards they had in the process, but one day, often with little provocation, they snap. It is the point where the insanity of the city has stolen too much joy from daily life. The most common reason for this epiphany is, I suspect, a traffic jam. As you sit choking down exhaust fumes, you hear that tired old voice telling you that this is the way things are in New York. There are millions of people. There is traffic. There is congestion. You must be patient. Sure, you can honk your horn like everyone else and dispel some aggression, but it won't get you moving any faster. Then that voice is drowned by another, a desperate voice that says there is more to life than this, that there is fresh air somewhere else, that you need to *escape.* So you do. You pull over and start driving down the sidewalk.

I witnessed this phenomenon once on Hicks Street, in front of the Cobble Hill

School, when I was walking home from work. There was a massive traffic jam due to some construction on the BQE entrance ramp—or at least some signs to that effect. Suddenly, someone reached that fabled point of no return, pulled onto the sidewalk, and drove down to the next corner, then turned in a joyous burst of acceleration that reverberated off the brownstones—one so inspiring that a few other urban soldiers broke ranks and executed the same maneuver, until there was an entire procession of Empire State plates roaring down the sidewalk. In the center of each plate, wedged between the numbers, was a little Statue of Liberty.

It was such feelings that led Sarah and me to get away from it all, once and for all, over her Christmas break. With the market in an uproar no one was going to train me anyway. Our destination was one of the emerging markets, Costa Rica, where we rented a four-wheel-drive vehicle and set off exploring with a map. Three years before, we had made a similar trip on our honeymoon, driving around Belize, and had found it to be a wonderful experience—getting off the beaten track, being spontaneous, really seeing another country. But after traipsing through a few rain forests we decided that something was missing. We had come to see Costa Rica when we really didn't want to. Somehow, in the move from Annapolis to New York, we had lost the desire to travel and developed the need for a vacation.

"It's all this driving," Sarah apologized. "I drive up and back to Columbia every day. I should have thought of it before, but I'm just sick of driving."

"I wouldn't mind parking myself on a beach either, come to think of it. I'm just having a hard time slowing down."

We took out our guidebook, intent on finding some remote beach on which to plunk ourselves for the duration. Northern Costa Rica was out. It had become a tourist mecca and was full of resorts. But in the remote southwest corner of the country, near Panama, was the Osa Peninsula, a large boot planted in the Pacific Ocean, covered by protected rain forest and mostly uninhabited. It was, the guidebook said, "the last frontier in Costa Rica."

We spent the next day on a long, jarring drive down a coastal dirt road, which ended at the Rio Sierpe, a wide, muddy river lacing the top of the Osa's boot. There we hired a precarious canoe to take us to a rustic lodge at the river's mouth five miles downstream. That night, New Year's Eve, we were the only guests. We stood out on the end of a wobbly dock at midnight, watching a crocodile float by and staring at the stars. Stars! I had forgotten them.

The next morning we began the second leg of our journey. A larger boat arrived from Sierpe town, and we headed out into the ocean, where we hugged the coastline for forty-five minutes. Our destination was Drake's Bay Wilderness Camp, which our guidebook described as a collection of tents on a remote beach accessible only by boat. The end, I thought, of the earth.

Turning into Drake's Bay, I anxiously awaited my first sight of this, the farthest outpost in my guidebook. What met my eyes was a stranger creature than I had ever imagined floating atop the water on huge paddling yellow legs: a water bike, peddled by a tourist in a Hawaiian shirt. Then there was another one, and another one, like beetles aimlessly circling a summer pond. Then I saw the thatched-roof bungalows where the parasol drinks were served; the three, or four, or five hotels flanking the river; the scores of people swimming, kayaking, fishing . . . It was, the guidebook should have said, a turbocharged tourist trap.

I turned to Sarah with a sigh. "I think the market got here first."


## 33

Back from Costa Rica, I returned to IEM ready to get to work. Barbero was back, as were all the traders, but the market was still a mess. I approached Barbero, wondering how to proceed. Should I keep calling the broker-dealers, sit with the traders, or what?

"We're not going to do that anymore," he said.

"What?"

"Your job. It's been eliminated."

I stood perfectly still.

"Now that the market is like this, we need to focus on other things."

"I see." I tried to appear unmoved. "So what do you want me to do?"

"I don't know yet. Give me time. Frankly, I've got other things to think about right now." He turned back to the screens.

I wandered off dumbfounded. One bid, one offer, and a trade while I was at lunch. The shortest trading career in Wall Street history?


Once again in limbo, I resolved to stay on the Trading desk instead of returning to my former position. My toehold was the temporary position I had assumed next to Forte's secretary. I held onto it tightly, reminding Barbero at every opportunity that I was looking for employment. Eventually he told me to sit with Richard Klausthaler, who had recently returned from IEM London and was trading the exotics.

Klausthaler had been jerked around as much as I had. In April he had left for Hong Kong, tasked with being our first trader there. With interest rates rising, he and others had argued that the time wasn't right for such a move, but Escobar had overruled them. To accommodate him, Klausthaler had moved his wedding up from July to February. Once in Hong Kong, however, he discovered himself in the midst of a major political battle for control of the Asian emerging markets. People in the Hong Kong office told him that he was working for them, not Escobar. Escobar, in turn, kept promising to visit and never did. By August the new venture was on the rocks. Klausthaler then moved to London to replace our Brady trader, who had quit, and stayed the next four months in temporary housing. Lacking confidence in IEM leadership, and with his wife pregnant, he finally asked to return to New York, where he was handed the exotics book.

In light of the current crisis, the risky exotics were dormant, giving Klausthaler time to train me. He hadn't been directed to do so, of course, but he wasn't averse to providing instruction in between calls. On the other hand, he did mind the trainee phone, since he spent a lot of time negotiating with other investment banks, trying to get himself out of IEM. Bonus season was over; it was time, as they say, for bids away. "I need the line," he would tell me, then lean over and whisper something about bonus guarantees and his P&L. After a while, it was so patently obvious that he finally admitted it. "Basically," he said, "I have no confidence in the leadership of this desk. I've got three different people telling me what to do. They always think they know better than you. And their attitude is getting really old. I walk into the conference room, and they stop talking. They don't even share trade ideas. How can you run a desk like that? They've been jerking me around for a year now, and I'm fed up. This isn't the only investment bank on the Street, you know."

His wasn't the only discontented voice. During the peso crisis, you didn't even want to get near the IEM traders. With their bonuses slashed, their market collapsing around them, losses mounting, and confidence in their management slipping away, their morale had reached an all-time low.

On January 31, things got even worse. With a Mexican default looming on the horizon, there were signs of panic in the market. The desk had taken out a large short position, expecting the crisis to deepen. Then the White House made a sudden televised announcement of its unilateral rescue plan, and the entire market rallied hard. Unlike the other trading desks on Wall Street, however, IEM didn't get the news until it came over the wire services precious minutes later. For all its high technology the group had no television on the trading floor. The desk got hammered. Buyers swamped the phone lines, each one a stake in the heart of our P&L.

Klausthaler turned to me, shaking his head, as we watched the carnage take place. "I suggested we get a TV months ago, but they wouldn't listen."


In late January, I was crossing the trading floor when I was intercepted by Savegre. "Well, I suppose I have to do this," he chirped. "Let's go to the conference room."

I knew what that meant: it was time for my bonus debriefing.

I followed his rapidly moving figure into Forte's empty office, happy to have reached this moment. After adding up all the trades the Middle Markets had done through December, my business had brought in well over a million dollars in commissions in six months. Compared with the Institutional salesmen, this wasn't that much, but in the worst bond market since the Great Depression, in the sector leading the plunge, in an office that had hindered more than it had helped, and without any previous experience, I thought it a minor miracle, justifying my promised fifty grand. I had earned my number, and now it was payday.

Savegre sat down behind the desk, and I faced him in a chair. Perhaps it was just the recent holidays, but when he lifted his balding head, a few hairs sprouting from the top, twisted his lips into a clever frown, and laced his fingers meditatively, I was immediately reminded of the Grinch—the Grinch Who Stole My Bonus.

"Let me get right to the point—Paul, your bonus this year is twenty-five thousand dollars."

"What?—What do you mean?"

"It's been a tough year—"

"You've got to be kidding me! I was told fifty!"

Savegre rose to go.

"Wait a minute! Wait! I made this group *a million bucks*!"

A flick of the wrist, a little shrug, and Savegre assumed his rock-hard, nothing-I-can-do expression. "It's been a bad year. The entire bonus pool is down." He edged past the desk.

I turned in my seat—"That's not what I was told!"—but he was gone.

I left the room in shock and tottered the length of the trading floor, hands clasped behind my head like a prisoner shot in the back. I had just lost twenty-five thousand dollars. *Twenty-five thousand dollars!* How? When? What about my number? My number! I was supposed to top 100! Now it was only . . . 80! *Eighty!* How could this be? *They had promised me!* I returned in a daze to my old position on Operations Island and sank into my chair with a groan. "I don't believe it," I muttered.

"Don't believe what?" asked my neighbor, an operations specialist.

"They just cut my bonus in half, the bastards."

He laughed. "At least you got one. We didn't even get one."

"Nothing?"

"Zippo. All of Operations."

A few minutes later I tracked down Plastino, the business manager, who was shuffling some papers in his office.

"Jack," I said, "what happened?"

"What happened with what, Paul?"

"My bonus. They cut it in half."

"Did they? Well, I know there've been some adjustments lately."

"But I only spoke to you a few weeks ago. Now it's twenty-five instead of fifty."

"Huh! That doesn't sound right. And after all that work on Middle Markets!"

"You're telling me! What happened?"

"It's been a bad year," he shrugged.

I lowered my voice. "Did Savegre say something?"

Plastino stared at me. "No—as a matter of fact, he spoke quite eloquently in your defense during the bonus meeting."

"He did?"

I stared at Plastino. Should I believe him? Should I believe anyone? Who could I trust anymore?

"Don't you think it's suspicious? I get promoted to Trading and my bonus gets cut in half by Sales."

"All I can do is talk to Lisardo."

"Could you?"

"Sure. Maybe he can do something." Plastino took out a note card from his shirt pocket. "Refresh my memory. What was the total comp you anticipated?"

"One twenty. But you told me it was at one-oh-five."

"That's right." He replaced the card, dropping his chin and mumbling into his pocket: "You're sure Kenny Breen told you that?"

"Yes, I'm sure!"

Plastino puckered his cheeks as if sucking on a sour ball. "I'll see what I can do."

I got up to leave. I was wasting my time.

"I wouldn't feel bad," he said. "It wasn't like last year. There were only three seven-figure bonuses in the group."


Before leaving for home that night I called my friend Jim in Tokyo and told him what had happened. "Man, tell me about it!" he said, providing some insight on Lehman Brothers. "You should have seen it here! It was *ugly*. I mean, I'm in a meeting with guys pulling down seven figures, and they're fighting over *ten grand*—and they're taking it from the guys who *work* for them, right on their desk!"

I hung up in anger. I knew what had happened, but I could never prove it. That was the ultimate reason for the secrecy of the Latin Mafia: so that when the money was divided, no one had grounds for questioning and fomenting unrest. Instead, in their silence, they preyed on a weakness that we all had, and which I saw in myself. Why was I so surprised my bonus had been cut in half? All the evidence had been there all along. And yet I had chosen not to see it. I wanted to believe in my "managers," to believe that there was sense and order in my little world and a place to put my faith, and they had encouraged that, keeping me constantly striving and treating them with respect, rather than challenging them, asking to see the numbers. Oh, what a colossal fool I was! Trusting people and the system!

And they had taken me to the cleaners. They were the insiders, getting rich; and once again, I was the sucker.

When I got home, I told Sarah right away.

"How can they *do* that?" she exclaimed angrily. "They told you fifty!"

"Caveat emptor," I replied.

Sarah's anger soon evolved into disappointment and finally resignation. She brushed off our loss as she had learned to brush off so many other losses in New York. It was the only way to get by. I followed her example, and by the time I went to bed, the whole thing was one big joke, allowing me to ponder a more serious question. What the hell had happened to me? A year ago, when I was unemployed, I would have been overjoyed to get a job paying eighty thousand dollars a year—ecstatic! Now here I was crushed by a bad number. My whole perspective had shifted. What a fool I had been marching down the trading desk like the walking wounded just because I wasn't in three digits! The important number wasn't one hundred—it was *thirty*, with maybe fifty left if I were lucky. It was a matter of birthdays.

The joke got even better at the end of the month. After federal, state, and city taxes were excised from my bonus, the ultimate fruit of my New York labors turned out to be just twelve thousand dollars. I even called my bank to make sure. Yes, they confirmed, at the standard rate of deduction you lose about half to taxes. Finally it was announced that Michael Stamenson, the salesman who had sunk Orange County, had received a million-dollar bonus. At least I knew what I had to do next year.


While I managed to drive my monetary loss from my mind, thoughts of my future wouldn't budge. In the past three weeks the market had collapsed, my job had disappeared, and my bonus had been cut in half. I had experienced a complete reversal in fortune and once again sat looking through job opportunities on Bloomberg. Meanwhile, the firm had begun eliminating five hundred people in a public mass firing announced in *The Wall Street Journal*. I decided to corner Barbero and find out what was going on.

At his request we met in a bar downstairs. With the descent of Forte, Barbero had one foot firmly planted in the inner circle. He looked the part, too, with heavy-lidded eyes, a sharp part down the center of his scalp, and the perpetual trader's sunburn. Once seated, he lit up a Camel and sagged back in his chair, his face flushed even more than usual. "So what's up?"

"That's what I'm hoping you can tell me."

"How are things going with Klausthaler?"

"Fine. Until I got my bonus, that is." I filled him in on some of the details. He smiled through the smoke and told me I wasn't alone. "You should have seen Fraga when I told him," he said, referring to our emotional Brady trader. "He kicked the garbage can across the conference room." He laughed, "So I said to him, hey Russ, that's just the business, it was a bad year. What else could I say? I know these guys are getting bids away. It's that time of year, no? If he wants to go to Chase or Chemical, there's nothing I can do. And Lisardo knows that. If he doesn't want to pay him, he can lose him." Barbero grinned through the smoke. "He can lose me too. I wasn't too happy. Maybe I'll get a bid away, who knows."

"I just want to know what my number means. Are they trying to tell me something, or not?"

"I wouldn't look at it that way."

"Frankly, I never know *how* to look at it. No one tells me anything. I've never even received a performance evaluation."

"You should have. Savegre did one on you."

That was a surprise. "He did? What did it say?"

Barbero took a long drag on his cigarette. "You got all the top marks."

I studied him a moment. "Then why didn't he show me?"

Barbero smirked, flicking his wrist dismissively. "You know Raoul."

"What's with that guy?" I burst out. "He left me on my own from day one."

"You know how the office works. No one has time—"

"Then why hire someone if you're not going to train him?"

"I didn't hire you. Miguel did."

"Okay, why did *he* hire me, then?"

"You'll have to ask him. I suppose he saw something in you. I don't know, that's just Miguel. I knew nothing about it. I remember the day I first saw you. Who is this guy, everyone was saying. Because, then, Miguel had decided to leave. Then you show up your first day, and we didn't know what to do with you. So you ended up working for Savegre."

"So no one is responsible," I quipped.

"I don't know what Raoul did with you after that."

"You could have trained me to do a job. Now where am I?"

Barbero bristled. "Wait a minute. You have to understand, you didn't—what's your salary?"

"Fifty-five."

"See?" Barbero shrugged, as if I didn't get it. "We can make that in one good trade."

At the end of January it was announced that Dave Komansky, the new president of Merrill Lynch, would address the firm on its performance in 1994. On the surface, this appeared to be quite a challenge for Komansky. After seven Fed interest rate hikes, Wall Street was a shambles. Overall pretax profits had fallen 87 percent in 1994; Salomon, still reeling from the enormous $290 million fine imposed on it for defrauding the U.S. Treasury, had lost a stunning $685 million, most of it in the bond market. The derivatives business had stumbled. Under-writing was down 33 percent. Bonuses had been slashed. Five thousand workers had lost their jobs. And Merrill had shared in the pain. The firm's net income was down 25 percent from the previous year. In the last three months, 250 people had been laid off and bonuses cut as much as anywhere.

Merrill had also shared in a year of scandal. Orange County's $2 billion lawsuit had capped off a year that had ended the long life of Kidder Peabody and seriously wounded Bankers Trust, whose derivatives debacles were still taking their toll. Many of BT's clients were now in rebellion, refusing to honor their contracts, while others had fled the firm's tarnished image. The bank's debt had subsequently been downgraded, 10 percent of its workforce had been slashed, fourth quarter earnings had plunged 64 percent, and employees were quitting high-level posts, including the leadership of its emerging markets group, which had defected en masse to Wasserstein Perella. Other houses were still paying for previous crimes. Prudential Securities, which had defrauded hundreds of investors in limited partnerships dur-ing the eighties, was busy writing out $700 million in settlement checks.

Beneath this skin of carnage, however, lay some deeper facts mitigating Ko-mansky's challenge. Merrill had vowed to fight the Orange County charges, which everyone agreed would take years of legal combat to settle. And financially, the firm was doing fine, to say the least. Strengthened by its diverse business portfo-lio, Merrill Lynch had just had the second-best year in its entire *history*, raking in $1.02 billion in profits and emerging the clear winner on Wall Street, a firm well ahead of the pack. The greatest challenge facing Komansky, most people felt, was explaining all the layoffs and slashed bonuses, given the firm's excellent operat-ing results. Rumor was, the firm had taken the market drop as an excuse to boost its stock price by cutting personnel. What was Komansky going to say about that?

I was interested to know. Komansky was a Merrill Lynch success story and known for his people skills. Like the chairman of the firm, Dan Tully, he had been raised in the working-class boroughs of New York and kept a photo on his wall of the Brooklyn tenement in which he grew up. He portrayed himself as a beer-drinking regular guy, an example of what hard work could accomplish. Like Tully, he was a loudspeaker for the Merrill Lynch Principles, always stressing that it was the culture of the firm that made it a success and that, as top dog, the firm's great-est threat did not come from #2 Smith Barney, but its own arrogance.

I had seen Komansky in IEM only once, a visit noted more for the reaction of Savegre, who surpassed all previous records of humility and earnestness. Dressed in black, he could easily have been a butler. At the time I had wondered what Ko-mansky knew about the way things really operated on a trading desk. A twenty-seven-year Merrill Lynch veteran, he had come from the Retail side, where he had spent the majority of his career, and taken over the helm of Capital Markets in 1993, a year in which he earned about $6 million in compensation before finally being selected president, Merrill's chairman-in-training. Did he know how the Latin Mafia operated, or did their modus operandi go all the way to the top?

The speech was given in an odd locale: a large, low-ceilinged room supported by numerous view-obstructing pillars, and temporarily filled with plastic chairs. For all its wealth, Merrill Lynch world headquarters had no sizable auditorium in which employees could gather. Komansky stood at a lectern in the center with a slew of video cameras upon him—the speech was being broadcast to offices worldwide—and a monitor by his side. He was a large man, six-four and well over two hundred pounds, with a tire of a neck and no chin. He read his statement, which sounded as if it had been lifted from the pages of the annual report—tough year, but we did great—and then showed a slick video—professionally produced, of course—in which the year's headlines, financial and otherwise, faded in and out, set to a rock-and-roll score. Until you've sat in a tightly packed room of glum Wall Street employees, their numbers slashed, listening to Michael Jackson sing "Thriller," you don't really know the meaning of the word "discordant."

Afterward Komansky took questions. One of the first was whether there would be any more personnel cuts. No, Komansky said, most of the cuts were over, in his opinion. A few market-oriented questions followed. And then some brave soul stood up in the middle of the plastic chairs and cleared his throat. "Mr. Komansky, if this is the second most profitable year in Merrill Lynch history, as you have just stated, why were our bonuses cut, and why all the layoffs?"

A rumble arose from the audience. Komansky produced a broad smile. "What a brave man you are," he replied, producing laughter. The rest of his response wasn't directed at the questioner, however, but at the row of plastic chairs in front, in which his top executives sat. "Sure, we've had to trim bonuses some, but, c'mon. So Edson won't get his plane this year, Rick won't get another house, Lonny's going to have to cut back on all that overseas travel, Herb won't get a new suit. Let's keep this in perspective, guys."

That was enough for me. I leapt to my feet, stood atop my chair, and screamed, "LET THEM EAT CAKE!"

Okay, okay, I just thought about that. But it was certainly feasible. Dave Komansky made $4.5 million in 1994. That buys a lot of cake.

## 34

While I was watching Klausthaler trade the terminally ill exotics and studying my flash cards, the unthinkable finally happened: IEM moved to Seven. The rumors had sprung up once again and been confirmed; we had all boxed up our meager possessions; and in the first week of February, I arrived Monday morning to find that the entire office had been transported downstairs over the weekend. Our new Trading desk was three hedgerows in the vast field of Merrill's bond farm. Two of these faced each other: one Trading, the other Sales, forming a thick wall of computers. Overlooking this lukewarm embrace was a third, one-sided row backing up to the windows. This was the home of International Retail and various odds and ends, such as myself. As a whole, IEM was flanked by other bond trading groups, though they remained nameless. That was the spirit of our move: there were no introductions made, no explanations, no talk, no nothing, aside from a woman who came around to brief us on our new phone system. We just came to work one day and started working in a different place, as if nothing had happened.

But, of course, something *had* happened. The move caused a great deal of whispering and wild rumors. One thing was clear: IEM would never be the same again. The Latin Mafia had been dislodged from their exclusive perch and were now mixed in with scores of other managing directors, many more powerful than they. Their free-wheeling days were over: they were part of Mother Merrill. This forced repatriation tarnished their shine and left them looking out of place. They had no private conference room to call their own anymore, no place to gather and smoke Camels and exclude the gringos. Our investment bankers—including Escobar— who were all Latin, weren't even located adjacent to the rest of the group. They had separate offices up a flight of stairs and down the hall from the rest of us. An era had come to a close.

There were a few other changes that struck closer to home. I wasn't sitting with the traders anymore. I had been given an old computer, rather then a promised new one. And I was way out on the end of my row.

In the new post-bonus, post-Sixteen, post-peso-crisis era, our numbers continued to dwindle. The managing director in charge of IEM's Hong Kong operations was fired, ending our expansion there. Our head derivatives trader quit for Smith Barney, taking my Achilles heel, Javier Pip, with him. One of our analysts wasn't hired on, and left for law school. Our most experienced International Retail trader, needing some sun in her life, took a retail job in Miami. Charles Post finally gave up and left to work with some investment bankers on another floor. And Savegre finally won his battle with Eduardo Salvador, who was replaced by a less combative research analyst—one with no experience in Latin America, aside from a few months in IEM, and with no Spanish-language capability.

As IEM's losses came to the attention of the firm, even larger heads began to fall. The first was Miguel Forte, who was rumored to have lost $10 million in the back book. He was relieved of all trading responsibilities. Diego Barbero assumed full duties as head trader and major Mafioso, leaving Forte in a limbo normally reserved for *Associatus rovingus*. While his losses were great, however, Forte still enjoyed an immunity that other traders—McCarthy, Weaver—had not. He stayed in IEM.

Savegre wasn't held accountable either. He was demoted to salesman but not fired, and Mickey Gurevich was made head of Sales. This put Savegre in a tough position. He had to come up with some new accounts—and fast—in a very bear market. But he quickly found a workable solution: he took his accounts from Middle Markets. The very first was Cargill. Then Gurevich fired Dick Sullivan, our fiery Irish American salesman, and Savegre got even more accounts.

Amid all this turbulence I had a job offer, of a kind. One of the remaining brokers called me in a rush late one afternoon and asked me out for an immediate drink. I met him in a bar downstairs fifteen minutes later. The man looked worried. He had just heard his longtime partner asking one of their clients for a job. "Just a half hour ago," he said. Then he started pushing the positives of his business, how the market was going to turn around, how much money they had made in '93. I wasn't interested. I couldn't even explain why. I was committed to seeing my IEM experience through to the end, whatever that end was, and it wasn't a job in Middle Markets. I felt, for no conscious reason, that I was on a trajectory to a different destination, some understanding that would be attained only by staying on my present course.

All the dislocation, the layoffs, the demotions, and the quittings, the slashed bonuses and the mounting losses finally led Lisardo Escobar to take another decisive step in early February: he called a second group meeting. The meeting was held on Eight, in a conference room we used twice a week for the morning call. This was itself a telling sign. In an organization where real estate was everything, we were playing musical conference rooms.

You could feel the hostility in that room the second you entered it. Unlike the moments before the morning call, there was no conversation. There was just a silent, windowless conference room full of people waiting for Escobar. He finally showed up, trailed by his new lieutenants, Barbero and Gurevich, sat down amid the silence, and immediately launched into a speech about the future of IEM. We had nothing to worry about, he said. The market had suffered a correction, the peso crisis had taken us by surprise, but hey, these things happened. We had lost some people, but there was nothing that could be done about that. He didn't see any need for more cuts. As he talked, he kept flipping his palms up and down like vacillating switches while interjecting the occasional careless laugh. Anyway, '94 is history, he assured us confidently. It was a bad year, but now it's over. The market is going to turn. In '95, we're all going to make the same bonuses we did in '93.

Given the weight of the statement, the silence in the room felt like shock. How

Escobar could say that we were about to repeat the best year in the history of the emerging markets, and all of Wall Street, was enough to baffle even the faithful.

"All we need to do is make three million in production per person," he explained. "That's it. We've looked at the numbers. Three million. Now, come on, guys, that's not a lot, is it? We can do that."

"How?" someone asked, releasing a pent-up flutter of laughter.

"Just through transactions. We're going to be transaction based from now on. That's it. None of this fancy stuff. We already talked it over"—he looked to Gurevich, sitting next to him, for support—"and we've decided there's no major restructuring needed."

So there had been another secret meeting. Escobar was right—nothing had changed. He went on, seemingly unaware of how he was being received—unaware of how a group of talented people felt when they weren't consulted on major decisions affecting their future, when instead of having input, they were subject to questionable decisions made in blithe secrecy. It was as if the boom were still on and Escobar could do whatever he wanted with us.

"We have identified some problems," he admitted. "But we're going to fix those. We need to start dealing better with our customers, for one. We need better sales and marketing, trade ideas. Mickey is going to be looking into that now."

Gurevich nodded. It was the only public acknowledgment that Savegre was no longer head of Sales and the first admission that there was a real problem in that department. Savegre, who was present, didn't move an inch. He just looked obediently at Gurevich as if he had been his boss all along, rather than someone he had once hired.

"And Diego will work with him on that."

Barbero, who was standing behind Escobar, stepped forward. Trading, Sales, and Escobar—the new leadership had been established. Identifying who ran IEM was like figuring out who ran China during the Cold War. It was all a matter of who stood next to whom.

I looked around the room: Forte was nowhere to be seen.

Escobar flicked a careless wrist at the crowd. "Okay? So that's it, unless anyone has any questions."

"Yeah, I do," said John Wesson, surprising everyone. A chiseled midwesterner long on muscles and mathematics but short on speech, Wesson rarely spoke about anything but the peso derivatives he traded. Now he faced Escobar from the other end of the conference table. "I don't know about anyone else here, but I don't think I got paid."

The question froze the audience like a flashbulb. Escobar's shoulders caved into a shrug, which ended with him dropping his arms forward on the table and lowering his head. He pulled back with a frustrated gasp, as if not responsible for the uncomfortable position he was now in, then lifted his palms to the ceiling as if asking why. "John, you got paid. Everybody got paid. We didn't get paid as much as we liked, but that's the market."

"I don't think I got paid. I don't think anyone else does either. I don't know, let me ask. Does anyone here think they got paid?"

This courageous act, the only one I ever witnessed in IEM, pulled everyone's eyes to Wesson, then drove them back to Escobar, whose hand flew up to rub his prominent jaw, hiding his lower face. Wesson's fixed gaze bore through it, and it was not a happy one. Rather, after a year's worth of highly pressured trading, he looked as though he could easily twist Escobar's head off.

"I did a lot of work over the past year—"

Escobar waved the point away with flailing arms. "John, hey, we all did."

"—and I didn't get paid for it, that's all I know. If people work, they need to get paid. I don't know about anyone else, but I get calls from headhunters all the time. I never took those calls."

"Good, you did the right thing."

"Why shouldn't we take those calls?" asked Justo Lamberti, turning Escobar's head to a second front. "Why shouldn't we take the next bid away?"

Escobar went on a brief offensive. "Justo, what good would that do? The Street is hurting all over, not just here. Merrill is the safest house on the Street. This is the place to be." He faced the rest of the group, who sat quietly watching him. Their collective indifference tore at his confidence, making him sound for the first time as if he were pleading. "And like I said, this is going to be a good year, a really good year. We have all the people we need, right in this room. Come this time next year, you're all going to be a lot happier, I *promise*. I'll tell you one thing— *I'm* not leaving. I'm right where I want to be. And if you'd just look beyond your number a minute, you'd see that you are too."

Escobar undoubtedly was happy. He was one of the seven-figure bonuses.


Later that day I finally saw Forte on the floor. He was sitting at the far end of the room, working half days now, his status unknown. I was sorry to see that. The one leader in the group, he had been pushed aside by the market and now sounded uncharacteristically cynical.

"How are things going?" I asked.

He snorted. "Like the market. How about you?"

I told him that, with things the way they were in the group, I was interested in looking at other options within Merrill. I thought that was safe: there was no denying that things were bad in the emerging markets, and I was displaying a desire to stay with the firm. I wasn't that worried about Forte breaking my confidence, but it was best to be cautious anyway, especially at such a delicate time in the group.

Forte thought a moment. "Why don't you see Lester Walker?"

Perfect, I thought. Lester Walker was the Undertaker.

"He knows a lot of people in the firm," Forte explained. "What do you want to do?"

"Go abroad," I said.

"Where?"

"Any crown colony except this one."

Forte laughed, wrote down Walker's number for me, and offered to call him on my behalf. I thanked him. Then I did something difficult to explain, for it worked on a subconscious level. I asked the same question of Savegre. I placed my trust in him, thinking that if he broke it I was not responsible for the repercussions.

"Why do you want to go overseas?" he asked. "The money is much better in New York."

I spit out something about wanting to live in London, where Savegre had once worked for Money Markets.

"I know lots of people over there," he said quickly, always eager to show his connections within the firm. "And Hong Kong too. Let me ask around."

I appreciated that. He sounded so sincere. And he looked so pathetic as a salesman, sitting there with the men he once managed, that the next day I even gave him some leads I had never pursued.

"Any luck with London?" I asked.

"Huh? Oh no—haven't heard back yet."

Meanwhile Klausthaler surprised me with his own lead one Friday, handing me a Post-it note with a number on it. "This is Roger Franklin. He's a friend of mine. He's looking for an emerging markets trader. I told him about you. He wants you to call him."

Franklin worked at a British bank that was well known in the emerging markets. I called him that afternoon and arranged an interview two weeks hence. I also faxed him my résumé when no one else was around. Standing there watching the paper go through, I noticed the résumé of Charles Post sitting on the windowsill.


The next Monday I walked in, stole a chair after the morning call, and assumed my usual seat at the exotics position. Klausthaler was late. I sat there for almost an hour while the market opened and the exotics began trading. One of the salesmen finally stood up and asked for a price on Ecuador from Russ Fraga, one of the Brady traders. As soon as the trade was done I slid my chair over to Fraga.

"When is Richard coming in?"

Fraga briefly lifted his head. "He's not. He's left the firm."

I didn't move a moment. "He didn't even tell me . . ." I said absently. "Where did he go?"

"Lehman, I think."

I sat contemplating Fraga's back. In a second, whatever meager reserves of energy I had left were drained from my body. Now what? I thought mechanically. That was the proper response in IEM: don't think about the meaning of things, just plow on, take the next step, react, before it's too late.

I considered Fraga. Our most emotional trader, he had built a wall around himself the past few months. I liked him, but the thought of starting from scratch with someone else was just too much. It took too much energy, at least in IEM. And I knew Fraga was in no mood to teach me. In addition to his Brady inventory, he had just been handed the specialized exotics book, with hardly an explanation.

I slid my chair back down to Klausthaler's old position and sat staring at the screens for a long time, seeing nothing.

Klausthaler called later that week and told me what had happened. The previous Friday, soon after handing me my job lead, he had informed Diego Barbero that he was leaving the firm. When a trader quits, he leaves the floor that day: traders are handling too much money to be left on the desk without a care—or worse. Barbero immediately arranged for an "exit interview," which was standard policy in such instances. This gave management a chance to either sever ties amicably or top a rival bid.

Barbero led Klausthaler up to Escobar's office and closed the door. Escobar was sitting behind his desk. Barbero informed him that Klausthaler was leaving. Klausthaler explained that he had another offer. Suddenly Escobar switched to Spanish and began talking to Barbero—about Klausthaler. This was extraordinary, not only because it was so brazenly tacky, but because, unbeknownst to Escobar, Klausthaler spoke fluent Spanish.

ESCOBAR: *Has he really got a bid away?*
BARBERO: *Yes, he's quitting.*
ESCOBAR: *I didn't realize they were getting bids away.*
BARBERO: *I told you they were!*
ESCOBAR: *So he's really quitting?*
BARBERO: *Yes, Lisardo, he's really quitting!*

Escobar made no counteroffer. Klausthaler left the building and went home.

The next day I asked Barbero what I was supposed to do. He told me to wait and see. I went back to my position and sat there flipping through the job advertisements on Bloomberg. Nothing reached out and grabbed me. Did I really want to work on Wall Street? In banking? I didn't know anymore. I wasn't sure of anything anymore.

It took a few days and some prodding for Barbero to get back to me. "Come on upstairs," he said, tapping me on the shoulder. I followed him to an empty office on

Eight where George Navarro was waiting. Navarro, who was in charge of the combined Eurobond/International Retail desk, was a hard read. He was of Spanish extraction and a favorite of Escobar's, but also allied with the larger firm, where other members of his family worked. He was the only person in IEM who seemed to consider Merrill Lynch a career. I had worked with him on occasion during the Middle Markets, and we had gotten along fine. He seemed at times to be a full-fledged member of the Latin Mafia, but maybe he just knew how to work the system.

The office overlooked the trading floor and had a small table near the window. Barbero sat across from me, and Navarro reclined on the windowsill, one foot on top of it, his back to the wall, and lit up a Camel. He handed one to Barbero. They muttered something back and forth in Spanish, Barbero talking over his shoulder, Navarro looking out the window. They were obviously talking about me. Naturally, I kept wondering what the hell was going on. But that was the point, wasn't it?

"Okay," Barbero said. "What we have decided is to offer you a position as a retail trader."

*A retail trader* . . . The words burned a hole in my head. All I could see was the fax I had received from Miguel Forte over a year ago now: *I am pleased to confirm Merrill Lynch's offer to you as an International Retail Trader for the International Emerging Markets Group* . . .

It was too much. I twisted in my chair, my head shaking.

Barbero went on. "This is a good opportunity. George's desk—"

"What happened to my trading position?" I shot back.

Barbero paused, his eyes fixed on me as if trying to figure me out. "We're not going to have any new positions open in trading. Not for a while. The market is too bad."

"It's a good opportunity for you," Navarro said. "You did a good job with Middle Markets. We can use that experience."

I kept squirming around, leaned forward, dropped my head in my hands, and lifted my head back up, eyes crossing the ceiling. Meanwhile I felt the same feeling that had taken me to Savegre, just a few days before, bubbling up. The feeling that I was done playing the game. That I was going to let the truth do my work for me.

"No—I need to think about it," I blurted out.

Navarro and Barbero both paused in surprise, staring at me. No one said that! Not in the market, not in IEM, and certainly not in a bear market. And not when you weren't an insider. It was professional hara-kiri. I had been given a job to do, and had no choice in the matter. It was simple.

"Do you realize that this is my *fifth job* this year?" I stressed.

"No," Barbero said, his ruddy face dry-cleaned of emotion. The emotional Darwinism of the market had long since sculpted his indifference.

Navarro took a quick perturbed pull on his cigarette. "Paul, this is a good opportunity. And, frankly, there's not much else out there."

I kept shaking my head. What was the point? What could I tell them that would matter?

Barbero stood. "Okay, you'll let George know, then."

"We need to know soon about this," Navarro said, swinging himself off the windowsill. "Think about it. If you want to be part of the desk, fine, I'd be happy to have you." He stabbed his cigarette in the ashtray and followed Barbero from the room.

I sat there alone awhile, looking through the glass at the furrows of Seven below. For once the trading floor was quiet.


Later in the day I spied Forte and told him what had happened. He laughed at some inside joke and said, "Take it." Then he began collecting his belongings to leave early for the day. "Have you spoken to Lester Walker yet?"

"Briefly. I went up to his office and told him I was looking to go abroad. He said to check back with him."

"Good luck," Forte said. He donned his coat, picked up his briefcase, and headed home. I never saw him again.

I thought about my options the rest of the day. There really weren't any, as far as I could see. The retail trader job was a giant step back, and without a single challenge; but if I didn't take it, that was it: I was another IEM casualty. And with Sarah in school, we couldn't afford that. I would have to take the position and look elsewhere in the meantime.

I caught Navarro before going home. "Okay," I said. "I'll take it."

"You're sure about that? We need your head in it one hundred percent."

I knew what he meant and agreed. "Don't worry," I assured him. "You just caught me by surprise, that's all."

"Okay, I'll tell the desk. You can start tomorrow."


## 35

I arrived for my first day on the Retail desk without the slightest rise in energy. It was impossible to motivate myself for the sixth time. I had wiped the slate clean and started over, mentally, upon my move to Trading, but you can only do that once. Now, instead of leaving the past behind, it pressed down upon my will.

Ironically, out of all the jobs I had held, International Retail had the best conditions. The retail traders were on the bottom rung of the desk, so they had nothing to prove. There were three of them, plus a secretary, and they were all supportive. The job was resolutely dull, however, which is why no one valued it. One of our many phone lines would blink. I would answer and talk with some broker in Merrill's international retail network, usually in one of the Latin financial capitals. He would ask for a bid or an offer on a bond. We had a marker board with all the prices. I would give the latest price. Sometimes I would call across to one of the traders if the board didn't have what I needed. Then I would fill out the trading blotter. It was a job that in more developed markets was done by computer.

After a few hours of this, I looked down at the traders' row and noticed Tommy Rana sitting at Klausthaler's old position. Rana was a young Indian investment banker who had recently returned from our collapsed Hong Kong office. He had never worked on a trading desk before.

"What's Rana doing?" I asked Julio, one of the retail traders.

"I hear he's trading the exotics now," Julio said.

I stared at him. "You've got to be kidding me . . ."

I stood up, fighting a wave of intense emotion, and thinking about nothing but finding Barbero. I spotted him speaking with another trader at the end of the desk and was by his side in seconds.

"Can you tell me what is going on?" I interrupted in distinct, barely restrained syllables.

Barbero immediately retreated into his impassive shell. "What do you mean?"

I pointed to Rana. "What is he doing there?"

"Trading."

"The guy doesn't have any experience!"

"We needed someone to fill in for Richard."

"I worked with Richard the last two months!"

"Tommy has experience modeling bonds."

"Diego, I did the Brady Sheet for *months*! That guy doesn't even know what a *Brady bond* is!"

Barbero stared dully back at me. "We just felt—"

"You could have told me. Why didn't you say something?"

"We hadn't made up our minds."

"You said there were no positions open!"

"No, now wait a minute!" Barbero objected, raising a finger in warning, "I said there would be no *new* positions."

I gasped incredulously. "You've got to be kidding me. You said that—"

"I *said* that—"

*"That's no way to treat people!"*

Barely in control of myself, I strode back to my position and sat down, overwhelmed by a sickening emptiness. What was wrong with these people? Didn't they have any—humanity? I felt a ripping and tearing inside, a tug of war between a powerful need for justice and the impotency of my position.

Later that day Klausthaler called me from home. He had yet to start his new job. I explained to him what had happened with the exotics book. "So the Latin Mafia are jerking *you* around now," he said, and suggested why. "Miguel's star has fallen. He was your mentor, right? Tommy Rana is Escobar's boy. He's from the banking side. Now that the market is down, everyone is vulnerable. Escobar is just putting him in a safe spot."

Was that it, I wondered? Klausthaler had been in Hong Kong with Tommy Rana. They were friends. Had he put in a good word for Rana over me? I didn't know what to think, and I wondered why he was calling.

"I have the name of a headhunter for you," Klausthaler said. I wrote it down and thanked him. "Now what's going on in the market?" he asked abruptly. "I'm a little out of touch." He went on to request some specific price levels, then hung up, our transaction complete. Two years in IEM, I thought, and he didn't have anyone else to call, or a better strategy to employ. But I wasn't surprised. Looking out across the trading floor, I realized I trusted no one.


In the wake of the Rana event I redoubled my efforts to find another job. It wasn't easy. After the peso crisis, the emerging markets had become the black sheep of Wall Street. Except for some high-paid talent—market disasters were viewed as a great opportunity to poach personnel from rival firms—the job market had dried up. I called Eduardo Salvador to see how his search was coming and found him at home: he had been unable to find a position. In addition to market obstacles, Savegre had been bad-mouthing him to other banks. I called headhunters in New York and London, and they advised me to wait a few months until the market quieted down. At the same time my efforts were halfhearted. I wasn't sure what I wanted to do, because I wasn't sure what was wrong with my life. Was IEM an exception or the rule? Should we just go abroad? How much of a factor was New York? Should I do something else?

One new option that presented itself—literally—was the wire services, which I figured could use someone with trading floor experience. So I pulled up a news story from the Dow Jones Emerging Markets Report and called their managing editor, Gordon Hawthorne, who agreed to see me.

I also returned to see Lester Walker, the Undertaker. Walker had an office in Risk Management, on Eight, whose interior windows overlooked Seven, giving him a view down the length of IEM. For a second, as I neared his door, I imagined him standing by the glass with his phone, listening to my calls. In reality, I found him sitting perfectly still in front of his computer, his back bolt upright, his fingers bridged in front of him. What he was praying for, I don't know. The screen provided no clues. There were just columns of numbers, scrolling down in a seemingly infinite loop, mesmerizing him.

"Lester?"

The Undertaker turned as if on a slow swivel, his owlish eyes blinking at me. "Yes, Paul," he said softly, placing his hands flat on his thighs.

"Ah—just wondering if you had any info on what we talked about the other day."

"No."

"Oh." I expected him to add something, but no additions were forthcoming. "Okay . . . I'll . . . just check back with you later then."

"Fine." He initiated his turn.

"Oh, Lester, I was wondering—"

He slowly rotated back. "Yes?"

"You're from Tasmania, right?"

"Yes."

"Does Merrill have an office in—"

"No."

"Right. Okay. Well—thanks."

I left, feeling a sudden relief in the hallway. The Undertaker was so circumspect, you might've thought I was a risk to the firm's capital.


Thursday finally arrived, February 23, and the midtown interview Klausthaler had arranged with Roger Franklin. I spent the day doing retail trades at a steady pace, hating it more and more. With their market getting crushed, the Latin brokers were in surly moods. They questioned your pricing, tried to talk you down, even threatened to complain to management. There was a different dynamic operating with them than had existed with Middle Markets. They were the kingpins of the Latin retail market, and they expected the International Retail traders to remember it.

By the end of the day I found my nerves wearing dangerously thin. It wasn't the stress of the job per se, it was everything, an indefinable accumulation of emotion that had no outlet. The thought of now rushing midtown for a six o'clock interview generated a new kind of response, one without a name. It was as if I were plumbing new areas of my mind. How was it that these regions existed? There were no fire walls in the psyche, only more rooms. And this one was a kind of rippling, anxiety-laden space, which caused a slight tremble in my fingers. I wondered how I was going to overcome this, and it only made things worse. Another door opened, into the fear-of-failure room. I was going to go to this interview, I thought, and really mess it up, because this place is really messing me up, and I'm not sure how to handle it anymore.

I reached into my desk drawer. My little bottle of Valium had made its way down to Seven, so I broke through the childproof cap and took a couple of those without thinking and felt better right away, before they even had time to do their work.

Then I went into the men's room to make sure I looked okay and went outside and hailed a taxi.

I arrived in midtown, near Central Park, and went into another bank, this one a lot smaller than Merrill Lynch, occupying a few floors of the usual glass Manhattan high-rise. Roger Franklin came to the elevator to meet me. He was a clean-cut young Briton with that professional trader air about him, all squared edges and focused, rapid-fire speech. He took me into a long conference room, which reminded me of Sixteen, and we sat and talked about my résumé. I was feeling pretty relaxed by now, and the interview went quite well. It turned out Franklin didn't need just any trader, though—he needed a head trader, which obviously I wasn't qualified for. However, he said, he had his eye on someone at another bank, and if this guy took his offer, he would need an assistant, and he would certainly like to recommend me for that on the basis of what Klausthaler had said about me. I said I would be very interested; it would be a good way to learn trading. The interview ended on that positive note, and Franklin led me to the elevator, where I agreed to call him the following week. On the way down, I felt pretty good. Maybe Merrill Lynch *was* the problem, I thought. Perhaps it would be better to work for a venerable British bank like Barings.

The next Monday I came into work feeling better than in weeks. I sat down at my monitor, per my morning ritual, and took a look at the latest financial news. BARINGS COLLAPSES, the top headline said. Collapses what? I brought up the story and read it in disbelief. Barings PLC had just suffered one of the most spectacular losses in financial history. Using a combination of derivatives and deception, a trader in its Singapore office, Nick Leeson, had built up a massive, secret trading position on the Japanese stock market and had been crushed following the Kobe earthquake. He had, quite literally, bet the bank for his bonus—and lost. Now Britain's oldest merchant bank, which had financed the Napoleonic Wars and our own Louisiana Purchase, and even managed the Queen's money, was bankrupt.

I held my head in my hands, stunned. This was not really happening. Then I laughed incredulously, hysterically. What else could you do, when faced with such absurdity? The world seemed bent on proving that there was no continuity, no meaning in anything. There was nothing to believe in, no point in extending trust. Tomorrow, everything would change. Like an idiot, all you could do was babble your way from one day to the next. It was perfect market management.

Meanwhile Nick Leeson was on the loose, having fled Singapore, setting off an international manhunt for the newly named "rogue trader." I tuned my wires to Nick's frequency and followed the stories with great interest. The press quickly vilified Leeson, turning him into a rich yachting playboy who lived an exotic lifestyle among the jet set of Singapore, rather than saying what he was: a working-class kid who had made far less than any IEM trader the previous year. At the same time the culture that produced him went unscathed, as if Leeson were some anomaly in the system rather than a man exposed by an act of God. There was a hidden assumption there, that the moral system inside the financial world operated the same as the one without; the same faith in moral equivalence seen in the media's treatment of Mexico. It was as if all these catastrophic events were unique, rather than products of a greater systemic picture no one wanted to admit—or judge.

From within that system, however, I found myself cheering Nick on, hoping his false passports would do the job. And why not? The system had finally gotten what it deserved. Why shouldn't Nick bet the bank for his bonus? What had the bank ever done for him? What loyalty did it inspire? Didn't the system operate on self-interest? What principles stood between him and the big bet? So Barings paid his salary—hey, caveat emptor, right? That's what it was all about. In the market there are always losses. I didn't hear anyone at Merrill chastising Leeson, either. But why should the Street care? After all, the trader who almost sank Merrill in 1987, Howie Rubin, was now making eight figures a year at Bear Stearns. That was the way the system worked, and all the insiders knew it. The only problem with Leeson was, he got caught red-handed.

The more I thought about Nick, the more I wondered how I would feel if I somehow hit the wrong key and triggered the collapse of my employer. It wouldn't ruffle my conscience much, I decided. There comes a point when destroying the system is justice.


After work on Wednesday, I took the train across the Hudson to meet with Gordon Hawthorne at the Dow Jones Emerging Markets Report. It occupied part of a long, tankerlike building in Jersey City, directly across from the World Financial Center. Hawthorne met me at the elevator and led me through a cipher lock to his new offices, which were still under construction. Tall, thin, and in his fifties, he had a strain of what is best called New England prep school headmaster in him, an attribute that is warming, as long as you are on the right side of it. The newsroom looked something like IEM. There were clumps of computers staffed by people either monitoring the news or writing it down. The room was less crowded, though, much quieter, and had a far more relaxed atmosphere; everyone was in casual clothes. It wasn't an especially warm place, but compared with Seven, it was positively refreshing.

Hawthorne led me to his own cubicle, where I sat down beside his desk. He took out my résumé, asked me about my past, and told me what he was looking for. The Emerging Markets Report was expanding abroad and hiring new people. It was a ground-floor opportunity to learn the news business. Most of the jobs were in exotic locales—Vietnam, Turkey, the former Soviet republics—how did that strike me?

"Just what I'm looking for," I said. "I'll take Istanbul over Brooklyn any day."

"This is also a good place to start if you're interested in working at the Paper one day," he added. "The *Journal*, I mean."

I flinched. I wasn't interested in working for *The Wall Street Journal*. The *Journal* was at the top of its field, and I didn't ever want to get near the Top again. In a second I imagined the entire trajectory: I would put in lots of hard work at the bottom, scrape my way up the ladder, and one day get to the Paper, where all the other reachers and strivers were, eyeing each other, trying to get ahead, elbowing their way up, and forgetting, by the time they got there, who they once had been. Then, disillusioned, I would seek out the quiet Emerging Markets Report, a place to hide from the Top and lead a sensible life. Hadn't my father told me that once before? It's not a question of getting to the Top; it's a matter of finding a place where the Top can't get you.

"So why do you want to leave IEM?" Hawthorne asked, fixing his eyes on me. "I have to say, we don't get many of your kind over here. There're not many bond traders who want to give up the perks, shall we say."

I said, in a few sentences, that there didn't seem to be a real values match for me across the river, that there were certain aspects of it I found disturbing. Meanwhile Hawthorne nodded, with an affirming hum. "Yes, I've dealt with enough people over there to know how they operate." He glanced at me with an inexplicable conflict on his face. I thought for a moment that we were seeing eye to eye—that Hawthorne wouldn't mind toggling the Merrill self-destruct switch either, given the opportunity.

"Have you ever heard of Foster Winans?" he asked.

"No."

"Foster used to work for me. I hired him for an equities news wire. Later on he went to the Paper, where he wrote a column that a lot of people read. It could effect the movement of stocks in the market. Then one day he went bad. He got in with some traders and cut himself a deal. He was leaking word to them in advance, before the stories were printed, and making money off them."

Hawthorne looked up from my résumé, his inexplicable conflict resolving itself as emotional strain, the strain of a man who sticks to his beliefs regardless of the stories he has read or written. Suddenly I realized that he was wondering about me, whether I were the next Foster Winans. What was my real story? Why had I come over here from IEM? He had launched the Winans tale to track my response, which was blank. And it was blank because for the first time in my life I was shocked to hear someone question me like that. As if I were a member of an untrustworthy element of society. And yet I knew he was right to think so, generating a mixture of shame and defensiveness all at once.

"You see, we're selling one product here," he said. "Integrity. That's all we've got. And we have to guard it every day. It sounds like mom and apple pie, but it's also true. That's why a lot of us still work here."

Integrity? It was so long since I had heard that word, I marveled at the sound. I had seen it on the walls of Merrill Lynch but never heard it mentioned in IEM, not once. At least the Latin Mafia had *some* shame. It seemed to have fallen out of American society as well. Not even the president had integrity—everyone knew that. I felt like telling Hawthorne that it was good to finally meet someone of his caliber, but I couldn't, of course, under the circumstances.

"That's refreshing to hear," I said instead, the words coming out in a whoosh.

The conflict on Hawthorne's face disappeared. We *were* seeing eye to eye. He understood now why I wanted to leave Merrill Lynch. He glanced down and told me he found my résumé interesting—market experience and foreign travel are pluses—and went on to describe some of the particulars of the job. I relaxed. Things were going well. Hawthorne said he usually didn't hire walk-ins like this but, under the circumstances, he might consider a six-month trial period here in New Jersey. It was important to see if I could do the writing.

"What kind of salary goes along with that?" I asked him.

"Thirty-five, once you're hired on for good."

My face said it all: thirty-five? What kind of a number was that? My God, I had made eighty this year, in the worst bond market since—

Hawthorne stiffened.

"Thirty-five," I said flatly.

Hawthorne shifted in his seat, moved by restrained irritation. He looked as if I had betrayed some confidence of his. "That's what we pay. People don't come into this business for the money the way they do on Wall Street. They do it for the truth. As I said, all we have here is our integrity."

In a society that doesn't care, I thought. Why should I suffer for that? Why should I be one of the suckers, while those bastards across the river—

The question unnerved me. I squirmed as much as Hawthorne, feeling a clammy shirt slide along my back. I felt slick and hot inside my suit and wanted to escape it. Could I? I had spent a year now almost exclusively with Wall Street bankers, and it showed. Hawthorne could see it, I could feel it. It tore my thoughts in two—was this man a fool for doing a job that didn't pay him, or honorable for doing what he believed in? Did honor even exist, or was it just more bull? Had I succumbed to the market, or had I finally figured it all out? The sweat rolled down my back. I cleared my throat, wiped my forehead. I wasn't sure what to think anymore, what to believe in. What kind of system was I in?

"So let me think about this," Hawthorne concluded, "and we can talk in a few days."

I quickly agreed, pushed myself hastily to my feet, held out a damp hand, cracked an uncomfortable smile, and walked awkwardly to the elevator, Hawthorne surveying me from his cipher-locked doorway. Once the twin doors snapped close, I collapsed against the wall, my chin sinking into my chest, completely still and exhausted, the silence magnifying the beat of my heart.

It was dark when I emerged to walk along the river. The World Financial Center was twinkling across the water, an impressive sight. As I said, New York always looks best at night.


The next day, Thursday, George Navarro stopped me while I was walking along traders' row. "I need to talk to you a second," he said, leaning back in his chair, phone to his head. I waited until he got off.

"So what's going on?" he asked.

IEM was hardly the place for casual chatter. Suspecting something was up, I smiled and said, "Nothing, things are just fine."

"Yeah? That's not what I've been hearing. Word is you're still unsure about what you're doing."

"Is it?"

"I hear you've been looking for a job."

I shrugged. What do you say to that?

"Are you sure you still want to do this? I need to know."

"I have a lot to forget about," I said.

"Okay, but I need to know. I stuck my neck out for you when no one else would, you know."

I bristled. "Like who?"

Navarro looked off. "Oh, you know, the usual people, I guess. Escobar, Barbero, Savegre."

*Savegre.*

"Listen," I bristled. "That's a little much. First of all, I get hired into this place as a retail trader, and instead I get stuck with Savegre, who blows me off for almost an entire *year*. Worse—the guy *stood in the way* of the Middle Market business. Now he's got the nerve—"

"Paul, look, that's all water under the bridge now."

"Is it? How do I know it's not going to happen again?"

"Because I'm telling you."

"I've been through this *five times* already."

"I know it, but that's all past now. You're not working for Savegre."

"It happened in Trading too. How can you expect people to work this way?"

"This is the market, you don't have any other choice. Now I've got a business decision to make. Do you want the job? I need to know."

Navarro had a new look in his eye, a terminal look. I was no longer an able pawn but damaged goods, a liability, someone who wasn't playing the game. It was a conditioned reflex: once the virus was identified, the system immediately developed antibodies. And yet on a subconscious level I welcomed them.

An idea presented itself, a way to make it easy for the both of us. "Okay, look, just assuming for a minute I say no, I can't do this. What then?"

"Then there's no alternative but to reduce head count."

*Reduce head count.* I loved that phrase: it was so surgically clean. The verbal equivalent of a scalpel. "Does that imply any severance pay?"

"I assume it would. I don't know—I'd have to check."

"I just want to know all my options. I don't want to jerk you around any more than I want to jerk myself around."

"Let me find out, then."

Navarro caught me later that afternoon. "Fourteen weeks, salary and benefits."

"Okay, thanks. I'll let you know tomorrow."

He dashed off.

## 36

Although our future had become a larger unknown with every passing day, Sarah and I avoided discussing it. It wasn't an inability to communicate, as before, but a lack of anything new to say. We understood the issues by now. There were only decisions to make. And when I arrived home after speaking with Navarro, it was finally time to make one.

"So what are you going to do?" she asked as we did the dishes.

"I don't know. What do *you* want to do?"

"It's up to you. It's your job. If you take severance pay, do you think you can find another job?"

"I don't know."

"Do you want to work in banking?"

"I don't know anymore."

"Do you want to work in New York?"

"I don't know—but Brooklyn is out."

"You said it."

Once the dishes were done, we went into the living room, sat on the couch, and had a frank discussion about the future, the one we had avoided for so long. There were a number of factors to consider, and I had analyzed each of them a thousand times. But I never felt, when my analysis was done, that I had a clear understanding of our situation. There was always something lurking beneath the surface that I failed to identify. I felt this way now, though I was able to phrase the most troubling question.

"Why are we here? That's what I want to know."

"What do you mean?" Sarah asked.

"I'm not sure why we're here anymore. Why am I working at Merrill Lynch and why are we living in Brooklyn?"

"We're here for the money."

"I suppose, but I've forgotten why."

"So we can buy a house."

"We could have bought a house in Annapolis."

She rolled her eyes. "Come on—let's not go into all *that* again."

"I'm serious. I think there's a lot more to this than we realize—than we ever considered when we were making the decision to come here."

"Like what?"

"Like why did I feel so much pressure to come to New York and make as much money as possible on Wall Street?"

"You wanted to retire by forty."

"There's more *to it* than that. I thought that Wall Street was *success,* didn't I? I think we both did."

"I never wanted to move to New York."

"But didn't you think—wow, we're moving up in the world?"

"Maybe a little," Sarah admitted.

"I know I felt it. And it's hard to say where it came from. I feel as though it's been bred into me my whole life, this vision of money as success."

"How? Your parents aren't like that."

"I know—that's the scary part. And Roxbury Latin wasn't like that either. And Harvard wasn't like that. And the navy wasn't like that. So where did that feeling come from?"

"Television?"

"That's what I was thinking. Television and advertising."

"You think we really listen to that, though? I just tune it out."

"You *think* you do, but do you really? What about all the subliminal messages about values, about what makes you happy, about what the good life is—how do we resist those?"

"Come on, television is not controlling my mind!"

"It's not just television, it's our whole market culture. Just look who we were before we came up here. We had our little cottage, we had a great view, a fine town, friends, we had paid off both cars—we were *happy.* But we were an advertiser's nightmare. We hardly went shopping at all. We enjoyed nature instead. We didn't watch much television. We hardly even got any mail. The whole economy *hated* us. Why? Because we were content with what we had. We were free from wants. We didn't need to buy anything."

"But we left Annapolis anyway."

"That's right! The market got to us. That's how strong it is. It was this whole vision of success I'm talking about. Some deep instinct driving me forward. I couldn't stay in that perfect spot—I had to go to New York! To Wall Street! That's where the action was! God, what a *fool* I was."

"Ha! And look at us now," Sarah said. "We have a pile of junk mail every day—magazines, credit cards, record and tape clubs, catalogs from everywhere—the only thing I've given up is my library card. I don't even know where the library *is* here!"

"Who has time?" I reached into my back pocket. "Look at my wallet! It's so big now it's wearing a hole in my pants. I'm serious! And it's not full of money either. It's full of junk."

"You should see my pocketbook. I've never had so much junk in my life. Where did it all come from?"

"That's my point. The market found us. It turned us into good consumers."

"This is really sick, when you think about it."

"It is!"

"We totally sold our happiness—for what?"

"For money! The system doesn't care about our *happiness*—it cares about our *productivity*. It's struggling to survive like the rest of us. And we weren't producing, so it redefined what our happiness was. Then we had to go in search of it—and here we are, living in this rat hole."

"The same thing happens to women," Sarah said. "The system says we're happy only if we're cover girls. So I'm supposed to go out and buy all this junk—shampoo, makeup, mascara, closets full of clothes—just so these cosmetics companies can make a fortune. Do you know how many women have self-esteem problems because of that?"

"You know how many men have heart attacks on Wall Street?"

"You're right, no one ever tells us how to be happy."

"Happy doesn't sell, honey."

"But happy is so simple!"

"That's why it doesn't *sell*. We all have to be reaching for something more *expensive*. Otherwise the whole engine would just *stop*."

"You know what's scary? I never even thought about this before. And I'm twenty-seven years old!"

"I know, I didn't either. The only reason I'm thinking about it now is because of all the stuff that's happened this year. It's shoving it in our faces."

"God, it's so slick!"

"Isn't it? Our whole culture is like a big propaganda machine. It's not *crude* propaganda, like what the Soviets used to broadcast—you could see through *that*. But that's what makes it so insidious. It's decentralized. No single person or organization is in charge of it. It just surrounds us everywhere, every day. And it seems to be harmless. How can you criticize a billboard? Yet when you add it all up, it's *controlling our lives.*" I grabbed my head in my hands. "It's staggering, when you think about it. We have literally been lied to for years."

"We have been! You know, when you're growing up, you take everything at face value. You think that companies are inventing products and offering them to you and pointing out their advantages and letting *you* decide—as if *we* are in charge. But in reality our society is programming us to want those products in the first place!"

"Look how it happens too. The culture preaches certain values—materialism, self-indulgence, instant gratification, ego—all those things that make you want to buy. It's turning us all into a bunch of economic robots. Produce, consume, produce, consume, produce, consume . . . Isn't that ironic? We think we're living lives of liberty when in fact we're all slaves to the system."

"The advertisers know that too. They're the ones selling freedom from inhibitions. Rebel!"

"That's right! They create the problem and then they solve it. Isn't that beautiful?"

"Tugger, get down. You're not supposed to be on the couch."

"When you get right down to it, we're all part of this huge, glitzy, complex, slick marketing engine. And we can't resist it, even when it starts bankrupting our own counties. Caveat emptor!"

"Look at the public schools," Sarah added. "When they have a budget problem, the first thing they cut is the art teacher. I see it all the time. And people wonder why the country is scarred by strip malls and ugly housing developments? *Hello*— could it be because children don't know what *art* is?"

"What about college degrees? I went to one of the best universities in the *world*—and all I'm supposed to talk about is *sports*? Why did I bother? The only reason I need a Harvard degree in my job is because so many other Harvard degrees *want* my job. And the only reason they *want* it is for the money. All I really am is a glorified grocer, moving products off the shelves. The whole thing could better be done by a computer."

"But they think it's success, the way you did."

"I keep thinking about what my dad said—if you're happy, you're a success."

"Isn't that strange? People say money doesn't buy happiness, then they spend their whole lives trying to earn as much as possible. Why don't they take their own advice?"

"Because we're all listening to this nameless, invisible force out there. Think how much better the world would be if all the commercials told you the truth: all you need to be happy is your family, a cottage, some woods, a few good friends, and some books."

"Don't forget Tugger!"

Ears raised, the Little Beast looked at Sarah with her big brown eyes, her head cocked at a curious angle. Sarah scratched behind her ears. "That's all right, Tugger—you can come too."


Later that night I was lying in bed on the verge of sleep when I was seized by an emotion that wouldn't let me go. It arched my back like a mine, lifting and breaking the back of a ship.

"What is it?" Sarah said.

"Sarah—"

"What? What is it?"

I sank back into a listless state. "I don't know if I can do this anymore."

"That's okay, that's okay—"

"I just don't know if I have it in me."

A warm hand rose to my face. "Hey, you have to do what makes you happy. Whatever it is, I'm with you."

# E P I L O G U E

## The World Financial Center
### March 3, 1995

The elevator splits, breaking the frozen quiet. The corridor is active. I weave among faceless people, pass through the double doors, and the great trading hall expands before me. The scoreboards are already rippling with news, the shouts have gelled into a steady clamor. I am late. The market is off and running. But this morning I do not care. Let it go.

Arriving at my position, I stand behind my chair. My long winter coat is warm but reassuring; I leave it on and stand perfectly still while all moves about me. The traders are chattering on the phone; the salesmen are asking for prices; bodies crisscross through the aisles; a piece of paper flutters to the floor in slow motion. One of the retail traders catches my eye, and I burn. All right! I take off the heavy woolen coat and drape it over my chair, not caring that he knows I am late, and lean on the backrest, my fingers strumming on the wool, while staring blindly at the monitor as if my answer lies there. Finally I slide resignedly into the familiar seat, feeling safer but far from relaxed. The touchscreen is blinking with calls from all over Latin America, begging me to answer, to begin. But I can't. My arms are heavy, my palms fixed to my side. I lean forward, bringing the lights closer to my eyes, mesmerized by flashes. What a strange morning it has been! When I got out of bed, I couldn't tell if I had slept. Was I thinking all that time, or really dreaming? Somehow I managed to dress and board the subway and arrive here, but I remember none of it. Now I cannot move. Inertia washes over me, a welcome comfort, though I refuse to admit why.

The lights turn hostile, and I straighten. I will go to the men's room, take a break. I leave the safety of my position and wade back into Seven. By the exit I pass Breen, who is leaning back in his chair, talking on the phone with his feet up on the desk. His shoe leather is torn. One sock has a hole. He swings the phone cord like a jump rope.

The men's room lies just beyond the exit. It has two doors like an air lock and in between I meet two guys talking about "a block of fifty IBM." The slam of the door cuts them off, leaving me in a pneumatic hiss of plumbing, which halts abruptly. In the long mirror over the sinks, a man is moving past. I pause to study him. What is that expression on his face? I lean on the counter, which is wet, and stare into his eyes, questioning the questioner. He tells me nothing, except that he hasn't shaved. The last time that happened, so long ago now, he went down into the lobby, bought himself a razor, and used the hand soap on another floor. This morning he lifts a hand to the stubble and laughs in the draining silence.

Back in the corridor I stop by the drink stand and buy a cup of hot tea, English breakfast tea. On this strange morning it has the power to evoke the strongest image. I lift the cup and stare into silver service sets, a grandfather clock ticking in a quiet drawing room, old women smoking and playing cards, and, beyond the window, a man atop an elephant, fading into mist. Then the cup falls, the image dissolves, and there is no place else to go except back to my position. I safeguard the cup with both hands, like a midsummer's game—it seems vitally important— back through the doors, and turn into the great trading hall of Seven. The sound of surf greets my ears now, and I float along the edge of a reef past identical coral heads of white, eels hiding among them. Then, from the crashing roar, another sound emerges, a private, coherent whisper, barely audible, which I have not heard in ages. It swirls around my legs and recedes.

Back at my position, the long hours ahead finally break through my resistance and I resolve to get to work. I have one last hope before doing so, and am rewarded. An E-mail message has arrived from Tokyo. I click it open.

```
Hey, pal, how are things with the bull?
```

Emotions rise and spill across the barriers. How is it? Do you really want to know? My fingers rest on the keys, but an answer eludes me. My thoughts descend into a swirling confusion, a noise as loud as the one without. It takes me minutes to set down the first line.

`Things have been better. I am thinking of leaving.`

Motionless, I ponder what to say next. It seems like an impossible task, explaining how I feel, but I want to set my thoughts down, I must. I make a number of attempts, erasing each one. They only lead me back to the confusion. How do I make sense of all this?

`Have you ever felt totally alone? I look out on this trading`
`floor and I wonder if anyone sees what I do.`

There, that is a start. Now all I have to do is explain why. But I can't. Once again my thoughts dissolve in the acids of emotion. My forehead turns clammy, and I break away from the screen, seeking distance. The plate glass behind me is mostly veiled, but through the cracks I watch the street below. Soundless people pass in and out of view, hurrying down sidewalks, pouring in and out of subway stations, pausing restlessly at street corners, dashing across the street. Where are they all going—and why? We no longer know. We produce to produce. We don't ask why; we just do what the system tells us. Look at them! Motion, motion, motion, money, money, money—as if speed and greed could buy you immortality. As if the dollar were God. The great bull has pulled free from its harness and runs amok. Productivity! Growth! Efficiency! Profits! Do we ever consider the cost? It's everywhere now—education, law, journalism, politics, art, literature—everywhere standards are falling, corrupted by the market. The church, the family, the community are weakening—don't we ask ourselves why? Or has profit made us blind? The gap grows between rich and poor, the movies sell violence, the prison population swells, the forests are knocked down, the gated communities proliferate—can't we draw connections? Everywhere market principles are choking moral principles, strip-mining substance, bulldozing beauty, razing reason, and we can't even summon any outrage anymore because we're so deafened by the roar.

Whatever happened to the Constitution? This country isn't about business—it's about principle. Principle! Otherwise America is just mere advertising, and we are mere consumers, tiny cogs in the world's most powerful corporation, a twenty-four-hour theme park called the U.S.A.

A stab of awareness penetrates my thoughts, the sharp end of an unblinking stare. I snap my head toward the eighth-floor windows towering over the end of the trading floor. A shadow figure stands there, framed in his perfect square, his owlish eyes fixed upon me, upon us all. He taps a finger on his blackened lips and turns away.

I quickly return to my idle computer, where my message still lingers on the screen. It is incomplete—woefully incomplete. But I haven't the energy to explain. All I add is this:

```
Time is short, my friend.
```

The message goes off to Tokyo, where Jim is still asleep. I hope he comes in early.

That accomplished, I don't know what to do next. It's close enough to lunchtime, but I don't feel hungry. I contemplate going to the cafeteria anyway, but I don't feel like moving. A brief shiver, an antishock, passes through me, scaring me briefly, but I dismiss it and try to focus on doing some work. The lines continue to blink, but I can't answer them. I sit still, and I wait.

"Paul, line two-four," one of the retail traders says.

"Who is it?"

"Lou."

I pick up the phone with a "Thanks." Lou is my old college roommate. He is in his first year of business school and looking for a summer internship. A few weeks ago, as a newly selected bond trader, I told him that I would help him as much as possible. Now I don't know what to say.

"So how's it going?" Lou asks.

I laugh painfully and tell him what has been going on. "So I don't think you're going to have much luck here," I say. "In fact, we have a hiring freeze right now."

Lou is despondent at the news, and I wonder what to say next. I want to tell him the truth but can't confront it. Who wants to face our misery, even when it's a fact? How much better it feels to tell those innocuous little lies, our bottomless hopes, as if they were reality! A few weeks ago, in the euphoria surrounding my new trading assignment, I played up my job to him. Now I cringe at the memory. How do I explain it?

I steel myself; it's time to be frank. In a few choice sentences, I tell Lou what life is like in IEM, how it really operates.

"I know it's pretty tough," he says.

I tell him I don't see a values match for him either.

"I worry about that sometimes," he admits, "but I want to work on the Street."

"Why?" I ask.

He laughs. "The money—what else?"

"You want to spend some of the best years of your life here?"

"I have to spend them somewhere—I'm fifty grand in debt."

The practical point stings me. "You're at the Harvard Business School," I counter. "You can do anything you want. Why not interview somewhere else?"

"I have. I interviewed with an equities firm in San Francisco last week."

"San Francisco!" I laugh. "Go! Go! Everyone loves it there."

"I know, but—it's not the Street."

"Who *cares*?"

Lou coughs. "Well . . . you know, Wall Street is where the action is. If I don't do it now, I never will."

"Lou—Wall Street is where *New York* is. Do you want to live *here* the next few years?"

"Why not? We'll be making enough money."

"No, you won't. You and Leslie will be living in a one-bedroom apartment—*and* paying back fifty grand."

"Well . . . I'll get used to it. Everyone else does. The other job is equity sales anyway. I want to trade bonds."

"Why?"

The question takes him aback. "You know—it's the thing to do."

I stop my rebuttals, conceding defeat. One voice cannot rise above a loud-speaker. And who am I to tell him how to lead his life? Perhaps he will find himself a better home than I have. Or perhaps he will find a different self and move on. That is just as important.

"Lou, all I want to tell you is what I've learned," I conclude. "The reward from graduating from a place like Harvard is that you get to pick the life you want. That's it. Everything else is propaganda."

He laughs. "Yeah, I know what you mean. . . . So do you think I should look at other desks at Merrill?"

I sign off presently, a knife working its way into my stomach. Is it just me, or what?

I rustle through my file drawer looking for something to read, hoping to take my mind off things. Transparencies, research reports, pamphlets—the remains of the Middle Markets Group. I spy an old copy of Merrill's in-house magazine, *We the People,* which I saved for an article on IEM, and force myself to reread it. Pictures of the Latin Mafia, glowing praise about the growth of developing countries—Can it be true? "Merrill Lynch is special," our top investment banker says. "In IEM, there's a lot of trust and a family-like atmosphere."

The sound of the trading floor breaks in; every sound is suddenly distinct. I stuff the magazine back in the file, slam the drawer, and the noises merge into a clamor. Reaching forward, I search blindly through the papers on my desk. Relax. Hang in there. It's not long now. The whole year is turning over in my head, prompted by Jim's message, Lou's call, and my approaching deadline, stirring a maelstrom of thoughts and emotions.

When my vision clears, I find myself holding onto the brand-new Merrill Lynch annual report. It is smooth and slick, glossy and bright. Inside are neat fold-out charts, gold-lettered slogans, line after line of capital and investments and acquisitions, and page after page of achievements, including the firm's recent selection by *International Financing Review* as Emerging Markets Bond House of the Year. Each page is full of smiling faces, too, representing all the major races and both sexes in just the right balance. In back, the small print reveals the name of the New York marketing firm behind it.

I flip through the pages in mounting dismay. It is so slick, it is good enough to make me wonder—am I right about all this or not? I feel very warm all of a sudden—what is wrong with me?—and then the two happiest faces of them all appear, staring confidently out from their introduction, the chairman and president of the firm, pronouncing their faith: "We are equally confident that the Merrill Lynch Principles, which have guided us successfully over the years, will continue to provide a solid foundation for our future success."

And there they are, taking up a whole page:

CLIENT FOCUS
RESPECT FOR THE INDIVIDUAL
TEAMWORK
RESPONSIBLE CITIZENSHIP
INTEGRITY

For a moment the trading floor is quiet. Then I hear it: a chaotic, hysterical laugh rising from all corners of Seven. I lift my head and the entire trading floor is bathed in red. It shakes, it clanks, it groans—and disintegrates completely. There is no sense, no order to it anymore. There are only millions of disparate fragments, fighting for their share of the market.

The Market!

The laughter rises to a crescendo. It screams—it roars! I stand unsteadily as the floor tilts, as the heckler chants, as the questions spin in a widening gyre—When do principles become propaganda? When does order become chaos? When does progress become decline? When does the system become the enemy?

Vertigo strikes, and I shove off in urgency, weaving past Corporates, dashing past Governments, pursued by a pack of rabid slogans gnashing at my heels: *E Pluribus Unum!* In God We Trust! Life, Liberty, and the Pursuit of Happiness! Truth, Justice, and the American Way! One Nation, Under God, Indivisible, with Liberty and Justice for All.

And the Market jeers! How can it not, when the rules to live by are the same ones we break to get ahead? And what does that say about the Market, when our values stand in the way of its efficiency? When it elevates the worst, building a society ruled by *slicks*?

I burst into the empty men's room and slam the stall door behind me, holding it shut as if keeping demons at bay. Then I slump against it, feeling the cold metal against my face, and think, no, no, I'm not going to end up like Holden, for Christ's sake. I hang there, but there is no relief. There is a tearing in my gut and a great sob of tension, but I am well beyond tears. The emotion rises like a hollow bubble, bursting in silence. Nothing can free me from the starkest vision, a picture of a world in which ideals are dead, where market principles rule, where democracy has fallen to marketocracy.

The door bursts open, covering my gasp.

"So did you sell those Ginnie Mae bonds or not?"

"Yeah, I did. Didn't I tell ya? I got lifted at one-oh-one. That was about ten o'clock. Then they went down two bips, so I bought 'em back. Now they're up five."

"Hey, that's a nice profit!"

My forehead bounces softly against the door, my features twist, and I scream inside. A nice profit! Jesus Christ! A nice profit! You *fools*! What about sunsets and rose-covered cottages? What about pounding surf, blazing fires, and the Milky Way? What about *life*? My God, how have we done this to ourselves? Instead of expanding our hearts and minds we have crafted a world where the less you think about life, the more you get *paid*. We have married ourselves to the *means*, as if the means could tell us the *ends*. We have put a naive faith in the system, and it has wrapped its fingers around our *throats*.

The voices dissipate amid the hiss of plumbing. And then there is silence once again. But it is a silence I share at last. I push myself away from the door and stand more easily now, my hands rubbing my face, awareness rising like steam. I can feel it now, dim but constant, and never to be removed, the product of the heat, the furnace, the crucible of the trading floor. It is the perfect Reason, the absolute Truth, the divine Order, the eternal One—it is He. He is *there*.


I return to my position, exhausted but revitalized, like stepping from a sauna into cool air. No one appears to have noticed my absence or the emotion behind it. But that is not surprising. Plenty of people hustle across the trading floor in a sweat. If anything, it makes you look good.

I decide to do some work. I have to do something. I take the next blinking light and trade with a broker down in Rio. Then it's on to São Paulo, Mexico City, back to Rio, on to Caracas. The last broker thinks my price is too high. I tell him I'm reading it off the board. He keeps arguing with me. I tell him I don't profit from this personally. He demands to speak with someone else. His whole tone, his whole obnoxious, overbearing ego, irritates me in a new way. "Sure," I say, "hold on." I put him on hold and sit back with my arms crossed, watching the line blink. I've wanted to do that for a long time. Eventually it goes dead, but another immediately springs to life.

I can do no more. The space between myself and the touchscreen has widened, and keeps widening, until the lights of Latin America are like stars. The Wall Street hangover has struck, the New York hangover, the hangover of reflection, of enlightenment, of awareness. The curtain of reason has fallen across this stage, ending Darwin's play. I have seen the truth, and now my ambition is dead. If the system were in equilibrium, I would not suffer from this problem. A healthy balance of work and home, of competition and cooperation, would reinforce the whole. But here there is no moderation. Here, in this high-tech world, life is digital. Either you play by the rules or you are cut from the team. So you do nothing but work until the thoughts of the day become the thoughts of the night, then the weekend; until the game is your life and the Market is your master. What way is that to live?

Now the hidden costs are apparent. I was just going to come here for ten years, make a fortune, and depart. But who wants to spend ten years of his life without living? Should I sacrifice years thirty to forty so I can have lots of money from forty to seventy? I could die of a heart attack in the meantime. And who would I be by the time I reached forty and the Market had done its work? There is a reason market people are paid so much—the price of a soul is expensive. But when looking at the rich, we never think about that. We just want their *things*. We stop our bicycles and watch the Rolls fly past. How many of the driven have paid a terrible price—minds that never grasp the meaning in life, families broken by fiscal disputes and market values, lives bound by cords of gold, enslaved by their own greed? If Wall Street is any measure, the difference between great riches and a decent living isn't a matter of effort and ability, it's simple perspective: how narrow you are willing to be, and how low you are willing to go.

I look down the traders' row and spy Navarro, who is on the phone. The afternoon is wearing on. I haven't gone to him, and he hasn't come to me. I suspect he is giving me until the end of the day, which is what I want. Hopefully, he won't come over in the meantime, because I still don't know what to tell him. I know what the traders would advise: at some point you have to cut your losses. But has that time arrived?

*Of course not*, a voice says. It echoes inside that tired cavern, coming from everywhere and nowhere all at once. *Are you crazy? What are you going to do if you leave here?*

I don't know.

*You have no equity on the Street. Not in this market.*

So I'll do something else.

*What? You have no training.*

So I'll get some.

*Oh, sure! You'll just start all over again at the bottom of some corporation! Think about it! What will that do to your head?*

All companies can't be like this!

*Sure they can! They want you to do what you're told and not complain about it.*

Why is criticizing the system complaining? This is *wrong.*

*Oh, now, that's going to look good on your résumé! "I left my last job because I had a disagreement with the system." You'll never get hired!*

But it's true!

*Who cares? What are you going to do if your severance pay runs out? You'll be unemployed.*

No kidding.

*Remember what that was like?*

You know I do.

*Then why go through it again? This time it will be even worse—Sarah's in school. How will you even pay for the apartment?*

Who knows?

*You'll have to move. Where will you go?*

I don't know.

*Somewhere deeper into Brooklyn—*

Never!

*Then why not just stay and do your job? Wouldn't that be easier? You've got a nice steady paycheck.*

I also hate it here.

*Hate it here!? This is the top of the pyramid! Do you know how many people want your job?*

They have no idea what they're getting into.

*They're getting rich, that's what they're getting into! Isn't that what you want too?*

Sure—but at what cost?

*There is no cost! The more money you make, the better off you are!*

I don't buy it. Look at these people—they're slaves!

*They're successful!*

Who says so?

*Everyone! This is America, hombre! This is what life is all about! Money is success. Success is winning. And winning is everything!*

But look what you have to do—

*It doesn't matter as long as you win! America loves a winner!*

There's got to be more to life than that!

*Are you sure?*

Think about it!

*Don't you remember all those years you spent playing lacrosse and soccer? What did you learn there? Compete. Win. Win! Winning is good! So why are you trying to change the rules now? Just play ball!*

Because this isn't a game—it's my life.

*So? It's a good life! You're a young man who is making it! Here in New York City! You can be king of the hill, top of the heap!*

I don't want to be top of the heap! I know what it's like there!

*So what are you going to do, just throw your future away?*

This one, maybe.

*After dragging Sarah up here and putting her through a year of hell?*

I can't help that! I thought it was a good decision!

*Think what it will do to her!*

She understands!

*Oh, sure, she understands now, but what about in six months, when you haven't got a job?*

Would you quit saying that? I'll get a job! I'll hold up my end!

*What do you think your parents will say?*

Nothing. They just want me to be happy.

*Won't they be disappointed this didn't work out?*

Maybe. I don't know.

*And what about everyone else—friends, relatives—how will you explain it?*

I'll tell them the truth—I quit.

*But what are they going to think? They all thought you were a winner!*

This isn't winning!

*Who's going to believe that?*

Not everyone thinks Wall Street is paradise!

*No? Look around! Some of the smartest people in the country are in this room. There are M.B.A.s lining up at all the top schools hoping just to interview with Merrill Lynch. There are parents fighting to get their kids into the right colleges, the right private schools, the right summer camps, the right nursery schools, for Christ's sake, just so they can get jobs at places like this and earn salaries like yours. That's the system, hombre: everyone wants a lucky seat on Seven.*

That doesn't mean it's right!

*Just think about what they'll say about you!*

*Stiles couldn't take it, they'll say. He couldn't take the heat. Wall Street is a tough place, isn't it? Only a tough man can hack it.*

Oh, give me a break.

*That's the truth, isn't it? You can't take it anymore. You've lost your nerve.*

I know what you're trying to do.

*What kind of man are you, anyway?*

My own man, thank God.

*Nah, you're just a quitter, that's all. Just look at yourself, sitting here whining about your job!*

I'm not whining, you asshole, I'm trying to figure out what to do!

*You know what to do! Didn't you bust your ass to get here?*

Of course I did!

*Then why throw all that away? Think how far you've come—all those interviews, those months scraping to learn the business, mastering the Brady Sheet, battling to survive derivatives, making your mark with Middle Markets, getting made a trader—hey! You're a survivor!*

Yeah, and look where it got me—back at the beginning!

*So? Mexico took a little turn for the worse—big deal. Things will turn around, won't they? Bear markets don't last forever.*

Maybe—

*All you have to do is hang in there. In a few months, this whole thing will be a bad memory. Then you can move back up, and things will improve. It takes sacrifice, that's all. You have to roll with the punches better.*

I guess so.

*Look down the road a ways, at the big picture. In a few years, you'll be on Easy Street. You'll have that house in Greenwich, you'll drive that Land Rover, you'll put your kids in the best private schools, you'll send them to the Ivies. Then they'll have a shot at a job like yours. So come on, listen to me: all you have to do is stop thinking. Do you hear me? Just do your job and stop thinking, stop thinking, stop thinking, stop thinking—*

The computer chimes, breaking my concentration. A box appears announcing a message from Tokyo. I click it open.

```
Just remember, a poet can always be a banker, but a banker can
never be a poet.
```

My hands reach out and embrace the monitor—the last place I ever expected to find salvation. He's right . . . he's right . . . Jim is right! This isn't the top—it's the bottom! *Choose life.*

I sit back, my eyes fixed on that golden line, but within seconds it begins to shimmer.

*Oh sure, you're just going to run off and be a poet! Ha! How the hell are you going to make a living?*

Quiet!

*You want to spend the rest of your life worrying where your next dollar is coming from?*

Leave me alone!

*Look at these people! They're all out for themselves—and they're getting paid!*

I'm not going to listen—

*You have no choice, hombre!*

Out of the corner of my eye, I catch the retail traders eyeing my inactivity for the first time. All right! All right!

I pick up the phone, tap an empty line, and listen to a steady dial tone. It is past four now, less than an hour to go before the market closes. Navarro's seat is empty. What am I going to tell him? An intense desire to flee overwhelms me—but where can I go? I am surrounded by steel-and-glass teeth, rising downtown, rising midtown, and hinged in between, the open jaws of an urban trap. A fist crashes down on the desk. What does economic theory have to do with this? A hundred years ago, I could have grabbed my rifle and loaded my family into a wagon and headed off into areas without maps, and possibly died, but at least I would have been free. Now, from the Catskills to Costa Rica, there is nowhere I can go, nowhere the Market cannot find me. I am trapped here by banks of technology, my rifle a phone, my wagon a desk, my liberty imprisoned by an enemy I cannot see—inside me, outside me, all around me—trapped in this mass hallucination, this megaphone of lies. What am I to do? Some hold the subway system hostage, others send bombs through the mail, lock themselves to a tree, confront a whaling ship—I know what they are fighting! But I choose a civil disobedience. Or it chooses me. A stalemate has occurred, bringing me to a halt. I sit perfectly still, refusing the one thing the Market demands: my incessant motion. And I wonder, as the trading floor screams, how long it will be before the Market comes for me.

Sweat breaks out, a hot clammy hand grips my brow, fingers tighten around my throat. I pull at my tie for air and tell myself to relax, relax, relax, everything is going to be all right. The phone lines flicker in front of me, so many fires in the rain forest viewed from space. The entire touchscreen is ablaze! I tilt my head back and the scoreboard flashes above in Times Square glory, first, G-E-T-S-O-M-E-P-E-R-S-P-E-C-T-I-V-E, then T-O-U-C-H-D-O-W-N! The artificial lights intensify into the blinding lamps of interrogation—*What have you decided, hombre?* Then the dial tone erupts in my ear in a piercing, off-the-hook staccato—*Dive! Dive!*—the phone falls into my lap, my head falls into my hands, and the sound of the trading floor rushes in with a fury, the rising fury of a great wave as it lifts above the plane, pausing for that eternal moment before smashing itself upon the beach.

"Paul."

A distant hiss; I do not move. My breathing is slow and steady but laborious, mechanical. My eyes are fixed on the desk. The weekend, I'm praying, just wait for the weekend. A few more minutes, that's all.

"Paul!"

The chair slowly swivels, bringing a face into focus. It is Plastino, the business manager, standing behind me with a folder clutched officiously by his side. He lifts an amused eyebrow, a reflexive rebuke for my transgression—reverie on the trading floor.

"I guess you know why I'm here—"

"Don't worry," I say hastily, "I'm going to speak with Navarro. I just thought I'd wait until the market closes."

Plastino firms his features. "Paul, you don't understand—they've already made a decision."

At first the momentum of my thoughts defeats comprehension. Then a tide of awareness floods in, and I rocket from my chair with explosive force, a tremendous, giddy smile on my face. "Oh! They finally made a *decision!*"

"I hate to be the one to do this—"

"No, no, don't worry about it!" I clap Plastino on the back so hard he pitches forward. "Don't worry about it at all!"

Plastino straightens in surprise, clamping down on a brief alarm. "Why don't we go upstairs to my office?" He gestures me forward with the folder, his voice cautious and formal.

"Sure! Sure!"

I spring ahead, Plastino accelerating to keep up. He herds me toward the stairs with his folder, and I pause at the top, my sense of direction overwhelmed. "Which way, Jack?"

"Right here, Paul."

Plastino opens the first office and allows me to enter. It is a tiny room. There is a chair, a small desk, the mandatory computer, and that's it. Plastino sits behind the desk, I drop into the chair, and he starts talking. I have no idea what he is saying. He is looking at me with clasped hands, he mentions Escobar, something about the Market, and stands, less than thirty seconds later, asking me to wait a minute. In the brief moment I am alone, my euphoria fades into a jittery, detached awareness of my surroundings, the beginnings of my separation.

Seconds later a young woman enters, her own folder pressed to her chest. She is an attractive brunette, dressed in a white silk blouse and a light skirt, and projects a confident, carefree mood, calculated to put me at rest. A hand closes the door behind her.

"Hello, Paul, my name is Kathy. I'm a Human Resources manager from the Fixed Income Division. I will be helping you with your out-processing today." She extends a buoyant hand while looking me in the eye, encouraging me to adopt her mood, to bond with her rather than see her as the enemy. She is surprisingly relaxed, under the circumstances, making me wonder how many times she has done this.

Kathy sits down crisply behind the desk and bounces forward into position. Her feet barely touch the floor. She opens her folder with the precision of a minister at the altar, adjusting it squarely in front of her, and consults her notes. Then she raises her face with a casual smile. "Well, I guess you know why I'm here."

"You're firing me."

She blanches, admits this with a nod and a strained smile, and lowers her face, but not before I see the line of her lips break. Pulling a form from the folder, she slides it across to me. "This is for the SEC. If you will just sign at the bottom. As you can see, you are officially being labeled a staff reduction." She quickly adds, "So there is nothing preventing you from getting a job with another firm, I just want you to know that. This just says that Merrill Lynch no longer supports you as a Registered Representative."

I sign, vaguely remembering some talk of this at my Series 7 course. So it was relevant after all.

Kathy shakes another document free and hands it across the desk. "This is the fact sheet on your SBC—your Salary and Benefits Continuation. Under the Standard Policy the firm will provide you with nine weeks of full salary and ben—"

"Wait a minute," I say sharply. "I was *specifically told* fourteen weeks. That was the deal."

An engaging smile snaps to her face. She is on my side! Everything is fine! "Yes, I'm getting to that. If you opt for the Transition Policy instead of the Standard Policy, you will get fifty percent more SBC, for a total of fourteen weeks." Her voice sounds disembodied, as if she were not attached to it physically—or morally. Just doing my job! Let's just get to the end of this without any problems! "To be covered by the Transition Policy, you must sign the Agreement and Release I will be giving you." The words trigger her to produce the necessary form, which she hands across to me. "You have twenty-one days to consider this. If you sign it and return it to me by then, the Transition Policy will go into effect."

"Okay. What is it?"

"You'll have to read it," she says firmly.

I flip through the legal document and finally come upon the key paragraph:

The employee, in consideration of the payments described herein, hereby releases and discharges Merrill Lynch, it subsidiaries and affiliates and their officers, directors, employees, and agents from any and all actions, causes of actions, claims, or charges arising out of Employee's employment and/or termination of employment, including but not limited to, wrongful or unlawful discharge, violations of Title VII of the Civil Rights Act of 1964 as amended, the Civil Rights Act of 1991, violations of the Equal Pay Act, Americans with Disabilities Act of 1991, the Age Discrimination in Employment Act of 1967 as amended, violations of any state and/or municipality fair employment statutes or laws, or violations of any other law, rule, regulation, or ordinance pertaining to employment wages, hours or any other terms and conditions of employment, and termination of employment.

"I see," I say. "In other words, I'll get my promised severance pay if I agree not to sue you for anything. The firm, I mean."

Her strained smile returns. "Something like that, I guess."

When you are facing unemployment, the decision is a simple one. "Where do I sign?"

"You don't have to sign now. You have three weeks to think it over. And we encourage you to have a lawyer look at it."

"Oh, I have no doubt it's legal."

Her head falls back to her notes, and bobs back up. "The severance pay is taxable, of course."

"Of course."

She hands me a thin marketing brochure next. "You will be contacted soon by Lee Hecht Harrison, an outplacement firm. They will support you for three months, at the firm's expense."

"They're a headhunter?"

"No, an outplacement firm is different. They, um, you know, they help you maintain continuity."

I lift my hands uncomprehendingly.

"They'll provide you with an office and a fax machine and all that."

"So it looks like I'm employed, you mean."

She blushes. "Right. They'll also help you with your exit statement."

Another lift of the hands.

"You know . . . why you left."

"I thought I got fired."

Her face falls back to her notes, hiding an emotion I cannot identify. "You can say that, if you wish."

I flip through the brochure while her pen skips down her checklist. Lee Hecht Harrison comes on like a MASH unit reviving economic casualties. "You will receive immediate advice on how to deal with business associates, friends, and neighbors," the brochure promises. "You will also determine how to best position your new status and how to enlist the support of family and a broad range of acquaintances. . . . You will compile a list of references and talk to them about what they will say on your behalf when contacted. This will prevent any unpleasant surprises when serious discussions with a new employer begin." The pamphlet concludes with a suitable analogy to American politics. "As you activate your job search you will use a Lee Hecht Harrison office as your 'campaign headquarters.' Your consultant will continue to meet with you, advise you, and serve as your campaign manager."

"Any questions?" Kathy asks.

"No. I'm ready to launch my campaign."

She smiles uncertainly and stands with her notes, taking me by surprise.

"What now?" I ask hurriedly, a disturbing suspicion grabbing my stomach.

"That's it, as far as I know. You're free to go."

Even after a year spent in this place, the news still manages to wound me. "No one else wants to talk to me?"

"I'll check, but I don't think so. You can just walk right out the door." She points cheerily down the hall. I'm a lucky man!

I roll my head back, eyes closed, and release a long groan. Disturbed, Kathy edges toward the door. "I'll check, okay?" She returns in silent seconds. "No, that's it, you can go!" She beams at me as I stand and extends her confident hand.

"What about my security pass?"

Her face falls. "Oh! I need that."

I take the pass out of my wallet, give it a final glance, and hand it over. One more happy face turned over to the Transition Policy.

She drops the pass in her folder and extends the hand again. This time I take it and hold it briefly. And for the first time, I notice her freckles.

"Hey, Kathy—when you were in college, did you ever think you'd end up doing this for a living?"

For a second her lips form a perfect circle, then deflate, a choir mouth compressed into a line. She looks down, slowly withdraws her hand, and dodges into the hall.


I remain standing, looking at her ghost in the doorway. The empty hallway beckons. To the left is the trading floor; to the right are the elevators.

I turn and pick up the phone.

"Hi," I say.

"Hi," she says.

"I just got laid off."

Silence, then a long sigh. "Well, that's that, I guess. Are you okay?"

"Yup."

"Do you want me to come get you?"

"Oh, that would be great, thanks. I don't feel like taking the subway."

"I'll be right there."

I hang up, finding myself in a different room. I am a visitor now, an unwanted guest. I do not belong here anymore. The empty chair, the spotless desk, face each other and whisper about me, monitored by the computer. What is he doing here? He should leave. But I feel that something is wrong, very wrong. There has been no closure. No one is coming to shake my hand, to say they're sorry things didn't work out, to wish me luck. The patient stands in the examination room, his diagnosis terminal, but the doctors are nowhere to be seen.

I sit down facing the desk. The sterile office is a library of silence, the computer a manual revealing their technique. They use the business manager, who acts as if he has no choice. Just doing his job, what the Latin Mafia tell him to do. He hands me over to a woman I have never met. She is just doing her job too, processing me. Then I am left here, stripped of all belonging, while a light shines on the exit. I will leave as anonymously as I arrived one year ago. How surgically clean. Fifteen minutes and a reduction in head count. No one has to face me and explain, or listen. I have worked here for three hundred and sixty-eight days now, I have worked hard under trying conditions, I have been bounced from position to position and done my job to the best of my ability. Yet now that they are done with me, none of that matters. No one has to take responsibility. They have left me here, just as they left me in IEM, to find my own way. And they do this, like anything else, because they think they can get away with it. They are confident there will be no repercussions, because the Market is on their side. Speed, complexity, and rapid change soon erase all evidence of the past and their responsibility for it. All they have to do is wait. As soon as I leave, I will quickly fade into dust, like the vast forgotten history of Wall Street, taking with me whatever happened in IEM and making it all right. They don't have the guts to face me and deal with the truth. I am a reminder that there is a cost to this business, a human face. I remind them of all those questions the Market raises, those they have suppressed or forgotten. I am a reminder of the impact of their methods, the decisions they avoided, the secrets they kept, the bonuses they stole, the lies they told, the lives they squeezed. So instead of coming here, instead of looking me in the eye, they hide behind their screens—proving, once and forever, that slick is just another word for coward.

I cannot accept this. Masculinity is not sacrificing others to get ahead, or compromising your principles for a buck. In the end, the tough man is the honorable one. I don't want them to think otherwise, to think that they have fooled me, that they have used me and thrown me away at will, that I am weak. I know that they carry no sword and would run without the Market behind them. I do not want to just walk out the door, tacitly approving their methods, leaving them the winners. I do not want it to end this way, on their terms. No—I want them to know that there is, or was, more to this country than money, and more to a man than the Market.

I go in search of Escobar.

The head of IEM is sitting behind his desk in his long office at the end of the hallway, leaning back in his chair with his socks up on the blotter and studying some papers in his lap, when I walk in.

"Lisardo."

Escobar looks up in surprise and watches me move toward him. When I am a few feet away, he snatches a piece of paper from his desk. "There was nothing we could do. We've already reduced head count by twenty-five percent—"

Sure, and almost none of the victims were Latin. I stop by his side and uncurl my fingers. My hand shoots out—

"No hard feelings."

Escobar stares indecisively at my open palm and smiles sheepishly. Without getting up or moving his feet, he extends a limp hand through his parted knees. I shake it. Then he reclines, and his attitude changes.

"We were thinking of doing this last summer, but then you started doing so well with Middle Markets . . ." He shrugs as if he doesn't understand what has happened since. He doesn't understand anything, I realize, like why I am here shaking his hand after he just fired me. Just more evidence, in his mind, that I am still a sucker. So be it.

"I just wanted to wish you good luck," I say.

Escobar stares at me. He doesn't know how to respond. I turn to go, and he doesn't move. He doesn't walk me to the door, wish me well, or even take his feet off his desk. He just watches my back in silence.

Three months later, following a devastating first quarter, Lisardo Escobar left IEM to form a new investment company, taking with him Mickey Gurevich and two IEM investment bankers, one of whom redefected within a week. He left behind a group that had lost an estimated $50 million over the past year. IEM was subsequently folded into Merrill's High Yield desk, where it enjoyed a market resurgence: exactly one week after my departure, Brady bonds began to rise, surpassing their record highs within eighteen months. I had caught the downturn almost perfectly.


Back in the hall, I find the stairs down to Seven. For a moment I stand at the top observing the scene below, a view forever imprinted on my mind. Then I take a breath and descend. I begin at the end of the traders' row, tapping people on the back, explaining that I am leaving the firm, eliciting speechless looks, uncomfortable handshakes, well-wishes, too-bads. I skip over some people, I wait for others to get off the phone. Their faces pass by in a jumbled blur while my consciousness draws up into a ball and retreats to a far-off corner of my mind. Our emotional Brady trader, Russ Fraga, is surprisingly distraught and whacks his phone into his hand. "Look, I'm really sorry to hear that, I really am, I wish you the very best, Paul, I do." He turns back to his screens, shaking his head. He will leave within the year. "Hey, it happens all the time, right?" another one says. "Don't worry, you'll find something soon. Something better than this, probably." One by one they pass by, until I reach the last man in the row, Barbero. He is standing next to his chair, talking with Escobar when I interrupt.

"I'm leaving," I say, hand extended. "I just wanted to say good-bye."

Escobar quickly departs without a word. Barbero shakes my hand, his eyes moving back to the screens. "Sorry it didn't work out. I—" He leaps to the broker microphone. "Sell DCBs! Sell DCBs!"

I wait.

"Russ! Venny is getting lifted!"

Barbero glances at me, returns his eyes to the screens. "Like I said, I'm sorry it didn't work out. But if you need any recommendations, anything at all, just let me know."

"Sure thing."

I return to my position via the retail traders, who all seem to know what is going on. One of them watches me closely, I suspect because he has been told to do so. But he has nothing to worry about. All I want is what is mine. I take out a paper bag and fill it with everything I own—papers, pamphlets, research, briefings, Transition Policy—and put it on the desk. Perhaps there is some poetry in it. Then I pick up the phone for the last time and call the Core. None of them is in, but perhaps that is best. Finally I look for Forte, but he has gone home already. According to a year-old promise, he is supposed to be leaving now to form his own investment company, funded by Merrill Lynch. Instead he has made a bad trade. The promise evaporates, and he is gone within a year.

I grab the bag and carry it to the last part of IEM, the Sales row. Now that the market has closed, there is only one salesman left: Savegre. He has a hunted, intense look when I arrive at his side, no doubt caused by a difficult search for new accounts. After Escobar's departure, he will once again be made head of Sales, but, like Forte's, his future is short-lived. He will depart within a year for a foreign bank.

I tap him on the shoulder. "Raoul."

Savegre spins around and nearly leaps from his seat, as if I am a ghost.

"I'm leaving the firm," I say.

He feigns surprise. "You're *leaving*?" An incredulous hand sweeps across his bald head. "No one told me."

"It's happening. As we speak."

His body twists in agitation, and his investor face emerges. "I had no idea—really." He frowns. "I did talk to those people in Hong Kong too—no opportunities, though."

"Too bad." I smile, hiding my thoughts. How could he possibly expect me to believe him?

I shake his hand, pick up my bag, and move down the aisle, wondering what Savegre is really thinking. A young man who worked for him almost a year, who sparred with him on occasion, who even respected him once, is walking away from him, never to be seen again. I feel his eyes boring into my back until my curiosity overcomes me. Reaching the stairs, I put my hand on the rail and spin around, shooting him one last glance.

He is bent over *The Wall Street Journal.*


The way out was shrouded in fog. I can barely remember it now. But a separation occurred there, of that I am certain. Today when I see the World Financial Center pop up on the nightly news, I feel nothing. Nothing at all. When I heard that our corner grocer in Cobble Hill, the man I bought milk from for a year, was gunned down in a robbery, I flinched, but quickly put it from my mind. It's better that way. For there's a point you reach when you've seen too much of the world—when the system no longer makes sense, when your trust is withheld by habit, when your country shimmers like a mirage, and the man you once were is a painful memory—a point where you stop reaching out and start withdrawing, for your own well-being. It is then that you build your own little world, a world of sense: a few good friends, your family, and some very high walls. You stop putting your happiness in the hands of anyone or anything else. You turn inward, reviving the life of the mind. And you reach out to that perfect truth, which is always there. Finally, you focus on finding a quiet niche where you can enjoy your fleeting moment on this earth—a moderate place, where people are still free, values are still strong, and life is still good.

I knew where mine was, and who would go with me. She was there on the street when I left the firm forever; and I was there in her arms, out where the buildings scrape the sky.

*—Annapolis, Maryland, January 1997*

## A C K N O W L E D G M E N T S

I have learned that writing a book is not the solitary task it appears to be. Throughout this project I have had the support of some terrific people, including some on Wall Street. I especially wish to thank William Powers of *The New Republic*, who edited the original book proposal. Bill's warmth, generosity, and unflagging friendship have meant a great deal to me. Likewise, I cannot thank my literary agent, Christopher Byrne at Harold Ober Associates, enough for the kindness and patience he has shown. Chris is the first-time author's best friend. I have also benefited from the guidance of an outstanding editor at Times Books, Karl Weber, whose insights greatly improved my work. Karl shepherded this project with great wisdom and the utmost professionalism. My parents, of course, have continued to support me at every opportunity, as has Tugger, who sat beside me these many months with nary a bark. Most of all, I have had the unwavering support of Sarah, who makes everything possible. You are holding the product of her love.